HOUSING THE CITY BY THE BAY

HOUSING THE CITY BY THE BAY

Tenant Activism, Civil Rights, and
Class Politics in San Francisco

JOHN BARANSKI

STANFORD UNIVERSITY PRESS

Stanford, California

STANFORD UNIVERSITY PRESS
Stanford, California

Printed in the United States of America on acid-free, archival-quality paper

Library of Congress Cataloging-in-Publication Data

Names: Baranski, John, author.

Title: Housing the City by the Bay : tenant activism, civil rights, and class politics in San Francisco / John Baranski.

Description: Stanford, California : Stanford University Press, 2019. | Includes bibliographical references and index.

Identifiers: LCCN 2018035360 (print) | LCCN 2018037791 (ebook) | ISBN 9781503607620 (e-book) | ISBN 9781503603257 (cloth : alk. paper) | ISBN 9781503607613 (pbk. : alk. paper)

Subjects: LCSH: Public housing—California—San Francisco—History. | Housing policy—California—San Francisco—History. | Housing Authority of the City and County of San Francisco—History. | Low-income tenants—Political activity—California—San Francisco—History. | Civil rights—California—San Francisco—History.

Classification: LCC HD7288.78.U52 (ebook) | LCC HD7288.78.U52 B355 2019 (print) | DDC 363.509794/61—dc23

LC record available at https://lccn.loc.gov/2018035360

Typeset by Kevin Barrett Kane in 10/15 Adobe Garamond

Cover design: Preston Thomas

Cover art: Schematic of Valencia Gardens housing project in the January 1944 issue of the architectural magazine, *Pencil Points*; (inset) 1965 civil rights protest to end discrimination in trade unions and SFHA employment. *San Francisco News-Call Bulletin*, Courtesy the Bancroft Library, University of California, Berkeley.

For Mary O. Furner

CONTENTS

ACKNOWLEDGMENTS

The path to my first book was a long one, with many people contributing and helping along the way. First, I want to acknowledge Mary O. Furner, to whom this book is dedicated. At UC Santa Barbara, she skillfully guided me through the Ph.D. program with a perfect mix of advice, encouragement, and trust. Her comments on the book manuscript helped sharpen the narrative and the analysis. Her own work serves as a model of intellectual inquiry that shapes how I approach the craft of history. Mary is a remarkable scholar, mentor, friend, and human being.

I also want to acknowledge and thank the generosity of the following individuals and institutions for helping to make this book possible. At UCSB, I was fortunate to receive financial assistance from several sources. The History Department, the History Associates, and the Interdisciplinary Humanities Center provided generous grants to assist me with research, travel, and rent. The University of California President's and Regents' Fellowships also helped to move the project forward. The Department of Housing and Urban Development provided a doctoral dissertation research grant that funded a portion of my research. Fort Lewis College, where I taught for a number of years, provided several travel grants to conduct research in California.

Several housing officials took time out of their busy schedules to discuss housing questions with me. Wolfgang Foerster, a senior officer in the Department of Housing in Vienna, met with me to discuss how and why his city and nation still value social housing in a neoliberal age. At the San Francisco Housing Authority, tenant and SFHA archivist Bea McQuaid graciously shared her knowledge of the office and its housing and records with me during the formative stages of the research. Michael Roetzer helped with locating materials and answering questions. Also at the SFHA, Glory Williams and Julissa Owens always lent a helpful hand in finding materials at the office. Linda Martin offered valuable suggestions for Chapter 8 and helped secure some permissions for images from SFHA annual reports. Carl Williams, former SFHA legal counsel and director, regularly sat down with me to discuss the challenges and promise of making public housing in the City by the Bay.

This book could not have been written without the assistance and support of archivists. Wherever I went, I consistently encountered supportive, dedicated professionals who steered me to relevant collections and individuals. I want to thank the archivists at Howard University's Moorland-Spingarn Research Center, the GLBT Historical Society in San Francisco, the California Historical Society, the California State Archives, the San Francisco Labor Archives, the Department of Special Collections at UCLA, and the Franklin D. Roosevelt Presidential Library and Museum in New York. At the University of California, Berkeley, the archivists at the Bancroft Library, Environmental Design Library, and Ethnic Studies Library all made my research trips to the Bay Area easier and more productive. Susan Palmer at Cornell University's Division of Rare and Manuscript Collections made sure that my visit to the archives was fruitful.

The National Archives is one of our more important institutions, and it is unfortunate that Congress treats this national treasure so shabbily. At the San Francisco National Archives (in San Bruno), Lisa Miller was very helpful in locating HUD and New Deal materials. On the other side of the nation, Janis Wiggins at the College Park National Archives provided similarly excellent assistance. In the San Francisco Bay Area, Chris Carlsson (at foundsf.org), Keith Baker, John Jota Leaños, and Al Rahm Lujan provided generous assistance with photos.

The archivists and librarians at the History Center, in the San Francisco Public Library, were exceptionally kind, supportive, and helpful over the many years I worked on this project. Tami Suzuki, Susan Goldstein, and Christina Moretta helped in finding materials and photos for the book and shared their knowledge of the city's historical record.

Early on, at Los Angeles Valley College, a number of faculty contributed to my intellectual development and my interest in becoming a historian. Three who stand out—Dr. Gloria Miranda, Farrel Broslawsky, and Lawrence Jorgensen—provided courses that opened up new ways of thinking about the past, and the present. I think of them often and am very grateful for all of the work they did in the classroom for their students.

I met many thoughtful and amazing people in UCSB's History Department; Joshua Ashenmiller, Mark Hendrickson, Jay Carlander, and David Torres-Rouff provided community and support. Beyond that department, I connected with a group of graduate students and union members who were deeply engaged with the world and worked on a number of projects to make our workplace and community more democratic. They were a constant source of inspiration, laughs, and mutual aid. Thanks to Samara Paysse, Glyn Hughes, Laura Holliday, Jay Stemmle, Ted Coe, Erica Hurwitz, Sara Mason, Keith Rozendal, Luis Prat, Molly Moloney, Joe Conti, Tiffany Willoughby-Herard, Jeanne Scheper, Gabe Cohn, Jessica Taft, and Ralph Armbruster-Sandoval. As the book neared completion, I reconnected with Laura Holliday who used her editorial skills to strengthen the book's narrative and analysis. Throughout the project, Gabe Cohn and Jessica Taft cheered me on as only friends can.

Also while I was at UCSB, Cecilia Méndez helped me understand how historians might use concepts and theories to better understand power and justice across time and space. I am also grateful for her support and encouragement as I made my way through graduate school. Mario García was always willing to share his ideas about the past and teaching. Randy Bergstrom and Zaragoza Vargas regularly provided kind words of encouragement and mentored me throughout my time at UC Santa Barbara. Eileen Boris and Nelson Lichtenstein were always supportive of the work I did on and off campus. Alice O'Connor excelled at helping me understand the inner workings of the historical profession, and she prepared me well for transitioning from student to faculty member. I benefited greatly from her research and teaching, and her comments on early drafts of this book made it much better. She is also a valued friend.

Sonoma State faculty across several disciplines but especially in the History Department helped me hone my analysis and improve my writing. Sonoma's history faculty Peter Mellini, Tony White, Stephen Watrous, and LeVell Holmes all kept me inspired about the past. At San Francisco State University, Robert Cherny's research and teaching gave me a deeper appreciation of California history. Barbara Loomis was a model of what teachers can do to make a difference in students' lives. Also at San Francisco State, Bill Issel took an interest in my academic work from the moment I arrived there—and it has thankfully continued to today. Bill has contributed to this book and to my growth as a historian in a couple of ways. His scholarship has shaped how many of us understand San Francisco and urban history. As a teacher and mentor, he has enthusiastically and generously supported my work, and his comments have strengthened the book manuscript significantly. I will always be grateful for his influence on my work and life.

At Fort Lewis College, my colleagues and friends Michael Fry, Janine Fitzgerald, Brad Benz, Phil Duke, and Doreen Hunter commented on earlier drafts of the book and all made it better. New colleagues at El Camino College have welcomed me to the campus and into their lives, and this has made finishing the book much more pleasurable. Orion Teal and Arthur Verge generously offered comments on some of the earlier chapters. My student Gavin Quan provided helpful assistance with gathering photos for the book.

I am grateful to Margo Irvin at Stanford University Press for taking on the project. Her active interest in the book from the start helped keep us moving forward. Nora Spiegel provided much assistance in moving the book to completion. The book benefited from the peer review process. Thank you to Barbara Berglund for making a number of helpful suggestions and to Nancy Kwak for providing astute comments on my efforts to reconstruct San Francisco's housing and tenant history. I also want to thank the anonymous readers who offered suggestions small and large. In the final stretch of the project, Jennifer Gordon used her excellent copyediting skills to make the book better. Of course, I alone am responsible for any errors in this book.

Friends and family have provided crucial support. Tim Wright gave valuable constructive criticism on my academic work for many years, and this book is better for it. In Santa Barbara, Michael and Louise Caccese welcomed me into their home during the early years of graduate school. Liz Caccese always encouraged me to finish the book. For the countless research trips to the Bay Area, friends and friends of friends were generous in offering floor space, couches, and sometimes spare beds. In Colorado, Keith Fox and I regularly compared housing and environmental policy in ways that helped untangle the past.

Finally, my family provided nothing but encouragement for me and this project. My parents, Leonard and Carole Baranski, have given their friendship, support, and love for as long as I can remember, and for that I am quite thankful. My brother Jamie always asked for updates on the book with the larger goal of moving me to finish it sooner rather than later. It is now done. My partner Annie Rose Stathes has enriched my life beyond measure, and I am very happy I completed this book with her by my side.

LIST OF ABBREVIATIONS

The following is a listing of some of the more frequently used abbreviations in the book.

ACLU	American Civil Liberties Union
AFL	American Federation of Labor
BAC	Bay Area Council
BACAD	Bay Area Council Against Discrimination
BART	Bay Area Rapid Transit
CCIH	California Commission of Immigration and Housing
CCU	Council for Civic Unity
CHPA	California Housing and Planning Association
CIO	Congress of Industrial Organizations
CREA	California Real Estate Association
FEPC	Fair Employment Practices Committee
FHA	Federal Housing Administration
FPHA	Federal Public Housing Authority
HHFA	Housing and Home Finance Agency
HOPE I	Homeownership and Opportunity for People Everywhere
HOPE SF	Homeownership and Opportunity for People Everywhere San Francisco
HOPE VI	Homeownership and Opportunity for People Everywhere VI
HPTU	Hunters Point Tenants Union
HUD	Department of Housing and Urban Development
ILWU	International Longshoremen and Warehouse Union
IWW	Industrial Workers of the World
NAACP	National Association for the Advancement of Colored People

NAHRO	National Association of Housing and Redevelopment Officials
NAREB	National Association of Real Estate Brokers
NHA	National Housing Association
NTO	National Tenants Organization
OEO	Office of Economic Opportunity
PHA	Public Housing Agency
PILOT	payment in lieu of taxes
PWA	Public Works Administration
RMC	resident management corporation
SCWC	Senior Citywide Council
SFHA	San Francisco Housing Authority
SFHRC	San Francisco Human Rights Commission
SFPHA	San Francisco Planning and Housing Association
SPUR	San Francisco Urban Renewal (Research) Association
SFPHTA	San Francisco Public Housing Tenant Association
SMUF	South of Market United Front
SRO	single-room occupancy housing
TODCO	Tenants and Owners Development Corporation
TOOR	Tenants and Owners in Opposition to Redevelopment
USHA	United States Housing Authority
WACO	Western Addition Community Organization
WPA	Works Progress Administration
YBTU	Yerba Buena Tenants Union

HOUSING THE CITY BY THE BAY

INTRODUCTION

SINCE THE 1990s, stories of San Francisco's housing shortage have regularly produced national headlines and reports of astronomical rent increases, million-dollar home prices, evictions, and tenant resistance. Almost immediately after a string of apartment purchases began in 2013, landlord Anne Kihagi made headlines for her brutal tactics used to evict tenants from rent-controlled units. Tenants—including a cabinet maker, a teacher, and retirees in their 90s—worked with City Attorney Dennis Herrera to fight the evictions. Herrera, who since 2001 had used his office to advocate for civil, consumer, and political rights, won a $2.4 million victory against Kihagi. Judge Angela Bradstreet ruled in favored of the tenants because "Kihagi and her associates had 'purposefully destroyed their tenants' quiet enjoyment and any sense of sanctuary through their long, continued and unrelenting campaign of harassment, reductions in services, and unlawful and fraudulent evictions. Their reprehensible conduct," Bradstreet emphasized, "had a terrible effect on the lives of multiple San Francisco citizens."[1] Amid soaring housing costs, the ruling against Kihagi offered a small victory in a much larger struggle over housing and neighborhood control, justice, and citizenship.

The difficulties associated with the city's housing have generated considerable discussion about the problem, its consequences, and, to a lesser extent, solutions. Residents and visitors alike love San Francisco for its quirkiness and diversity, its neighborhoods, and its civic life, but the loss of residents due to the lack of affordable housing has undermined many of the city's communities and charms. Importantly, the shortage of safe, affordable housing and its consequences are not new. Since before the 1906 earthquake and fire, the city's residents have grappled with high housing costs and with finding ways to expand affordable housing in their city. Of their varied efforts, the city's public housing program has been one of the more important.

Many people equate public housing with misguided government action. News editors, especially since the 1950s, have run sensational stories about public housing's spectacular failures. Housing projects in these narratives are sites of poverty, vice, and despair; they frequently link the "ghetto" and urban problems to public housing, reinforcing stereotypes about urban space and the poor in addition to those about public housing. Housing officials at every level of government consistently make the news for corrupt and scandalous behavior. Some editors portray public housing as just another government program for dependent clients who traded hard work and skill acquisition for free government handouts. News stories have sometimes blamed the programs for maintaining racial and class segregation and for warehousing poor people rather than providing high-quality homes. Cherry-picked tenant opinions legitimate these negative stereotypes. Public intellectuals and urban professionals have criticized government homes for their design and social goals, and they have sometimes conflated the effects of urban renewal with public housing in poor neighborhoods. The media have disseminated research from institutes, think tanks, and sometimes government agencies and commissions that have highlighted the problems associated with government social programs.[2] Novelists have described the projects as dangerous and crime infested, as have movies, television, and documentaries.[3] All together, these sources have contributed to a negative image of public housing and presented public housing tenants and their neighbors as the "other," as a social group apart from mainstream society and less deserving of government programs. Perhaps just as important, public housing, in theory and practice, runs counter to classical liberal economic values and assumptions about the superiority of privately owned homes and limited government.[4]

Scholars have also documented problems associated with public housing. The academic narrative of government housing often tells the story of a federal program that began in the 1930s with the promise to solve the nation's housing shortage, create jobs, and play a positive role in urban planning. Across the country, public housing programs did build quality homes for a diverse but usually segregated tenant population and put many people to work transforming neighborhoods and city infrastructure alike. But, to continue the conventional academic narrative, by the 1950s the housing program began to suffer from insufficient funding and political attacks in addition to many of the problems causing the prevalent negative images of public housing mentioned above. Scholars of public housing have connected the rise and fall of support for public housing to the arc of support for government social programs and the welfare state.[5]

This narrative needs refinement. Despite its flaws, government housing has generated jobs and provided homes as well as a wide range of social services to low-income residents (mundane but important accomplishments often ignored by the media and in common perceptions of the program). By 2015, roughly 3,300 local public housing authorities were in charge of about 1.2 million units nationwide, though that was down from a peak of 1.4 million units in 1994.[6] Government housing has supported city governments financially, increased the number of housing units under the public's control, and removed property from the speculative market. Remarkably, this government program has constructed housing for use, not profit, in a nation that rewards individual and speculative homeownership. In addition to these material benefits, the program, especially as it was administered through local housing authorities, has provided opportunities for supporters and opponents, tenants and non-tenants, experts and non-experts to participate in the policymaking process.

Even though experts and local elites have dominated this process, ordinary residents have turned to the program to debate issues ranging from the role of the state and the legitimacy of private property to the economic and civil rights of residents. This participatory process has included both advocates and opponents to the public housing program, which has generated a high level of political engagement in part because housing and neighborhood are so closely tied to one's identity, economic interests and security, and community.[7] Compared to private housing, government housing as a publicly funded program provided a higher level of access and accountability that allowed the city's residents to influence their housing and some of the major issues of the twentieth century. Tenants—and women especially—have exercised power through this program. For many, the program became closely tied to the civil and economic rights of citizens and some of the other social movements of the twentieth century. *Housing the City by the Bay* develops this more complex narrative of public housing by balancing a recognition of the contributions of government housing with an acknowledgment of policy mistakes and political and economic limitations.

San Francisco's public housing program captures this complexity. One year after the creation of the United States Housing Authority in 1937, San Francisco residents worked with the city's political leaders to establish the San Francisco Housing Authority (SFHA), which became the local institution in charge of building and managing the city's public housing. In 1940, the SFHA completed the first public housing project west of the Rocky Mountains. Built in the working-class Bernal Heights district, Holly Courts offered 118 two-story row houses that resembled the popular garden-style government homes constructed in England. Apartments with three bedrooms, a dining room, kitchen, bathroom, and living room rented for $21.20 per month, which included utilities and a host of modern amenities. Tenants also had access to landscaped grounds, a space for political and community meetings, public transportation, and a park with great views of the city. Rent-dollar for rent-dollar, Holly Courts provided a better value than what was then available from private landlords. Applications to live in Holly Courts, like those for later SFHA projects, always outpaced supply.[8]

The SFHA was not free of policy mistakes. Its leadership sometimes missed opportunities to expand the program and, with few exceptions, brought a limited analysis of the housing problem and role of government in the economy.

Holly Courts

Figure I.1.
First public housing project west of the Rockies, Holly Courts in Bernal Heights.

For example, SFHA officials failed to secure all available federal housing funds, either because they neglected to apply for them or they ineffectively navigated the federal political landscape. Few SFHA officials questioned the fundamental principles of liberal economic values, especially the sanctity of private property rights and the idea of a limited government. The power of eminent domain, for example, was rarely used.

The SFHA program never came close to providing enough housing to meet demand because public housing advocates could not muster the legal, intellectual, or political power to articulate, in law and practice, a right to housing that superseded the power of private property rights. On issues of discrimination, the SFHA leadership structured many of its early policies to reinforce privileges for members of some social groups while shutting out individuals from other social groups. The doors of Holly Courts, for example, remained closed to nonwhites for more than a decade before a San Francisco Superior Court decision forced the SFHA to integrate the project, and in the post–World War II era, war veterans received favored status over nonveteran SFHA housing applicants. Although the SFHA provided an active site for policymaking, bringing in many participants and political views, politically appointed commissioners and SFHA staff have generally limited tenant and resident power in their city's housing. And in recent decades, the loss of public housing units has contributed to less diversity in the city and a drop in participatory politics.

It is here, at the intersection of San Francisco's changing demographics and politics, that the SFHA program provides insight into historical struggles for economic and civil rights in the United States. *Housing the City by the Bay* connects a hundred years of housing reforms to some of the larger questions related to citizenship and housing that U.S. society has wrestled with since its founding. What economic rights and protections should nation-states provide their citizens? Who is a full political citizen? Who is eligible for those rights and protections? Who is deserving? Undeserving? If not every citizen receives the same rights and protections, then why? Should housing be privately owned? Or, are there nonspeculative public and cooperative alternatives to housing the nation? These very questions have shaped discussions and U.S. political struggles to define the proper role of government and the rights attached to citizenship—and they have motivated many of the larger social movements in U.S. history, including those connected to the provision and ownership of housing. This case study explores how San Francisco residents engaged with these discussions and movements.[9]

Significantly, from its inception, the city's public housing program became an important institution in the political debates surrounding housing, planning, and citizenship. To examine both the debates and the policies that followed in the city, I have applied a methodological approach similar to that used by historian Lawrence Vale called "design politics." Design politics highlights the ways political culture, as much as urban space, shapes not only which housing and redevelopment projects get approved, but also what these projects look like and whom they serve. Design politics reveals how political and economic elites have exercised power in shaping these processes, from how they used language and symbols in urban development to drawing on and reinforcing stereotypes about social groups and communities. This approach also focuses attention on how ordinary individuals and their communities were part of the process even though the effects of their participation were limited by unequal distribution of power and resources.[10]

The "design politics" approach helps illuminate three issues needing interpretation: housing policy in relation to the changing political and ideological content of U.S. liberalism over time; race relations and discrimination; and the important role of political activism. Liberalism comes, of course, in varied and nuanced varieties. As the dominant public philosophy in the United States through most of the twentieth century, liberalism has combined assumptions and values centered on a faith in capitalism and private property rights, representative government, and political equality for citizens. Yet some liberals have turned to government to achieve economic security and social justice, whereas others have preferred to rely as much as possible on nongovernmental organizations, private philanthropy, and the so-called free market to achieve a good society. These alternatives—between government and nongovernment solutions, a statist liberalism and classical liberalism—animated public discussions about the proper role of government from the long progressive era through the decline of the New Deal order, marked by the shift in the Carter–Reagan years when government turned to deregulation, lower taxes, and reductions in government social programs.[11]

The persistence of inequality and injustice has focused the nation's attention on the extent to which government should address such problems to serve the public good. From the 1860s through the Great Society until the legislation of the 1960s, political support overall increased for government programs and regulations and the expansion of political, civil, and economic rights. The state did expand in this period to bring about a greater degree of justice and equality, as the nation's residents and political leaders modified their values and assumptions by supporting a more active government in their daily lives, especially in the economy, even when those beliefs led to public policies that challenged private property rights.

By the 1960s, adherence to a stronger state liberalism began to shift again, this time retreating from a vision of government that provided a growing list of economic and civil rights. Scholars have noted that resistance to civil rights legislation, a declining standard of living, and a loss of faith in the federal government have been crucial to this shift. These neoliberal preferences for smaller government shaped legislation at all levels and led to defunding and dismantling of government regulations, programs, and civil and economic rights for citizens. Public housing scholars have documented key aspects of this evolution of liberalism as have others interested in social policy and civil rights.[12] The ebb and flow of federal housing legislation often defined what happened in San Francisco.

Housing the City by the Bay contributes to this discussion of the public policies associated with the varied iterations of U.S. liberalism through an examination of San Francisco elites and nonelites, homeowners and renters, as these different groups debated and defined the proper role of government in housing, civil and economic rights, and urban development. From the debates and social movements at the turn of the twentieth century that expanded government into urban space, to the scaling back of some urban programs in the 1960s, *Housing the City by the Bay* offers a history of the ideological defense of public housing in San Francisco. The book contends that many city residents, especially nonelites, articulated a broad set of economic and civil rights through their discussions of and struggles for public housing. This history captures ideas and actions by the city's tenants and gives us a richer, more complete picture of twentieth-century urban liberalism. By putting the topic of housing activism at the center of Bay Area politics, *Housing the City by the Bay* complements the work of Robert Self, Christopher Agee, Chester Hartman,

William Issel, and Rebecca Solnit, scholars who have found an active citizenry in the Bay Area struggling to shape the role of government.[13]

A focus on civil rights and the historical construction of race make up the second strand of *Housing the City by the Bay*. Neighborhoods have done much to shape individual and group identities in cities. San Francisco scholars—including Albert Broussard, Judy Yung, Nayan Shah, Estella Habal, and Tomás Summers Sandoval—have highlighted the ways these connections have contributed to racial identities and urban demographics and politics. Living in particular neighborhoods and housing can also limit or expand an individual's access to public and private resources, opportunities, and safety. In different ways, the confluence of inequality, race relations, and civil rights struggles often coalesce around housing and redevelopment projects. The SFHA program was regularly at the center of these battles. To be sure, many white San Francisco residents used public housing to maintain segregation in the city, as did their counterparts across the nation. But as a public agency, the SFHA also became subject to activist and legal challenges of its segregationist policies. Almost from the SFHA's inception, city residents used the agency to promote and deny equality in public policies, to influence who had access to SFHA jobs and training, and to pressure labor unions and other private institutions to integrate. By examining these processes, *Housing the City by the Bay* also reconstructs the evolution of race relations in a multiracial city and weaves a range of social groups' experiences into a single case study that focuses on the intersection of civil rights, urban space, and power across a hundred-year period.[14]

The third theme of the book is political activism. Every chapter follows the housing-related movements launched by reformers and radicals, tenants and property owners, nonelites and elites. This focus on competing class politics builds on the many histories of active civic and working-class life in the city.[15] *Housing the City by the Bay* documents the ways tenants organized to influence housing policy, advocate for justice and democracy, and define citizenship; it connects tenant activism at the project level to broader city and national movements; and it shows how property owners and developers pursued their own class interests through SFHA policymaking. San Francisco's housing-related social movements show how federal policies, especially those tied to economic and civil rights, attracted people not only to join the debate but to engage in the policymaking process. These movements also show how institutions and laws can blunt, absorb, and sometimes reflect the goals and desires of individuals in social movements. Importantly, the highest level of political activism followed the growth of SFHA permanent units—and as the number of permanent SFHA units declined, so too did tenant political activism.

In San Francisco, as in other cities, public housing programs have encountered very real problems, ranging from underfunding and structural inequalities in implementation to tenants and their allies not sustaining their participation and influence. Public housing supporters and opponents, scholars, and editors of popular media have, by highlighting these problems, contributed to negative stereotypes of government housing. Critics of the program have blamed public housing for problems created by structural problems in the economy, for perpetuating inequality and discrimination, and for a host of social evils. Yet San Francisco's public housing program delivered housing and services to low-income residents not served by the private sector, contributed to improving the social and physical landscape of the city, and provided space and resources for residents to participate in decisions, small and large, that affected their lives, housing, neighborhoods, and city.

Most importantly, the SFHA program became a focal point for debates and struggles over economic and civil rights attached to citizenship. The history of how San Francisco's residents have shaped this program—how they worked with federal public housing officials, how they thought about policies and their implementation, how they envisioned the civil and economic rights of citizens—suggests ways to design public housing and other social programs around the nation to encourage greater equity through enhanced public participation. For residents and housing officials alike, the history of the SFHA offers examples of urban housing becoming more inclusive, more democratic, and more responsive to the needs of residents.

CHAPTER 1
PROGRESSIVE ERA HOUSING REFORM

[U]ntil certain fundamental evils have been remedied it is futile, or worse, to adopt the methods of housing reform which may be said to belong to the post-graduate period rather than to the kindergarten stage of a community's development. In other words, we must get rid of our slums before we establish Garden Cities; we must stop people living in cellars before we concern ourselves with changes in methods of taxation; we must make it impossible for builders to build dark rooms in new houses before we urge the government to subsidize building; we must abolish privy vaults before we build model tenements. When these things have been done there is no question that effort can be profitably expended in the other directions mentioned.

Lawrence Veiller[1]

APRIL 18, 1906, 5:13 AM. An earthquake rolled along 200 miles of the San Andreas Fault so powerfully that an observer noted that California "shook as a house shakes in a heavy wind." Indeed, instruments as far away as Tokyo and Potsdam recorded the vibrations that leveled Santa Rosa and other northern California towns. In San Francisco, about 45 miles southwest of the epicenter, the temblor cracked the earth and asphalt roads and uplifted sections of brick and stone sidewalks. Shoddily constructed homes and tenements collapsed, burying working-class residents and their belongings. Telephone service shut down, and the city's famous open-air cable cars stopped in their tracks. Three hours later at 8:14, an aftershock destroyed another round of buildings. Dozens of fires broke out, and for three days the city was aflame. All but a few of the salons and brothels, gambling halls and opium dens in the infamous Barbary Coast were burned to the ground, leaving visitors and residents without the district's services. Chinatown was leveled, as was City Hall, save its dome, which hovered eerily in midair above a bare steel frame. The disaster demolished 5 square miles of San Francisco's downtown and more than 28,000 buildings, exceeding in size and cost London's fire of 1666 and Chicago's of 1871. At least 1,000 people died and 200,000 were left homeless.[2]

Figure 1.1
Remains of San
Francisco's City
Hall after the 1906
earthquake and fires.

There were varied responses to this urban crisis. The hilly streets bustled with activity. Dogs "wild with fear" whimpered and roamed the streets, some heading for higher ground where they joined confused and shaken residents dressed in robes and pajamas. Some people wondered about the extent of damage and queried their neighbors for answers. Others, drawn as people usually are to catastrophe, toured the city surveying the devastation. The injured and displaced found assistance in dozens of temporary health clinics and soup kitchens constructed by local social and public health workers. In the three days following the quake, 300,000 people fled the city on the Southern Pacific Railroad, which offered free transportation to those in search of housing and stable ground. Many sifted through the rubble for necessities or loot. In the instability, officials called in federal troops from Fort Funston, and Mayor Eugene Schmitz declared martial law and instructed the police and soldiers to shoot all looters on sight, though this directive apparently did not apply to the police or wealthy women caught picking through Chinatown rubble. The federal government sent tents and other vital supplies. Developers sped north to Marin and Sonoma counties to obtain materials for rebuilding the city, and soon they were reconstructing many of the homes, good and substandard alike, that had been destroyed. Landlords raised rents and drew up plans to subdivide their buildings; they also continued the local custom of discriminating against nonwhites, whose difficulty in finding housing steadily increased after 1906.[3]

The quake intensified an existing housing problem. Indeed, once the immediate task of providing food, health care, and emergency shelter passed, a small group of social reformers in the city returned to housing and urban reform. Like many throughout the Atlantic World, they asked how should the state be used to make government more responsive and democratic to ordinary people, to develop land and resources in rational ways, and to improve the standard of living and health of workers? Those questions, generally called the "labor question," guided reformers and radicals who conducted social research, advocated public policies to protect workers and tenants, and built organizations such as political parties and labor unions. In San Francisco, a group of reformers, made up mostly of middle- and upper-income white women, worked to improve housing and planning and in the process acquired a degree of expertise based on their political experiences and their utilization of social scientific research.

In the aftermath of the quake, these housing reformers advocated for an expanded government role in housing and planning, including public housing, and aimed to pass new regulations and laws contributing to new housing reform institutions. However, their failure to inspire and work in cooperation with nonwhites, with workers and their labor unions, and with tenants in a meaningful way limited their achievements in housing reforms. Property owners retained their power over housing and urban space. Still, the reform efforts in this period did lay important intellectual, political, and organizational groundwork for New Deal housing initiatives in the 1930s and contributed to the rise of the new liberalism amid the debates about the proper role of government in ensuring the economic rights of citizens. This chapter places the work of San Francisco's reformers in the context of the international reform community and housing reforms of the 1920s, following developments in the housing reform movement into the first years of the Great Depression.

As news of the 1906 disaster spread around the world, individuals, relief organizations, and governments—local, state, and national—donated more than $10 million in cash and goods to assist San Francisco residents. Debates over how to use the donations for relief and housing illustrated a general reluctance among the city's elites to help ordinary people and expand the economic rights of citizens. The American Red Cross sent in "professional charity men," some from as far away as New York

City, while San Francisco leaders and social workers formed the Finance Committee and the Finance Corporation. These two quasi-public organizations drew from the city's business and political elites (male only), local social workers, and Red Cross staff. Social workers and Red Cross staff set up dozens of soup kitchens and gave modest cash grants to businessmen and "deserving" individuals. Administrators viewed their relief work as essential for humanitarian reasons and for stimulating the local economy, but the distribution of relief also challenged prevailing ideas about individual responsibility and the proper role of charity and government. Many San Francisco merchants thought that the distribution of subsidized and free goods hurt their businesses. Social workers, for their part, expressed concerns that not all recipients were deserving and that they might become dependent on assistance. When Katherine Felton, who was a leading social worker in San Francisco and California, worried aloud about a recipient's "willingness to lean on public aid indefinitely," she was stating a popular belief both inside and outside of San Francisco.[4] These ideas about individual responsibility and the role of private and public assistance influenced attempts to address the labor question.

After the quake, the pressing problem of housing led some reformers to advocate proposals outside of the speculative private housing market, and the discussion of these solutions reflected the uncomfortable but evolving relationship that such reformers had with relief and social programs. With the housing crisis increasing homelessness and residents' flight from the city—among them construction workers needed for rebuilding—the Finance Committee and Finance Corporation took immediate measures, including arranging for construction of temporary tents in parks and vacant lots and providing grants and low-interest loans to homeowners for rebuilding. But clearly a more long-term solution was needed. Dr. Edward T. Devine, a New Yorker sent to San Francisco by the American Red Cross and a member of the Finance Committee, had the most ambitious proposal.[5]

Devine called for the establishment of a nonprofit public corporation with the power to build, sell, and rent permanent housing. The housing would be not just for the usual long-term dependents of city government—such as the aged, infirm, and invalid—but also for workers who did not earn enough money to rent or buy their own homes. He recommended using $3 to $4 million of the committee's money for housing. His program was designed to put money into circulation, create jobs, and make housing for residents who might otherwise leave for want of shelter. Inherent in Devine's program was the conviction that public agencies should provide model homes and communities. "The intelligent and efficient carrying out of the plans proposed," he wrote, "will enable the community to set a standard of attractive, sanitary, safe, and yet comparatively inexpensive dwellings which will have a beneficial effect not only in the immediate future but for the coming generation."[6] There was also the recognition that

Figure 1.2
San Francisco neighborhoods.

private landlords and developers would not provide enough safe, affordable housing. "Private enterprise," his Red Cross report noted, was "not providing for this necessity."[7]

Others agreed. Among San Francisco social reformers, Alice Griffith and Elizabeth Ashe fully supported Devine's housing plan. Born into prominent San Francisco families, Griffith and Ashe in the 1880s volunteered for benevolent societies and were motivated by Social Gospel—a movement grounded in Christian values and addressing social problems through voluntary charitable work. By the turn of the twentieth century, they turned to social reform and settlement house efforts and combined their charitable work with a belief in government regulations and public programs to address the labor question. Their expertise was enhanced by trips to Europe, where they observed the latest progressive reforms and shared stories of their own community work.

Figure 1.3
Residents in front of a temporary cottage being moved to a lot in the city.

Griffith became known as the Jane Addams of the West Coast. In 1902 she and Ashe cofounded the Telegraph Hill Neighborhood Association based on the Toynbee Hall and Hull House settlement house models. The Telegraph Hill settlement house, located in the largely immigrant North Beach district, became the first settlement house on the West Coast; it provided health care, adult education such as English classes, nursery school, daycare, and safe play areas for children. Telegraph Hill's programs aimed to deter crime, bohemianism, and radicalism by promoting Americanism, but they also met some of the immediate needs of residents that were not provided by employers, government, and fraternal associations.[8]

The two women gained widespread respect for their dedication to fighting for the underdog. Knowing the benefits that municipal housing had brought to English cities, and moving from a faith in charity to government provision, Ashe and Griffith lobbied political and economic leaders for Devine's housing plan. Significantly, the two did not attempt to mobilize tenants and workers behind these housing plans. Those they did lobby—San Francisco's elites—by and large remained unconvinced that a public agency should build permanent low-income housing.

In the end, Devine's plan for permanent projects was reduced to 5,610 temporary cottages and 19 two-story tenements for sale to the private sector. Demand for the cottages was "enormous," according to the Red Cross, and many of the 17,000 residents housed in these buildings across the city regarded them as better than their pre-quake housing. By the summer of 1907, the tenants were given a choice: Either purchase and move the dwellings to individual lots or be forcibly removed by city park authorities.[9] As thousands of families were forced back into the private housing market, the city's first experiment with nonspeculative, social housing came to an end.

The damage from the earthquake also revived interest in a major redevelopment plan. While Finance Committee and Finance Corporation members dispensed relief and built temporary homes, some of the city's leaders worked a scheme called the Burnham plan, which, like Devine's housing plans raised larger questions about the economic role of government. Two years before the quake, James Phelan, former San Francisco mayor and one of the city's largest landowners, led a group of businessmen and politicians who hired Daniel Hudson Burnham to redesign the city. An architect and city planner, Burnham was a leading figure of the City Beautiful movement, whose participants viewed urban planning as a way to enhance a city's physical design and foster social harmony. His plan for San Francisco drew inspiration from Europe's imperial cities and called for wider boulevards, majestic public parks, a civic and culture center to serve the needs of residents and businesses, and planned residential developments. City leaders hoped the plan would help to maintain San Francisco's edge and power over West Coast competitors, such as Los Angeles and Portland, and impose social order in a city marked by class conflict. The Burnham plan incorporated these hopes and reflected the latest ideas in international and large-scale urban planning.[10]

Prior to the 1906 fire, the implementation of the plan had languished because of its cost, its fifty-year time frame, and the need to put massive tracts of land under public control. The earthquake and fire renewed hope for the Burnham plan: Supporters saw in the rubble and ashes a chance to reinvigorate interest and debate. A public information campaign urged San Franciscans to approve the project, but the plan never found the necessary popular and political support. According to historians William Issel and Robert Cherny, "[n]either the strongest supporters of the plan nor its staunchest opponents would agree that city government ought to exercise the sweeping powers over private property necessary for the implementation of a comprehensive city plan." Without the implementation of the Burnham plan or government housing programs, private developers and landlords controlled the shape of housing and urban development, and in the process they left substandard housing across the city.[11]

To reformers who believed dark, poorly ventilated, and shoddy housing generated social and civic problems, the post-quake housing conditions gave new urgency to housing reform. Alice Griffith wrote, "To one with eyes trained to seek for all that makes for the welfare of the people, the fire has left a print which will not be eradicated for years. The houses are rebuilt, but such has been the demand for homes, that both landlords and tenants have overlooked all but the barest needs of shelter." Griffith worried about how these homes influenced an individual's character. "The greatest want in this district, as in other parts of the city, is the social work. The existence of the camps, living in the shacks, drives the people—particularly the younger members of families—into all kinds of ill-advised amusements."[12]

The city's housing reformers followed their counterparts in other U.S. cities by focusing more on regulating the quality of housing than on pursuing large-scale housing projects. Despite the allure of public and cooperatively owned housing and limited-dividend housing,[13] these large-scale projects did not have much popular or government support in the United States. New York City housing reformer Lawrence Veiller, who wrote extensively on housing laws and was part of the international housing reform community, knew the benefits of large-scale housing projects and admitted that a focus on the physical nature of housing did "not touch the questions which most vitally concern the welfare of the great mass of people." And yet, for the practical Veiller, the creation of government regulations and building codes to ensure safe housing was a good first step. As he put it, housing reformers needed to be "interested . . . in the quality of brick and mortar, in methods of fire-proofing, . . . in rivets and flanges of iron beams and columns." He thought a gradualist approach to the housing question, through civic education and legislation, would slowly and continuously expand the role of government in housing and make housing better and safer.[14]

San Francisco and California housing reformers pursued his approach: In July 1907, the city of San Francisco passed the Tenement House Ordinance, which required builders to leave at least 30 percent of a lot open; and in January 1909, the state legislature passed the State Tenement House Act, which established standards to improve the health and safety of the state's housing. Unfortunately, neither the city nor the state allocated adequate resources to enforce this early housing legislation, which meant that virtually no inspectors could be hired, leaving local residents and voluntary associations with the burden of enforcing the new laws. Nevertheless, in spirit if not in practice, the laws were the kind of legislative efforts promoted by housing reformers such as Veiller in the short term.[15]

To help build support for local and state housing legislation, San Francisco reformers used social science research methods to study California's homes. These "social surveys" modeled those being conducted in rural and urban areas on both sides of the Atlantic and had the same purpose: to agitate those who were interested in problems of social welfare and get them involved in organizations working for social reform.[16]

In San Francisco, Alice Griffith used Telegraph Hill Neighborhood Association resources for a 1909 housing survey in the North Beach district. Under her direction, twenty-six students from a University of California, Berkeley, ethics class conducted a door-to-door survey. They recorded the size and number of rooms, the quantity and quality of water closets, and rents in every building, as well as the age, sex, ethnicity, and number of boarders living in the mostly Italian immigrant community. Photographs of the housing conditions complemented the data and text of these studies. San Francisco civic and religious groups conducted similar research in other parts of the city. The vivid reports confirmed what San Franciscans knew and saw: Since the 1906 disaster, the number of dark, unsanitary, overcrowded rooms had not only grown at an alarming rate but had spread "over every hill and into every valley of the city."[17]

Aroused by this proof of the city's deplorable housing and a sense of justice, representatives from civic and religious organizations—including the Council of Jewish Women, Women's Public Health Association, Catholic Settlement and Humane Society, Commonwealth Club, and the Telegraph Hill Neighborhood Association—formed the San Francisco Housing Association on April 10, 1910. As in other cities in the United States, this voluntary organization aimed to improve the housing stock by strengthening the language and enforcement of local and state laws.[18]

Dr. Langley Porter, the San Francisco Housing Association's first president, lamented that government's failure to enforce housing legislation had "practically nullified the law." The association also launched a public information campaign, complete with social surveys and exhibits, to persuade the public of the benefits of rational housing and planning. With their association, San Francisco's housing reformers built a local housing reform community.[19] They joined a larger community of housing experts who belonged to the National Housing Association (NHA), a New York-based organization founded in 1909 with Russell Sage funding. Alice Griffith served as the city's representative to the NHA, which brought international reformers together to develop solutions to the housing question while providing mutual support to members who saw few tangible victories.[20]

The San Francisco Housing Association influenced the shape and enforcement of government housing legislation. Working with Lester Burnett, a state senator from San Francisco, and the San Francisco Labor Council, the San Francisco Housing Association drew on Lawrence Veiller's New York laws to draft legislation for California. Burnett successfully overcame California's real estate interests by passing the 1911 Tenement House Act, which strengthened the state's 1909 building, health, and maintenance codes. According to later surveys, the law helped reduce the number of crowded and poorly built and ventilated homes. In 1912,

San Francisco created a planning commission, which enacted its first zoning laws in 1921.[21] In these ways, the new liberalism began to expand the regulatory role of government.

Yet, improvements in San Francisco housing conditions were slow. In a typical response to one of Griffith's many letters complaining about a documented building violation in San Francisco, John P. Horgan, chief building inspector of the Department of Public Works, wrote: "As to the granting of permits in violation of the law, I assure you it is not, and never has been, the policy of this office; it is possible, however, that a slight error may occasionally occur."[22] In 1913, San Francisco Housing Association President Langley Porter complained that the "state tenement house act was being perfunctorily enforced." It was "impossible to enforce the State law without an adequate inspection force, yet even the modest request of the Board of Health for one or two inspectors has been refused by the Board of Supervisors."[23] The lack of enforcement showed. When Griffith compared San Francisco housing surveys to New York, Boston, and Chicago surveys, the statistics gave "foundation to the belief that San Francisco conditions, unless checked, will, as the years pass, rival those of the large Eastern Cities."[24]

By the eve of World War I, several reform traditions motivated the city's housing activists. Certainly, the reformers wanted to improve the quality and safety of low-income housing and bring justice and government protections, however limited, to workers and their families. They believed that dark and crowded dwellings bred immorality, vice, and disease—at the individual, family, and neighborhood level. For some, they also wanted to use housing reform to spread Victorian ideas of gender roles and urban aesthetics to produce virtuous middle-class citizens and neighborhoods that looked like theirs.[25] These ideas firmly connected home, traditional gender roles, place, and values to the republic. Langley Porter put it this way:

> Next to "mother," "home" is the most sacred word in our language . . . to guard the home of the family has been an instinct of every right-minded human male. It has been the ambition of every far-seeing statesman to make his land a land filled with family ties, and his cities, cities of homes. From the foundation of the family rooted to its own home rises the permanence, the glory, and worth of this republic. Yet today rampant greed threatens this foundation.[26]

With San Francisco at the perceived edge of a closed frontier, the city's reformers viewed healthy homes as a concrete way to reverse a decline of the nation's political virtue while also advocating for economic justice.[27]

San Francisco reformers were motivated by a moral imperative to save the republic, improve housing, and bring about economic justice, but they also drew inspiration from a community of international reformers who promoted government housing and planning. Members of this group included community activists, intellectuals, architects, and planners: Lewis Mumford, Edith Wood, and Frederick Law Olmsted in the United States; Ebenezer Howard, Sidney Webb, and Raymond Unwin in Britain; and Albert Südekum and Hugo Lindemann in Germany. Their work focused on research and theory as much as on building codes, zoning laws, and urban planning. In the area of housing, they saw limited-dividend, cooperative, and public housing as ways to lower rents while at the same time improving the quality of working-class housing and neighborhoods.[28]

In England, municipal governments influenced by Sidney Webb and other socialists built public housing (known as council housing) and planned communities (garden cities), while on the continent government housing programs emerged. In the United States, housing policies did not extend much beyond building codes and zoning laws, though a few labor unions and private organizations experimented with model tenements and cooperative housing. Whether in San Francisco, London, or Berlin, members of this housing and planning community thought government, not landlords and developers, held the keys to improved housing.[29]

Even so, in California, housing reformers continued to take a gradualist approach to involving the state in housing. Rather than seek support for broader housing reforms and programs, reformers focused instead on housing legislation at the local and state level. They used their own and the public's anxiety about and concern for the foreign-born population to push for a state commission to work at the confluence of immigration and housing.[30] San Francisco reformer Katherine Felton thought that a state immigration and housing commission with the right director could rouse "public opinion to the sentiment of preventing bad housing" and "be able to exert far more influence than a private citizen." Otherwise, she contended, the "tremendous influence brought on building inspectors by architects and owners of property" at the local level would continue to diminish low-income housing quality.[31] Across the state, citizens pressured Republican Governor Hiram Johnson (Rep. and Prog., 1911–1917) to create a commission on immigration and housing. As one of the state's leading progressive voices, Johnson had built a political career railing against government corruption and the monopolistic practices of the Southern Pacific Railroad, while still putting his faith in government to further the general welfare. In 1913, he responded with the creation of the California Commission of Immigration and Housing (CCIH), which expanded the state's regulatory role in housing.[32]

The CCIH leadership and staff worked at several levels. Johnson appointed Simon Lubin—a progressive businessman, economist, and reformer—to run the commission, a post he held for ten years. Nearly all of the new agency's staff came from housing and planning organizations around the state. The CCIH staff tried to improve the living and working conditions of workers in the state in part to reduce the growing number of strikes, especially those waged by the Industrial Workers of the World (IWW) and immigrants. CCIH efforts often involved both collaborating with and coercing employers to provide better housing, edible food, and higher wages. Meanwhile, the CCIH worked to Americanize immigrants through English and civics classes.[33]

Lubin and the commissioners collaborated with local reformers to produce surveys of urban and rural housing. As a result, the CCIH became a clearinghouse, both collecting and distributing this local research and information coming out of national and international housing circles. The CCIH's dissemination of this knowledge helped educate the public about housing problems and solutions, which in turn led to tougher state housing laws—but the CCIH still lacked the funding required to follow up on housing violations. Even in 1923, the CCIH only had three inspectors for the entire state, far fewer than the twenty the CCIH director believed were necessary for San Francisco alone. Not surprisingly, the state's low-rent housing remained substandard and inadequate to meet the population's needs.[34]

Besides the CCIH, San Francisco's housing reformers looked to the 1915 Panama–Pacific International Exposition as an opportunity to build support for their efforts. Held in San Francisco, the world's fair became a venue to raise public support for housing and social policies. Planning for the fair, commemorating the opening of the Panama Canal, had begun in 1904. Working through the San Francisco Civic League of Improvement, the city's leaders hoped to showcase new products and the value of private–public partnerships to civic unity. After the 1906 earthquake and fire, they also wanted to show the world that their city had not only recovered but remained the cultural and financial center of the Pacific Rim. Nearly a third of the city's 450,000 residents turned out for opening day, and, in the next 288 days, 15 million visitors passed through the gates into a constructed world with sights common to world's fairs: corporate promotions of goods and gadgets; replicas of classical Roman buildings; a 120-foot golden Buddha statue; gaudy, racist simulations of indigenous villages from Africa, Asia, and the Americas; and a "Race Betterment" booth sponsored by California's eugenicists.[35]

The 1915 exposition also included less carnivalesque exhibits, such as displays of social surveys and promotions of public health, transportation, utilities, and even planning of industrial and agricultural resources. Labor experts presented information on how to improve the economic security of workers through higher wages, cooperative insurance and banks, and various kinds of social insurance. For their part, housing reformers promoted regulatory legislation, cooperative housing, and establishing local offices to build government housing.[36] These displays of social policy alternatives to classical liberal economic practices aimed to expand economic rights and security connected to citizenship—and although they did not lead to a burst of housing and social legislation in San Francisco, their presence did make city-owned projects easier to justify.

With direction from Mayor James Rolph (Rep., 1912–1931), a banker and businessman, the city built a new civic center based partly on the Burnham plan, including a new City Hall to replace the one destroyed in 1906. San Francisco's government purchased the city's railway system and became the first municipality in the nation to own its transportation system. San Francisco also began planning the construction of the Hetch Hetchy reservoir, which promised to fill a beautiful valley with water in order to provide the city with a public alternative to the water monopoly held by the Spring Valley Water Company. With federal assistance and city bonds, Rolph moved these municipal projects forward. The projects reflected the demands from local progressive and radical organizations, such as the Bay Area's Public Ownership Association, for greater government control of sectors of the economy.[37]

World War I provided another opportunity for expanding the role of government, though this expansion happened more at the federal level. During the war, U.S. government officials sought industrial peace and increased production across the nation. To avoid labor unrest, especially in the defense and other critical industries, they took social policy cues from progressive reformers and labor leaders by regulating wages and hours and supporting collective bargaining agreements between the American Federation of Labor (AFL) unions and employers.

The housing shortage, especially in war-production areas, posed another challenge. Without decent homes, workers were less productive and more likely to strike or leave the area. AFL President Samuel Gompers, who chaired the Health and Welfare Committee on the Council of National Defense, appointed a committee to investigate national housing conditions. While Gompers's committee found shortages across the nation, housing reformers lobbied Congress for programs modeled on Europe's experiments in public, limited-dividend, and cooperative housing. Congress responded with two major housing appropriations: $75 million to the U.S. Shipping Board and $100 million to the Department of Labor. The Shipping Board lent money to private real estate and ship companies to build company housing. In contrast, the Department of Labor's United States Housing Corporation, under the direction of Frederick Law Olmsted, built and administered dozens of quality public housing developments modeled on the garden cities in England.[38]

Residents and housing experts praised Olmsted's villages, but real estate representatives launched a vigorous campaign against the public housing program, chastising officials for, as housing expert Edith Wood put it, "building better houses than workers were accustomed to, for wasting time on town planning." Tellingly, the finished and unfinished federal housing units were sold after the war. But the program revealed, on one hand, the capacity of government, if given a chance, to build high-quality housing and communities, and on the other, the opposition to government involvement in the housing sector.[39]

Although World War I expanded federal housing programs, at least temporarily, the war slowed down housing reform in San Francisco. The city did not receive federal war housing even though from 1910 to 1920 its population increased 20 percent (from 416,912 to 506,676), and new and old residents strained the housing supply.[40] Many members of the San Francisco Housing Association abandoned housing work in favor of war service, either locally or in Europe, through organizations such as the Red Cross. Regular meetings stopped, though Alice Griffith remained active on the National Housing Association (NHA) board. Some San Francisco Housing Association members worked with the CCIH, which continued its education and regulatory efforts. The California government passed three regulatory housing laws in 1917, though without the funding for more inspectors, but rejected CCIH recommendations for limited-dividend housing and low-interest government home loans. CCIH staff did improve some rural labor camp housing, mostly because employers wanted to prevent labor disruptions and more state regulations. By the war's end, housing reform in California had slowed to a trickle, following national trends. NHA members put their faith in planning commissions and zoning laws, building codes, and state housing commissions to stamp out substandard housing. To keep alive housing alternatives, the NHA's education program championed European large-scale housing models.[41]

Housing reformers, in and out of San Francisco, failed to accomplish more because they failed to articulate a compelling alternative to private housing that would mobilize the public. In San Francisco, a city noted for its politically active residents, that failure was especially important. Without popular support, broader housing and urban reforms did not stand much of a chance against the power of the landlords, the real estate industry, and a political culture and legal system that supported private property rights over the economic rights of citizens.[42]

Without more government legislation, San Francisco's housing and neighborhoods during the 1920s reflected household income, racial discrimination, and the decisions of property owners. Some San Francisco homes rivaled the best urban housing in the world—elaborate and spacious Victorians with private gardens and ritzy mansions sporting spectacular views. But the city's worst dwellings were on par with the worst dwellings in the nation—dark, dangerous units without running water or bathrooms. Chinatown and North Beach had some of the most deficient housing, including the legendary subterranean units disparaged by the press and housing reformers. In the Western Addition and Mission districts, row houses and Victorians by and large survived the earthquake and fires. After

1906, when demand for housing soared, many property owners subdivided their homes or replaced them with apartments, and housing quality often diminished with higher population densities and reduced upkeep by landlords. Of the two working-class districts, the Mission had a higher rate of homeownership, but often what appeared as well-kept homes had crumbling and unhealthy interiors. San Francisco then, like today, was a city of renters who in some districts outnumbered homeowners nine to one.[43]

San Francisco's districts also reflected the cultures and circumstances of the many ethnic groups that populated them, from the Western Addition to Chinatown, and growing racial segregation. Although black residents were not limited to a single block or district in San Francisco before World War I, housing discrimination against black residents steadily increased in the 1920s, leaving the Western Addition to become one of the few districts open for African Americans and other nonwhites.[44] As San Francisco lawyer and African American civil rights activist Edward Mabson remarked, housing discrimination against African Americans and other nonwhites made it "almost impossible for us to find places to live" anywhere but the Western Addition.[45]

A Works Project Administration travel guide noted that the district's black population was international in nature, represented nearly every "State in the Union, Jamaica, Cuba, Panama, and South America." When these residents were combined with a large Japanese community and immigrants from around the world, the district represented one of the most diverse urban spaces in the city if not the nation.[46] The Chinatown district was perhaps the most segregated in the city, and, as in other ethnic neighborhoods, many settled there to ease the transition to a new life and nation. But when Chinese residents attempted to expand their residential boundaries or move to other districts, whites often greeted them with "threats, bombs, and open violence."[47]

The substandard housing and racial diversity in many of these working-class districts contributed to negative narratives that paved the way for slum clearance and public housing. Landlords built units below ground, which contributed to rumors of a vast underground network of tunnels and rooms. The press sensationalized these subterranean spaces and linked them to Chinatown's alleged vice, disease, and exotic rituals and practices—even though district businesses catered to all ethnic groups, and underground rooms existed in other parts of the city.[48] In other parts of the city, housing reformers highlighted the growing problems of crowded, low-quality housing conditions and warned that San Francisco would suffer the social as well as physical consequences of bad housing. Narratives of the "slum" and its negative social consequences proved important for both public housing and urban redevelopment policies in the coming decades.[49]

The substandard homes in San Francisco neighborhoods and the growth of racial discrimination did mirror national trends, but the political climate in San Francisco, like that of the nation as a whole, ensured little government intervention into the real estate market. Across the Atlantic in Europe, housing reformers were more successful, tapping the power of labor unions and political parties to build what became the Modern Housing movement. To achieve their goals, Europe's housing reformers publicized the social costs of substandard housing and promoted a vision of economic rights for citizens that included quality housing and well-planned neighborhoods. Their vision involved building mass-produced working-class housing (public, limited-dividend, and cooperative) that would include space to foster working-class solidarity and culture. Meeting space in housing projects, for example, would bring tenants together to discuss art, politics, and community. Architecture and planning, these reformers believed, could create a shared experience among tenants that would increase civic and political participation.

The Modern Housing movement did not solve Europe's housing problem, but it did bequeath council houses in England, worker palaces in Vienna, cooperative developments in Sweden, mass-produced apartments in the Soviet Union, and modernist projects in Weimar Germany. In addition to providing attractive living environments, gardens, and units with plenty of light and space, these projects typically offered space for social events and private and cooperative businesses. The environment was conducive to civic and political participation for tenants living in and near them—all at affordable rents. And the Modern Housing movement helped make housing an economic right of citizenship across Europe where nations were building welfare states through social programs and legislation.[50]

In the United States during the 1920s, builders added homes and apartments to the nation's housing stock, yet homeownership was out of reach for two-thirds of workers, and at least a third of the nation's population, including San Francisco's, lived in substandard dwellings—rented or owned. U.S. Secretary of Commerce Herbert Hoover approached the nation's housing problem as he had approached problems in other industries. Guided by a vision of associative liberalism, Hoover believed government officials should work with private sector associations, such as business groups and civic organizations, to formulate a voluntary, collective plan to address economic problems. In housing, he created the Division of Building and Housing to encourage industry leaders to make homes more efficient, more affordable, and easier to finance. Hoover also worked with a number of private housing organizations to promote private homeownership and a suburban ideal grounded in traditional gender roles and good housekeeping. Working with these institutions, Hoover brought some standardization to the home construction and finance industry, but affordable homes remained

Figure 1.4
San Francisco residents
taking shelter in "pipe
homes" during the
Great Depression.

unavailable to many households, while substandard housing dotted neighborhoods across the nation.[51]

The unresolved problems in the housing sector contributed to the Great Depression but also reinvigorated interest in housing reform. In the early years of the crisis, home construction plummeted, and foreclosures of non-farm homes skyrocketed. Housing insecurity added to the stress of families already suffering from unemployment and underemployment. In 1931, Herbert Hoover, by then U.S. president, sponsored the White House Conference on Home Building and Home Ownership, though he remained committed to private sector solutions even after several years of industry failure. At the conference, according to housing and social reformer Loula Lasker, Hoover "urged upon the hundreds of delegates present—architects, city planners, social workers, et al.—to push home-ownership, dramatically inferring that only in his own little home could a real American be happy." Researchers presented reports on the social and economic implications of a failed housing sector, including an entire volume on how discrimination and housing shortages compounded the problems of African Americans.[52]

Despite Hoover's pitch for private sector solutions, the conference participants produced a list of policy proposals that included government-secured home loans, slum clearance coupled with a vigorous public housing program, limited-dividend and cooperative housing developments, and neighborhood planning initiatives.

Figure 1.5
Feeding San
Francisco's
unemployed in 1932.

Of these recommendations, Hoover supported two: the Federal Home Loan Bank Act of 1932, which provided both credit and capital for mortgage lenders, and the Emergency Relief and Construction Act of 1932, which created the Reconstruction Finance Corporation, a body that made loans to limited-dividend corporations for constructing low-income housing. Both pieces of legislation, however, had so many strings attached that few applications were approved.[53] Still, the national-level discussion of government alternatives to privately built and owned housing, and the federal policies themselves, signified an intellectual link to progressive housing reforms on both sides of the Atlantic and a slight shift in how best to use the federal government to improve the housing sector and house the nation.

Depression-era San Francisco faced housing and larger economic crises similar to those occurring across the country. In San Francisco, business failures produced unemployment and underemployment. Social unrest increased as public and private relief failed to meet demand. In 1931, more than a thousand demonstrators marched to City Hall under the Communist Party banner, and protests and mass assemblies became routine.[54] By the spring of 1932, the caseload of destitute families served by Katherine Felton's Associated Charities had risen to 8,000 from pre-1929 levels of about 300. Daily she heard "familiar chronicles of disaster—jobs lost, savings wiped out, credit stopped at the corner grocery,

Figure 1.6.
San Francisco residents protest for economic security and rights in 1931.

furniture sold piece by piece, sickness, unpaid doctors' bills, debt." It was so bad that Felton changed the name of her organization to the Citizens' Agency for Social Welfare because she wanted to eliminate the stigma associated with citizens receiving relief.[55]

San Francisco's housing situation was grim, and the private housing market was suffering. San Francisco real estate agent Kernan Robson spoke of tight credit markets, growing slum conditions, and how his office was only selling lots "without street work, without gas, and even without sewers."[56]

The deepening economic crisis affected the 1932 election. Millions of people filled social halls and attended forums in urban and rural areas to debate the proper role of government in the economy. Housing reformers promoted government intervention in the housing sector as a means of both employing and housing people. In her *Recent Trends in American Housing* (1931), the distinguished housing expert Edith Wood highlighted the benefits government housing had brought to national economies in Europe, especially after World War I. She asked, "Can we not have vision enough to re-build our Devastated Regions without waiting for a war to destroy them?" She ended her book by writing: "Wanted: A Major Statesman to make Housing on the Grand Scale the chief plan in his platform."[57] Hoover, however, remained reluctant to use federal power to address the housing and unemployment problems of ordinary citizens. His inaction contributed to the success of his opponent, Franklin Roosevelt, in the 1932 presidential election.

The 1906 earthquake and fire, and the low-quality housing that followed in many city neighborhoods, inspired San Francisco reformers to focus their attention on the housing question. Nearly all of the city's housing reformers were white elites with ties to reform organizations, business associations, and government agencies. Female housing reformers outnumbered men, yet the latter usually filled most of the leadership positions. Alice Griffith, Elizabeth Ashe, and Katherine Felton contributed to the formation of reform organizations that would be part of international housing reform discussions and efforts. These connections provided a wide range of ideas and legislation for improving the city's housing. Through their knowledge and their organizations, San Francisco reformers acquired a degree of housing expertise that allowed them to work on local and state housing legislation, including the creation of the CCIH.

Importantly, San Francisco's housing reformers proposed several different ways to use government to improve the city's housing and built environment. Of their various policy proposals, their plans for public housing after the earthquake and limited-dividend and cooperative housing through the CCIH were the most ambitious in using government in new ways. But in San Francisco, as in other cities in the United States, the call for such alternatives to private housing did not take hold—because the reform communities failed to include the very workers they tried to house; because housing knowledge, such as that exhibited at world's fairs, did not win over the public; and because the legitimacy of private property in law and political culture was too powerfully entrenched, especially outside of the housing reform community.

With limited public support, early government housing policies at the local and state level led to building codes, tenement laws, and zoning laws. But, as housing reformer Edith Wood noted at the time, such a regulatory policy "may forbid the bad house, but it does not provide a good one."[58] Nor did these reforms have the power to help the home construction and finance industry during the early years of the Great Depression. As Franklin Roosevelt prepared to occupy the White House, housing reformers around the nation began to agitate and organize for federal housing legislation. With Roosevelt, housing reformers hoped that their statesman had arrived.

CHAPTER 2

THE SAN FRANCISCO HOUSING AUTHORITY AND THE NEW DEAL

San Francisco is not going to be a bigger city; it can be made a better city.
Wayne F. Daugherty, Works Progress Administration[1]

IN 1930, CATHERINE BAUER, a recent Vassar College graduate, toured Europe to study trends in architecture, housing, and urban planning. As she mingled with Europe's leading architects, housing experts, and planners, she became particularly interested in the Modern Housing movement, which had produced more than 6 million public housing units. Although Europeans had not solved all of their housing problems, their accomplishments impressed Bauer. From the attractive garden cottages in England to the majestic "worker palaces" in Vienna, European social policies were addressing the housing question and adding housing to the rights of citizenship. Why, she wondered, had housing in the United States remained so expensive, so poorly planned and shoddy, so tightly controlled by landlords and developers? She answered those questions in *Modern Housing* (1934), which critically compared the strengths and limitations of Modern Housing in Europe to private housing in the United States. Bauer contended that the kinds of large-scale housing projects produced in Europe did not take hold in the United States because the idea of individual homeownership "has been exploited so intensively that a very large proportion of the population still tends . . . to approach the housing problem in the role of petty capitalists rather than as workers and consumers."[2]

The widely acclaimed book made the 29-year-old author a star in the field of housing and planning. For the next three years, Bauer promoted the ideas and accomplishments of Modern Housing in the United States at conferences, committee hearings, and packed union halls. She became one of the leading advocates for public housing and helped make the idea of government housing more acceptable to a broader audience and to New Dealers interested in housing and planning as much as job creation. The push for government housing in and out of Washington drew on local, national, and international networks of housing reformers and tapped the resources of the growing labor movement. The political movement for federal housing encouraged the nation's population to back a government solution to the nation's job and housing problems.[3]

Figure 2.1
Catherine Bauer, author
of *Modern Housing*
(1934).

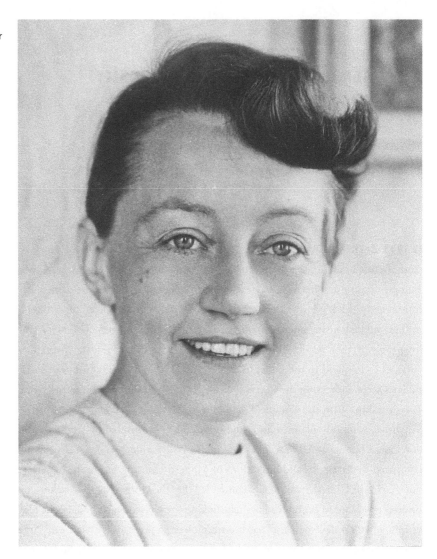

San Francisco residents embraced New Deal housing, first with Public Works
Administration housing and then with the United States Housing Authority (USHA)
and their own public housing authority. San Francisco housing reformers drew on
earlier settlement and public health notions of the social ills of substandard housing,
but many also envisioned a public housing program that combined the best elements
of Modern Housing with New Deal economic planning.

In creating the San Francisco Housing Authority (SFHA), proponents of
public housing faced several obstacles. Housing officials and advocates, and the
legislative frameworks (local, state, and federal) they worked under, had to navigate the politics of creating public housing within a legal and cultural system
that prioritized private homeownership and private property rights. Limited

federal funding and changing federal guidelines constrained what San Francisco's residents accomplished, especially given the high cost of land in the city. Racial discrimination also polluted the policies of the San Francisco Housing Authority in its early years.

This discrimination fueled the Bay Area civil rights movement and led to greater involvement of nonwhites in the city's housing decisions. Through the process of expanding public involvement, the SFHA contributed to the development of a local New Deal coalition that was committed to building public housing, chipping away at segregation, and making housing an economic right. San Francisco's housing and planning experts championed government planning through the production of housing knowledge, political engagement, and the expansion of the SFHA program. They also thought that housing authorities such as the SFHA could lead public works projects beyond housing. The political conversation in San Francisco about economic rights was thus part of the larger transformation of, and expansion of, the meaning of citizenship and government in the decade. As a public program, government housing provided opportunities for public accountability, participation, and responsiveness that the private housing sector lacked. In this way, San Francisco's residents gave meaning to the "public" in public housing.

In 1933, the Great Depression remained the most challenging public policy problem facing the nation. The economic crisis had taken a serious toll on private and public relief agencies. In San Francisco, a native of the Mission District, Frank Quinn, remembered how the resources of local charities "proved to be inadequate as the number of the unemployed grew and grew."[4] A similar drain on city coffers led Mayor Angelo Rossi (1931–1944) to threaten the closure of parks and libraries. Members of the San Francisco League of Women Voters worried about the loss of public services and "wholesome recreation." As the league's president, Mrs. Earl Treadwell told the mayor, public recreational services employed workers and provided "a valuable safeguard against social unrest." Public services continued, but the high unemployment rate, lack of resources for relief and assistance, and levels of social discontent concerned many in the city.[5]

San Francisco was not unique. Across the nation, the unemployed and hungry stood in breadlines, customer withdrawals shut down banks, business owners closed doors, bankers foreclosed on homes and farms, and marshals evicted families. Mutual aid societies and local governments crumbled as need outstripped resources. Unemployed Councils, organized through the Communist Party, marched for relief and jobs with dignity; labor unions grew; and tenant unions demanded renters' rights, rent reductions, and cooperative and public housing. Meanwhile, business and apartment owners strengthened their associations, in part to resist mounting pressure that threatened their power over workers and tenants.

Within this context, President Franklin Roosevelt initiated a series of federal programs known collectively as the New Deal. His administration created financial and banking regulations and reassured the public that bank deposits were safe. To farmers and landowners, the Agricultural Adjustment Administration provided cash subsidies and price supports. The National Industrial Recovery Act set up a voluntary system for business leaders to stop overproduction, harmful competition, and price instability and also gave some workers legal protections for concerted activity and collective bargaining. A variety of relief and work programs provided some of the unemployed with emergency funds and jobs while improving the nation's infrastructure. In all of these areas, new federal programs generated national discussions and political engagement about expanding the role of government in the economy.[6]

For the housing sector, the Roosevelt administration created two types of programs. The first type assisted private property owners and developers. The Home Owners Loan Corporation provided affordable mortgages to struggling homeowners, while the Federal Housing Administration insured, supported, and regulated FHA home mortgages. These loan programs benefited many middle- and upper-income white households, bankers, and builders, though the loans did little to end substandard housing or prevent the many forms of housing discrimination experienced by nonwhites and women.[7]

Roosevelt's second type of program funded limited-dividend and government housing projects. Administered by the Housing Division of the Public Works Administration (PWA), these projects were intended to create jobs, provide low-rent homes, and clear slums. Harold Ickes, PWA administrator, appointed Robert Kohn, a New York architect with decades of housing reform experience, to be the Housing Division's first commissioner. Kohn offered a broad vision for the program. He thought "shelter must be provided for all the people," and this housing must include the nation's "mixed racial, social and economic groups." The housing program had to be funded nationally, but "its inception and management must be local" and "its design in the hands of specially trained technicians." The biggest challenge, Kohn thought, was cultural and political. "We must," he wrote, "go a long way to revise our national viewpoint regarding ownership rights as against community rights in land." Government had to "be able to regain the control of the land needed for housing." The goal, Kohn wrote, was to "create an intelligent social control of our new low-cost housing so that we may make the most of the opportunity to learn how to build a community of the spirit as well as one of brick and stone."[8]

Kohn and the PWA Housing Division mobilized the nation's housing reformers, including those in San Francisco. On November 10, 1933, twenty-five housing reformers from the San Francisco Bay Area and Housing Commissioner Kohn gathered at 1010 Gough Street, San Francisco, at the Associated Charities building. It was the first meeting of the San Francisco Housing Association in more than a decade; its purpose, Alice Griffith told the audience of social workers, architects, and planners, "was the discussion of the need for a survey of housing conditions in San Francisco." Kohn spoke next, describing the recent federal housing legislation and making a pitch for a "responsible group of disinterested citizens" to "study the housing problems in its city." The goal of that research would be to provide support for PWA applications to build new housing "for the type of people not heretofore provided for at a low rental." He found a receptive audience. By December, Griffith was the newly elected president of the reactivated San Francisco Housing Association, and she enlisted her friend Elizabeth Ashe to assemble a survey committee.[9]

After more than four decades of social reform work, Griffith and Ashe knew well the city's housing and the political importance of social research. Griffith and Ashe trained twelve investigators from the Civil Works Administration in survey methods and building and public health codes. The team, armed with data cards and a Department of Public Health letter to facilitate indoor inspections, headed for the Western Addition to gather data. This block by block survey was so well done that it set the standard for similar investigations by the Civil Works Administration and the Public Emergency Housing Corporation.[10]

Housing knowledge, and proof of substandard housing in particular, served several purposes. The housing surveys refuted claims by city and neighborhood boosters, who feared the stigma associated with reports of slums; they also contradicted real estate industry claims that private housing was succeeding in providing safe, affordable housing and that government housing was therefore unnecessary. The narrative of slums made it easier to justify clearing parts of communities for housing projects. Ultimately, the research made up a key component of PWA housing applications, which had to persuade PWA officials of local need, political support, and expertise in the housing field.[11]

But in San Francisco these studies initially failed to motivate local elites. Compared to efforts in other cities, such as New York and Oakland, the San Francisco Housing Association had a slow start in rallying support for their campaign to bring New Deal housing to the city. In March 1934, Kohn told a PWA field representative that San Francisco's mayor and leading citizens denied "there is a slum condition anywhere in the city." Unless the San Francisco Housing Association "has a definite plan which appears to you worth while," Kohn added, "I would not spend much time over S.F. I understand, however, that there are some sites in the Oakland district that somebody wanted you to see."[12]

San Franciscans did propose PWA projects. The San Francisco Housing Association submitted two applications for limited-dividend housing. The first application, Candlestick Point (near the southeastern part of the city), offered the benefits of inexpensive land and proximity to a municipal railway line and industrial jobs. The second application—known as Jefferson Park and designed by San Francisco architects Albert Evers, John Bakewell, Warren Perry, and Frederick Meyer—was for a 1,400-unit development to be constructed in the Western Addition. This project proposed replacing eight blocks of old wooden structures with modern three- and four-story apartments with large courtyards. Both projects met with broad public support, though they involved clearing out residents of both neighborhoods. San Francisco Housing Association members used civic organizations to publicize the social and economic costs of bad homes and the benefits of the proposed ones. The San Francisco Chamber of Commerce, the A. H. Wall Post No. 435 American Legion (whose African American membership badly needed housing), and the Telegraph Hill Neighborhood Association urged Mayor Rossi and federal officials to approve the projects.[13] But in the end PWA officials rejected their applications for not conforming to federal guidelines. What the process revealed was that the San Francisco Housing Association as an organization of volunteers did not have the capacity—human or resources—to act quickly and effectively in the competition over federal funds.[14]

San Francisco residents increasingly showed their support for public housing and other government measures designed to expand their economic rights. The streets of San Francisco were alive with regular protests demanding government relief and jobs. The waterfront strike, sparked by dockworkers' demands for control over their work and union, spread across the city into the 1934 General Strike with broad public participation and support for change.[15]

Also that year, author and radical Upton Sinclair ran for governor on his End Poverty in California (EPIC) platform. Although he lost the election, his campaign—like so many of the popular movements in the era—coalesced around the desire for government programs to transform the economy into one operated for use, not profit, and did much to change the minds of Californians about the role of government. Even some of the city's elites, many of whom were influenced by a mix of Catholic teachings and anticommunism, recognized that citizens deserved economic security even if it meant greater government involvement in the economy.[16]

Across the nation, the PWA housing program did increase public demand for a better federal public housing program. The 24,244 PWA units built nationwide embodied many of the democratic and social purposes of Modern Housing, including communal and social space, modern architectural designs, and amenities such

Figure 2.2
San Francisco dockworkers gather for a meeting during the 1934 General Strike.

as onsite laundry facilities. Labor unions used PWA legislation to build cooperative homes.[17] But the program suffered from underfunding, legal and political attacks by the real estate industry, and voluntary housing associations such as the San Francisco Housing Association that did not have the capacity and expertise to win government housing contracts.[18]

These shortcomings motivated the nation's housing reformers to work even harder for stronger federal legislation. In 1935 New York Senator Robert Wagner introduced a bill to create a permanent public housing agency, but, shaped more by public health traditions than by Modern Housing ideas, his bill failed to excite housing and planning advocates or organized labor. It did not pass. The next year Wagner and Congressman Henry Ellenbogen of Pittsburgh—who, born in Vienna, Austria, knew firsthand the benefits of government housing—worked with Catherine Bauer on public housing legislation. Supporters campaigned for the Wagner–Ellenbogen bill by promoting the benefits of government housing. For example, they displayed exhibits of Modern Housing projects from Europe and PWA housing at community forums. Catherine Bauer used the AFL's housing division to reach union members, speaking at packed union halls around the Midwest and East Coast and convincing labor leaders to support the bill. The Wagner–Ellenbogen bill won the support of fifty-one national organizations, including the NAACP, the Federal Council of Churches, and the Conference of Mayors.[19]

The Wagner–Ellenbogen bill also benefited politically from support from New Deal agencies, research, and supporters. The National Planning Board funded local and regional offices and strengthened the nation's networks of planners, including some with intellectual ties to the City Beautiful movement of the progressive era. During the 1930s, New Deal planners researched social and economic problems, and their reports advocated public works to employ workers, build the nation's infrastructure, and stabilize the economy and environment. They pointed to examples of federal planning such as the Tennessee Valley Authority (TVA) to illustrate the value of public works.[20]

The Roosevelts and other New Dealers celebrated the ways New Deal agencies improved the lives of citizens, who became more willing to accept federal intervention in the economy and supported a growing list of federal programs that expanded their economic rights. Catherine Bauer later noted that the TVA was successful

> because Americans *can* get excited about the idea of using a great natural resource for the benefit of the people . . . and enjoy even the nastiest fight against the "power interests" or . . . "the big farmers." They both fit right in with our entire radical heritage, the political traditions of a frontier country always more interested in development than in reform.[21]

Or, as a housing pamphlet stated, the provision of decent housing "is recognized as a social necessity similar to education, public health, social security and other public services."[22] New Deal programs, including government housing, demonstrated the power of the state to shape political culture and public engagement through a combination of knowledge and material benefits tied to citizenship.

In San Francisco, as in communities across the nation, public housing advocates promoted the Wagner–Ellenbogen bill.[23] The San Francisco Housing Association sponsored a series of talks for the bill. At a forum on May 31, 1936, Griffith delivered an impassioned speech in support of the bill. "In England and the Continent of Europe such progress in slum clearance and low cost housing has been made that American visitors can only hang their heads in shame, that our much vaunted advance in civilization has hardly produced a block of good houses in which people of the lower wage scale can afford to live."

She spoke of San Francisco tenements having thirty apartments without a single bathroom for the entire building and of dark, crowded homes unfit for human habitation. "Housing the unemployed," she continued,

> is the most difficult problem. . . . Families become nomads moving from house to house as the rent collecting time approaches. Now, how can we Americans solve the problem? We have been brought up on the American tradition of

freedom. We have been taught that our forefathers left their native lands to establish themselves on a new continent where liberty would be secure for all time. We abhor fascism and Communism—they both spell to us the destruction of individual liberty and the sanctity of the home. Bad homes are the worst national menace. In the dark are incubated the germs of disease, the maggots of crime and anarchy. If this democracy is to live the free citizens who compose it must have sanctified homes.[24]

Griffith's speech, infused with warnings of fascism and communism, reflected well the city's political shift that had emerged after the class struggles of the early 1930s. A majority of the city's leaders and residents increasingly accepted government intervention for jobs, economic rights, and housing and planning because they saw that kind of involvement as needed for both social stability and the public good.[25] The efforts of Griffith helped mobilize popular support for public housing and social programs, as did labor unions and mass movements such as Upton Sinclair's EPIC and Dr. Francis Townsend's Old Age Revolving Plan, which called for a federally funded pension plan.[26] The importance of popular support for government housing was not lost on New Dealers. Director Langdon Post of the New York City Housing Authority cautioned President Roosevelt in 1936 that "[t]o go into the campaign without a program for publicly subsidized low rent housing would be great folly—the demand for such a program is far greater than many people would lead you to believe."[27]

President Roosevelt listened and added housing reform to his campaign promises, easily winning the 1936 election, but his lukewarm support for the Wagner–Ellenbogen bill emboldened opponents and southern representatives on the House Banking and Currency Committee to kill the measure. The next year, the persistent Wagner, now working with Congressman Henry Steagall, introduced another public housing bill that met with greater success. Roosevelt fully supported this bill, helping overcome opposition from Southern Democrats and the National Association of Real Estate Boards, the U.S. Chamber of Commerce, the U.S. Building and Loan League, and the National Retail Lumber Dealers Association.[28] The passage of the 1937 United States Housing Act created the United States Housing Authority (USHA).

Although many housing reformers were pleased with the new legislation, many thought the program had been diluted in several ways: First, the USHA would be primarily used for slum clearance and housing lower-income families; second, meager funding meant the program would not meet housing demand or build anything more than basic housing; and third, because the USHA did not directly build projects, it relied on state legislation to enable local governments to create local housing authorities, thus devolving responsibility and initiative first to the states and then to local officials.[29]

That latter concern played out in California throughout 1937, as state legislators battled over the enabling legislation needed to empower local governments to move forward with public housing. Considerable opposition came from Republican Governor Frank Merriam, but the state's real estate industry and business groups, especially from southern California, also stalled the legislation.[30] Finally, in January 1938, a special session of the California legislature passed the Housing Authorities Law, giving local governments the legal means to participate in the USHA program. For the next three months, Bay Area housing and planning activists pushed San Francisco Mayor Rossi to establish a housing authority and appoint commissioners with "a broad social view point."[31] On April 18, 1938, at Rossi's urging, the San Francisco Board of Supervisors created a housing authority.[32]

In order to maintain support from the city's political and economic leaders, Rossi strategically selected the five commissioners. Two appointees, businessman and real estate leader Walter H. Sullivan, and L. M. Giannini, whose family controlled Bank of America, had publicly opposed the USHA program. The other three commissioners supported public housing: Businessman Marshal Dill represented the enlightened businessman and civic leader, and Alexander Watchman represented the San Francisco Building and Trades Council and the AFL. For the fifth commissioner, Rossi appointed Alice Griffith.[33] The appointments reflected the city's dominant coalition of liberal labor, business, and civic leaders and were similar to those being made in other cities—in fact, when an MGM studio writer asked Catherine Bauer for a composite housing authority commission, she recommended three businessmen, one labor man, and a woman social worker (or, alternatively, an African American civic leader).[34] The appointments legitimated the new institution and gave it powerful political connections to local and national organizations. But, as in other cities, the appointment process—as opposed to holding general elections for these positions—was a missed opportunity to raise public awareness and encourage participation in the new institution.

The new agency got off to a relatively good start. The commissioners met weekly to build the authority. They established its name—the San Francisco Housing Authority (SFHA)—and approved bylaws and its official seal. With the help of the mayor, the commissioners received a $5,000 loan from the city that enabled them to rent an office and hire staff. Because the USHA did not give seed money to local authorities, this initial capital was crucial for competing with other cities for federal funding; as a 1938 USHA survey reported, thirty-eight of the first fifty-two authorities were effectively paralyzed by lack of funds.[35]

SFHA commissioners hired a four-person staff and a lawyer, William O'Brien. The first director, A. D. Wilder, had a budget of $30,000 that drew on future rents and federal subsidies. USHA officials supervised the making of the authority, sharing their field experience and ensuring a degree of accountability and conformity with USHA guidelines.[36]

In June 1938, the SFHA and city entered into a contract by which they promised to eliminate "unsafe or insanitary dwelling units" and showed a spirit of cooperation that would last for decades.[37] The SFHA, like other authorities, was established as an autonomous "public entity," free from the charter provisions that governed other departments of the city government. As such, the SFHA had political and financial autonomy, though its leadership certainly responded to the political dynamics of the city. The SFHA would make a regular payment in lieu of taxes (PILOT) for city services to the city government, an arrangement in line with national practices. The Department of Public Health (which provided the legal power of condemnation), the Department of Education, the Commission of Parks and the Commission of Recreation (two separate entities until their merger in 1950) also pledged assistance to the housing authority.[38]

The formation of the SFHA provided the city's housing reformers with a powerful vehicle for improving San Francisco's housing stock and expanding the number of participants in housing policy. In contrast to the San Francisco Housing Association, the SFHA had resources to plan, build, and manage a public housing program and to accomplish "softer" ends, such as information gathering and communications, via staff to conduct research and public information campaigns to educate and agitate the public in favor of large-scale public housing. The SFHA also set a new standard for public participation in housing policy. For example, the commission meetings were open to the public, and, because of public funding, the public had a right to participate in the decision-making process. The SFHA's legal relationship with the city and federal government also gave it a power that voluntary organizations lacked. Finally, as historian Gail Radford has noted, public authorities, like the SFHA, by the 1930s had become legitimate structures to provide goods and services that the private sector failed to deliver.[39]

With an institutional and legal framework in place, SFHA commissioners and staff set out to create public housing. Several discourses shaped their goals. Commissioners Giannini and Sullivan viewed public housing as a way to bail out landowners, rid the city of slums, and put men to work. As well, they saw sitting on the commission as a way to monitor plans and policies and to restrict the program if it competed too vigorously with the private housing market. Commissioners Dill, Watchman, and Griffith drew from the Modern Housing traditions and the emerging New Deal liberalism that lodged greater faith in government to redress the shortcomings of the market. To prevent perceived and real social ills, they thought

SFHA housing had to be modern in style, serve working-class families, have ample sunlight and ventilation, and provide community services such as health centers and nursery schools as well as space for social and political purposes.[40]

Griffith, whose reform work had given her a deeper understanding of the degree and effects of housing discrimination, wanted to assure that nonwhites had access to public housing. The New Deal emphasis on public works to improve the material lives of citizens and to employ people also influenced SFHA commissioners. With construction for the 1939 Golden Gate International Exposition nearing completion and unemployment remaining in double digits in 1938, the commissioners tried to enlarge "the Authority's program in order to put men to work."[41]

National-level pressure prompted local action and revealed local challenges. USHA officials pressured commissioners to submit at least one application as soon as possible. "Washington wants action," a USHA regional land advisor told the commissioners in June, "and the sooner we get things going the stronger we will be with Washington."[42]

To submit an application, commissioners had to find lots, preferably empty or occupied by substandard housing, and then begin negotiations with the property owners. At the same time they made rough architectural designs and cost estimates. If negotiations secured options for properties, commissioners turned an application in to the USHA, whose officials approved, revised, or rejected it. The challenge for many authorities was purchasing land at or below the USHA limit of $1.50 per square foot. USHA officials, including USHA Administrator Nathan Straus, regularly rejected SFHA applications for not meeting USHA guidelines, especially land price limits.[43] As Commissioner Dill told a USHA land advisor, working within federal limits was challenging "because San Francisco is of such a small area, the land is much higher in value than in other cities."[44] Negotiations with landowners consumed vast resources and time and, on many occasions, leaked news of a proposed site sent property values soaring beyond USHA limits.[45]

New leadership pushed for faster progress. In September, Director Wilder left the authority to become the director of public works of San Francisco. His replacement was Albert Evers, a San Francisco architect and planner who had worked on the PWA housing application for the Western Addition.[46] Evers stressed to the commissioners "the urgent necessity of actually starting on a project in order to obtain money for administrative office expenses."[47] Two weeks later he again underscored the need for action, this time "in order to put men to work."[48] Evers commissioned a citywide survey of properties to update the agency's understanding of the housing situation. The SFHA hired Wayne Daugherty, who had directed similar surveys in other cities. He used SFHA, the Works Progress Administration, and city resources to hire 507 researchers who for the next year canvassed the city, block by block, dwelling by dwelling.[49]

New information helped to offset resistance. As had been the case with earlier research done by Griffith and Ashe, the housing survey would help build support for USHA applications and counter SFHA opponents who claimed their neighborhood or city had no slums. Even Mayor Rossi, who supported the SFHA, sided with city boosters on this point, claiming that "[w]e do not have slums here," though he was willing to concede that "nevertheless there are areas of substandard housing in the city."[50] Such remarks were so common among city boosters that Nathan Straus dedicated a chapter from his book *The Seven Myths of Housing* (1944) to disproving these kinds of claims. (Significantly, in the postwar era, boosters and local elites would rediscover the value of the term "slum" as a way to prepare the public for redevelopment and housing projects that often displaced poor residents.)[51] By October, such debates over the existence or nonexistence of slums threatened federal funding, prompting USHA Director of Project Planning Jacob Crane to urge the SFHA leadership "to avoid delay in procuring sites" because some or all of the $15 million earmarked for San Francisco could "be diverted to other cities."[52]

With much federal prodding from above, the SFHA staff scoured the city for available properties and eventually submitted two applications to the USHA. Holly Courts, a 118-unit development in Bernal Heights, was small by USHA standards. Small projects, USHA officials thought, risked being consumed by the slums around them, whereas large projects transformed a greater percentage of built space in a neighborhood, produced economies of scale, and provided more open space, jobs, and units. SFHA commissioners argued that their local knowledge and expertise informed the Holly Courts project. As a compromise, the commissioners also submitted an application for a 469-unit project named Potrero Terrace. This project, which required the acquisition of seventy-six parcels on Potrero Hill bordering McLaren Park, lined up better with federal ideas about the scope and role of public housing in low-income neighborhoods. In December 1938, the USHA approved both projects at a total cost of $2.5 million.[53]

Success bred institutional stature. Holly Courts and Potrero Terrace substantially strengthened the SFHA. The commissioners hired more staff, secured financing from Bank of America, and reinforced ties with the San Francisco Building and Trades Council with construction contracts. The city's newspapers ran positive stories about public housing, and the SFHA leadership pledged that their agency could provide not just housing and jobs, but "opportunities for the growth of a better community life."[54]

Yet resistance to public housing did not fade away. Neither Holly Courts nor Potrero Terrace had encountered much organized support or opposition at the application stage, but that quickly changed. In March 1939, just months after the

Figure 2.3
Health Director Jacob
C. Geiger (*left*), Mayor
Angelo Rossi (*center*),
and San Francisco
Housing Authority
Director Albert J. Evers
(*right*) inspecting Holly
Courts in 1940.

approval of the two projects, SFHA Commissioner Watchman reported that the
San Francisco Apartment House Owners Association was "organizing opposition
to the Authority's program."[55] The San Francisco Real Estate Boards, the Federation
of Taxpayers, and the Central Council of Civic Clubs joined the fight against such
projects. These organizations claimed that public housing "socialized real estate" and
threatened the apartment house industry.[56] They found support in organizations
such as the National Association of Real Estate Boards, the United States Chamber
of Commerce, the National Association of Home Builders, the National Retail
Lumber Dealers Association, and the National Apartment Owners Association.
These national organizations distributed information kits with samples of anti-
public housing billboards, pamphlets, and newsletters, all aimed at undermining
public perceptions and support of government housing.[57]

Opposition materials argued that public housing was another New Deal step toward socialism, antithetical to the legal and cultural traditions of private property, a misguided effort at social engineering, and unfair to private landlords. According to opponents, housing authorities, despite contributing PILOTs, skirted their tax responsibility and consumed more public services than they paid for. The most effective argument claimed that public housing brought nonwhite and poor tenants to neighborhoods, thus threatening property values and racial and class integration; it skillfully played on the fragile racial and class identities of white homeowners. To solve the nation's housing crisis, public housing opponents proposed instead a renewed faith in free enterprise and, paradoxically, greater government support for private property owners, developers, and bankers.[58] The anti-public housing campaign reflected a larger campaign against radicalism, the New Deal, labor unions, rights and protections for nonwhites, and the ways liberalism itself was evolving in the decade.[59]

To counter the attack on government housing, the SFHA commissioners, with the encouragement of USHA officials, launched their own public information campaign.[60] Catherine Bauer, Bay Area public housing advocates, and agents from the Works Progress Administration (WPA) discussed the benefits of public housing on Bay Area airwaves with program titles such as "Slums Cost You Money" and "Low Rent Houses Will Not Be Competition to Private Builders of Small Homes But Act as Spur to Build More Homes."[61] At the request of a WPA art project supervisor at the University of California, Berkeley, the SFHA contributed to two films that played to large audiences locally and nationally.[62] The commissioners also spoke at community events and met with members of civic, labor, and business organizations. The campaign plugged public housing as a way to raise private property values, improve social conditions, reduce city government expenses, and put people to work. Local newspapers emphasized the benefits of public housing and argued that the SFHA would not engage in social experimentation. As one article claimed, tenants would not be used as "sociological guinea pigs." The campaign also tried to convince nervous property owners of the value of public housing in their neighborhoods.[63]

The campaign and the results of the SFHA 1939 *Real Property Survey* helped justify the expansion of the SFHA programs, but project by project, the agency continued to draw both opponents and supporters into the policy process and provide opportunities for residents to discuss their civil and economic rights. Public debates over a proposed Chinatown project illustrate how the SFHA opened up the housing policy process. The 1939 survey found 85 percent of Chinatown's housing to be substandard and overcrowded, a figure in line with popular perceptions of the district's housing. When the SFHA proposed a project there, only a few older residents and affected property owners offered any resistance.[64]

Supporters in and out of the district mobilized behind the project. Emily Lee Fong, of the Chinese Young Women's Christian Association, who had done progressive reform work in Chinatown, urged the SFHA to "make every effort to remedy the social situation of overcrowded homes in the Chinese section of the City."[65] Chee Lowe—representing the Chinese Chamber of Commerce, Chinese Six Companies, and Chinese Native Sons—called attention to the "social problems of Chinatown and the dire need of low rental housing in that area."[66] Lowe convinced the SFHA commissioners to create a Chinese Advisory Committee, which worked closely with Chinatown residents, SFHA staff, civic groups throughout the city, federal agencies, and municipal departments—especially the Department of Public Health. Together, they proposed a 350-unit project. As historian Nayan Shah has shown, Chinatown housing reformers and their allies used the housing project to transform the negative images and rights of Chinatown's population from undeserving bachelors and prostitutes to commendable, modern, stable nuclear families deserving of equal rights.[67] At the same time that Chinese families made new claims on the state, the housing program drew Chinese residents into the New Deal coalition. In light of Japanese atrocities in China and a growing distaste for discrimination at home, San Francisco public housing became a site for confronting and even breaking down negative Asian stereotypes in the city and expanding support for the New Deal.[68]

Supporters of the Chinatown project overcame some of the political and social obstacles associated with public housing, but the high land costs were a significant challenge. Chinatown properties averaged $3.00 per square foot, double the USHA limit of $1.50 per square foot.[69] Based on the logic that "Chinatown being an historical spot, known to the entire U.S., there might be a special dispensation granted by the USHA," Commissioner Dill made a request to the USHA for flexibility.[70] Federal officials acknowledged the high land prices but told the commissioners to keep looking. SFHA Director Evers responded that because "there is no land at the lowest prices," it might be possible to have properties "condemned by the Health Department" for eminent domain proceedings.[71] To condemn a building through eminent domain, SFHA staff had to find replacement housing for any displaced tenants (as per USHA requirements) and justify the use of government power to take private property for the public good. For the SFHA, as with other public agencies, the use of eminent domain was often a costly and lengthy process because it challenged private property rights.

By February 1940, the frustration over land acquisition produced a policy innovation. Evers and Lowe pitched the idea of using $75,000 from city funds to supplement USHA funding. After San Francisco Supervisor Alfred Roncovieri presented the Evers–Lowe plan for the 1940–41 city budget, the board approved the resolution, paving the way for USHA approval of the Chinatown project.[72]

Yet even with city funds, the SFHA reduced the size of the project to 250 units because securing properties through purchase and eminent domain was so difficult.[73] The project became known as Ping Yuen or "peaceful garden." Ping Yuen's architects fused Chinese architecture and interior design styles with Modern Housing features. The design offered a Chinese-inspired façade that satisfied local residents and maintained the district's attractiveness to tourists. Yet it also preserved popular stereotypes of Chinatown's residents as foreigners with different, even exotic, values and tastes.[74]

The SFHA plans for the Western Addition, where the majority of the city's African Americans lived, encountered similar challenges. Deteriorating housing, job discrimination, and increased segregation severely limited the housing choices of African Americans in the city. In May of 1938, African Americans began lobbying the SFHA for housing assistance, and soon after the Negro Women's Housing Council took the lead in urging SFHA commissioners, especially Griffith, to build public housing for African Americans. Negro Women's Housing Council President Sara Jenkins, along with others, regularly met with SFHA officials and stressed that African Americans "cannot get a decent place to live."[75] Jenkins requested adding an African American to the commission and creating an African American advisory board. She had the support of commissioners Griffith and Dill, but other SFHA officials were less receptive. Director Evers warned Jenkins that continued agitation "would militate against the possibility of a project in the Negro area."[76]

Undeterred, the Negro Women's Housing Council sponsored "forums, public meetings, public and private conferences, and lectures in fostering a constructive activity in favor of public low-cost housing."[77] In 1940, the Negro Women's Housing Council also applied for WPA funding for twenty-six staff members to conduct a socioeconomic survey of the city's growing African American population. The results of this social survey, Jenkins hoped, would support an education campaign to counter the "social evils" associated with racial discrimination.[78] The WPA never approved the study, but with the assistance of Griffith and the San Francisco NAACP, the SFHA established a Negro Advisory Committee. Its first members included Reverend J. L. Boyd, Revels Cayton, Welford Wilson, William H. Henderson, and Jenkins, and these leaders worked with the commissioners on land acquisition and community and race relations.[79] As was the case with the Chinese community, African Americans influenced the direction of the SFHA and saw in public housing a way to expand their civil, political, and economic rights in the city.

Their efforts also encountered racism, which became a key factor in developing the profile and story of the Western Addition public housing project. In contrast to the Chinatown project, which everyone in the city knew would house tenants of Chinese ancestry, the Western Addition project raised the thorny issue of tenant selection for this and other SFHA projects. Residents of all races wanted to know the answer to two questions. Would SFHA housing be open to all qualified residents regardless of race and ethnicity? And, conversely in important respects, how would SFHA tenant and site selection affect the racial and ethnic composition of neighborhoods?

The SFHA chose not to pursue a policy that outlawed segregation. Instead, the commissioners pledged to follow the spirit of federal guidelines that allowed authorities to select tenants based on a neighborhood's existing racial and ethnic patterns. Because it reinforced existing patterns, which were already segregated, this neighborhood pattern approach amounted to segregation by a publicly funded institution. As in other cities, the SFHA strategy was used because it reduced opposition from white residents to public housing and because it aligned with some SFHA officials who believed in segregation. In San Francisco, the Negro and Chinese advisory committees reluctantly accepted this segregationist policy in exchange for desperately needed housing projects in their communities. In a pattern typical of race-related struggles during the New Deal, they prioritized the housing program and new economic rights over civil rights.[80] By following the neighborhood pattern approach, the SFHA decreased the chances of alienating white residents, who would nevertheless benefit from new jobs and PILOTs to the city government. The SFHA reinforced other public policies that maintained segregation as well, from discriminatory mortgage lending to the legal enforcement of racially restrictive covenants in property transactions.

What scholars of public housing have often missed in discussions about using a neighborhood pattern to select tenants, and maintain segregation, is how housing authorities generated political activism and engagement. Prior to the Great Depression in San Francisco, a relatively small group of affluent white reformers organized housing knowledge and their social networks to address the housing question. They did not meaningfully include nonwhites and workers. For their part, tenants and workers might participate in labor unions and political parties, but they did not generally organize around housing as an economic right.[81]

With the creation of the federal public housing program, the diversity of individuals participating in policymaking began to expand. In San Francisco, African Americans and Chinese residents were drawn into the SFHA and New Deal policy process, and unions, civil rights organizations, and veterans groups increasingly mobilized their members in support of public housing. San Francisco property owners created new homeowner associations to protect their neighborhoods from public housing, nonwhites, and poor tenants. Some of these groups joined local and national organizations in the fight against public housing. In these ways, residents converged on the SFHA, where they discussed, debated and defined the economic and civil rights of citizenship and the role of government in the economy. This broadened discussion was certainly not democratic, but it did expand the level of participation for debates concerning public and private housing policy.

The Western Addition project illustrated this expansion of political engagement. It took two years to secure the land options for Westside Courts, which was planned for a neighborhood with 60 percent substandard housing and a working-class population of white and nonwhite families.[82] With only 2 1/2 acres of land, the 136-unit project paled in comparison to the PWA proposal earlier in the 30s. Still, the architects of Westside Courts planned modern amenities, a social hall, and open space for children.[83] Throughout the city, support for Westside Courts poured in from unions, civic organizations, and political leaders. African American organizations raised community awareness about the district's dire housing situation. San Francisco's four daily newspapers, and even San Francisco Chamber of Commerce President Walter Haas and San Francisco Bank President Parker Maddux were "favorable to the project."[84] With such community support, the USHA approved the application in September 1940.[85]

As the construction of Westside Courts moved forward, the opposition mobilized. Property and business owners in the Central Council of Civic Clubs and the Divisadero District Merchants Improvement Association (DDMIA), which had fought integration for two decades, urged the SFHA commissioners, the San Francisco Board of Supervisors, and Mayor Rossi to abandon the project. In response, the SFHA commissioners held several well-attended public meetings. Landlord Emma Cougle complained that, upon hearing of Westside Courts, one of her tenants left and that the SFHA "project has greatly depreciated" her property's value. Ben Vladov, another property owner, did "not believe the slums are in his district except one or two locations." John Reagan said he owned "property in the proposed site and will not sell it or give it up under any circumstances."[86] The "project will deteriorate the whole district," former DDMIA president Michael Kelly stated. "Public housing," he warned, "is bringing on a tax strike."[87]

But the opponents were too late. It "was a practical impossibility to do otherwise than continue development of this project," the commissioners explained. "The USHA has advanced money on the project, land purchase is almost complete and architects plans being made." They suggested that organized "protest on the project might better have been made when the first publicity appeared in the newspapers."[88]

Two weeks after the public meeting, a delegation representing the Western Addition Housing Council and Fillmore Merchants Association "asked the intent of the Authority regarding additional projects in the Western Addition, as they find people moving away and the merchants suffering thereby." Mrs. Fletcher asked "if any of the racial groups had applied as tenants and had been accepted."[89] Despite this pressure, the SFHA moved forward with the project, emphasizing federal obligations and showing their commitment to providing some (though certainly not enough) housing to Western Addition residents.

SFHA plans for two projects in the Mission District also inspired city residents to engage in debating housing policies. SFHA applications for the Valencia Gardens and Cogswell projects had the support of more than twenty-five organizations in the district. After two years of planning, the USHA approved both projects in March 1940. White residents, merchants, and property owners claimed the projects were "rushed through . . . without reasonable notice." Opponents distributed antigovernment housing handbills and literature, comparing SFHA decision making to the "sort of 'blitzkrieg' that is fashionable in Europe" and "as un-American as the Gestapo or the OGPU [Soviet Union secret police]." Public housing, to them, was a wrongheaded social plan that injured "homeowners in the area selected for experiment." "The trouble with our current breed of social planners," they said, was "that they conceive their authority to be OVER the people instead of FROM the people."[90]

The opponents demanded the resignation of SFHA Commissioner Dill. They also mobilized residents, and for the first time opponents and supporters reached a political parity, as evidenced by a divided press and a divided Board of Supervisors. If the SFHA abandoned the two projects, the authority stood to lose $2.5 million in federal funds and much-needed housing units. Mayor Rossi worked out a compromise. The commissioners abandoned the Cogswell site but continued with Valencia Gardens.[91]

Valencia Gardens highlighted the connections between Europe's Modern Housing and the U.S. public housing program. The SFHA selected architects Harry Thomsen, Jr., and William Wurster to design the project. Wurster (who married Catherine Bauer and was an influential western architect) and Thomsen were part of the international housing and planning community who worked on New Deal programs.

The two architects, influenced by the promise of Modern Housing and large-scale housing, designed housing units to "stress the dignity of the individual."[92] They arranged six low-rise buildings into a serpentine-shaped complex that surrounded two service courts and three garden courts landscaped with trees, statues, and benches. The shape of the complex prevented tenants from seeing the whole project, thus giving each court "the feeling of a small neighborhood," and it helped buffer the winter and summer winds that blasted the rest of the city. When coupled with amenities not found in low-rent housing of similar

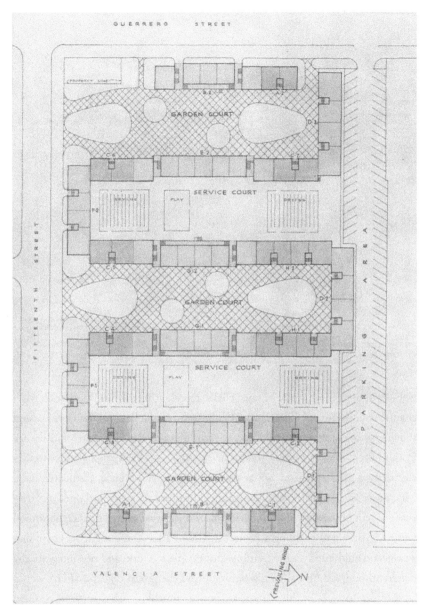

Figure 2.4
Plans for Valencia
Gardens housing
project, highlighting
common courtyards.

cost, the popular project was well received in the housing and planning community, and later by tenants themselves. Wurster and Thomsen also understood that well-designed projects such as Valencia Gardens could help build support for public housing and planning, as well as legislation to expand the economic rights of citizens.[93]

The SFHA had learned to respond effectively to overtures from a neighborhood that desired public housing. On August 29, 1940, a delegation from the Glen Park Community Club asked the SFHA commissioners "whether or not a project could

Figure 2.5
Valencia Gardens
housing project
completed in 1942.

be built in their community." Elmer Hicks, representing the neighborhood's Merchants Association and Community Club, "presented a letter to the Commission showing 100% of their Organization in favor of a project." The water and sewage in this outer Mission neighborhood, he stated, "was already installed, as well as electricity, and . . . the land will be reasonable in price." Frances Carpenter and a Mrs. Anna said, "a project in Glen Park will improve the neighborhood." A forty-year resident of the area, Winifred Morrill, said she was "sure all the neighborhood will be favorable to building a project in Glen Park." These residents knew that a project would improve the housing, put people to work, and not integrate the neighborhood. Commissioner Watchman told the group that the SFHA would look into a "project in this district as soon as possible."[94] In their visits to Glen Park, SFHA commissioners found, as the 1939 *Real Property Survey* had, roughly 15 percent of the single-family, working-class row houses in substandard condition.[95]

Just three months after residents asked for a project, SFHA commissioners submitted an application for Glen Crags. Residents and business owners asked local and national politicians to approve the development, and civic and labor organizations followed suit. The USHA approved Glen Crags.[96]

But opponents of public housing had also developed new tactics for blocking such efforts since the early years of the SFHA. Before construction began, the Glen Park Property Owners Association stopped the project by claiming it violated the city's zoning laws for multi-residential buildings. For the next year the lawyers battled it out in front of the San Francisco Planning Commission, which ruled in favor of the authority.[97] The legal strategy and then the shortages of World War II delayed Glen Crags long enough for property owners to raise a successful legal challenge in the late 1940s.[98]

Federal officials also made decisions that limited the growth of San Francisco's public housing program. In 1940 the SFHA commissioners submitted two applications for projects, in North Beach and Rincon Hill. Both areas had blocks of substandard housing, but North Beach's high land prices and Rincon Hill's dearth of facilities (churches, schools, playgrounds, and so on) led federal officials to reject the two projects without much consideration for local and regional expertise. As Catherine Bauer told Nathan Straus,

> I really must register my hearty disagreement with the action of the Washington office in disapproving the SFHA application for two small projects in the North Beach and Rincon Hill areas respectively.
>
> For one thing, I'm sure I don't know what we have all this complicated mechanism of Regional Offices and local authorities for, if we don't trust their judgment, by and large, on site selection—provided, of course, their selections are reasonable with respect to cost, convenience and other matters of broad national policy and necessity. Beyond such matters, there *is* great variety in local situations: factors enter in which simply cannot be judged except on the spot.[99]

Bauer was not alone in resisting authority from Washington, DC. At the 1940 National Association of Housing Officials–USHA Committee meeting, SFHA Director Evers and his counterparts at other authorities discussed local versus federal expertise with Straus and his staff. "The whole meeting was devoted," Evers recalled, "to a discussion of simplified procedure and more autonomy for Local Authorities." Discussions did not lead to significant changes in the working relationship between local authorities and the USHA, however. Although the Rincon Hill project was rejected, the USHA allowed a modified North Beach application to move forward, something that must have delighted Alice Griffith, who had for four decades worked to improve the homes surrounding her Telegraph Hill Neighborhood Association.[100]

By the end of 1940, the SFHA had five other projects in various stages of planning and development. In Visitacion Valley, a suburban district in the southeastern part of the city, the USHA approved the Sunnydale project for 772 units on 49 acres of green meadows. To build the two-story apartments, the SFHA planned to bring roads, sewer system, and other infrastructure to the area, and because of this planning, many in the housing and planning community began to envision a much broader economic role for public housing authorities.[101] Just to the east of

Figure 2.6
Elizabeth Ashe (*left*),
Alice Griffith (*middle*),
and Mrs. Harry M.
Sherman, née Lucia
Kittle (*right*) at Social
Service Clubs, February
28, 1940.

Sunnydale in the Hunters Point district, the SFHA planned row houses on land currently used as cow pasture. Federal officials approved the SFHA project called Bernal Dwellings, a 201-unit project in the Bernal Heights neighborhood, and De Haro Plaza, a 135-unit project near Potrero Hill. In total, the eleven approved projects would add 3,600 units to the city's housing stock.[102] For all of the projects, SFHA staff also promised to "integrate the life of the project into the larger social life of the community around it. Whenever possible project facilities will be made available to the general neighborhood."[103]

The first SFHA project to open its doors, and the first public housing west of the Rocky Mountains, was Holly Courts. Completed on May 31, 1940, Holly Courts offered 118 two-story units in the Bernal Heights district. The units had large windows, electricity, gas heaters, closets, private bathrooms, hot water, and fully equipped kitchens. Outside, each unit had an individual garden plot for flowers or a vegetable garden that also opened up to an attractively landscaped courtyard. There was a common meeting room for tenants. The layout of the row houses provided lots of open space, and the project, like the interiors of the units themselves, revealed the influence of the Modern Housing movement. Holly Courts tenants were screened by SFHA's John Beard, who selected tenants based on income, current housing conditions, family need, and, in keeping with the practice of tenant selection by neighborhood pattern, race. At least one of the adults in the household had to be a U.S. citizen. By 1941, the average monthly income for families at Holly Courts was $72.30 a month while monthly rents averaged between $17.95 and $21.20 a month. Tenant satisfaction, based on SFHA interviews, was extremely high.[104]

The SFHA used Holly Courts and an array of social services offered there to improve the lives of tenants and their neighbors and the public image of the housing program. The two commissions—Recreation and Parks—provided staff and activities for children who could choose from eight onsite play areas or Holly Park down the street. The SFHA sponsored gardening clubs, consumer education and organizing, and efforts involving tenants in housing councils.[105]

The Department of Health offered onsite health and baby care to residents of the neighborhood, and the SFHA hired social worker Else Reisner to enhance public housing through "education, demonstration, and advice." Her education program blended settlement house traditions, Modern Housing experience (especially from Vienna's housing program), and Victorian attitudes about gender roles. Reisner furnished a model unit and brought in experts whose slide lectures covered topics such as arranging furniture, making household budgets, and performing housework efficiently. Other lectures focused on "child education, recreation, art in the home, and adult education facilities." Education on domestic activities aimed to reduce mothers' "fatigue and strain" and expand "time for their own education and recreation," though the messages reinforced traditional gender roles, a gendered division of household labor, and, despite SFHA staff proclamations to the contrary, a degree of institutional paternalism and surveillance.[106]

Even so, these services did much to foster a feeling of civic responsibility, friendship, and cooperation among tenants. SFHA staff also made an effort to remove the stigma of charity that was often attached to these services by highlighting the multiple benefits of public housing and the need for government intervention in the housing market—just as New Dealers highlighted the need for government jobs and planning when the private sector failed in those areas.[107] Tenant satisfaction was crucial to the larger SFHA program. As Reisner put it, "public housing is still in process of development, there is still much opposition to be overcome. *Happy, satisfied tenants constitute the most important factor in a sound and effective public relations program.*"[108]

Holly Courts ushered in a period of rapid expansion for the SFHA. Not long after Holly Courts opened, construction workers completed Potrero Terrace and Sunnydale, adding 1,243 units to the city's government housing stock, bring the total to 1,361 SFHA units. Potrero and Sunnydale provided the same sort of amenities and services as Holly Courts, and by 1941 more than 3,000 residents had applied to live in one of the three completed projects.[109]

Figure 2.7
The Sunnydale housing
project created jobs for
city residents.

Demand for SFHA housing reflected several factors. The SFHA's 1939 housing survey estimated that at least 40,000 substandard housing units existed in the city; comparatively, SFHA units offered a better and healthier alternative to private housing.[110] SFHA rents, set at 17 to 20 percent of tenant incomes, made public housing a cost-effective alternative to private housing. Finally, the stigma associated with using public programs, whether in the form of government housing or employment, diminished greatly during the economic crisis. More and more, ordinary people believed that citizenship rested on a growing set of protections and rights, including access to housing.[111] The SFHA's second annual report stated, "As the program of the Authority progresses greater numbers of citizens are becoming interested; as they become acquainted with the true objectives and guiding principles, their enthusiasm and support grow proportionately."[112]

To be sure, some local and national opposition to public housing continued. But local housing authorities and the USHA had done much to change public attitudes toward government housing. Catherine Bauer compared the housing program to an inoculation. "I think the USHA and the local authorities have in 28 months," she wrote, "done an almost superhuman job of inoculating this great jittery cow of a country with a healthy serum." That inoculation of the body politic attacked "many

Figure 2.8
The large Sunnydale
housing project
exemplified San
Francisco Housing
Authority planning in
the 1940s.

of our most cherished national prejudices and sentiments. . . . In my opinion the injection has unquestionably taken, occasional eruptions and twitchings merely indicating the successful working of the fluid. Succeeding operations can only be easier."[113]

× ✕ ×

New Deal legislation acted as a powerful force in turning the city's reform community toward the housing question. Even though the San Francisco Housing Association's initial PWA housing applications were not approved, the application process revitalized reformers in the city and broadened their vision of housing reform and the relationship between their city and the federal government. That transformation in some ways followed the new relationship that citizens began to forge with Washington, DC. In San Francisco, the making of public housing attracted a greater number of participants, whether public housing opponents such as Emma Cougle and Ben Vladov or supporters such as Sara Jenkins and Emily Lee Fong. As with the cases of Jenkins and Fong, the SFHA's program drew nonwhites into the New Deal coalition and expanded the number of individuals demanding an expansion of the welfare state to include economic and civil rights. The public nature of the SFHA, in contrast to the San Francisco Housing Association, facilitated increased citizen participation in housing policy in their city and expanded citizen expectations of government.

In a review of the SFHA's early years, Alice Griffith acknowledged that the authority could have done more had it "been freed from the necessity of combating ignorant prejudices and active antagonisms fostered and promoted by selfish property holders, the Real Estate Board and the Apartment House Organizations." More time, she said, could "have been used to hasten the acquisition of needed properties and thus furthered the construction of several more projects."[114] She might have mentioned the federal obstacles placed in front of local authorities, particularly inadequate funding and the inflexibility of USHA officials who rejected local judgment. She might have also commented on how the political culture of liberalism, however much it was evolving, still did not offer an analysis of the structural problems caused by private property rights. On civil rights, she blamed SFHA officials and staff for bowing to white pressure to use the authority to maintain segregation—just as New Dealers did in other programs administered around the nation. By doing so, however, the SFHA did two things. It gained the support of many white residents for the idea and enactment of public housing while laying the foundation for the civil rights struggles that would erupt during the Second World War.

Despite obstacles and problems, the SFHA had achieved several major accomplishments by 1941. It had completed three permanent projects and had eight others in various stages of planning and construction, putting thousands of people to work. This $15 million program had grown with active input from the community, and the SFHA had become a vital part of the city's social and political landscape. Emboldened by the completion of three projects, empowered by their growing institution, and armed with the knowledge of housing needs in their city and how to navigate the USHA, SFHA commissioners approached their program with confidence, ready to build large and small housing projects alike. Not every city could make such a claim. On the eve of the Second World War, there were many possibilities for the city's public housing authority.

CHAPTER 3

PUBLIC HOUSING, RACE, AND CONFLICTING
VISIONS OF DEMOCRACY AND THE STATE

In the post-war world there must be work for all who are able to work.
There must be homes, worthy of the name, to which the workers may
return when their tasks are done. These goals are complementary and
the aim of good government should be to ensure them both.

Nathan Straus, U.S. Housing Authority[1]

ON JANUARY 25, 1943, hundreds of residents gathered on Post Street between Market and Kearney to kick off "War Housing Week." San Francisco Mayor Angelo Rossi, members of the Board of Supervisors, and federal officials spoke at the downtown rally. Comedians Jack Kirkwood and Tommy Harris, actors, singers, municipal and U.S. Army brass bands, and even a Franklin Delano Roosevelt impersonator entertained the crowd with housing jokes and patriotic pageantry.

The gathering was aimed at raising awareness of the seriousness of the metropolitan area's housing shortage. Few in the crowd needed to be told about the problem. The migration of civilian, military, and government workers to the San Francisco Bay Area for jobs and opportunities had exhausted the supply of local housing at all price and quality levels. Housing was so tight that one San Francisco family was sleeping in an old icebox. Across the bay in Richmond and Oakland, war workers lived in converted sheds and chicken shacks. Even individuals and families in higher income brackets had trouble finding housing. By 1943, the housing crisis in San Francisco threatened the war effort and the city's social and political fabric. No wonder that the federal government stood "ready"—not only to lease rooms and homes but to "advance all costs of converting" attics, rumpus and game rooms, and basements into war apartments.[2] Government officials even discussed relocating the elderly and other residents not directly contributing to the war effort if they could not find enough homes for San Francisco workers.[3]

Local and federal officials used these rallies and public information campaigns to build support for housing legislation and to gain greater cooperation from private property owners who were reluctant to put the nation's housing needs before their own interests. Some of these property owners aligned themselves with real estate, banking, and construction industry leaders who wanted government subsidies and

Figure 3.1
Rally for War Housing
Week, January 25,
1943.

lower taxes, but not regulations or public housing. This chapter describes the many ways that this political push against public housing and expanding economic and civil rights reflected a national movement against the New Deal and civil rights. Nonetheless, during this same period, public housing and planning advocates, government officials, and tenants increased their support for government-owned housing and additional New Deal policies to expand economic and civil rights.

During the war years, this group of housing and planning experts worked with local and federal officials to develop solutions to the housing crisis, and many of them kept track of advances in the field outside the San Francisco Bay Area. Federal officials set up clearinghouses to identify, register, and allocate private housing, occasionally leased converted rumpus rooms, and expanded public housing. As in the First World War, federal officials justified expanding the government role in the economy using the language of national security and patriotism, though now the idea of economic and civil rights permeated discussions of federal housing policies.[4]

The SFHA responded to the challenges presented by San Francisco's rapid population growth during World War II, including planning for demobilization effects at war's end. The wartime expansion of the SFHA, like other housing authorities, continued New Deal goals and provided a laboratory for improving public planning, expanding social welfare programs, and examining the state of race relations. In the preceding decade, the SFHA had already developed the institutional capacity to plan and manage a program of large scope and depth, though procuring needed labor and materials even for approved projects became more difficult during the war. Some New Dealers envisioned using housing authorities for postwar urban development, regional planning, and rounding out a comprehensive welfare state. These proposals were driven by worries of a postwar recession, but also by a vision of government that blended economic planning with expanding economic and civil rights of citizens.

For many San Francisco residents, the wartime language of fighting for democracy abroad also became a powerful weapon to challenge discrimination in jobs and housing at home. Civil rights activists targeted public housing and turned the SFHA into a site for contesting the nature and meaning of citizenship. As a result, as they had in other cities, efforts to integrate SFHA housing contributed to tensions among civil rights advocates and housing officials. Those tensions over civil rights, as well as debates about the economic role of the SFHA, led to a power struggle within the authority, leaving in its wake a regime hostile to the social and economic goals proposed by the progressive housing and planning communities in the West. This change in direction in SFHA leadership meant that members of California's housing and planning community would lose a powerful institution in their push for civil rights, public planning, and guaranteed full employment in the postwar era.

When national governments mobilized for war, their spending pulled many parts of the world out of the Great Depression. The Golden State was well suited to attract these war dollars: It offered natural and human-made ports in the San Francisco Bay Area, Los Angeles, and San Diego, and its mild climates made year-round production possible. California farmers and agribusiness resumed full production following a decade of crop destruction, fallow fields, and labor stoppages. Weapons companies already dotted the state, and administrators of California's private and public universities made faculty and facilities available to the war efforts, including the Manhattan Project. Throughout the state, city boosters and business organizations sold California's natural and human resources to companies and government agencies. By the end of the war, more than $19 billion from the U.S. government alone had flowed into the state for defense contracts, new military bases, and war-related goods and services.[5]

In this climate, the San Francisco Bay Area economy boomed. The Kaiser Shipyards and San Francisco Naval Shipyard won federal contracts; public agencies such as the San Francisco Housing Authority and the University of California also secured federal money to provide goods and services from housing and roads to development of atomic weapons. The demand for labor caused population shifts as individuals and families predominantly from the U.S. South and Southwest flocked to the Bay Area. Many of these new residents were married and in their 20s and 30s. Nonwhites made up a large portion of these new residents, who hoped to find a safe and friendly climate in which to live, work, and raise their children.[6] From 1940 to the end of 1942, San Francisco's population rose 15 percent to a total of 728,236; by 1945 it reached 827,400 residents. The city's African American population surged by 600 percent from 4,802 in 1940 to 32,001 in 1945. Bay Area homes and rental units became scarce, and vacancy rates in San Francisco regularly dropped below 1 percent.[7]

SFHA commissioners and staff found themselves at the center of the housing shortage, and wartime scarcity of materials made their work challenging. Citizens, civic groups, and military and federal officials took an active role in expanding the city's government housing stock. The SFHA commissioners tried to complete their eight permanent projects, but the diversion of materials and workers to the war effort drove up construction costs and caused crippling material shortages. By early 1941, the deficiencies had stalled the SFHA program, and in August the commissioners stopped work on all projects. In December, they described spending resources on the projects as "useless" unless they were given federal priority for materials and workers.[8]

The first step toward obtaining labor and materials was for federal officials to declare San Francisco a "congested production area," and the government obliged. With that designation, the city became one of ten national congested production areas (along with four other West Coast cities: San Diego, Los Angeles, Portland, and Seattle). But this designation still required residents to apply political pressure and navigate numerous government agencies to obtain the release of materials for every housing project. SFHA commissioners did some of this work, as did a host of local civic, labor, and political organizations. The San Francisco Housing and Planning Association, the San Francisco League of Women Voters, the Congress of Industrial Organizations (CIO) and AFL locals, and the California Housing and Planning Association (CHPA) all lobbied the federal government by urging "the immediate construction of [the Authority's] projects."[9]

Because there was little chance of getting federal priorities for all of the SFHA's eight projects, the SFHA made Westside Courts in the Western Addition a priority. The district remained one of the few housing options for nonwhites, who were excluded from a majority of the city's neighborhoods, and high rents ensured overcrowding, even after the internment of San Francisco's 5,300 Nisei and Issei residents, most of whom lived in the district. Western Addition properties were known for substandard and even dangerous conditions. In 1943, for example, Director of Public Health Jacob Geiger ordered 288 structures in the district to be

"vacated and remodeled or torn down because of fire and health hazards." Through
the Western Addition Housing Council, the Negro Women's Housing Council,
and local and state organizations, African Americans and their allies pressured local
and federal officials to complete Westside Courts.[10] Commissioner Marshal Dill
urged Leon Keyserling of the United States Housing Authority (USHA) to classify
Westside Courts as a priority, and SFHA commissioners coordinated an active letter
and phone campaign. Washington approved both the 135-unit Western Addition
project and Valencia Gardens, a 246-unit development in the Mission District,
leaving the six remaining permanent projects, however badly needed, shelved for
the duration of the war.[11]

Material shortages still delayed Westside Courts and Valencia Gardens. SFHA
Director Albert Evers worried that, given public expectations, the delays threatened
the SFHA's credibility. Evers felt compelled to give the "press a true picture of the
situation so that the public would be informed of the reason completion of this
sorely needed housing is being delayed."[12] Part of the delay, according to Nathan
Straus of the USHA, was based on the way other federal agencies gave bankers and
private homebuilders priority access to labor and materials.[13] SFHA commissioners
did eventually get the needed materials, and they renegotiated labor contracts to
meet USHA, War Production Board, and labor union approval. With the delivery
of materials and workers, and a redesign of basements to double as air raid shelters,
workers completed Valencia Gardens in December 1942 and Westside Courts in
1943, giving the SFHA five permanent projects with 1,741 units.[14]

The five projects offered tenants several aspects of Modern Housing. Many SFHA
units had private gardens (which became Victory Gardens), electricity, refrigerators,
and indoor plumbing and private bathrooms. Artist Beniamino Bufano—who was

Figure 3.2
Dedication of Hunters
Point housing project,
November 27, 1943.

fired from the WPA for creating politically charged art that commemorated workers such as Harry Bridges and critiqued fascism, modern warfare, and capitalism—provided large-scale statues of animals for SFHA project courtyards.[15]

Along with the physical and cultural amenities, SFHA projects provided space for social programs. Nursery schools, health clinics, social halls, recreation areas, and adult education classes were available to tenants and neighbors alike. Morse Erskine, a Bay Area lawyer and civil rights activist, brought cooperative stores and a collective spirit to San Francisco's public housing.[16] Combined, the social programs and efforts to make public housing a collective institution offered tenants something much different from what they experienced in the private rental market, and demand for San Francisco's public housing, as in other cities, far outpaced supply.

Figure 3.3
Mrs. Barbara Corbin and Judith Ann, 4 months old, wait for Mr. Corbin to return from work. They were among the first occupants in the Hunters Point project.

In addition to its permanent housing program, the SFHA also received federal contracts for temporary war housing units. Planning for construction of federal war housing reflected the debates over what role public housing would play in the nation. Funding for war housing came from the Lanham Act, which was sponsored by Texas Representative Fritz Lanham (Dem.) in response to the national housing shortage. No friend of the USHA, Lanham made nearly all war housing temporary and portable to appease the real estate industry, and he assigned the Federal Works Agency the responsibility of spreading the funds across multiple federal agencies rather than having the USHA and its 600 local authorities manage the Lanham program. Non-USHA agencies, working with local communities and unions, generally did a poor job with design, safety, and accountability. After reports of these kinds of problems emerged, Nathan Straus testified before Congress, recommending that the USHA program be given responsibility for all war housing, but he failed to convince members in Congress, who worried about the growing role of the USHA in the housing market.[17]

Still, Lanham funds did go to the USHA, and these funds were funneled to local housing authorities, especially in San Francisco and other defense areas. The SFHA still had trouble acquiring land within price limits, but the financial and legal support from the federal government during wartime made it easier to acquire property for Lanham housing.[18] The SFHA leased and acquired small lots across the eastern side of the city, but it selected the cow pastures in the southeastern part of the city for its largest development, called Hunters Point. The availability of 500 acres of mostly undeveloped land close to the San Francisco Naval Shipyard was unusual for San Francisco. George Thomas, a real estate appraiser, noted that Hunters Point residents "were few and of very limited means, some employed in the slaughter houses, others in the Yards, and some followed fishing for a livelihood."[19] Putting the war and SFHA goals before the needs of these residents, SFHA lawyers removed the few tenants and property owners who resisted moving to make way for the new housing.[20]

Figure 3.4
Wartime portable trailer units were set up on lots near the shipyards in the southeastern part of the city to meet housing needs.

With the Hunters Point location and other smaller, scattered sites, the SFHA staff dramatically expanded its program and budget. The SFHA installed two types of Lanham Act housing. Temporary dwelling units (TDUs) were built on-site in either dormitory or family style. The other type, portable dwelling units (PDUs), were mass produced offsite, then shipped to locations for installation. Local trade unionists loudly protested the use of PDUs even though the shoddy construction produced an endless stream of maintenance work. SFHA commissioner and member of the Plumbers and Gas Fitters Union No. 442 John Spalding critiqued the PDU heaters and stoves for being fire hazards. Unless they were changed, the plumber warned, a fire could break out, as had happened in similar units in Richmond, California. The commissioners responded by distributing fire prevention pamphlets to tenants and taking out personal liability insurance policies, while Spalding lobbied without success for federal permission to change the devices.[21] Many tenants found portable dwelling units to be "the least desirable of all temporary housing."[22] Still, the SFHA installed nearly 8,000 TDUs that, when combined with the PDUs, added 10,492 Lanham housing units and $20.5 million in federal money to its program.[23]

The SFHA took the leading role in planning the infrastructure and coordinating the services for sites with temporary units. The transformation of Hunters Point into a habitable neighborhood illustrated the economic planning capacity and expertise of the SFHA and its staff. Working with city officials and departments and trade unions, SFHA commissioners brought roads, sewers, schools, and police and fire services to Hunters Point. A branch of the public library was established. Social halls and a gymnasium provided space for choir practice, indoor volleyball, dances, and meetings. SFHA officials even refereed well-attended boxing matches in the gym. Government-funded daycare centers were provided, though they did not meet demand.[24]

Working with the city's public health department and the U.S. Public Health Service, the SFHA delivered a well baby clinic, a health center, and an infirmary to the area's workers. To improve transportation, the SFHA returned to service an old steam-driven train that carried workers to and from the shipyards. The SFHA also funded the *Hunters Point Beacon*, a neighborhood newspaper, and a Junior League office. The SFHA commissioners brokered deals with individuals and companies to provide goods and services such as barber shops, drug and department stores, a laundry, cafeterias, food markets, and a movie house. The public and private services eventually supported a population of 35,000, and Hunters Point became "a city within a city."[25]

In addition to planning and building infrastructure, SFHA commissioners and staff also demonstrated a knack for fiscal administration. Throughout the war, the

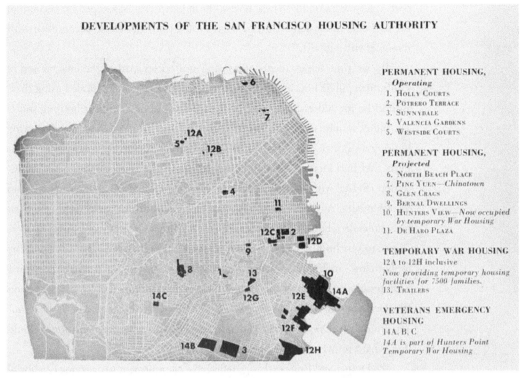

DEVELOPMENTS OF THE SAN FRANCISCO HOUSING AUTHORITY

PERMANENT HOUSING,
Operating
1. Holly Courts
2. Potrero Terrace
3. Sunnydale
4. Valencia Gardens
5. Westside Courts

PERMANENT HOUSING,
Projected
6. North Beach Place
7. Ping Yuen—*Chinatown*
8. Glen Crags
9. Bernal Dwellings
10. Hunters View—*Now occupied by temporary War Housing*
11. De Haro Plaza

TEMPORARY WAR HOUSING
12A to 12H inclusive
Now providing temporary housing facilities for 7500 families.
13. Trailers

VETERANS EMERGENCY HOUSING
14A, B, C
14A is part of Hunters Point Temporary War Housing

Figure 3.5
Map of San Francisco Housing Authority projects in 1947.

authority operated without federal subsidies and generated an operating surplus from its permanent and temporary housing. In addition to its regular payments in lieu of taxes (PILOTs) to the city government, which by January 1947 topped the million-dollar mark, it contributed more than $400,000 in extra payments to the city. The SFHA also sent more than a million dollars to the federal treasury from temporary housing rents. This surplus was achieved by paying union wages, having a degree of public participation in the policymaking processes, and working with private and public agencies to meet the changing needs of tenants.[26] It was also achieved by raising income limits to allow higher income tenants to qualify for public housing, a policy change in response to pressure from labor and military leaders who wanted more public housing for union members and veterans—and against the wishes of real estate interests and SFHA commissioner and landlord Edgar Nichols Ayer.[27]

During the war, SFHA staff also oversaw the construction of nearly 11,000 permanent and temporary government units; meanwhile, all of San Francisco's homebuilders combined built only 6,000 private homes.[28] Other California housing authorities achieved similar or even more dramatic accomplishments. By 1944 the Los Angeles Housing Authority built 4,000 units, and the Richmond Housing Authority built 24,000 units. (Before the war, Richmond's entire population had been less than 24,000!)[29] These federal–local partnerships, ramped up because of the national crisis, demonstrated what local authorities could accomplish with resources and support.[30]

The wartime achievements of housing authorities sparked the imagination of California's public housing and planning advocates. Many envisioned using these authorities for addressing what they believed would be a postwar housing shortage and economic recession. SFHA Director Evers promoted the idea of putting housing authorities in charge of urban development and regional planning. As Evers told Earl Draper, assistant administrator of the Federal Housing Administration (FHA), with a few "slight changes in the United States Housing Act and State Housing Authority Enabling Acts," local authorities could form "the basis for wholesale rehousing and replanning." If land acquisition and building were "timed to synchronize with the end of the war," he contended, large-scale housing for both low- and middle-income groups was "the most logical means of providing widespread post war employment."[31] Draper agreed, noting that he "saw no reason why local housing authorities should not be authoritative in every sense of the term." Yet, ominously, Draper admitted that in some localities housing authorities would find it hard to overcome "the prejudice against their work."[32]

The Draper and Evers exchange reflected a commitment to continue left-liberal New Deal economic efforts, among them the push for legislation to do more economic planning to improve the physical landscape (rural and urban) and expand economic rights. California's housing and planning community members nurtured their ideas in committees, departments, commissions, boards, and public housing authorities. By 1943, many California public agencies and civic organizations had added planning to their purview. To give just three examples of civic organizations in this vein, the League of Women Voters expanded its housing committee to include planning; the San Francisco Housing Association became, with Morse Erskine as first president, the San Francisco Planning and Housing Association; and the California Housing Association changed its name to the California Housing and Planning Association.[33]

The closing of the National Resource Planning Board in 1943 by congressional conservatives intensified the search for public institutions to conduct research, plan, and manage large-scale public works programs in the postwar era. Housing authorities, many believed, could continue the federal–local partnership for improving regional economies with capital projects. California's housing and planning community members also wanted to ensure that postwar urban housing, renewal, and planning stayed as much as possible in the hands of government staff and experts, in part because they believed private property owners would put profit before the needs and rights of residents and communities.[34]

Also by 1943, there were vigorous discussions about postwar economic development and who would control urban planning. Some held that public agencies such as housing authorities should have the power and resources to oversee housing and public works and even expand civil rights, while others put their faith in a private sector subsidized but minimally regulated by government.[35]

In September 1943, the California Commonwealth Club arranged a forum in San Francisco to participate in the national discussion about the future of housing and planning. David D. Bohannon, a Bay Area home and commercial builder and former president of the National Association of Home Builders, presented a report that described recent planning efforts. Although he was critical of some wartime projects, he argued somewhat surprisingly that New Deal and wartime planning efforts offered much promise for long-term urban and regional economic planning. "We have developed advanced ideas in housing, architecture, and city planning. Modern design," Bohannon continued, "is being dictated by maximum livability, and a desire to relate the house to the neighborhood, and the neighborhood to the city and regional plan." Long-term public planning in conjunction with private industry would, he said, revive cities and stem the flow of capital and whites to the suburbs. "Most American cities are decaying within. . . . We cannot afford to build out into the periphery and let the heart of the community decay." Bohannon concluded by saying, "Perhaps the greatest asset municipalities will receive from the present public war housing program will be the availability of large tracts of land." These public lands, he thought, could be used for industrial expansion, permanent public housing projects, parks and recreation, and private home development.[36]

But Bohannon's openness to public housing and planning was refuted. The second presenter was Ray Smith, vice president of the San Francisco Real Estate Board. Smith recommended what would become a post–World War II approach. Voicing a business conservative view, he criticized the growth of state economic power during the New Deal, especially the use of eminent domain and public works, as assaults on private property rights. For the postwar era, Smith proposed what business and property owners often wanted (and often got) from government: direct and indirect subsidies with few or no regulations. Postwar planning, Smith said, "must be a joint enterprise for government, private enterprise and the citizen to work out together, under the political philosophy of private enterprise." Smith wanted no role for public housing and planning advocates who, influenced by the civil rights movement, envisioned government plans to integrate neighborhoods and embark on public works. Smith explained that plans of "checkerboard housing of non-assimilable races are not compatible with the temper of most of our people. . . . A time may come when infiltration does not immediately cause reduced values and a complete readjustment of neighborhood occupancy, but we are not yet ready."[37]

Discussions of public housing featured prominently in this forum in part because of its growing influence and popularity. Yet while the record of housing authorities inspired housing and planning advocates, it clearly struck fear in the real estate industry. Public housing advocates promoted the idea that landlords had not, and would not, deliver enough low-rent housing to meet demand, which clearly justified government intervention.[38]

Against this reality, predictably, the real estate industry stepped up its two-pronged attack on public housing as a threat to the traditions of private property and all-white neighborhoods. Smith and other real estate representatives effectively used the threat of integration to stir up white opposition to public housing and planning. Smith's reference to "checkerboard housing" did not refer to any actual civil rights or fair housing policies, but it did reflect the shift in thinking among housing and planning advocates who had incorporated civil rights into their vision of government.[39]

Such was not the case among those who made the key decisions regarding who got housing and where. In the 1940s, racial discrimination was practiced by San Francisco private property owners and SFHA staff who relied on both laws and enduring customs. In the private sector, homeowners used restrictive covenants and neighborhood associations that, when coupled with real estate industry practices (red lining, not showing properties to some social groups, and so forth), helped maintain segregation in the city. With the advent of FHA mortgages, FHA officials approved or rejected mortgages to ensure neighborhood homogeneity.[40]

Demand for public housing units exceeded supply, and SFHA staff ranked applicants based on deserving and less deserving social groups. For example, veterans, if their income was not too high, got preferences, as did those who lived in substandard housing. The household income of applicants also influenced SFHA tenant selections: During the 1940s, the SFHA picked working-class families with children who were not the poorest residents of the city. Noncitizens were ineligible, and nonwhite applicants did not have access to many public housing sites. Following the agency's informal prewar policy of segregation, SFHA staff selected tenants on the basis of preserving the existing racial composition of neighborhoods. The first three permanent projects in operation—Holly Courts, Sunnydale, and Potrero—only housed white tenants.[41] The effects of housing segregation in the private and public sector constructed visible color lines throughout the City by the Bay.

Those color lines energized civil rights advocates in many areas of public and civic life. Activists looked especially to the problem in public housing because it was more accountable than private housing. Beginning in 1938, civil rights activists had first challenged discrimination in the SFHA by demanding the right to advise the SFHA through committees. As projects opened up and tenant selection began, civil rights advocates challenged SFHA tenant selection policies that maintained segregation in the city's public housing. Their efforts for equal rights and fair housing found little support among the commissioners and staff, with the exceptions of commissioners Dill and Griffith. In 1942, with Westside Courts nearing completion, the SFHA staff began selecting nonwhite tenants for the new project and hired an African American manager, Robert Flippin.[42]

Westside Courts mobilized both opponents and defenders of civil rights. White residents in the neighborhood, who opposed opening a racially integrated project and extending full citizenship to nonwhites, warned the SFHA leadership of racial strife and actions similar to the white hate strikes sweeping the nation to counter workplace and neighborhood integration. To emphasize their point, they handed the SFHA commissioners a 1942 newspaper article about the growing racial conflicts in Detroit sparked by whites opposed to African Americans in public housing.[43] In response, the Jefferson–Lafayette Improvement Club, the Western Addition Housing Council, the Bay Area Council Against Discrimination (BACAD), the NAACP, and the Communist Party mobilized to keep the project open to nonwhites. The San Francisco ACLU office threatened a lawsuit against the SFHA if it did not permit "commingling in all the projects."[44]

Support for housing nonwhites at Westside Courts also came from the CHPA, whose members included Alice Griffith; Catherine Bauer; Oakland-born Edward Howden, who would later direct the Council for Civic Unity (CCU); Morse Erskine; and Dorothy Erskine of the San Francisco Housing Association.[45] The controversy at Westside Courts intensified the struggle for civil rights at the SFHA even though none of the permanent project tenant populations, including Westside Courts, altered the racial and ethnic makeup of any neighborhoods.[46] In an effort to codify what had been an informal approach to tenant selection, the SFHA commissioners passed the following resolution:

> this Authority shall act with reference to the established usages, customs and traditions of the community and with a view to the preservation of public peace and good order and shall not insofar as possible enforce the commingling of races, but shall insofar as possible maintain and preserve the same racial composition which exists in the neighborhood where a project is located.

The policy affirmed the SFHA position on tenant selection and segregation that had been in place since the opening of Holly Courts.[47]

The passage of this discriminatory policy, often called a "neighborhood pattern" policy, outraged the San Francisco Bay Area housing, planning, and civil rights activists who launched a publicity campaign against the SFHA calling for what they called "democratic housing." Democratic housing was defined as nondiscriminatory and was also connected to a broader use of public planning and housing to revitalize cities and provide economic security to citizens. They promoted their program at luncheons, community gatherings, and in print. They even worked with San Francisco school district officials on classroom materials (fact sheets, exhibits, and lessons plans) for imparting their ideas to the next generation of citizens. Through the CHPA, they coordinated a statewide effort to pass civil rights and planning legislation in Sacramento. The proposed civil rights legislation, according to Augustus Hawkins, a leading Los Angeles Democrat in the struggle for economic and civil rights, would "remove restrictions within our democracy that are contrary to the ideals and purposes for which we are fighting on the far-flung battle fields of the world."[48]

The stepped up activism for democratic housing and employment in California reflected national civil rights trends. Organizations such as the NAACP and the League of United Latin American Citizens experienced dramatic growth, and professional associations intensified their demands for equality. The creation of the Fair Employment Practices Committee in 1941 and the 1943 repeal of the Chinese Exclusion Acts were examples of civil rights progress, as were the many ways workers, especially in CIO unions, pushed for fair employment practices and integrated unions. Yet meaningful state and federal civil rights legislation remained out of immediate reach across the nation, and white resistance and violence in workplaces and neighborhoods intensified.[49]

An important dimension of the civil rights movement during World War II was the use of social scientific research on intergroup relations. Sponsored by public and private institutions and building on five decades of research methods, social scientists conducted case studies to document the color line with an eye toward social and political equality and understanding the dynamics of intergroup relations. These researchers unpacked the deep racial prejudice in the dominant culture and institutions and the social and political costs of discrimination.[50]

Although the bulk of these studies focused on Midwest and East Coast locations, some of this research examined intergroup relations in the West. In 1943, San Francisco reformers invited sociologist Charles S. Johnson to oversee a study of the city's African American community. The list of sponsors and researchers on this project included a who's who of the city's progressive reformers. The 98-page report, entitled *The Negro War Worker*, grappled with the complexities of social relations and racial stereotypes in a metropolitan environment undergoing significant growing pains. Within this context, Johnson's report focused on racial discrimination against African Americans and other nonwhites in housing, education, recreation, employment, and labor unions. Following similar social science work, his study also explored juvenile delinquency and the process of rural migrants adjusting to urban living.[51]

Johnson's report found that the massive influx of migrants, white and nonwhite, to the city during the war magnified social and racial tensions. Some of the tensions revolved around the competition for housing, jobs, services, and public spaces, especially for whites who felt they were losing their power and privilege. Other tensions arose from cultural differences. Many long-term residents blamed the new migrants for the city's social problems, with nonwhites often singled out. One respondent told Johnson's field researcher, "Negroes now coming in are rowdy, thievish, drunken, and quarrelsome. They are dirty." It was not only whites, however, who were uneasy with new residents. Katherine Flippin, an African American San Francisco civil rights activist, recalled that "San Francisco's Negro community had exploded. All of a sudden it was filled with people with whom we had difficulty identifying, because they spoke a different language, their behavior was unlike ours. They came from a different . . . world."[52] Across the bay, in Richmond and Oakland, historian Marilynn Johnson found similar social chasms. Established residents, she wrote, "tended to blame newcomers for ruining their cities, attributing trash, crime, immorality, and a host of other urban ills to outsiders who had 'invaded' their communities."[53]

For established African Americans, some of these tensions resulted from their trying to maintain status and recent gains, leading them to display a paternalistic attitude toward working-class black migrants.[54] Wartime unleashed a heightened racial consciousness among members of social groups, and whites especially reinforced their racial identity through neighborhood segregation and holding onto racial stereotypes. To combat self-interest, fear, and stereotypes, Catherine Bauer, who chaired the interim steering committee of Johnson's report, wrote that there should "be a broad community organization mobilizing all the elements of the community to meet effectively the problems of group inter-racial, inter-cultural relations."[55]

The housing section of Johnson's study documented widespread discrimination against nonwhites. When Johnson asked for an explanation of housing discrimination, the majority of whites cited concerns about falling property values. "The mere fact that there is a Negro or Chinese family in a block," one man remarked, "immediately depreciates property values . . . and the area becomes undesirable." Others used popular stereotypes to justify discrimination. One respondent commented, "Negroes are lazy and dirty. It's bad to have them living around white girls." Another man proclaimed, "I wouldn't even want Marian Anderson as a neighbor." Many whites, Johnson found, held similar attitudes toward people of Chinese, Mexican, and Filipino descent.[56]

The wartime migration of whites and nonwhites, the city's housing shortage, and the civil rights challenges to the color line heightened prejudice and deeply held stereotypes. To shore up their neighborhoods and racial identity, whites organized at the block and neighborhood level and increased their use of racial covenants.

Here—more than in workplaces, recreation areas, and public accommodations—was where whites fought hardest to preserve white neighborhoods and by doing so white privilege and power.[57] On both sides of the bay, segregation was becoming more entrenched as a result of federally insured loans and tenant selection by those in charge of public and private housing. Johnson's study warned that racial ghettoes forming in Hunters Point and the Western Addition might rival those in the Midwest and East Coast, or the Chinatowns and barrios in the West.[58] Private landlords and their agents contributed the most to segregation in the city, but the SFHA's tenant selection did much to reinforce these larger trends.

Because of its public nature, civil rights organizations continued to apply pressure on SFHA leaders to integrate the city's public housing. But their efforts, within the context of wartime strains in race relations, produced, in the short term, the opposite response. Mayor Rossi's appointments to the SFHA commission created a deck stacked against civil rights. Dill and Griffith were sympathetic to civil rights, but the other three commissioners—Edgar Nichols Ayer, William Cordes, and Timothy Reardon—plotted to shore up the program's ability to resist changing its segregationist policies. Working with SFHA's tenant manager John Beard, commissioners Ayer, Cordes, and Reardon staged a series of crises between SFHA project and division managers and SFHA Director Evers. On August 17, 1943, with tensions mounting at the authority, Commissioner Dill called a special commissioner meeting to discuss a reorganization of the Maintenance Department. Ayer, Cordes, and Reardon, citing what they claimed was a failure of leadership, asked Evers to resign. Shocked, Evers demanded a chance to defend his record, but his request was denied when the three commissioners outvoted Dill and Griffith on the matter. Next, the three commissioners declared his position vacant and promoted John Beard, who had worked with tenant selection, to be the new SFHA director. Beard had no formal expertise with planning or architecture, though his experience with filtering out nonwhite applicants from white-only projects certainly helped his candidacy.[59]

The ouster of Evers and the promotion of Beard estranged many in the housing and planning community, both locally and nationally. Dill and Griffith were so infuriated by these "unfair practices" that they resigned on August 18, the day after Beard's installation as director. Dill wrote Rossi to express his disapproval "of the ruthlessness of the Commission's procedure" in firing Evers who Dill claimed had "intelligently and unselfishly given some of the best years of his life to the creation of a monumental San Francisco asset."[60] Housing activist Edgar Zook told Evers, "It is a shame that our Mayor and his Commission have to indulge in such rotten politics."[61]

Local, state, and national organizations sent letters of support for Evers to the SFHA, the mayor, the press, and federal officials. Many noted the loss of Dill and Griffith as well. PHA Regional Director Langdon Post described Griffith's departure as "irreparable" while Bauer, who frequently contributed to the SFHA's program, felt it was a "real shame" for Griffith to resign and to "hand Beard such a complete victory."[62] Griffith also asked Bauer to intervene, writing that Ayer "will kill post-war housing if he can—but I maintain we can prevent that—and Langdon Post can take the war housing right away from the Authority if he is dissatisfied." Bauer was sympathetic, but she did not get involved.[63]

After two months of reflection, Griffith publicly attacked not only the proceedings but also Mayor Angelo Rossi's deleterious appointments to the commission. Griffith told the press that Evers was fired "without just cause" and that she considered Beard "a man without wide experience and no background for a position of such importance." She documented the chain of events and stressed the importance of the public housing program to the city. She hoped to spark a movement to remove Beard and the remaining commissioners and return the authority to its purpose. Griffith, then 78, was the most prominent housing figure in the city, and her report was discussed widely.[64] Although many in the press and housing community shared Griffith's views, sufficient popular and political support for Evers never materialized. Griffith, Dill, and Evers never returned to the authority. With their departure, the SFHA lost decades of knowledge in the housing, urban planning, and architectural fields—and its key advocates for using the SFHA to advance civil and economic rights and urban planning.

The reconstituted SFHA, with Beard at the helm, refocused the institution on slum clearance. To fill the two vacant seats, Rossi appointed Katherine Gray, a San Francisco social worker, and labor leader John Spalding. Gray was a member of the SFPHA and the CHPA, though she drew more from the public health tradition of public housing than from the Modern Housing and planning traditions. She also favored a gradualist approach to civil rights. Spalding represented the American Federation of Labor wing of organized labor in the Bay Area and, as noted earlier, brought construction expertise to the city's public housing. Although he supported public housing for creating union jobs and low-cost homes, he could not push for civil rights in the housing program without drawing attention to discriminatory practices in the building trade unions.[65] With these appointments, Rossi ensured that the SFHA leadership would not push against the city's color line and would maintain public housing leadership from the usual social and political groups.

As the new SFHA commissioners pursued their vision of public housing, city leaders limited the agency's economic power still further. At a June 1944 meeting, the commissioners discussed the role of the SFHA and agreed "that any additional housing in this area, when and if allocated[,] should be constructed on a definite slum clearance basis, on locations of structures condemned by the Board of Health action rather than scattering the units throughout the City." Commissioner Gray emphasized that "the public housing program should be carried forward with the real purpose of its creation—that of actual slum clearance." With eliminating slums as their goal, they joined the San Francisco Real Estate Board, the City Planning Commission, and the city's Master Plan Committee in forming an urban renewal plan. As part of that coalition, the SFHA proposed to expand permanent public housing and make the authority the "land-acquiring agent" to assist "private enterprise in demolition and rebuilding of blighted areas." This role would hand control of planning and building to the private sector.[66]

However, even with this newly limited, passive role, the SFHA was not a welcome participant in any urban renewal plans. San Francisco Real Estate Board representative Raymond Smith "took exception to the participation by the Housing Authority" because the SFHA wanted the opportunity to add public housing to renewal projects. Smith lobbied local government to remove the SFHA from the coalition. The San Francisco Board of Supervisors responded with legislation to "exclude participation of the HOUSING AUTHORITY" in urban renewal planning. The supervisors' rejection of scattered SFHA sites was a response to neighborhood association and real estate representatives, who saw public housing as the Trojan horse of integration (despite the new commission's clearly segregationist orientation) and a threat to the private housing sector.[67]

The new SFHA leadership represented a turning point in the program's history, as they steered the program away from the intellectual and political movements for economic rights and an expanded economic role for public housing authorities. In this case, political leaders in and out of the SFHA and business groups pushed back against expanding government's role associated with New Deal liberalism.

The SFHA leadership also resisted the growing civil rights movement. While the nation remained at war against fascism, the SFHA presented a harmonious picture of race relations in their program. "We deliberately allowed a few white families to the Westside," Director Beard explained, "so as not to establish a purely Negro project." Tenant selection at temporary units in Hunters Point reflected the multiracial flood of workers into the area during the war. These units provided relief for African Americans, who otherwise were confined to substandard housing or forced to leave the city. The authority's staff estimated that, by 1945, 10,000 African Americans would live in Hunters Point, and the other 22,000 African Americans would compete for the few units in neighborhoods open to nonwhites.[68]

SFHA reports showed whites and African Americans working, playing, and living together in Hunters Point.[69] A consultant to the authority, Mr. Andrews, said in his report to the commission: "Well, frankly, I think [race relations] have been handled damned intelligently . . . by the Housing Authority and by the Navy. I really think that the racial situation there is much less of a headache than any other projects I know of."[70] But the reality was much different. Outside of an interracial athletic program, which was not without racial tensions, whites and African Americans in Hunters Point lived separate lives, and many of the civic organizations excluded African Americans or at best provided limited interracial socializing.[71]

Along with the change in SFHA leadership and focus, the demographic changes in SFHA housing and the city during the war and persistence of racial discrimination produced heightened tensions and a call to action by the city's civil rights organizations. At a September 1944 conference at San Francisco State College, 10,000 "interested individuals and representatives of organizations" met to "discover ways for building a more democratic community." Discussion groups wrestled with "the most serious problems facing the city." To reduce racial discrimination and tensions, one of these discussion groups created the Council for Civic Unity (CCU), which became a leading interracial civil rights group in San Francisco. CCU members believed their organization could "perform the same function for this city as the United Nations Organization can for world unity and security."[72]

As the CCU began its work, rumors of an impending race riot in Hunters Point spread throughout the city on Halloween day. On November 2, 1944, Mayor Roger Lapham created the Mayor's Committee on Civic Unity, a temporary committee of the city's leading civil rights and housing activists. Oleta Yates, Henry Shue Tom, and Robert Flippin, for example, served on both the CCU and the mayor's committee. Eneas Kane, who went on to become SFHA director in 1965, was the city's representative, while the former dean of Hastings College of Law, Maurice Harrison, chaired the committee. The Mayor's Committee on Civic Unity focused on race relations in and around public housing.[73]

The committee's investigation found that the rumors of a race riot "originated in a few words of idle gossip," though it still recommended putting resources into improving race relations given the wave of race riots across the country.[74] SFHA Director Beard agreed, noting that there was "no immediate danger of race riots but . . . the problem is growing and giving us much concern." As to the source of tension, he said, "Generally speaking, there is no evidence of Negro discontent on the project, but rather discontent among the whites."[75] Beard's acknowledgment of whites as the cause of racial tensions was remarkable, but so was his failure to understand the deep discontent among African Americans fueling the civil rights movement in the city and nation.

The Mayor's Committee on Civic Unity and the CCU worked together on community relations, though the CCU generally took the lead in integrating the SFHA program. Both groups asked newspaper editors to "be most cautious in the printing of any racial material" and "check with the Chairman or the Mayor's Office before publishing stories on subjects closely allied with the work of the Committee." Kane urged the city's department heads to treat nonwhites fairly, while the Mayor's

Committee on Civic Unity enlisted Langdon Post and other sympathetic federal officials to end discrimination in public programs. Some CCU members queried housing officials and experts from other cities on the race question; other members reported on the latest social science research on race relations; and still others investigated race relations around the state. The CCU found white attitudes to be the main problem, though mutual distrust between whites and blacks and tight housing conditions also contributed to racial tensions.[76] Lucy McWilliams, chair of the CCU's housing committee, reported that racial tensions were "accentuated by the lack of decent and adequate housing."[77]

The CCU recommended desegregating the SFHA program and using authority resources and space (on and off public housing sites) to facilitate tenant associations. The recommendation required the SFHA leadership to change its prohibition of tenant meetings of a "political nature" in SFHA projects. The CCU based their recommendation on Modern Housing ideas and on experiences in other West Coast cities. In Los Angeles, Marin City, and Seattle, where similar in-migration and racial tensions existed, public housing tenant associations provided a framework to discuss common issues and improve interracial understanding. When the CCU asked Hal Dunleavy of the Public Housing Administration about tenant associations, he said that his agency always encouraged forming voluntary groups in housing projects, which he believed significantly reduced racial tensions. They were, he said, "comparable to the old 'Town Hall Councils' of New England." In Marin, "the council is responsible for much of the community welfare." Members elected their officers, who in turn met with management "once a week to iron out their difficulties."[78] Nationally in 1945, public housing tenant associations existed in 76 percent of permanent housing and 90 percent of temporary war housing.[79]

The SFHA leadership was not so inclined. Beard resisted local and federal pressure to facilitate tenant associations and to do more to integrate the city. The housing authority, Beard said, looked "with disfavor on any effort to organize the tenants for political reasons."[80] Furthermore, he believed that the formation "of any tenant organizations was unnecessary and undesirable."[81] Beard worried that SFHA tenants might follow the example of Richmond's tenant associations, which had a number of African American organizers with membership in the Communist Party and experience fighting discrimination in the boilermaker's union. In Richmond, tenant associations demanded more public housing and an end to discriminatory policies and evictions. When the Richmond Housing Authority leadership did not budge after two years of negotiations, tenants conducted a rent strike to move negotiations forward. Across the nation, this sort of direct action in public housing appeared frequently and provided tenants with a way to influence race relations, housing conditions, and community and workplace issues.[82] Beard's belief in handling tenant concerns individually, rather than collectively, was grounded in traditions of management rights and aimed at dividing tenants and workers to limit collective and democratic power.[83]

In these ways, the SFHA leadership slowed progress in race relations and contributed to segregation. Lester Granger, a New York African American social worker who was organizing the San Francisco Urban League branch, warned, "San Francisco's Negro district is today right where the New York and Chicago districts were 40 years ago. In the East there were no civic plans to help the Negroes find suitable housing and their own efforts resulted in the present New York and Chicago Harlems." Granger thought that the SFHA should take "the first step" in integrating neighborhoods so that African Americans had more housing choices than Hunters Point and the Western Addition.[84] Others agreed. In November, representatives from the CCU, the CIO, the NAACP, and the Communist Party asked the SFHA leadership to change its tenant selection policies. But Commissioner Ayer stated that as "a public body this Authority must follow the will of all the people. This has been the policy in the past and must necessarily be the policy in the future."[85] If the SFHA contributed to segregation, so too did private property owners. Nonwhites found it almost impossible to locate housing. African Americans, a CCU report noted, had the fewest choices in housing, and they were "not inclined to leave" public housing, "for no other housing [was] available."[86]

The intransigence of the SFHA leadership, Mayor Roger Lapham's refusal to do more to end discrimination, and the absence of federal civil rights legislation combined to spur Bay Area activists to focus on state legislation for changes in policy. At a statewide conference in January 1946, 699 delegates from 366 California labor, religious, civil rights and women's organizations gathered for a two-day event billed as "a powerful instrument of the rank and file of the people of California, in meeting their most serious economic and political problems." Attendees hoped to craft an alternative program to the "halfhearted" proposals that they believed Republican Governor Earl Warren would soon propose. California Attorney General and New Dealer Robert Kenny spoke on the importance of public planning and full and "democratic" employment in the postwar economy. The conference's housing committee, which included New Dealer Langdon Post, called for both more and "democratic" public housing. Democratic housing for these folks generally meant the elimination of racial discrimination in housing rather than giving tenants the power to make decisions in their housing. Other committees forwarded policies for full employment, public works, expanded Social Security and unemployment coverage, public health insurance, childcare, cheap public power, and city–farm cooperation. There was even a committee to free California from economic dependence on eastern capital. Each committee proposed legislation, with each receiving

95 to 99 percent approval from the attendees.[87] Housing authorities remained an important part of this vision, for they were already providing many of these social and economic programs.

After the conference, the California Housing and Planning Association (CHPA) launched a campaign to build support for state and federal legislation.[88] The CHPA developed lesson plans and textbooks with K–12 teachers in the San Francisco School District that covered public planning from the ancient Romans to the 1940s and showed the benefits of such planning.[89] Although these various efforts revealed deep support among labor and civil rights organizations in California for continuing the New Deal and civil rights legislation, progressive legislation was not forthcoming. Governor Warren's proposals fell short of the broad goals of the January conference, and no legislative proposals discussed at the conference came out of Sacramento.[90] California's legislation followed the federal trend as business leaders and their political allies attacked the New Deal and civil rights legislation for being antithetical to free enterprise and aligned with Soviet communism.[91]

The lack of state and federal civil rights legislation kept San Francisco residents focused on the local SFHA program. Opponents and defenders of segregation took part in shaping the direction of the authority. The San Francisco Urban League, American Veterans League, CCU, and San Francisco Council of Churches all urged the mayor's office and the Board of Supervisors to force the SFHA to make tenant selection on "a non-color policy of first come, first serve."[92] In response to growing public pressure, Mayor Roger Lapham appointed Dr. William McKinley Thomas to the SFHA commission in 1946. McKinley, the first African American on the commission, replaced Katherine Gray after her term expired. A doctor in the U.S. Army, he, like so many other African Americans from Texas, migrated to the Western Addition during the war. He became active in public life, the Republican Party, and civil rights.[93]

His appointment was significant, but SFHA policy on segregation remained hotly contested. At one of a series of June and July meetings, Sam Herman, representing the Veterans of Foreign Wars, said

> I believe everyone has a right to choose his associates. There is a big difference between segregation and discrimination. You are trying to solve a problem that has been going on for hundreds of years.
>
> I believe the Negro is just as good as the white man. But does that compel us to break bread with him. I don't think so.[94]

When some in the audience laughed at Herman's statements, he warned that "a policy of non-segregation would 'result in race riots like they had in Detroit.'"[95] Herman was part of a vocal minority in favor of segregation by any means necessary, but his comments reflected the worst of white fears. Still, the San Francisco Planning and Housing Association recommended that the SFHA should not only "greatly expand its program for housing members of the minority groups" but also "revise its racial policy to permit minority groups in all public housing in line with our democratic principles."[96]

Federal Public Housing Administration (FPHA) officials such as Langdon Post and labor and civil rights activists continued to put pressure on local officials to change SFHA policy, and at times they met with some limited success. On July 15, 1946, the San Francisco Board of Supervisors voted nine to one for a resolution calling for the end of segregation in the SFHA.[97] SFHA leaders did nothing until November 1947 when Commissioner Thomas introduced a resolution to eliminate discrimination in housing authority policies. He found no second for his motion and it, like the Board of Supervisor's resolution, died. San Francisco housing and civil rights advocate Marion Howden complained that the mayor talked about integrating public housing but then did not back those words with action: He refused to ask sitting commissioners for their resignation or to appoint more commissioners to integrate the program. Howden charged that it was "wheels within wheels, of course, and it all stinks."[98]

To many outside of the SFHA, the failure to do more on civil rights with the SFHA program was a lost opportunity to improve race relations in San Francisco. The leadership at other authorities, for example, used policies and tenant associations to break down the color line. Catherine Bauer told Ed Weeks at the *Atlantic Monthly* how, just to the north of San Francisco, Marin County's housing authority during the war chipped away at prejudice by demanding integration of its tenants. Whites and African Americans, she wrote, can

> live amicably in the same neighborhood. I know plenty of examples myself, both in older areas (even in Washington, D.C.) and in new slum-clearance and war-workers housing projects.
>
> It might also be worth while to point out that apparently a firm and consistent public policy is the prime requisite if one seeks to avoid segregation and "trouble." The Detroit situation he mentions was almost entirely due to the vacillation of the local Housing Commission, which first designated the project for whites, then tried to open it to Negroes. The administration of war housing in the SF Bay area provides another laboratory test. In Vallejo and Richmond, the local housing authorities tried to evade the issue and have had constant trouble, resulting finally in a high degree of segregation for minority races. But the Marin County Authority, serving exactly the same kind of shipyard immigrants (with a high percentage from the South)[,] handed every housing applicant a slip right

at the start, saying in effect: We're all fighting the same war and this authority recognizes no racial discrimination whatsoever: if you don't like it, lump it. And as far as I know they've never had any trouble at all; indeed Marin City is a model of community cooperation and morale in war housing.[99]

Sociologist Charles S. Johnson agreed that Marin had "gone the full mile of integration and its experience has been gratifying."[100] Others pointed to the Los Angeles and Seattle authorities for taking similar stands with similar results. By integrating neighborhoods and by supporting tenant associations, a few housing authorities had helped to give tenants a common identity as residents with mutual goals and interests, and in the process they improved understanding between whites and nonwhites. Social group formation often divided individuals, but intergroup communities also demonstrated that they could bridge gaps that had existed, as Sam Herman pointed out, for hundreds of years. Bridging these gaps in San Francisco's public housing could, many thought, improve race relations in other areas while giving public housing a shot of democracy.[101]

If the SFHA leaders did not move much on civil rights in the immediate postwar era, they did work on adding more housing to address the city's acute shortage. The city's growing population hit 775,357 in 1950, while new housing construction, private and public, hardly dented demand. Rental vacancies remained less than 1 percent. When Elmer Robinson ran in the 1947 mayoral race, he stated that San Francisco was "suffering from the worst case of growing pains it has experienced since the turbulent days of the gold rush."[102] San Francisco District Attorney Edmund G. Brown put out a 1947 report on the social costs of the housing shortage. Catholic Charities, according to the report, received daily calls from people who wanted to "place their children in foster homes because they have no housing in which they could keep their children. This agency also has applications from families who literally have no place to live." Catholic Charities placed a few of the "extreme cases, but was powerless to help most of the applicants." Brown's report concluded that "housing difficulties and unemployment" remained the top problems in the city and that a large percentage of the city's welfare cases "stemmed from inadequate housing."[103]

SFHA commissioners did focus on expanding temporary projects. The Lanham Act required temporary units to be dismantled after the war, but with the national housing shortage, federal officials extended the life of existing units and allowed authorities to add more of the low-quality units. In 1946, SFHA commissioners added 1,200 temporary units to existing SFHA sites.[104]

Amid the intense housing shortage, more residents, especially working-class residents, turned to the SFHA for housing. To manage its limited supply, the SFHA leadership regularly determined tenant requirements. Because of inflationary wage increases after the war, more than 50 percent of SFHA tenants exceeded income limits and were in danger of eviction. This was a national trend, something that led to political pressure on the federal government to put a moratorium on income-based evictions in public housing despite vigorous opposition from the real estate industry. SFHA commissioners too responded to public pressure by raising income limits to give more workers, especially veterans, a chance at living in government housing. Roughly 4,000 SFHA tenants stayed in their homes as a result. The idea of avoiding throwing mostly veterans "into the street" reflected the view of veteran-headed households as a deserving social group.[105]

Workers on strike were treated very differently. During the 1948 maritime strike, the Waterfront Employers Association wanted to expand on the recent business victory of the Taft–Hartley Act (1947) and reduce the power of the International Longshoremen and Warehouse Union and more generally the New Deal itself. As the strike wore on, ILWU member Mansfield Davis, who lived in the SFHA Wisconsin project and had organized tenants against attempts to relocate mostly African American tenants to make way for a proposed highway, came before the SFHA commissioners as part of a delegation of union members and Veterans of Foreign Wars. His delegation asked for rent reductions, an extension of credit, and no eviction notices for SFHA tenants on strike. The commissioners ruled against assisting the strikers, a position they maintained for the entire strike.[106] The managerial approach to tenants—one that put social control and stability before economic rights and democracy—caused tensions between tenants and the SFHA leadership, especially Director John Beard.

The postwar housing shortage also focused the city's attention on the building of permanent projects, including those delayed by the war. Higher construction costs had made prewar bids and construction plans impossible to implement. By 1947, the Chinatown project, for example, was $1.3 million more than its original contract. Similarly, real estate demand and speculation drove up the price of land in San Francisco, as in other major cities, without corresponding increases in federal formulas.[107] Responding to such pressures, SFHA leaders considered tower apartments. In a December 1948 meeting with the San Francisco Department of City Planning Chief Sydney Williams, Director Beard indicated that "if sites for further public housing did not seem to be available, they [SFHA] would simply double up on the old sites." Williams, who, like many in the housing and planning community thought high-density towers flawed, wrote to Catherine Bauer for advice on how to respond to these kinds of public housing proposals, even though he admitted that his department had little "applicable legal control."[108]

Bauer faulted urban planners in her reply. She contended that urban planners themselves contributed to the trend by focusing on "central reconstruction" rather than regional planning. Bauer pleaded with Williams, "*do* try to keep the SF Housing Authority from going the way of the NYCHA [New York City Housing Authority], which is now constructing some 20,000 dwellings *entirely* in elevator apartments."[109] But Williams and his office did not limit the plans of the SFHA, which along with the San Francisco Redevelopment Agency began planning for taller housing projects in a pattern that followed commercial real estate.[110]

The U.S. Congress also shaped permanent public housing in San Francisco. Federal legislators tried to balance the competing demands of housing and planning advocates and private real estate interests. In 1947, the Taft–Ellender–Wagner (TEW) bill, for example, called for a complicated mix of public housing and urban renewal projects to be built by the public and private sector.[111] Katherine Gray, now chair of the housing committee for the San Francisco League of Women Voters and more open to a broader role for housing authorities, complained that getting the public to understand or support this bill was "a very real challenge," despite the nation's desperate need for housing.[112] The SFHA commissioners and staff limited their lobbying to making small financial donations to the National Association of Housing and Redevelopment Officials (NAHRO) and phone calls to federal officials. Voluntary housing associations and labor unions did a better job of mobilizing political support for the bill.[113]

At the national level, discussions of the TEW revealed the spectrum of postwar federal housing visions. The CIO wanted $600 million "for housing to be built by housing authorities without respect to income limits."[114] In their lobbying against the bill, representatives from the National Association of Real Estate Boards and National Association of Home Builders denounced the TEW bill as one of many incremental steps toward socialism. One National Association Real Estate Board official declared,

> If there is one thing clear about socialism, it is that it has never gained ascendance in one full blow. It always moves in bit by bit, eating away one area of free effort at a time until finally the people wake up and find that everything is controlled at a central political headquarters.

Nathan Straus, former USHA administrator, dismissed the claims, saying that the bill "would provide nine times as many private as public housing units."[115] Amid all the claims and counterclaims, the struggle over who controlled public housing and urban redevelopment stalled the federal legislation.[116]

Debates continued, but support for public housing, coupled with political compromise, eventually produced housing legislation. When Harry Truman emerged victorious in the 1948 presidential election, he promised to make housing a key part of his Fair Deal.[117]

Figure 3.6
City housing inspectors in search of slums at the rear of 2062 1/2 Pine Street. Arrow 1 points to basement living quarters, and arrow 2 shows the location of the lavatory for the basement tenant. The third arrow points toward where the tenant's bathtub is located—across the yard, up a flight of stairs, in a corner room of the second floor.

Discussions of housing in the nation also got an international boost from the 1948 United Nations General Assembly's adoption of the Universal Declaration of Human Rights, which declared housing—among a host of other economic rights such as food, health care, and financial security—a basic human right. But the TEW legislation stalled in the U.S. Congress because of disagreements over civil rights, public planning, and the shape and purpose of public housing itself. These disagreements mirrored those in San Francisco during the decade. Truman pressured reluctant Democrats, especially in the South, to support new housing legislation, and, when combined with popular demand, the Housing Act of 1949 passed. The preamble of the 1949 Housing Act stated that the nation had "to remedy the serious housing shortage, to eliminate slums and blighted areas, and to realize as soon as feasible the goal of a decent home and a suitable living environment for every American family."[118]

The act authorized 810,000 new public housing units, but in many ways it had conceded much to private developers and realtors. Funding for government units was neither immediate nor sufficient to meet the nation's low-rent housing needs. The 1949 act gave local redevelopment agencies, not housing authorities, "maximum opportunity for the redevelopment of project areas."[119] In practice, this legislation would build more market-rate apartments and commercial projects than low-rent housing and would limit the U.S. government in providing citizens with economic and civil rights. It also reflected a legislative and political turn away from the New Deal.

Making public housing in San Francisco during the war years followed national trends and patterns. The SFHA staff added both permanent and temporary homes to its stock during a period of inflation, population shifts, and material and labor shortages. In the process, the SFHA demonstrated an administrative capacity for running an efficient public housing program that benefited both new and existing residents. For both SFHA residents and their neighbors, public housing offered a range of economic and social programs that drew heavily from Modern Housing and expanded the New Deal welfare state. Inspired by these accomplishments, housing and planning advocates hoped to see public housing authorities maintain their influence in the postwar planning process, not only in matters of housing but to push for broader economic development and civil and economic rights. Legislation at the state and federal level, however, was not supportive of such goals.

What stood out most in this period was the increasing political engagement of residents with the SFHA and housing policy more broadly. To many, the SFHA program offered an opportunity to struggle for civil rights and improve race relations in San Francisco. But many white residents remained very committed to segregation, especially if they perceived integration as affecting their own neighborhoods. Civil rights organizations encountered obstacles both inside and outside of the SFHA, despite the wartime ideals of equality and democracy, a loosening of racial barriers in work and civic life, and a growing civil rights movement. As Historian Albert Broussard has noted, for whites to "maintain the illusion of civility was one thing. Living with blacks in an integrated, egalitarian environment was quite another."[120] The SFHA leadership and staff regularly sided with the customs of many whites and used the SFHA to reinforce racist patterns of segregation and inequality. But after the war, this position became increasingly difficult to defend. In San Francisco, and throughout the West, the battle for civil rights began to grow as it did in the South, and the SFHA was often at the center of that battle.

CHAPTER 4

PROSPERITY, DEVELOPMENT, AND INSTITUTIONAL RACISM IN THE COLD WAR

*If we need housing, we need housing. And if we have needed a bold
housing program ever since 1945, we need it double now. For by now it
is absolutely clear as crystal that private enterprise will not and cannot
solve the housing shortage by itself, that private enterprise will not and
cannot get rid of the slums, that private home-building enterprise can
only serve a very limited segment of the housing market.*

John F. Kennedy[1]

*Down in Alabama, where we come from, you know your place, and
that's something, at least. But up here it's all a lot of camouflage.
They grin in your face and then deceive you.*

Mrs. Willie Mays[2]

ON OCTOBER 22, 1951, SFHA commissioners and staff joined 5,000 residents to
dedicate Ping Yuen, or "peaceful garden," the long-awaited public housing project
for Chinatown. At a cost of $3.5 million, the three six-story buildings were the tallest
public housing west of Chicago. To bring good luck, event organizers lit 100,000
firecrackers on the central building above a stage with "a dancing lion wearing Keds."
The vibrant color scheme drew attention to Ping Yuen's most striking feature—a
blend of Chinese and Modern Housing architecture. In front of the middle building,
workers built a Pailou Gate, which in Chinese culture is often used to commemorate
historical events, with an inscription by philosopher Lao Tse that read "Peace and
Prosperity Prevail Among Virtuous Neighbors."[3]

To Chinatown residents, especially Ping Yuen's new tenants, the opening of
the project was worth the wait. The new buildings provided 234 modern units at
an average monthly rent of $37, which was less than 25 percent of tenants' house-
hold average income of $202.[4] The SFHA hired Anna Lee, a counselor, to be the
first onsite manager. At the dedication ceremony, SFHA commissioners handed
out miniature models of the Pailou Gate and remarked on the ways Ping Yuen
improved the district and reduced slum conditions. The ceremony aimed to boost
local views of public housing and serve as a positive example of race relations for

observers at home and abroad. "Newsreel cameras, television and radio programs recorded the dedication," as the 1951 SFHA annual report stated, "and newspapers and periodicals as far away as China and Europe devoted space to the dedication." Even the Voice of America network, the U.S. government propaganda arm in the fight against communism, "beamed the story to far points of the world."[5]

Ping Yuen reflected many trends in public housing and urban renewal, civil and economic rights, and the Cold War. Demand for Ping Yuen and other SFHA housing always exceeded supply, and in terms of quality, amenities, and cost, public housing compared favorably to housing in the private sector. Ping Yuen's high-rise design and high-density units followed national public housing trends even as many housing experts worried about the potential negative social effects of concentrating poor tenants without support and good jobs. The justification for public housing continued to depend on assumptions about the failure of the private housing sector and the need to clear perceived slums, but increasingly SFHA housing became entangled in the local politics of urban redevelopment. And the city's leaders used the language of slum clearance to support urban renewal plans across the city rather than expanding public housing.[6]

In the early Cold War years, the SFHA expanded its program to become the largest landlord in the city and continued to play a vital role in the city's urban development and broader discussions about the economic and civil rights of citizens. The climate of fear in the Cold War diminished the political commitment

Figure 4.1
More than 5,000 people attended the Ping Yuen dedication ceremony in 1951.

to New Deal public housing, planning, and full employment and steered New Deal advocates into universities and safer professional positions. During this time, public housing tenants and housing and planning advocates had limited influence on the economic role of the SFHA. Instead, the economic role of the SFHA increasingly served the needs of urban redevelopment as local political and economic elites used federal legislation and the SFHA program for urban redevelopment projects. As in the previous decade, the SFHA often took center stage as the city's residents debated the degree to which government should be involved in housing.[7]

The SFHA's role in the city's civil rights struggle, on the other hand, was clear. Although the number of social groups eligible for SFHA units expanded in this decade, the tenant selection process still favored applicants from "deserving" social groups. Veterans remained more deserving of SFHA housing than nonveterans, and seniors gained access to SFHA housing for the first time. Poorer applicants began edging out higher-income applicants, thus concentrating the very poorest tenants in some projects. Nonwhites remained shut out of white-only housing projects. SFHA tenant selection thus preserved the racial composition of neighborhoods (Chinatown being one example) and assisted in maintaining segregation in the city—much to the consternation of the city's civil rights activists who made civil rights the most contentious issue in the housing program in the 1950s. As the Cold War intensified, SFHA leaders offered pluralistic and egalitarian images

Figure 4.2
The first Ping Yuen tenants, Mr. and Mrs. Henry Wong and their children, Beverly and Calvin. Henry was a World War II veteran.

of their program to the world in the fight against communism. Yet that cultural sensitivity on display at Ping Yuen masked the racial discrimination in the SFHA and the city at large.[8]

Excitement about the opening of Ping Yuen was in part related to postwar demographic shifts and the national clamor for more and better housing. A 1950 poll found that "75% of the population of the U.S. would live on the Pacific Coast if they could live anywhere they chose."[9] Not everyone followed their dreams to live in Washington, Oregon, and California, but millions did make the move. From 1940 to 1960, the combined population of these states grew from 9,733,262 to 20,339,105. California's population doubled. In the 1950s, the population of the San Francisco Bay Area's nine counties passed the 3 million mark, with much of the growth occurring in suburbs, where homebuilding reached record highs (see Tables A.1, A.2, and A.3 in appendix). Some corporate leaders also set up administrative and manufacturing facilities in suburban areas rather than in core cities such as San Francisco, Oakland, and San Jose. Government subsidies for wider highways, the Golden Gate Bridge and the Bay Bridge, and cars and ferries made possible some of this suburban expansion.[10] Government legislation and court decisions also shaped the housing industry by assisting white homeowners, disadvantaging nonwhite households, and maintaining racial segregation. As in other metropolitan areas, the process of suburbanization generally disadvantaged nonwhites in the public and private sectors in terms of lower-quality schools and public services and unequal opportunities for jobs and housing. These disadvantages shaped long-term patterns of economic inequality and damaged race relations by maintaining segregation.[11]

For all races, housing remained tight. In a 1949 national opinion poll, people ranked housing second, after the high cost of living, as the most important issue for government to address. Famous pollster Elmo Roper reported, "Majorities want a program of slum clearance and low-cost public housing."[12]

San Francisco had its own suburbs, patterns of inequality, and housing shortages. The city's suburbs siphoned off some of the housing demand from more crowded neighborhoods. The Richmond, Sunset, and Park Merced districts on the western side of the city added tracts of single-family homes and upscale apartments such as Stonestown and Park Merced to existing bungalows. A majority of residents in these districts still worked and shopped downtown, but they also patronized neighborhood establishments and the new Stonestown Shopping Center, located near Lake Merced. For entertainment, the western half of the city offered Golden Gate Park, the zoo, and Playland-at-the-Beach, which was the city's version of Coney Island.[13] Real estate agents and property owners helped to maintain a high degree of racial and income segregation in these districts by fighting integration and low-income apartments. For low- and middle-income residents, especially nonwhites, quality housing remained tight and expensive.[14]

Another problem was the scarcity of vacant land. A 1951 Department of City Planning study showed that from 1921 to 1948, the city's vacant residential land supply declined from 8,397 to 2,962 acres (see Table A.4 in appendix). By 1951, only 1,800 acres remained. Annexing land to the south in San Mateo County was not realistic. The only land-generating options, outside of redevelopment or condemnation, included tideland reclamation and the removal of cemeteries—two strategies that since the 1850s had netted 3,160 acres. Within these land constraints, developers did not find profit in building low-income housing on the available but costly land.[15]

The other problem facing low-income residents in San Francisco was the quality of housing. Of San Francisco's 265,000 dwellings, a 1950 Census Bureau report found almost 25,000 units "unsafe, rundown, in need of major repairs, or lacking in ordinary plumbing facilities."[16] In May 1950, the Department of Health launched an experiment to work with property owners, landlords, and tenants in low-income neighborhoods to ensure health code compliance. Health inspectors began in the Western Addition where they found outdoor alley baths and families living in basements "partitioned with tarpaper and beaver board to make two dark rooms and a kitchen with a cold concrete floor." One family paid $40 a month for a backroom with an adjoining "rat and roach infested kitchen" where the oldest son slept when he was not "working his way through college." The health inspector advised the mother to try "more roach powder around the damp, rotting sink and maybe another dose of rat poison in the corner where the children would not get at it." She agreed to do that, but also noted, "Maybe if they'd build some kind of housing project for people like us that want to live decently but can't afford high rents. . . . I've tried to find a better place but they either want $100 a month or won't take children."[17]

The Health Department's experiment did not clean up the city's housing stock. Instead, the high-profile campaign condemned low-rent homes and provided sensational stories to complement the slum narratives being produced by local and federal agencies.[18]

Combined, the narratives helped to justify the redevelopment projects in the works. Federal and state housing policies did not address the housing problem in San Francisco and other urban areas. If anything, they favored bankers, developers, and white property owners. The 1949 Housing Act allocated $1.5 billion for redevelopment and public housing, though only a small portion went to public housing authorities. Federal redevelopment programs marshaled public and private capital, knowledge, and political support for projects that became famous for displacing poor residents from their communities and clearing the way for high-end residential housing, convention centers, highways, and sports stadiums. The Housing and Home Finance Agency (HHFA) and the Veterans Administration (VA) offered mortgage and tax subsidies to home buyers, though redlining practices typically denied nonwhites from using these programs. Federal highway and water projects coupled with favorable tax policies also assisted the private housing industry, especially suburbs in the arid West.

On these programs, Catherine Bauer commented that the federal government was "inextricably involved in the housing business."[19] In 1950, she and others in the housing, planning, and organized labor communities did push for a federal cooperative housing program, modeled on European examples, to serve the bottom two-thirds of households. President Harry Truman, like the public, gave the cooperative housing legislation lukewarm support. The campaign instigated by the real estate, construction, and banking lobbies, in contrast, showed its collective strength by killing the legislation, often with claims that cooperative housing was "communistic, socialistic, and insidiously un-American."[20]

That pro-business political coalition worked its class politics at the state level, too, by putting Proposition 10 on the 1950 California ballot. Proposition 10 would require local voter approval for new public housing, thus making local housing authorities spend additional resources on political lobbying and delaying applications for federal housing funds. At the urging of the San Francisco Building Trades Council, the SFHA commissioners stated their "unqualified opposition" to the measure and declared that Proposition 10 would hurt a proven program "of immeasurable value to the citizens of this State in providing decent, safe and sanitary homes for families of low income whose needs cannot be met by private enterprise."[21] Despite a well-coordinated campaign against Proposition 10, voters passed it.[22] Catherine Bauer, who was living in California, wrote New Dealers Mary and Leon Keyserling to say, "Housing, city [planning] and redevelopment are in a dreadful state."[23] Indeed, it was becoming more difficult to muster state and national support for expanding the welfare state as the media and business groups pushed back against the New Deal.[24]

The views of a majority of San Francisco's voters about the SFHA and government bucked some of these trends. During the 1940s, the SFHA had grown steadily under Director John Beard, who gradually learned the housing field. He visited other housing authorities to observe their practices, followed housing and redevelopment legislation, and attended regional and national housing conferences. However, he managed the SFHA more like a business than a social program. In April 1951, the SFHA issued a report on the previous eleven years of operations.

During that period, the SFHA had housed 173,750 residents and become the city's largest landlord. The SFHA had revenue of $28,607,000 and returned "net profits" of $5,087,000 to the federal government. The authority also paid the city $2,631,000 in lieu of taxes (PILOTs), employed thousands of workers, and brought public and private services to low-income neighborhoods.[25] Beard's tight budgets eased the concerns of taxpayer groups and still maintained quality housing, but his budgets severely limited the SFHA's capacity to meet future large-scale maintenance costs. Still, the services at SFHA projects, the persistent housing shortage, and the city elite's support for growth gave the SFHA program a degree of legitimacy not found in other cities such as Los Angeles.[26]

Beard also revived the deferred permanent projects (Ping Yuen, North Beach Place, Bernal Dwellings, Glen Crags, De Haro Plaza, and Hunters View). Each project required amending pre–World War II contracts, revising costs upward to account for inflation, and updating architectural drawings.[27] In the case of Glen Crags, SFHA commissioners also resumed the fight with the Glen Park Property Owners Association (chapter 2), whose members stalled the development by claiming the neighborhood was not zoned for multiunit developments and that the development would "produce traffic hazards and a bulging school population." But the Glen Crags dispute was not about zoning or traffic or school populations. According to Miriam Weber of the League of Women Voters of San Francisco, the position of the Glen Park Property Owners Association was about fears of racial integration, lower "property values," and "an influx of low-income families."[28] The League of Women Voters and the Glen Park Residents Committee mobilized support for the project, while the SFHA leadership took a cautious position. Opponents convinced the planning commission to stop the project, and the SFHA transferred the Glen Crags federal funds to the 164-unit Alemany project in the southeastern part of the city.[29]

While the permanent projects moved forward toward construction, Beard requested a design change to minimize meeting space in public housing projects. Looking at the plans for Ping Yuen and North Beach Place, the first two deferred projects to be restarted, Beard wanted to convert onsite meeting space into apartment units. He argued that in the past, such space in SFHA projects had not been used properly, was costly to maintain, and duplicated Department of Recreation and Park facilities. Finally, the conversion of this space, he said, made possible the "construction of additional homes."[30]

Beard's motives influenced his preferences. He knew that tenants used space for political organizing, something he opposed. News of Beard's plans for additional homes in lieu of community space spread quickly. The city's youth councils, Alice Griffith (still going strong, although 84 years old), the SFPHA, and community groups demanded that the meeting space be preserved. They wrote letters, spoke with SFHA commissioners and Beard, and conducted research on tenant use of community space at permanent and temporary projects. In the last six months of 1949, they estimated, nearly 200,000 people attended adult classes, lectures, and children's activities. At the five permanent projects, they found that onsite facilities "have been used to capacity." They also noted that social spaces kept children off busy streets and out of trouble—a point sure to resonate with an audience concerned with juvenile delinquency.[31]

The commissioners nevertheless sided with Beard. "The function of this Authority," they said, "was to provide housing for low income families and . . . the provision of recreation facilities was the responsibility of the Recreation Commission."[32] For Ping Yuen, the commissioners did keep the health center, a decision in response to the public health fears of whites and the real health needs of the neighborhood. They also added a mural—not the initial sketch depicting nineteenth-century violence against the Chinese by members of the Pick-Handle Brigade and Workingmen's Party, but one "of a more constructive nature with regard to the Chinese people" that highlighted their labor, art, and families. The mural, created by James Leong, was more in line with the views of SFHA leaders who favored projecting themes of consensus rather than the political and historical sensibilities of Chinatown's residents who gave the mural and muralist a cold reception.[33]

As Ping Yuen moved forward, SFHA leaders had to manage tenant demand for public housing, which compared favorably to private sector housing. As one tenant at Westside Courts said, "I don't think any [private] landlord would do what they [SFHA] do here about fixing the place up. It's always clean and you don't have to argue about repairs. You just call them, and they come do the job." The waiting period for eligible applicants often surpassed three years for SFHA units.[34] To manage demand, the SFHA leadership created deserving social groups to determine eligibility. Applicants currently living in substandard housing continued to have high priority, but so did nuclear families headed by employed veterans with low incomes. Even though the Federal Public Housing Administration in 1954 waived the citizenship requirement for heads of families (in response to State Department requests to house political refugees from eastern Europe), the SFHA commissioners continued the citizenship requirement.[35]

Reflecting Cold War concerns, the SFHA did follow the 1952 Gwinn Amendment, a federal law requiring housing authorities to evict tenants with subversive ideas and associations. On at least one occasion, Beard ordered background checks, but not evictions, for five SFHA tenants who attended a forum at the International Longshoremen and Warehouse Union Hall 150 on the theme "Federal Housing or Federal Concentration Camps?" The Supreme Court ruled the Gwinn Amendment unconstitutional in 1956, but it, like the many other classifications governing tenant selection in public housing, illustrated how the SFHA tried to manage its multiyear waiting list of applicants and how applicants' socioeconomic position and, for a short time, their politics influenced access to public housing.[36]

If the SFHA, Congress, and the Supreme Court created categories for deserving and undeserving applicants, a combination of SFHA and federal changes during the 1950s elevated seniors to the deserving category. Since the start of the federal housing program, the elderly had been locked out of public housing. The New Deal and the United Nations Declaration of Human Rights contributed to the growing debate about economic rights, one that seniors engaged with as well. Catherine Bauer noted that senior housing had

> suddenly become a hot issue all over the country, and . . . a lot of states have been giving official attention to the problem, also the Federal Security Agency, the UN, and even HHFA. . . . And all the redevelopment people are interested because it turns out that an enormous proportion of the occupants of blighted areas are single old people.[37]

In San Francisco, 10 percent of the population was elderly and many lived in the city's rundown single-room occupancy hotels (SROs). In 1954, the SFHA won federal approval to reclassify the elderly as deserving of public housing, two years before the 1956 U.S. Housing Act made the nation's elderly eligible for government housing. Also in 1954, the federal government approved a SFHA project designed for the elderly. The plans featured studio and one-bedroom apartments and amenities to enhance the safety and comfort of older people. As many in the housing and planning community acknowledged, this population (one in six by 1960) across the nation needed not only affordable housing, but housing designed for a community of seniors. The SFHA was ahead of the national curve in terms of serving the needs of the elderly.[38]

SFHA tenant selection based on race remained the most contentious issue at the SFHA in the 1950s. The SFHA used tenant selection to maintain the racial and ethnic composition of a neighborhood and, while doing much to reduce opposition to public housing from white residents, contributed to segregation in the city. Because public housing operated with government funding, the SFHA became a key target for civil rights organizations. The Council for Civic Unity (CCU), whose members often came from the housing and planning community, continued to lead many of the struggles against the SFHA.[39] Under the leadership of Edward Howden, CCU education efforts included forums, luncheons, and publications, which often used the language of "democratic housing," "democratic jobs," and "white supremacy" to challenge Jim Crow policies and practices.[40] In a letter Howden penned for the *San Francisco News,* he put the city's reputation on the line:

> Nonsegregated housing is successfully operating in many cities. The SF Housing Authority is capable of equally successful administration of such housing. All that is needed is a new, clear policy. . . . Virtually all San Franciscans reject the doctrine of "white supremacy." Let us decisively reject as well that doctrine's chief weapon—race segregation—in the new communities we shall create.[41]

In addition to education efforts, the CCU also engaged in politics. The 1949 Federal Housing Act assigned 3,000 units to the SFHA, but the San Francisco Board of Supervisors had to approve all SFHA applications to the Public Housing Administration. In November 1949, when the SFHA submitted an application for 3,000 units to the supervisors, Howden convinced George Christopher, supervisor and future mayor, to add an antidiscrimination clause for SFHA projects. The Board of Supervisors approved the clause and application. Shocked, Beard and the commissioners postponed submitting the application to the PHA, drawing criticism from the press, civil rights organizations, housing and planning advocates, and union leaders. All worried about the loss of 3,000 homes and $30,000,000 worth of construction jobs to another city.[42]

The recently formed San Francisco Redevelopment Agency, whose plans depended on large quantities of low-income units to house residents displaced by redevelopment, also supported the application, revealing how fair housing legislation moved some institutions to support civil rights, even if economic interests drove that support.[43] On the defensive, SFHA commissioners made their own gesture at democracy by polling the city's business and homeowner associations that had supported the application before the antidiscrimination clause was added; support from these groups dwindled after the inclusion of the antidiscrimination clause. Howden claimed that the SFHA "poll" was not only "unnecessary" but biased for relying on "organizations either 'uninformed, unconcerned or opposed' to nonsegregation."[44]

The struggle for civil rights and housing continued in backrooms, public meetings, and the press. Supervisor Christopher labeled SFHA tenant selection a "policy of discrimination" and blasted SFHA commissioners and Beard for "jeopardizing the whole program." "If I were Mayor," Christopher continued, "I'd ask them to resign."[45] Alice Griffith told Mayor Elmer Robinson, whose fence-sitting amounted to a pro-segregation position, "Much has happened in San Francisco and in the world since this segregation policy was adopted." Knowing the social costs of discrimination and the benefits of public housing to the city, she asked Mayor Robinson to "call publicly upon the Housing Commission to approve immediately the pending resolution."[46] Selah Chamberlain, president of the San Francisco Planning and Housing Association, told John Beard that the SFHA was a community institution, one "for which all of us have worked," and therefore had to respond to community pressure.[47] But the SFHA commissioners stood firm. Commissioner Edgar Nichols Ayer, an apartment owner, remarked that change was not easy. "We've followed a community practice acceptable for many years. To change it at one man's suggestion is a little abrupt." The commissioners also claimed that a change would generate white opposition to the program.[48]

When the delay threatened the city's federal allocation and thus threatened more public housing, jobs, and redevelopment plans, the city's newspaper editors turned against the SFHA leadership. A *San Francisco News* editorial contended, "Under American constitutional standards and the rules of fair play, governmental agencies cannot justify discrimination against any group of citizens where public monies, provided by the citizenry as a whole, are being spent."[49] The *San Francisco Chronicle* asked, "Who is boss, the Housing Authority or the Supervisors?"[50]

Although the SFHA leadership depended on local agencies, it was not accountable to the Board of Supervisors or even the mayor. In February, behind closed doors at the SFHA office, Supervisor Joseph Sullivan offered a compromise that would keep the status quo of segregation in existing projects and already programmed projects, but select all tenants regardless of race or color "in order of application" in future projects. As the *San Francisco Chronicle* noted, the first-come, first-placed policy "represented little compromise at all." Nevertheless, the deal allowed the SFHA application to move forward for Washington's approval.[51]

The deal did not prevent the city's civil rights movement from challenging segregation in the SFHA program. North Beach Place, a $3 million development near Fisherman's Wharf deferred during the war, opened in 1952. The very popular project offered 229 units with monthly rents from $11 to $51, which included utilities. As in Chinatown, architects originally designed North Beach Place buildings for the neighborhood's dominant ethnic group, Italians. A SFHA project description read,

> San Franciscans can now look forward to a low rent housing project that will accomplish as much for North Beach as Ping Yuen promises to do for Chinatown. . . . All apartments will have cross ventilation to provide a maximum of fresh air and sunshine. Architecturally the project will be along modern lines and will achieve its Mediterranean feeling in the use of color and landscape gardening.

Architect Thomas D. Church "attempted to capture the Old World feeling in large continuous areas done in color and accentuated by plantings typical of Italian gardens." In both Chinatown and North Beach, SFHA officials used an architectural narrative to reinforce their selection of tenants. In the case of North Beach Place, SFHA staff only selected whites even though the neighborhood composition was far less Italian and much more racially diverse than it had been when the SFHA originally planned the housing.[52]

The whites-only selection for North Beach Place prompted a legal battle. In 1952, the SFHA denied three African Americans—Mattie Banks and her husband, James Charley, Jr., and Tobbie Cain—apartments at North Beach Place, even though Charley and Cain had veteran status and met SFHA income requirements. The CCU launched an information campaign while the NAACP assembled a legal team that included Loren Miller, Terry Francois, and Nathaniel Colley. Their case became *Banks v. SFHA*. Throughout the trial, they highlighted discrimination at the authority. Beard, in his usual frank manner, admitted, "At present, Negroes are admitted only to Westside Courts." The SFHA's five lawyers invoked the legal doctrine of separate but equal to justify Jim Crow, and they smeared the character of Banks and her husband, portraying them as criminals, debtors, and out-of-control consumers. Beard claimed Charley committed polygamy and was thus ineligible for veteran benefits. The authority's strategy focused on portraying Banks and Charley as undeserving individuals who threatened the moral order. When pressed, however, Beard conceded the overall tenant selection policy was "designed to localize Negroes to occupancy in the Westside Courts project."[53]

Beard's testimony did not help the SFHA's defense. San Francisco Superior Court Judge Melvyn Cronin recommended that the SFHA set aside twenty North Beach Place units for African American tenants, and then on September 1, 1952, he declared the SFHA tenant selection policy in violation of the Fourteenth Amendment and the "laws and general public policy of the State of California and the City and County of San Francisco."[54] The SFHA leadership appealed the decision and continued to deny Banks and her husband public housing, although commissioners Charles Jung and A. F. Mailloux of the AFL dissented. The district court of appeals upheld the lower court's decision. The California State Supreme Court refused to hear *Banks v. SFHA*; in 1954, so did the U.S. Supreme Court.[55]

Thus defeated, Beard and the commissioners agreed to "comply 100 percent with the court's ruling." It was a significant victory for public housing tenants and the civil rights movement in and out of San Francisco and helped fill in the national chronicle of racial progress during the Cold War. The San Francisco NAACP, whose stature grew from the victory, called unsuccessfully for the resignation of commissioners Edgar Nichols Ayer, Byron Haviside and Lloyd Wilson, whose support for Jim Crow was so consistent that "they could not now administer a program in accordance with enlightened and democratic principles."[56]

Discrimination in the private housing sector was even more pervasive. Restrictive covenants had been declared illegal in 1948, but property owners and their real estate representatives continued to steer nonwhites away from properties in many of the city's white neighborhoods. When San Francisco Giants centerfielder Willie Mays, and first wife Margherite, moved to San Francisco for the team, they tried to buy a home on Miraloma Drive near Mt. Davidson in November 1957. Neighbors protested the sale, claiming that their property values would decline. The seller, Walter Gnesdiloff, delayed the sale of his home to the couple because he worried about his neighbors and possible boycotts of his construction business by the real estate industry and homeowner association members. Mayor George Christopher invited the Mayses to live with him until they had a house, and the press welcomed the couple to the city. Edward Howden met with Gnesdiloff's neighbors and eased their fears. The sale went through and added another anecdote to the narrative of racial progress. At the time, though, many commented that San Francisco residents should not feel too smug about the outcome. The *San Francisco Chronicle* noted, "We strongly suspect that the outcome might have been less happy, less comforting to the city's self-esteem, had the house-hunter been an obscure and unsung—though equally exemplary—member of Mays's race, whose rebuffs drew no public notice and aroused no public outcry."[57]

The persistence of discrimination in public and private housing remained a key factor in shaping the city's social landscape in the 1950s, although practices ranged across the city. Within this dynamic social landscape, a number of distinct communities were flourishing despite the presence of low-income homes and buildings often labeled as slums ready for redevelopment.

In Chinatown, crowded housing conditions still captured the imagination of commentators, but the district's population underwent important changes. A combination of new immigration laws and a baby boom boosted the city's Chinese and Chinese American population to new highs. From 1939 to 1956, the Chinese population grew from 13,000 to 38,000 as families of naturalized citizens immigrated and as annual births rose to over 1,000 per year in the 1950s, up from 230 in 1940.[58] A majority wanted to remain in or near Chinatown, where there were jobs, community institutions, and ethnic businesses. Offering further enticement, the SFHA's Ping Yuen continued to provide social, health, and educational services to the area. After the New Deal, Chinatown leaders were better connected to the city's political committees and commissions, a notable example being SFHA Commissioner Charles Jung. The district's housing shortage created such strong demand for public housing that in 1956 the SFHA stopped taking applicants because 500 families were on the waiting list for Ping Yuen. This demand helped SFHA leaders convince the federal government to approve another 194 units for Chinatown in 1958.[59]

Some residents left the district for the Richmond district on the western side of the city, for Hunters Point, and, in an effort to stay close to Chinatown, for North Beach. By the end of the decade, the SFHA's tenant selection had integrated North Beach Place, with positive results for tenants; the racial and ethnic diversity in that project followed the demographic changes in the North Beach district, which became one of the more diverse neighborhoods in the northern part of the city.[60]

Population patterns in the Mission and South of Market districts were similar to those in North Beach. The SFHA integrated the Valencia Gardens project, while many Irish Americans left the district. In their place, immigrants from the Pacific Rim (especially American Samoa), Latin America, and Europe began populating the flatlands of the Mission district and spilling over into the Potrero Hill neighborhood. Some African Americans and Asians also took up residency in the area, making the Mission the postwar cosmopolitan workers' district. Latinas/os dominated the district, and Spanish became the area's second language. As more and more of the district's aging housing was classified as substandard, and as nonwhites replaced whites as the dominant social group in the Mission, city boosters and economic leaders began targeting the district for urban redevelopment, and newspapers and planning reports described sections of the district as slums.[61]

The South of Market district was home to the city's unskilled and migratory workers, who lived hard (and sometimes short) lives in SROs and boardinghouses. The male workers provided essential labor in warehousing, dock work, and small factories. African Americans and Europeans, native born and immigrant alike, joined Filipinos, Japanese, and Chinese in the district. Filipinos had the highest family residency rates in a district overwhelmingly populated by men. Nonwhites remained trapped in the lowest paid and least secure jobs, save unionized dock work, and during economic downturns, they remained the first fired and last hired. When not at work, the district's workforce filled many of the area's greasy spoon diners and bars. Like other low-income districts, the South of Market district came under attack from the press and political leaders who declared the area a slum and ripe for redevelopment. In contrast, during the 1930s and 1940s, the local press and political leaders would have rallied around the SFHA program to replace this substandard housing with public housing.[62]

The press and political leaders also targeted the Hunters Point and Western Addition districts for redevelopment, something that would have both short- and long-term consequences for the city's African American community. African Americans occasionally found housing in neighborhoods across the city, but nearly all of the 74,383 African Americans recorded by the 1960 census lived in these two districts. The Hunters Point area had grown quickly in the 1940s, despite the district's geographic distance from the city center, in part because the SFHA staff built up the area's infrastructure and transportation services to support the tenants in its 993 permanent units and 1,400 temporary units. The SFHA built a $250,000 recreation center with services offered by the Department of Recreation and Park as well as nonprofit organizations such as the Boys Club. The district was integrated, but the whites, Asians, and African Americans who lived there typically lived in segregated blocks. By the end of the 1950s, whites increasingly moved out of Hunters Point, and the quality of public and private services, including SFHA housing, began to decline with a shift in military, government, and business priorities.[63]

For its part, the Western Addition was the center of African American political, cultural, and economic activity in the city. During the war, African Americans, many from the U.S. South, had migrated to the Western Addition because discrimination kept them out of other districts. Throughout the district, the influence of southern migrants could be seen in business names such as S. Goree Jackson's Creole Cleaners and Wesley Johnson's Club Flamingo: The New Texas Playhouse. By the 1950s, African American–owned businesses, clubs, and churches were also important to the district's vitality and energy. Jazz clubs in the Fillmore neighborhood attracted audiences from around the nation. Housing for African Americans remained challenging in the district. The SFHA's 136-unit Westside Courts put a small dent in their housing needs, but with citywide housing discrimination and postwar housing demand, the district's landlords customarily added 15 percent to the rent of nonwhite tenants. Housing in the district was generally poor and was regularly targeted by city officials for slum clearance. By the 1950s, many African Americans in Hunters Point and the Western Addition found themselves out of work at double the rate of white workers, excluded from many labor unions, and limited to low-wage jobs. African American household income began to drop in this era.[64]

In an attempt to publicize discrimination in the city and improve race relations, the *San Francisco News* (1956) and the *San Francisco Chronicle* (1959) each ran a multipart series about African Americans. The papers focused on Hunters Point and the Western Addition and included interviews with whites and African Americans, workers and community leaders, native-born San Franciscans and recent migrants. The articles, especially the later ones in the *Chronicle*, contrasted respectable and responsible African American professionals and community leaders against unemployed and alienated African American youth who fit the stereotypes that many whites held of them. The articles often associated the latter group with vice, violence, and crime and presented them as irresponsible, angry, and, as a veteran San Francisco police officer put it, "children."[65]

Despite perpetuating negative stereotypes, the articles also highlighted African Americans' longing for full equality and equal opportunities. As the opening of the *San Francisco News* series stated,

To be a Negro in San Francisco is to live somewhere between the magnolia-scented despair of the South and the unfulfilled promise of the North. It is to see opportunity, but be unable to take it, to taste freedom but not swallow it. . . . It is to face discrimination of a subtler kind than the violence threatened by aging men playing with white sheets and burning crosses.[66]

The articles also emphasized the structures of inequality. African Americans were excluded from the better jobs and labor unions, save a few token positions; from "voluntary associations that make up a democracy; and from the kind of housing, medical care, and education that Americans expect."[67] San Francisco bankers and real estate brokers described maintaining segregated neighborhoods because they feared white homeowners who threatened boycotting their businesses, while white labor union members, often in collusion with employers, resisted integration. One personnel director said, "We'd like to hire freely. We just aren't sure how other workers would respond." The articles noted that young African Americans lacked opportunities and experienced frequent arrests and problems with police. Together, the two series provided a comprehensive case for how and why San Francisco's African Americans had yet to achieve "full rights as a citizen."[68]

The newspapers' series also reinforced narratives about slums in these two districts and thus provided a rationale for redevelopment projects. The *San Francisco News* article succinctly described Western Addition housing this way: "Overcrowded, with a high crime and disease rate, it is a blight San Francisco knows it cannot afford."[69] The description of the slum in San Francisco in the 1950s served a slightly different purpose than it had in earlier decades. Before World War I, the slum narrative justified the expansion of government building codes and zoning laws and (unsuccessfully) public housing and planning to achieve better homes, health, and rational use of urban space. During the Great Depression and Second World War, the concept of slums helped to mobilize support for government programs to create jobs, more housing, and a welfare state. Many also began to think of housing as an economic right for citizens and as housing authorities being a vehicle to carry out large-scale public works and planning projects. But this sentiment changed after the war. Legislation favored urban redevelopment agencies and projects that put economic growth and private real estate investment values before economic rights and the needs of low-income communities. As a result, the popular and professional descriptions of slums became a crucial tool in the justification of redevelopment projects.[70]

Such was the case in San Francisco. In 1945 the California legislature passed the Community Redevelopment Act to enable localities to create redevelopment agencies with sweeping legal and economic powers. Three years later, in anticipation of federal legislation, the San Francisco Board of Supervisors created the San Francisco

Redevelopment Agency. The mayor appointed the agency's commissioners who, unlike SFHA commissioners, were approved by the Board of Supervisors. Civil rights organizations pushed the Board of Supervisors to add a nondiscrimination clause to redevelopment agency projects, while the federal government required the provision of equivalent housing for anyone displaced by redevelopment activities.[71] Otherwise, the agency operated with a high degree of autonomy and found support from several powerful groups.

Pro-growth politicians and labor leaders lined up behind the agency to create jobs and economic development, as did local real estate investors such as Ben Swig and William Zeckendorf. Support also came from the Bay Area Council (BAC), which was the institutional arm of the region's business leaders. Representatives from Bank of America, American Trust Company, Standard Oil, Pacific Gas and Electric, U.S. Steel, and Bechtel Corporation, among others, made BAC's primary goal the expansion of San Francisco's position and power in the Pacific Rim economy. The San Francisco Redevelopment Agency offered a powerful tool for elites to reshape the city's urban space by razing neighborhoods and then constructing office and commercial buildings, convention centers and housing.[72]

In the agency's first years, it slowly built the technical expertise and knowledge to navigate local and federal laws and programs. Some members of the Bay Area housing and planning community saw promise, and employment opportunities, in large-scale urban renewal. Members of the SFPHA and a few New Deal planners, such as Van Buren Stanbery (formerly an official for the National Resource Planning Board), did research for the agency's early proposals. Their reports reinforced popular narratives about slums and the problems in low-income districts and how new physical structures would bring order, economic growth, and progress to those urban spaces. Little attention was given to the social world of these spaces, the social consequences of the redevelopment plans, or expanding the economic rights and security of residents in these areas.[73] As with the changing narrative of the slum, this shift in housing and urban planning stood in contrast to many of the social goals of New Deal housing and planning efforts.

In 1959, the city's economic leaders established the San Francisco Planning and Urban Renewal Association (SPUR). SPUR assembled teams of researchers to conduct studies about urban problems, from housing to traffic, and then disseminated that research to the public, along with solutions to the problems. Framed in objective, social scientific language, SPUR research aligned with the San Francisco Redevelopment Agency agenda. SPUR also organized individuals and groups to support the growing number of redevelopment agency proposals. When combined with research and support from the Federal Housing Administration (FHA) and HHFA, the redevelopment agency had powerful local and federal support for moving forward on some of the largest and most profitable urban renewal projects in the city's history.[74]

Some of the Bay Area's New Deal housing and planning advocates steered away from the redevelopment agency work and toward the University of California, Berkeley. Architect William Wurster, who had designed SFHA's Valencia Gardens and married Catherine Bauer, became dean of architecture at UC Berkeley. He—along with Bauer, T. J. (Jack) Kent, Mel Scott, Paul S. Taylor, and Albert Lepawsky, to name just a few—built a thriving intellectual community in and around the university. They had social and intellectual connections to MIT and Harvard, where Wurster and Bauer often taught, and they continued to draw on international sources for ideas and inspiration.[75]

Serving as public intellectuals, this community wanted practical knowledge, not simply unusable theories, to improve the physical and social landscape, and they envisioned urban and regional planning that would meet the needs of all citizens. In 1950, Catherine Bauer presented a paper at the annual meeting of the American Institute of Planners called "The Increasing Social Responsibility of the City Planner." In it, Bauer encouraged planners to rethink the purpose of public planning and to focus not only on the best in building design but on the social and economic needs of citizens of all races and classes. Rather than talking among themselves about city planning or staring at "faceless statistical abstractions" (a growing trend in urban planning), Bauer urged planners to engage with ordinary people, no matter where they wanted to live (downtown, surburbia, or rural areas), and importantly plan based on how people wanted to live and use the space around them. She thought planners were unfortunately not up to the task.[76] Bauer's proposals predated a similar call by urban writer and activist Jane Jacobs in 1961 and, as Bay Area planner Mel Scott later noted, "foreshadowed much of the important research undertaken in the next few years if not in the next fifteen or sixteen years."[77]

Academic planners used the Bay Area and California as their laboratory for research on housing and planning, traffic, and suburban and economic development. Increasingly, they added conservation and preservation of historically valuable spaces and structures and the natural environment to counter the negative forces of growth and development. Compared to parallel studies in the East, this West Coast research focused less on deindustrialization and slums than on the problems—pollution, loss of open and public space, traffic, and so on—threatening the quality of life in the Golden State. They also explored ways to empower public agencies to oversee projects that would transcend traditional political boundaries (city, county, state), deliver coordinated and integrated alternatives to the uncoordinated efforts common in the private sector, and serve the general welfare. At a minimum, Bauer thought that agencies in the right hands and with sufficient resources could "pose the *big alternatives* so that responsible, reasonably enlightened public decisions at all levels of government are at least possible."[78]

After a decade of discussions and research, Bauer concluded that planning intellectuals had made "little headway in building up the kind of solid practical *knowledge* that would clarify policy and perhaps even help to unify expert and public opinion."[79] That failure of knowledge, when coupled with their lack of power in response to Cold War urban policies, limited the influence of academic planners on urban institutions such as the San Francisco Redevelopment Agency and the SFHA, and they failed to impact some of the larger private projects in the city.[80]

Meanwhile, the San Francisco Redevelopment Agency expanded its staff and resources for three projects. The Diamond Heights site was slated for the rugged, open hills near the city's center, just south of Twin Peaks. This area represented some of the last remaining open space in the city. Compared to other redevelopment projects, Diamond Heights required the destruction of fewer homes and commercial buildings. Still, the agency's report described these structures as blighted (much to the surprise and outrage of the owners) to get government approval and prevailed in a lawsuit from the area's property owners to stop the project. Victorious, the agency moved forward with its plans to build on the contoured landscape 3,000 suburban tract homes, duplexes, apartments, and townhomes—none of them intended for low-income residents. The project also included schools, shopping centers, and playgrounds.[81]

The two other redevelopment agency projects were located in the South of Market and Western Addition districts. Dubbed the San Francisco Prosperity Plan, the South of Market project would build commercial buildings and a sports stadium, parking for 7,000 cars, a luxury hotel, a convention center and auditorium, and fountains on a par with those in New York's Rockefeller Center. The federal government approved a revised version of the Prosperity Plan known as Yerba Buena Center.[82]

Mixing business goals with an ethnicity angle, the Western Addition project included high-rise apartments and a Japanese cultural and trade center, complete with a movie theater (the Kabuki), commercial and cultural space, and Japanese businesses and organizations. At the request of Honolulu banker Masayuki Tokioka, a Pagoda of Peace to honor victims of the atomic bombs also became part of the project. The Yerba Buena Center and Western Addition sites depended on the redevelopment agency's acquisition and destruction of many homes and small businesses, and to win public acceptance for those actions, their staff championed the economic benefits of the project and reminded the city's residents about the dangers of slums to them and the city at large.[83]

The Yerba Buena Center and Western Addition sites depended on SFHA housing for federal approval, and so the agency tailored its claims for these projects accordingly. The San Francisco Redevelopment Agency estimated that the South of Market project would displace 4,000 residents and the Western Addition 10,000 residents. These people—often old, poor, nonwhite, and immigrant—had few realistic housing options in the city. From its start, the agency staff made inflated claims about using SFHA housing to satisfy federal rehousing guidelines. In a 1952 report, the agency wrote, "low-rent public housing dwellings will be available to all eligible occupants who wish to exercise their statutory preference." For displaced residents ineligible for or not interested in SFHA housing, the report estimated, "There will be many times as many vacancies as needed for Western Addition project families in the existing supply of private dwellings in the City."[84]

In fact, even with a slight decline in the city's population in the decade (see Table A.2 in the appendix), few public or private low-income housing units existed in the city for these residents. In 1958, SFHA Director Beard said, "demand for permanent and temporary housing in SF is at the highest peak since WW II demobilization." Beard, who supported the larger goals of the redevelopment agency, worried about how the lack of public housing stock would "slow up the relocation activities of the San Francisco Redevelopment Agency." As a short-term solution to house displaced residents, he refused to demolish temporary wartime housing units and instead made those substandard units—which were miles from the Western Addition and South of Market districts—available to the San Francisco Redevelopment Agency.[85]

Even so, at the end of 1959, the lack of affordable housing threatened the redevelopment agency's projects. In November 1959, the agency still needed 2,600 homes for displaced Western Addition and South of Market residents in order to comply with federal requirements.[86] Justin Herman, the director of the San Francisco Redevelopment Agency, came before the SFHA commissioners to explain the dire situation. His staff had contacted 448 property owners with housing for rent, and of those, only 8 buildings met "the standards of [federal] law." "Private housing is simply not available to these families at rents they can afford to pay," and this situation, he concluded, was costing the agency "large sums of money." Commissioner Jacob Shemano asked Herman if "racial discrimination was not largely responsible for the lack of private housing for these families." "It was," Herman replied. He then noted that "so many of the families are poor and financially unable to pay the rents for such housing, even if it were made available to them."[87]

Racial discrimination, poverty, shortages in affordable housing, and redevelopment agency relocation failures influenced the SFHA program in the city. In response to Herman's request, and in keeping with the goals of the city's economic and political elite, the SFHA commissioners raised household income limits to accommodate some of the higher-income displaced residents, though the SFHA tenant selection process continued to favor applicants with the lowest incomes. Many of the displaced residents and businesses never returned to their communities, and, importantly, these residents often furthered the concentration of poor, mostly nonwhite residents in SFHA housing, especially in Hunters Point. The SFHA program, through its control of housing units, became a vital resource for the redevelopment agency and the investors and city leaders it served.[88]

The SFHA in the 1950s increased its capacity and added to the city's low-income housing, though the gain in SFHA units masked a curtailment of the program. Between 1951 and 1957, the authority had funded 18 percent of the city's residential construction and 7 percent of all construction in the city, creating both jobs and new homes. In 1960, Beard managed more than 8,000 permanent and temporary units with 30,000 tenants, which made the authority the city's largest landlord.

But the SFHA could have grown even more. Throughout the decade Mayor George Christopher, the San Francisco Redevelopment Agency, and the Board of Supervisors—along with civil rights, labor unions, and religious leaders—urged construction of the 538 units remaining from the authority's 1949 federal allocation. SFHA leadership instead slowed the pace of new public housing construction in an effort to provide steady work to union members throughout the decade and to limit expansion of the program. SFHA Director Beard also reduced SFHA staff and delayed needed maintenance, which contributed to the physical decline of some projects.[89]

These local budget priorities mirrored federal public housing trends at the national level. From 1954 to 1960, Public Housing Administration Commissioner Charles Slusser reduced the number of agency workers "by more than sixty-seven percent, cutting the number of employees from 4,523 to 1,477."[90] At times, the reduced federal staff caused delays at the local level, "broke down the morale" of SFHA staff, and limited the quality and quantity of public housing in San Francisco.[91] Significantly, the cuts hurt the quality and image of public housing, but also created the conditions that led to the tenant organizing of the 1960s.

Given their differing incentives and interests, government officials, developers, and public and private landlords could not agree on a formula to provide enough housing for low-income households in San Francisco. Demand for public housing remained high throughout the 1950s, causing the SFHA leadership to adjust categories of eligible and ineligible citizens. Elderly and higher-income applicants, especially veterans and those displaced by redevelopment projects, became "deserving" applicants in terms of policy, though SFHA tenant selection followed that of other housing authorities as the poorest residents came to make up a higher proportion of the public housing population. San Francisco's civil rights movement used both political and legal strategies to make SFHA's housing more democratic and integrated. On the civil rights side, this was an important victory in the broader struggle for equality in the Bay Area. The struggle over civil rights was also a struggle over economic rights for people who thought about housing as an economic and human right.

Public housing continued to play a role in urban development and planning, but that role changed in two important ways. With a push from federal legislation, redevelopment agencies emerged as the center of postwar planning power, eclipsing the possibility of using local or regional housing authorities to conduct large-scale planning. That shift meant that large-scale projects that benefited elites and the private sector more than working-class residents would be pursued, often at the cost of poor and nonwhite communities—as was evidenced in the Western Addition and South of Market district developments. This shift, when combined with the impact of conservative SFHA leadership and Cold War politics, led many California housing and planning advocates to gravitate to the university, thus disengaging from the SFHA.

Planners in professional circles continued to write about public planning as a way to address complex social and urban problems and to improve the general welfare, but their influence in government agencies such as the SFHA had waned. The San Francisco Redevelopment Agency drew on popular narratives of the slum and technical knowledge to justify some of its larger projects. These projects did not reflect the Modern Housing concept of making housing an economic right for all citizens. Nor did the redevelopment agency officials think highly of the rights of residents to determine what happened to their homes, neighborhoods, and city. It would fall to ordinary residents and SFHA tenants to advocate for economic rights and a voice in urban policymaking. And in the 1960s, they began to organize in earnest.

CHAPTER 5

SOMETHING TO HELP THEMSELVES

*California, as well as many other states, is faced with the paradox of
pockets of poverty within an otherwise prosperous and affluent
society. Many of the individuals in these poverty areas are not
participating in the general prosperity enjoyed by the majority of
people. Long deprived of many of the socio-economic opportunities
necessary to become self-sufficient, plus the impact of the automated-
computerized commercial world, these people have been left in dire
need of remedial programs to overcome serious disadvantages in
education, employment, etc.*

California Governor Edmund G. Brown
to HUD Secretary Robert Weaver[1]

*The Welfare Rights Committee will continue to raise hell with the
Housing Authority whenever necessary. The Committee holds that
militant tenant organizations are essential for solid and constructive
discussion between tenants and the Housing Authority.*

Helen O. Little, Chair of Welfare Rights Committee,
Haight-Ashbury Howard Presbyterian Church[2]

IN THE EARLY HOURS OF FRIDAY, JANUARY 5, 1961, a fire began near the front desk of
the San Francisco Housing Authority central office at 440 Turk Street. With the
fire raging, seventy-five firemen rushed to the scene, where they battled to contain
the flames. By the time daylight arrived, the fire had gutted the cashiers' and inter-
viewers' offices and destroyed the switchboard and office machines. The smoke and
heat did considerable damage, but the firefighters saved the charred building from
total destruction. The fire inspector thought the blaze had started from either an
electric heater or a carelessly discarded cigarette. The two-story building suffered
$110,000 in damage, though SFHA Director John Beard assured the public and
tenants that because the authority stored its records in fireproof cabinets, "there
need be no disruption in collection of rents."[3]

At 8:30 am, truckloads of SFHA maintenance staff rolled up and "energetically turned to cleaning up debris and beginning fire damage repair." The Fire Department battalion chief, awed by the scene, remarked "This is the first time in 20 years that I have seen fire repairs begun before the firemen had left the building." Throughout the day and weekend, "men passed buckets of hot water from a nearby Chinese laundry to wash down the heavily smoked walls." SFHA officials arranged temporary phone service and rented office machines and furniture. On Monday morning, after a weekend of cleanup, the authority reopened to continue service to the public without interruption.[4]

As they had during World War II, SFHA officials that weekend demonstrated what they could accomplish when they made something a priority. But their priorities were increasingly out of step with SFHA tenants and the city's residents alike who in the 1960s began organizing to make the SFHA more responsive and democratic. Several developments help us understand the rise in organizing. Tired of declining SFHA housing conditions, discrimination, and top-down decisions, SFHA tenants formed tenant unions to influence the SFHA and the city at large. These tenant unions grew strong in part because tenants had a shared identity and common goals. New SFHA commissioners were more open to giving tenants opportunities to participate in decisions. Lyndon Johnson's Great Society programs, which expanded the civil and economic rights of citizens, also provided staff and resources to help with community organizing. Similar to the New Deal legislation in the 1930s that assisted housing reformers in bringing about public housing, the Great Society in the 1960s assisted low-income residents in organizing in new and powerful ways. Lastly, the social movements of the era encouraged the city's residents to mobilize for political power and to seek a more just and liberated society.

Guided by their goals, SFHA tenants contributed to the social movements of the decade to make government, employers, and landlords more responsive to the needs of residents. Their participation in the SFHA came at a time when housing and social programs enjoyed local support, though federal housing funds remained insufficient to maintain existing public housing or to build enough public housing to meet demand. Federal legislation also continued to favor private sector housing and redevelopment. However much local and national political elites discussed the importance of ending poverty, in practice legislation underfunded antipoverty programs, and economic insecurity remained a reality for millions across the nation. Within this context, San Francisco tenants and their allies organized for civil and economic rights.

As the 1960s commenced, federal officials began to promote a set of civil rights and social policies to tackle the problems associated with demographic shifts, poverty, and discriminatory housing and employment markets. These policies reflected the growing awareness of inequality—brought about by the civil rights movement and writings such as Michael Harrington's *The Other America* (1962). In the area of housing, Housing and Home Finance Administrator Robert Weaver and Public Housing Administrator Marie McGuire both stressed the importance of promoting existing federal programs while being open to alternatives to the 1950s initiatives of public housing and redevelopment. Weaver spent decades studying the causes and effects of housing discrimination, while McGuire's expertise was in senior housing. The two officials led a campaign to promote senior housing, scattered public housing projects (instead of concentrating them in a few districts), and a new leasing program to be administered through local housing authorities. The 1965 leasing program, known as Section 23, encouraged housing authorities to lease private rental properties for low-income tenants. This program marked the beginning of transferring federal low-income housing funds from public housing authorities to landlords in the private sector.[5]

These federal programs—along with the political currents of the 1960s—moved the SFHA in new directions. Mayor George Christopher (1956–64) appointed SFHA commissioners whose visions more closely aligned with the 1960s social movements than had commissioners from the 1950s. None of the new commissioners were housing experts, but they did follow academic and federal housing trends. They questioned John Beard's reluctance to build federally allocated housing and perform needed repairs on the authority's housing. They also supported low-density housing projects, civil and economic rights, and greater responsiveness to tenant demands. Commissioners Jacob Shemano and Charles Greenstone initiated a public relations campaign to emphasize the ways the SFHA contributed to the city and offered new possibilities for the program.[6]

Their campaign reflected what they had seen on their recent tour of East Coast public housing, especially in New York City where, instead of building many high-rise towers, the authority renovated brownstones and apartments around the city and selected tenants to ensure a mix of income levels. Shemano became a vocal champion of ending what he called "massive concrete camps." He thought institutional public housing led tenants to "identify themselves as different from the rest of the Community" and contributed to the formation of distinct social groups that negatively affected intergroup relations and mutual understanding. Shemano recommended that the SFHA follow the practices of the NYC Housing Authority, especially scattered housing.[7] SFHA staff and Beard thought that scattered housing would exceed federal cost limits and hinted that such projects might integrate white neighborhoods. This housing, like all new SFHA projects, also needed the Board of Supervisors' consent and a ballot measure approved by a majority of San Francisco voters. Despite the political challenges, the commissioners instructed staff to work on adding scattered housing to the program.[8]

The SFHA leadership also expanded its housing for the elderly. In 1961, the SFHA dedicated two projects (each eleven stories and reflecting 1950s design trends) with units especially outfitted for the elderly. Yerba Buena Annex, located at Golden Gate and Buchanan Streets, had 211 units with 43 units for the elderly. Five hundred people attended its dedication, including Mayor Christopher, who handed out golden keys to tenants and pronounced, "This is only the beginning. San Francisco plans to have many more low rent apartments for its elderly citizens who have done so much for the city."[9]

On Yerba Buena's first floor, the city sponsored a senior citizen's center with a paid director from the Department of Recreation and Park. Significantly, SFHA commissioners let tenants "themselves actually run the Center."[10] Two of Yerba Buena's first tenants, Miss Elsie Allen and Mrs. Powers, praised their units, which they "were enjoying very much."[11] Later in the year, on Pacific Street near Stockton, the opening of the Ping Yuen Annex added 194 public housing units, of which 44 were for seniors. The Chinatown development had a dedication ceremony with firecrackers, music from the St. Mary's Girls Drum Corps, a dancing dragon, and publicity materials for the U.S. Information Agency to distribute globally.[12]

Demand for the units at the two projects exceeded supply. SFHA staff estimated that 50,000 seniors were eligible for public housing in San Francisco. Congress did expand funding for senior public housing in the 1960s, although it limited overall public housing funding due to other priorities—such as Great Society programs and U.S. military spending for the Vietnam War and the Cold War.[13] As Congress set national priorities, San Francisco resident H. J. Hickox thought the government should focus on the nation's public housing program. As Hickox wrote, "Just when they are getting started in the direction of some low cost housing for San Francisco, particularly for the senior citizens, [there were calls] to 'cut out the housing program,' because of mounting military costs." Hickox thought the need was "particularly urgent here due to the great number of older persons living in this area and the very high living costs with low cost housing nonexistent."[14]

As SFHA commissioners worked to increase senior housing, they also coordinated a number of services for all SFHA tenants and their neighbors. SFHA commissioners and senior tenants developed a lunch program, and the SFHA contributed food and gifts to holiday celebrations at the projects. Yerba Buena tenants used the senior center for a vaudeville show to raise money for tenant needs such as a communal wheelchair.[15]

To shape the values and behavior of working-class youth, especially boys, the SFHA leadership created programs at SFHA projects, "particularly in those areas with high juvenile delinquency." The SFHA still sponsored the Hunters Point Boys Club, pushed the city library to bring books to Hunters Point, and arranged art programming and activities such as Jamaican steel drum lessons. The authority sponsored "Community Clean Up Days" in Hunters Point, providing staff, trucks, and lunch to several hundred kids, whose volunteer labor did what city workers should have done.[16]

As final planning progressed for the Alice Griffith Garden Homes (named in memory of Griffith, who died in 1959) in Hunters Point, commissioners included community space for "a variety of purposes—nursery school, child care center, recreation center, well-baby center, and so on." At all of its projects, the SFHA provided free, or nearly free, space to city programs (Education, Health, Public Welfare, Recreation and Park) and charity groups. By 1961, 70 paid staff worked with an average of 1,279 residents at SFHA facilities every day. Of the authority's 150,000 square feet of community space, roughly 85 percent was located in Hunters Point, revealing how the SFHA provided services that went unmet by public and private institutions.[17]

Figure 5.1
Alice Griffith Garden Homes in Hunters Point in 1962.

The SFHA also provided job training and jobs to its tenants. The SFHA ran summer employment programs for teenagers, who typically worked part-time SFHA jobs for minimum wage. Some tenants worked at the SFHA through grants. A three-year Ford Foundation grant, for example, funded the Hunters Point Youth Employment Center that included work training. The grant tried to steer youth away from what the funders considered nonproductive activities and instead prepared them for the world of work.[18] In some ways, the SFHA expanded on progressive era settlement house traditions, though with greater government and foundation support. No wonder that Commissioner Greenstone claimed the "provision of housing is just a very small part of the whole program."[19] The SFHA's programs tried to assist the tenants and their neighbors who had not been served by New Deal programs, or who were typically not addressed by the Eisenhower and Kennedy administrations' programs. Both Eisenhower and Kennedy focused their administrations on macroeconomic policies (fiscal and monetary policies) more than on social programs to expand the welfare state that would root out the structural inequalities based on unemployment, maldistribution of income and wealth, and racial discrimination.[20]

The experiences of nonwhite San Francisco Bay Area workers, especially African Americans, illustrated the limits of federal macroeconomic policies. A 1963 California State Employment Service report documented the growing number of nonwhites in better-paid jobs, but also their limited job opportunities. Nonwhites accounted for 25 percent of all employable persons in the Bay Area, yet their 11 percent unemployment rate was double that of whites. African American workers earned on average $1,000 less than white workers in every category (unskilled, semi-skilled, skilled, professional), were concentrated in low- paying occupations, and were subject to frequent layoffs and longer durations of unemployment. "The most striking feature of the labor force participation among the nonwhite population (more than 2 out of 3 of whom are Negroes)," the report noted, "is the generally lower participation of persons in the younger age groups." That disparity, the report found, was "undoubtedly a reflection of the greater difficulty these young people have in securing employment, since many of the industries which usually employ younger workers, employ very few nonwhite workers." Most troubling to the report's authors was that these employment trends existed for a full generation. The authors recommended a "two-fold attack" on these problems. First, "there must be a concentrated effort to upgrade the Negro labor force" so these workers would have the skills to compete in the labor market. Second, "there must be a strong program designed to increase opportunities for Negro workers in apprenticeship programs and in occupations and industries which heretofore have been barred to Negroes."[21]

Affordable and open housing was just as important as fair employment for the economic security of low-income residents of all races in San Francisco. Many San Francisco whites continued to protect their neighborhoods and channel nonwhites to inferior housing or to the long waiting list at the SFHA. With public housing segregation outlawed (though still practiced in the SFHA), civil rights organizations stepped up their efforts to end discrimination in the private sector. In May 1961, Blanche Brown took her friend Dorothy Lincoln to look at new homes in the Forest Knolls housing development. Located in the geographic center of the city, the hillside homes on fogless days offered spectacular views of the Pacific Ocean. The upscale homes were also in a protected neighborhood. When the two African American women arrived, the salesmen fled, and everyone else "literally ran out of the house."[22]

It was the third time that week Brown had generated visible white flight. Her husband, William "Willie" Brown, Jr., a young attorney and future San Francisco mayor, and their friends began what the press called an "impromptu 'sit in,'" closing the sales office for the day. But the event, as William Brown's biographer tells it, was anything but impromptu. The Browns astutely brought their kids and civil rights activists, including California Senator John Burton; future Supervisor, Mayor, and U.S. Senator Dianne Berman [later Feinstein]; lawyer Terry Francois; and jazz pianist Oscar Peterson. The press supported the family's struggle. Mayor George Christopher appealed to builder Carl Gellert to at least show a home to the Browns. Despite the headlines, and in contrast to Willie Mays's experience four years earlier, Gellert refused to open the Forest Knolls homes to Brown's family. The incident fueled demands for fair housing legislation while also thrusting Willie Brown into the public limelight, where he built one of the more powerful political careers in postwar California.[23]

Brown's case was one of many that California civil rights organizations, progressive labor unions, and religious groups leveraged to push for fair housing legislation. Their efforts encountered stiff resistance. In 1961, for example, California Assemblyman Augustus Hawkins (Dem., Los Angeles) proposed a bill to make it illegal to discriminate in housing based on race, nationality, or religion. The response from the real estate lobby and homeowner associations was swift. The San Francisco Real Estate Board sent forty members to Sacramento to protest what they called "discrimination against the majority." Standing in front of the capitol with a 15-foot "San Francisco Real Estate Board" banner, Vice President Don Klein said, "We are not against integration. . . . But we feel the bill would take away the right of the individual to do with his property as he seems fit." President William Hogan argued that the bill would give "minorities the right to dictate to majorities, and that is not the American way."[24] The real estate industry saw in fair housing an attack on their private property rights, their right to segregate, their rental profits, and ultimately their power. All were more important than civil rights. The Hawkins bill died.

But the next year, the California Real Estate Association (CREA), working with the National Association of Real Estate Board and the Apartment House Owners Association, created its own state measure to preempt future fair housing legislation. The backers of the CREA measure believed a legislative win would "once and for all" stop attempts at passing fair housing legislation in California and around the nation. Before the CREA introduced their measure, however, William Byron Rumford (Dem., Berkeley) successfully sponsored the California fair housing bill. The Rumford Act, as it was called, made illegal acts of discrimination in sales or rentals of private housing. The California legislature passed it in June 1963, and Governor Pat Brown signed it into law. Even though the Fair Employment Practices Committee (FEPC), which enforced the law, did not have adequate funding to fully enforce the legislation, the agency did investigate violations of the law, and, as is often the case with California politics, it inspired other states to pass their own versions.[25]

The San Francisco civil rights movement also continued to target the SFHA for not integrating some of its projects and failing to expand employment opportunities for nonwhites. SFHA commissioners left intact its tenant selection policy of first come, first served that had been established by the deal with the Board of Supervisors, backed up by the *SFHA v. Banks* case, and later supported by President Kennedy's 1961 executive order 11063 to make segregation illegal in public housing.

The first come, first served policy helped smaller and senior projects achieve a tenant distribution of roughly one-third African American, one-third white, and one-third Asian or Latina/o tenants. But, contrary to integrationists' hopes, that policy also helped to sustain segregation in other SFHA projects. Hunters Point, Potrero Hill, and Western Addition tenants were nearly all African American, Chinatown tenants nearly all Asian, and Holly Courts tenants nearly all white. This distribution of tenants resulted because some applicants turned down the "first choice" offered to them by SFHA staff and—in the case of Hunters Point, Potrero Hill, and Western Addition—because of the applicant demographics and racial and class segregation in the city. Roughly 85 percent of the 5,000 applicants on the SFHA waiting list were African Americans, and many of them, shut out of racially protected and higher-income neighborhoods, had to take housing in the three larger projects already populated by African Americans. After looking at these trends and the persistence of racial discrimination in his city, NAACP lawyer Terry Francois encouraged the SFHA leadership to do more to promote not only integration at all projects, but "wholesome intergroup relations" in the city.[26]

The NAACP also called on the SFHA to expand African American employment opportunities by changing its own hiring practices and by pressuring trade unions to open up their membership to nonwhites. African Americans made up roughly 11 percent of the city's total population, and although the SFHA workforce was 24 percent nonwhite, nearly all of these workers did menial, low paid jobs. For over two decades, the city's building trades enjoyed a steady stream of SFHA maintenance and construction work, but only the Laborers Union offered any of this work to nonwhites.[27]

Civil rights activists acted to combat such discriminatory practices. In April 1964, Allan Brotsky, who represented the NAACP and its community organizing offshoot the San Francisco United Freedom Movement, met with Beard and the commissioners to improve SFHA hiring practices and to implement a fair employment proposal to end discrimination in unions whose members worked on SFHA construction contracts. These two changes, Brotsky noted, were "not only sound but actually required under the laws of the United States and the State of California."[28] The larger goal of his proposal was to chip away at the structural unemployment and underemployment in districts where public housing was located. The proposal also aimed to integrate the building trade unions and open up more union work for nonwhites on private and non-SFHA public projects. Members of these unions were reluctant to sign up nonwhite men, or women, but they did not want to end two decades of harmonious labor relations with the SFHA.

The struggle over fair employment in SFHA relations with the city's unions highlighted the sticky nature of race relations, privilege, and power. In 1964, Joseph Mazzola, the chair of the SFHA commission and member of the Plumbers' Union, attempted to bury the NAACP's proposal in committee, an action supported by commissioners Melvin Swig and, to a lesser extent, T. Kong Lee. Commissioners Stephen Walter and Solomon Johnson continued their support of the NAACP proposal. Through strategic appointments since 1943, San Francisco mayors had maintained segregation in SFHA housing through a delicate balance of commission members and their viewpoints. But the civil rights movement made this balance increasingly untenable. SFHA commissioners Johnson, Lee (who switched his position), and Swig tried to remove Mazzola from the chair position, but the cagey plumber won back the loyalty of Lee by admitting the first two Chinese apprentices to the Plumbers' Union. Commissioner Johnson pleaded with Mayor John Shelley, a former president of both the San Francisco Labor Council and the California American Federation of Labor, to intervene. But Shelley stood in solidarity with his white union brothers. Commissioner Johnson resigned, and Shelley filled his slot with Reverend Hamilton Boswell, a leader in the Western Addition African American community, who immediately landed on a committee with Mazzola to study SFHA labor practices.[29]

In response to the SFHA stalling the NAACP proposal, the city's civil rights organizations, notably the United Freedom Movement, threatened a lawsuit. Commissioners Mazzola and Boswell met with trade union leaders to find a solution. Union leaders were unwilling to compromise, even after Boswell pointed out the damning patterns of racial exclusion in their unions at the local and national levels, including Mazzola's own Plumbers' Union. Mazzola defended his union, and the other trades, stating that "Negro people had not made themselves available to trades and crafts as qualified employees," and "the trades and crafts unions have always been in full compliance with State and Federal regulations." Boswell relented. He said it "was not his responsibility to ferret out alleged racial discrimination in unions nor should the Authority itself become a battleground in this matter." Commissioner Stephen Walter agreed, adding that the authority did "not have the funds, ability or time" to do an investigation. But, he stated, "Since a charge of alleged discrimination in hiring practices had been made . . . the Authority had a responsibility to the public." He suggested turning the matter over to the state's FEPC and, to prevent further conflict and a possible lawsuit, his fellow commissioners agreed.[30] Despite its influence, and increased protests in 1964 and 1965, the SFHA failed to change union policies.

Figure 5.2
Civil rights protest for fair employment at the San Francisco Housing Authority main office in February,1965.

As the FEPC carried out its investigation of the unions, civil rights leaders asked the commissioners to fund a tenant-relations position. In April 1964, after months of negotiations, the commissioners created a new position, director of human relations and tenant services, and hired Effie Robinson. Robinson was the first African American born in the California town of Healdsburg (70 miles north of San Francisco) and had earned a master's in social welfare at UC Berkeley in 1945. By 1964, she had nearly twenty years' experience in intergroup relations and elder care.[31]

Just months after the 1964 New York City race riot, Robinson attended the National Association of Intergroup Relations Officials conference in New York City. Her report on race relations captivated the commissioners. Recent African American violence against whites, or "the symbol of white power, the police," she said, was rooted in anger accumulated from centuries of humiliation. These facts had to be faced with "courage and honesty" and "be taken into account in any program organized to improve Negro-White relations. They must be taken into account in any program set up to help Negro youngsters or adults climb out of the slums." Moreover, white policymakers had to conceptualize civil rights not as individual but as group rights because, Robinson insisted, "every ethnic group

Figure 5.3
Civil rights protest in April, 1965 to end discrimination in trade unions and San Francisco Housing Authority employment.

that has moved into the mainstream has done so through group power. . . . Power is what the Negro revolt is all about. The revolt is a long suppressed reaction to a serious imbalance of power. Power cannot be acquired without conflict."[32]

After being schooled on contemporary ideas in the Black Power movement, the commissioners "deputized" Robinson to represent the SFHA at civil rights events. Through public education, Robinson tried to mitigate any negative psychological effects on tenants who lived in public housing and provide children with the knowledge to "be good citizens." She served on the city's newly created Anti-Poverty Council, which was gearing up to coordinate Lyndon Johnson's Great Society programs, and began representing the SFHA at community meetings. As her job developed, she brought these programs to tenants, and most importantly, she plugged tenants into the community activism that produced the flurry of tenant organizing in the decade.[33]

Robinson also coordinated community efforts to bring more public housing to the city to alleviate the affordable housing shortage. As the 1964 election neared, antipoverty and civil rights organizations pressured the SFHA leadership to sponsor a measure for 4,000 public housing units on the next local ballot. The estimate of 4,000 units was based not on need but on what they thought was politically possible. The redevelopment agency, the Board of Supervisors, and Mayor Shelley, as well as trade unions and civic groups, also asked the authority to add public housing to the ballot.[34]

Beard and the commissioners moved slowly on the issue—so slowly that the mayor threatened to replace the commissioners with redevelopment agency officials if they did not move more quickly. The SFHA commissioners asked Federal Public Housing Authority economists to research the city's housing needs. The FPHA's "A Study of the Current Public Low-Rent Housing Market in San Francisco–July, 1964" estimated the city's need at 1,500 elderly and 1,000 family low-rent housing units.[35] When questioned about how the federal economists calculated 2,500 units (1,500 fewer than what was proposed), Mr. Huber, the assistant director of the FPHA Regional Office, told the commissioners, "This would be the maximum amount of additional low-rent housing the Public Housing Administration would be willing to approve at this time."[36]

Critics identified several flaws in the FPHA study, and they showed up to the next SFHA commission meeting. NAACP spokeswoman Dorothy Lathan said that FPHA's 2,500 units would not "serve the needs of the city." Making a lawyer-like argument, Lathan said that the FPHA study missed the city's 10,569 substandard housing units and the people displaced by redevelopment, freeways, and public transportation projects. Nearly 1,200 families, she noted, still lived in temporary war housing and were eligible for permanent public housing that did not yet exist. Nor did the report consider the 50,000 families making less than $5,000 a year who were likely eligible for public housing, or the needs of military personnel. The federal "recommendation" for 2,500 was less than the average number of applications (2,762) for housing the SFHA received each month. The report, Lathan concluded, "just does not plan for the future. If we add up all the categories that stand outside the report, a need for 10,000 units of public housing units can be justified." The NAACP reaffirmed its recommendation of 4,000 units "as a bare minimum."[37]

The SFHA commissioners agreed with the NAACP recommendation, but at the urging of the mayor's office they turned over the final decision to the Board of Supervisors. The supervisors agreed to the FPHA's recommendation for 2,500 units because they thought that was the realistic number given the federal study. The campaign for 2,500 units became Measure H, the biggest political campaign ever undertaken by the authority.[38]

Mayor Shelley assembled a citizens' committee for Measure H, while Mazzola wrangled $2,500 from the Plumbers and Steamfitters Union Local 38, endorsements and financial support from the Building Trades unions and Labor Council, and hundreds of union members to canvass precincts for Measure H. Trade union support was certainly about jobs, but, as Mazzola put it, it was also about the ways "individually and collectively, the Housing Authority has served to elevate the dignity and stature of many citizens in our community." The League of Woman Voters, the Chinese Consolidated Benevolent Association, the Chinese Community for Low-Rent Housing for Senior Citizens and Families, the NAACP, and the San Francisco Ministerial Alliance endorsed the measure and promised to mobilize their members. The city's newspapers ran favorable coverage of the measure. The broad support was necessary to counter the real estate lobby and homeowners associations that attacked public housing as unnecessary and misguided.[39]

The 1964 election also gave California voters a chance to decide the fate of the Rumford Act. As implementation of the Rumford Act began, the California Real Estate Association (CREA) added a ballot initiative known as Proposition 14 that would amend the state constitution to make housing discrimination legal. The CREA campaign spent millions of dollars, some of which came from national real estate organizations, and used the networks of the real estate industry—from mortgage brokers and real estate agents to landlords, who mailed pro-Proposition 14 materials to their tenants. They also worked with neighborhood homeowner associations that organized at the block level.[40]

In San Francisco, Louella Hayes, president of the All Neighborhoods Improvement Club, directed her block-by-block organizing toward the state campaign. In response to the California League of Women Voters opposition to Proposition 14, Hayes wrote the league a blistering letter. "We were APPALLED and ASHAMED...."

We had the highest regard for your group and even had intentions of joining," she wrote. She listed the travails of property ownership and compared the Rumford Act to the sort of state authoritarianism practiced in the USSR. She reminded the League about the sacredness of property rights, stating that

> a property owner, who is interested in his investment, HAS and SHOULD AL-WAYS HAVE THE RIGHT TO DISCRIMINATE against WHITE, BLACK, YELLOW OR ANY OTHER COLOR who he feels will not be suitable for his apartments or houses.

She enclosed a pamphlet from the statewide campaign entitled "Some Questions and Answers Demonstrating the Need for a 'YES' vote on Proposition 14."[41]

Proposition 14 opponents responded with a statewide campaign that framed the battle as the major civil rights issue west of the Mississippi River. Church, labor, business, academic, and community organizations coordinated the Californians Against Proposition 14 campaign, which pleaded with the public to vote no on the "Hate Amendment." One of their posters beamed "NO MISSISSIPPI HERE!" and claimed, "Even the worst state in the Deep South has no law as bad as Proposition 14. If racism is legalized, it would be a victory for bigots. Fair employment laws would be next." Segregation in schools would increase and California "would become another Mississippi."[42]

Governor Pat Brown denounced the initiative. The San Francisco Committee for Fair Housing Practices urged sponsors to donate money for "radio-TV spots, advertisements, publicity, speaker's bureau, mailings" to counter the "distortions playing on fear and prejudice."[43] Through organizations such as Mexican American Political Action and League of United Latin American Citizens in the Bay Area, Latinas/os mobilized a political coalition against Proposition 14 that built on decades of fighting for civil rights, and they registered 130,000 new voters.[44]

Urban policymakers, no matter where they stood personally on Proposition 14, worried about how the passage of Proposition 14 would affect federal funding. Government lawyers agreed that "the language of the proposed California constitutional amendment, if taken literally, would bar local public agencies from complying" with federal nondiscrimination requirements.[45] San Francisco Redevelopment Agency Director Justin Herman thought that Proposition 14 "was not a good piece of legislation" because it threatened his agency's applications for federal subsidies.[46] The measure, Frank Quinn of the San Francisco Committee for Fair Housing Practices said, had national importance, for "As California votes in 1964, so may go the nation."[47]

The 1964 election results highlighted the ways white voters in California reflected conflicting visions of government in ensuring both civil and economic rights. When San Francisco's citizens cast their ballots, they approved Measure H

(148,218 to 116,764); favored Lyndon Johnson (Dem.), who promised to expand economic and civil rights, over Barry Goldwater (Rep.) by a count of 230,758 to 92,944; sent William "Willie" Brown to the state legislature; and a slight majority voted in favor of Proposition 14. Support for Proposition 14 ran eight to five in the Bay Area and two to one in Los Angeles and all of California. When African and Mexican Americans votes were excluded, the measure passed by a three to one margin (see Table 5.1 and Table 5.2). As Edward Rutledge, Director of the National Committee Against Discrimination in Housing, put it, "Voters were able to vote their prejudices on Proposition 14 and at the same time serve their self-interests by voting overwhelmingly for President Lyndon Johnson."[48]

Governor Brown said the election showed that the "majority of the whites in this state just don't want Negros living in the same neighborhood with them." President Ed Mendenhall of the National Association of Real Estate Boards (NAREB) framed it differently at his group's 57th annual convention, declaring, "Those voting against forced housing consider the right of decision in private property a liberty essential to the preservation of their most basic human right."[49]

The passage of Proposition 14 set several developments in motion. Aiming to uphold federal nondiscrimination laws, Housing and Home Finance Administrator Robert Weaver stopped sending federal urban redevelopment funds to California. Of the dozens of projects halted across the state, several were in San Francisco, including a $38 million project in the Western Addition.[50] The National Association of Real Estate Boards took its "property rights" model to other states with the goal of preventing fair housing laws across the country. Thirteen other states followed

1964 Election Results for Proposition 14

	Yes	No
San Francisco	165,155	147,151
Bay Area Counties (excluding San Francisco)	808,740	549,629
Los Angeles	1,802,620	870,342
California	4,526,460	2,395,747

Table 5.1
Data from the California Statement of Vote, San Francisco Registrar. Bay Area counties include Alameda, Contra Costa, Marin, Napa, San Francisco, San Mateo, Santa Clara, Solano, and Sonoma.

1964 Presidential Election Results

Candidate	San Francisco	California	National
Barry Goldwater (Rep.)	92,994	2,879,108	27,178,188
Lyndon Johnson (Dem.)	230,758	4,171,877	43,129,566

Table 5.2
Data from California Statement of Vote, San Francisco Registrar.

California with their own anti-fair housing laws.[51] The real estate lobby tapped into and also fueled a growing movement of white voters against civil rights legislation that chipped away, however slowly, at racial inequality. Meanwhile, NAACP western regional counsel and Sacramento lawyer Nathaniel Colley began preparing a legal case to challenge Proposition 14 in California's courts.[52]

In the wake of the election, President Johnson worked with Congress to pass the largest batch of social legislation since the 1930s. Known collectively as the Great Society, the programs expanded consumer, civil, and economic rights as well as funding for education, arts, and job training. From Head Start and Medicare to food stamps, Great Society programs tried to patch some of the holes in the New Deal welfare state and address poverty and the crumbling conditions in many urban and rural communities. Programs housed in the Office of Economic Opportunity (OEO)—Volunteers in Service to America (VISTA), Legal Aid, and the Community Action Program (CAP)—assisted low-income rural and urban residents to participate in the decisions that affected their daily lives. More specifically, VISTA and CAP staff hired community organizers to mobilize poor, underserved populations through voter registration drives, public rallies, and neighborhood councils. Legal Aid armed these individuals and their organizations with lawyers.

Across the country, many low-income residents found in these programs resources to improve their housing, neighborhoods, and cities and to expand the economic and civil rights attached to citizenship. They wanted institutions to square with a global discourse of equality, human rights, and self-determination. Many aimed for participatory and democratic decision making and as a result ended up reimagining who made public policy, how, and for whom.[53]

With the Great Society, President Johnson raised the status of urban development and housing programs. On September 9, 1965, just weeks after the Watts riot, Johnson created the Department of Housing and Urban Development (HUD). The creation of HUD made formal the federal–urban relationship begun during the New Deal. Robert Weaver headed the new department. Born in Washington, DC, Weaver earned a Ph.D. in economics at Harvard (1934), became a New Dealer and civil rights activist, and wrote regularly on the condition of urban African Americans. As the first African American to hold a cabinet post, his appointment helped to cement the Democratic Party's connection to civil rights and the African American community. Under Weaver, HUD programs continued to support the private housing sector and urban redevelopment projects while only slightly boosting spending for public housing. Public housing authorities across the nation, meanwhile, struggled to maintain their programs and housing.[54]

For SFHA tenants and their allies, the Great Society programs and HUD priorities produced an environment ripe for organizing. In many ways, the 1960s were a turning point not only for SFHA tenants but for the SFHA and the city's political dynamics. Tenants organized around a broad vision of public housing in the city and the nation, a vision that fulfilled some of the progressive and even radical goals of Modern Housing and New Deal advocates. That is, these public housing advocates from earlier in century believed in designing public housing projects that not only provided housing but brought tenants together socially and politically.

SFHA tenants worked with SFHA's Effie Robinson to improve their housing and intergroup relations, but they also added three distinct approaches to building their power and participating in the decisions that affected their lives, housing, and economic and civil rights. First, they packed SFHA commission meetings in order to monitor policy discussions and press the commissioners and Beard to make quality public housing a priority. When elites in and out of the SFHA excluded them from the political process, they let the commissioners know. At a February 4, 1965, meeting, SFHA tenant and Hunters Point community activist Elouise Westbrook told the commissioners, "Tenants residing in the Hunters Point Area are vitally interested in plans being formulated by the Economic Opportunity Council" and "inquired why tenants had not been contacted so they may become involved in any proposed plans."[55] Tenant pressure became so great that the commissioners passed an "Orderly Conduct of Commission Business" policy to limit agenda items and comments from the public.[56]

As a second strategy, SFHA tenants took positions with organizations and served on SFHA and city committees. In the 1950s, low-income residents and SFHA tenants had sat on redevelopment agency committees to satisfy federal requirements, but they were often handpicked or were denied a real voice in decision making. In the 1960s, San Francisco Economic Opportunity Program staff coordinated resident input on housing, education, and employment policies for the city's master plan and worked with Effie Robinson and tenants on committees in Chinatown, Hunters Point, and the Western Addition. Tenants contributed to setting the goals for the SFHA's proposal that was "a part of the Master Plan for San Francisco under the Economic Opportunity Program." Tenants worked in community centers receiving federal support and on projects ranging from job and daycare programs to neighborhood beautification.[57]

The third and most powerful strategy was forming tenant unions. For decades, tenants had met to influence SFHA policies, and in a few cases they had taken collective action, but Beard discouraged, red-baited, and retaliated against tenant activists. With tenant unions and a supportive political context, tenants began to challenge his power. SFHA tenants embraced the union structure for its democratic possibilities and for its ability to harness collective power. On December 3, 1964,

North Beach Place tenant Marjorie Bezzone became the first tenant association representative to address the commission. The North Beach Place Neighborhood Improvement Association, she said, aimed to

> improve conditions in the immediate area by providing activities for young people of each group from pre-school to young adulthood; improve general living conditions; improve relations among the tenants; and improve relations with the community at large.[58]

Across the city, tenants embraced the strategy. Bezzone's appearance opened the floodgates of tenant demands on SFHA and city leaders. Tenants appeared regularly before the commission, demanding better building maintenance, a more responsive SFHA staff, and better lighting and playground equipment. Nearly all of these representatives were women. Tenant unions published newsletters, organized social activities, and made policy recommendations to the SFHA and city agencies. Alma Burleigh, secretary of the North Beach Place Neighborhood Improvement Association, told the commissioners that our tenant union has improved the

> living conditions within our project. We have an exciting program of activities for children and adults. We have initiated new and more friendly relations between all tenants, between tenants and management and the Commission. The tenants in this project have begun to develop a new spirit of enthusiasm and optimism concerning their homes and their whole way of life. For the first time in this city, people in public housing have begun to do something to help themselves.[59]

SFHA tenant unions joined the civil rights movement and formed an alliance that allowed tenants and their neighbors to address decades of neglect and discrimination by elites in private and public institutions. In February 1965, the NAACP again accused the SFHA leadership of not doing enough to integrate the projects, the SFHA workforce, and union membership in the trades. Rather than let the issue be buried in committee, the NAACP asked for the removal of Beard and commissioners Mazzola, Lee, and John Gurich, as well as for corrective policies. "If something isn't done to change the 'repugnant practices,'" the NAACP threatened to launch a wave of direct actions, including picketing and sit ins.[60] Terry Francois, who successfully litigated the Banks case and who was now on the San Francisco Board of Supervisors, commented on the NAACP demands by telling the press "Beard should have resigned a long time ago."[61]

When the commissioners lagged in taking action, the NAACP worked with tenants, young and old, to protest in Hunters Point to "bring some Democracy within the Authority."[62] Direct actions followed at other SFHA projects and at the main office. In response, the SFHA leadership offered to monitor the racial occupancy of its projects, do more staff training, and work closely with tenant unions. SFHA tenants, the NAACP, and the San Francisco Board of Supervisors pointed to the recent FEPC report on the hiring practices of the SFHA and San Francisco Building Trades as evidence of the need for action. The 1965 report recommended that the SFHA produce a quarterly employee report broken down by job title, job status (temporary, part-time, full-time permanent, and so on), turnover, and race and ethnicity. The report also called for hiring more nonwhites for white-collar positions and exploring new ways to recruit nonwhite blue-collar union workers or get those workers "from other sources if unions can't supply them." Finally, the FEPC report suggested that the authority work with an independent agency to implement these changes.[63]

The SFHA leadership resisted the use of an independent agency to evaluate the authority's progress on civil rights. Commissioner Mazzola lashed out at the FEPC, NAACP, and Board of Supervisors for making integration "a political football" and then recommended a study of discrimination law to determine the authority's responsibility and culpability.[64]

Figure 5.4
Civil rights activists demand John Beard be fired in 1965.

The other commissioners, however, heeded the FEPC recommendation by bringing in the San Francisco Human Rights Commission (SFHRC) as the independent agency.[65] Of the various city agencies, the SFHRC, which had been established in 1964, had staff with the expertise and local knowledge to address the institutional racism in the SFHA and unions. In May 1965, the SFHRC recommended two courses of action for the SFHA. It wanted detailed quarterly reports on SFHA personnel (as the FEPC report had recommended) and on those of the private companies with which the SFHA contracted for services. It also recommended the implementation

Figure 5.5
San Francisco Housing
Authority Director John
Beard in 1965.

of an affirmative action program for recruiting nonwhite workers. The SFHA commissioners buried the two proposals in committee—which only intensified the civil rights campaign and negative publicity for the authority. Mounting political pressure forced Mazzola to resign in May.[66]

His replacement, Harry Bigarani, who headed the Painters Union Council, was slightly better than Mazzola on civil rights. Commissioners Bigarani and Boswell worked with SFHRC staff, C. L. Dellums of the FEPC, and HUD to make recruitment and hiring fairer and to expand the SFHA job training programs. Significantly, the new procedures only applied to white-collar positions, allowing the trade unions to continue their discriminatory practices and providing another example of gradual but frustrating progress on civil rights.[67]

SFHA Director Beard had always been a key obstacle to progress on civil rights, and SFHA tenants worked with a number of individuals and organizations to oust him. On October 7, 1965, SFHA tenants and their allies filled the SFHA commissioner meeting. Audrey Smith of the Yerba Buena Plaza Tenant Union, Mary Louise Paddock of the Sunnydale Citizens' League, Mrs. Washington of the Bayview-Hunters Point Block Organization, and Constance Lotti of the North Beach Place Neighborhood Improvement Association stood together at the podium to present a list of grievances to the commission. When Paddock, who represented 3,000 tenants, took the microphone, she demanded immediate action on repair orders, more effective pest control, new paint and clotheslines, and additional lighting for safety. She also expected more childcare in the projects. Smith, Washington, and Lotti expressed similar concerns and expectations.[68]

Their collective testimony prepared the audience for the reading of a telegram sent by Assemblyman John Burton (Dem., San Francisco) and read by Burton's assistant Sam Ridge. The telegram expressed support for the tenants and conveyed Burton's "unhappiness with the manner in which the San Francisco Housing Authority treats its tenants." Citing the FEPC report, Burton blamed the administration for "totally lacking not only in the understanding of the purpose of public housing laws, but also [for being] inept in its day-to-day functions." Director Beard, Burton said, "must bear the responsibility for a third rate operation." He told the commission to "find a new [director] who is not only well versed as to public housing but also has an understanding and feeling for the needs of people." He emphasized that the SFHA must have a "full commitment to human dignity and equality." SFHA staff defended their work, blaming the tenants for the repair and maintenance backlogs at the projects, but it was not enough to save Beard.[69]

In Beard's place, the SFHA commissioners hired Mayor Shelley's aide and friend Eneas Kane. Born, raised, and educated in San Francisco, Kane had attended law school at the University of San Francisco with Shelley, then taught English, public speaking, and social ethics at Saint Ignatius High School and the University of San Francisco. From 1936 to his 1965 appointment, the tall, redheaded Kane did public relations work in the private and public sector.[70] Kane brought a friendly and sympathetic approach to the position. Commissioner Walter conceded that Kane "might lack some technical knowledge" in agency management, but on the whole he thought Kane was "well qualified in the field of housing" and that "his well-known sympathies for matters of civil rights will be able to help us immeasurably." Civil rights organizations did not oppose Kane, though they questioned the selection process and asked why the commission did not do a national search. In response, Commissioner Walter said, "When you have a pot of gold buried in your back yard, you don't go around the world to look."[71] In contrast to Beard, Kane expressed a compelling commitment to a "new approach to the authority's dual obligation to its tenants and the people of San Francisco."[72] That approach, the new director said, would focus on "the twin goals of reorganization within and reaching out beyond."[73]

The "reorganization within" focused on administration. Kane saved over $1 million the first year through centralized purchasing, staff reductions, vehicle maintenance, reduced PILOTs to the city (Beard had overpaid for years), and oversight mechanisms to stop improper spending and theft. Even so, the savings did not keep pace with rising costs, especially in maintenance. From 1963 to 1966, maintenance costs increased an average of 13.2 percent while rental income rose only 3.2 percent. Rising vandalism also hurt the authority's budget: In one six-month period, replacing broken windows cost 94 cents per unit per month (4,106 windows for a total of $42,000) at a time when per-unit monthly rent averaged $58.63.[74]

The SFHA's budget faced further constraints because federal formulas did not cover major repairs on aging permanent projects. To supplement the program, the SFHA requested 500 units in the Section 23 leasing program, and by 1967 the authority was leasing 133 such units from private landlords. In terms of personnel administration, Kane clarified SFHA staff duties and improved morale. He directed staff to reduce discrimination in tenant selection to integrate SFHA projects. Kane pressed contractors and unions to hire nonwhites, though progress on this goal moved at a glacial pace. In his area of expertise, Kane used radio, newspaper, and television coverage to improve the authority's image.[75] Many were optimistic. The SFHA was, according to SFHA Commissioner Bigarani, emerging from "ice-age inertia" and enjoying a "renaissance."[76]

In terms of "reaching out beyond," Kane built closer ties with tenants and provided SFHA resources to build tenant capacity to participate in the decisions that affected their lives. He hired more project managers and instructed them to have "more direct and frequent communication with, by and among tenants." He worked with the twenty-two SFHA police officers to do more to fill in the gap between their role and that of the San Francisco Police Department and to improve their relations with tenants. SFHA employees attended required workshops on "easing social problems within projects." Kane expanded social services at the projects and increased the number of SFHA representatives on city agencies.[77]

In stark contrast to Beard, Kane welcomed "tenant councils to join with the Authority in the solution of joint problems." He set up a tenant organization program to develop tenant associations where none existed, and he created committees that worked with social groups (youth, elderly, parents). SFHA staff became more involved in grant and program development and even ran voter registration programs.[78] In June 1966, the Tenants' Advisory Committee held its first meeting for "the purpose of improving communications between the Housing Authority and tenant organizations." Kane worked with Larry Jack Wong and Father Joseph Wong of the Chinatown-North Beach Area OEO office and Ping Yuen Residents Improvement Association to provide community space for tenants and offer onsite vocational and educational programs, citizenship and English classes, and a nursery school. By welcoming tenant unions, improving communication, and expanding social programs, Kane helped to fulfill many of the social and political goals of New Deal housing advocates.[79]

Establishing lines of communication in particular was well timed. Of all the districts with SFHA housing, Hunters Point had been the most neglected by Beard and the city's public and private institutions. Police brutality there only exacerbated racial tensions and ill feelings that residents harbored toward the city's institutions. The Hunters Point Tenant Union (HPTU) emerged as a leading advocate for tenants and the district's residents. On September 22, 1966, HPTU Chairman George Earl penned a letter to Kane with a list of questions and demands. If the SFHA did not answer by October 15, the tenants threatened a rent strike. Then, on September 27, 1966, before Kane responded, a rebellion broke out in the district after a white police officer shot and killed 16-year-old African American Matthew Johnson for running away from a stolen car. It took three days for the National Guard and police to stop the unrest, but as was the case in cities across the nation, the protest-producing socioeconomic conditions remained.[80] After consulting with SFHA staff, on October 11 Kane met with the six-member HPTU Executive Committee. He told them the SFHA had applied for a $3.3 million emergency federal appropriation to fund backlogged maintenance at Hunters Point and other projects. At the next HPTU meeting, members discussed the SFHA application and then called a rent strike for November 1 as a "pressure move to assist the Authority in obtaining funds for rehabilitation purposes."[81]

However sympathetic to the tenant strike, SFHA commissioners and Kane were limited in what they could do. The SFHA used its monthly rent statements to tell tenants about SFHA procedures for obtaining emergency maintenance, about steps taken by the authority to secure federal renovation funds (of which $600,000 was earmarked for Hunters Point), and about the authority's eviction policy, which would use due process to evict tenants for not paying rent. When asked about responding to tenant demands, Commissioner Boswell said the authority "should not yield to pressure, particularly 'when we feel we are trying to sympathetically and honestly meet the needs of our tenants.'"[82]

In November, HUD denied the SFHA's application for emergency funds because the federal agency did not provide renovation grants for existing housing. HUD officials recommended that the SFHA take out loans for the renovations instead. But the SFHA's weak balance sheet made such loans impossible, so Kane submitted a grant application to the U.S. Department of Health, Education, and Welfare for the repairs needed in Hunters Point. Despite support in the House and Senate, this grant, too, was denied. Meanwhile, 900 Hunters Point tenants, acting with counsel from the federally funded San Francisco Neighborhood Assistance, deposited their rent into a tenant-controlled escrow account, which was used to pay for painting and renovations at their buildings. SFHA Counsel John Sullivan won an injunction against the tenant union and filed charges against eleven tenant union officials who, according to Sullivan, were wrongly acting as SFHA agents by collecting and using SFHA rent money. But tenants ignored the injunction and continued to divert their rent into their escrow account and to paint and repair their units.[83]

The HPTU leadership demonstrated flexibility during the strike. They enlisted the support of the San Francisco Human Rights Commission (SFHRC) to help find funding for the repairs. SFHRC representative Edgar Osgood wrote the SFHA on the "urgent need for repair and maintenance in permanent and temporary projects at Hunters Point" and suggested that if other funding did not come through, the SFHA should use its reserves and seek funding from the Board of Supervisors.[84] Hoping to both legitimate the strike and get federal funding, HPTU Chairman Earl provided HUD officials with a list of problems—building by building, repair by repair—to demonstrate the need for $600,000 worth of maintenance. HUD did not provide any funding, but in March HUD officials did approve a SFHA request to use city funds for repairs in Hunters Point. In April, Mayor Shelley pledged $350,000 of city money and Kane $150,000 of SFHA money for renovations in Hunters Point. Kane worked with tenants to set priorities for the money while Sullivan won a legal case against the tenants. By court order and negotiation, HPTU officials transferred the escrowed rents to the authority, tenants resumed their rent payments to the SFHA, and city–SFHA renovation money allowed work to begin.[85]

The formation of the HPTU, and the willingness of the tenants to act in solidarity, provided tenants with a degree of power unseen in the history of the SFHA.

Although the tenants did not secure all the funding their community needed, they did improve their housing conditions. And although the HPTU showed the promise of tenant unions, the strike and its outcome demonstrated the policy constraints under which its members and local housing programs operated. Tenants grabbed the attention of the city and the surrounding communities and secured vital funds for long-overdue repairs. But those funds, which only scratched the surface of needed repairs, jobs, and resources for the community, came from local sources: Federal agencies and the California government ignored the needs of Hunters Point tenants. The unwillingness of federal and state officials to fund Hunters Point repairs pointed to a bleak financial future for the SFHA program and reflected a growing political sentiment that urban programs and residents were not a priority.

The 1966 gubernatorial California election, which handed Governor Brown a defeat by actor-turned-politician Ronald Reagan (Rep.), reflected that shift too. Reagan's campaign attracted voters with a platform of law and order and reduced taxes, regulations, civil rights enforcement, and social programs. Reagan had also championed Proposition 14. The 1966 election illustrated a broader political shift among many white voters, especially throughout the South and West, who began to reject the Democratic Party's attempts, however inadequate, to end poverty and racial and gender discrimination.[86] Within this political context, the nation's public housing program would not have the federal support necessary to address the many problems facing low-income households and neighborhoods. For Kane and SFHA tenants, this political reality led to new demands and challenges heading into the 1970s.

The forces that influenced the SFHA program throughout the 60s reflect some of the major developments during the decade. As 1967 came to a close, SFHA tenants were working collectively with their allies to offer a vision of economic and civil rights unseen in the city's history of tenant activism. With support from Great Society programs and the SFHA, public housing tenants organized tenant unions, staged direct actions, and removed John Beard. Women supplied the most energy for tenant organization and participation in the policy decisions that affected their lives, homes, and city—and by doing so, made tenant's rights women's rights. As in the past, the organizing targeted the SFHA as a strategic site to challenge customs and policies that perpetuated inequality, especially the structural shortages of jobs and housing. SFHA tenant union experiences in this era demonstrated the growing power of tenants and new forms of public housing and urban decision making.

Yet, they faced legislative and political constraints. Those constraints highlighted two national trends facing the urban poor. Federal programs, existing and new, did not do enough to eliminate structural economic and racial inequality. Urban residents organized to put pressure on local and federal institutions and individuals, and in response, the federal government began to devolve its housing responsibilities to local governments and the private sector, as evidenced in the Hunters Point rehabilitation, redevelopment programs, and the growing use of Section 23 leased housing. Low-income tenants bore the burden of these changes and of the underfunding of public housing.[87]

The other trend was the backlash against programs for the poor and civil rights efforts to end discrimination. More and more, white voters and politicians began to associate Great Society efforts as too costly and too threatening to customs that maintained racial segregation and white privilege. The programs were also cited as the source of the problems facing many white voters, who began to experience a declining standard of living and a loss of faith in government. When San Francisco resident Mr. L. George wrote Lyndon Johnson to voice his concern about the high levels of public housing in his Potrero Hill district, he captured increasingly popular views of the recent expansion of government and the Democratic Party:

> We have 25% of all public housing of San Francisco right in this District, which has run the neighborhood to the ground. Filthy streets, Dice Games on Street Corners, Run down unpainted War Type Units, no landscaping, Broken windows in the School. And we have to support this by taxes. How much do you think the average homeowner can take.

He blamed local politicians and federal officials for running "us old timers off" and thanked "God we have Elections so we can remove these people from office next term. . . . I've been a Democrat for 30 yrs, but no more."[88]

Not every Democrat held that sentiment in San Francisco, but many urban and suburban whites, as the vote for Proposition 14 illustrated, could identify with George's critique of Great Society liberalism. Yet in many of the city's districts, including Potrero Hill, a growing interracial and intergenerational movement of tenants aimed to expand the role of government and make it more responsive to the needs of the nation's citizens.

CHAPTER 6

OUT OF STEP WITH WASHINGTON

The housing crisis in San Francisco, the Bay Area, and the nation
can be solved only if the federal government concentrates the same
degree of manpower, money and will on urban life as it now spends
on war, military programs and space. The housing shortage, together
with rising unemployment and continued inflation, produces human
suffering and increased tensions.

San Francisco Human Rights Commission[1]

IN APRIL 1970, a *San Francisco Bay Guardian* headline read "Roaches, Rents, &
Repairs: Tenants Are Striking All Over . . . 'They Won't Be Pushed.'" Tenant strikes
responded to the "acute housing shortage" and the ways landlords exercised power
over not only low-income households but also "middle and upper class residents."
Decorated with drawings of militant cockroaches carrying picket signs stating "Rent
Is Theft," "People Not Profits," "Unfit Even for Roaches," and "Strike," the *Guardian*
article identified several causes for the housing crisis: "Vietnam war inflation," "a
long-term influx of blacks, Chicanos, and students," "Nixon cuts [to] the Housing
and Urban Redevelopment budget," and "high interest rates."

The *Guardian* focused on the ideas and actions of tenant union members in
the Bay Area's private housing, but public housing tenants were expanding their
power, too. Private and public housing tenants fought for more housing (especially
for nonwhites and families), rent reductions, rent control, and an end to evictions
and unsafe units. They wanted "self determination" in their housing and the "right
to make decisions about the place they live in." They were, as one tenant put it,
"multiracial" and "proud to get it on." According to organizers, through the process
of collective struggle, tenants

> recognize the nature of landlord "exploitation" . . . [and] extend this analysis to
> other parts of the "system." They increasingly view federal and city governments,
> banks and insurance companies as the landlord's accomplices.

Some tenants linked housing to "human rights" and a rejection of "private property." Bill Hite, an elected tenant representative from the Haight-Ashbury neighborhood in San Francisco, saw tenant organizations as a "grass roots movement toward a socialist city structure."[2]

Not every tenant thought rent was theft or envisioned a red San Francisco. But the collective pursuit of profit and control over urban space by landlords, developers, and government officials contributed to the housing crisis that gave rise to tenant organizing in private and public housing. Public housing tenants' mobilization differed from that of their counterparts in private housing in several ways. SFHA tenants organized at the building and city level and connected themselves more effectively to national tenant networks and organizations. Because of the public and participatory nature of the SFHA, these tenants had access to human and financial resources as well as to a wide range of programs and services. SFHA officials did not always share the same vision as tenants, but they all worked together to address issues related to the program.

SFHA tenant organizing also reflected and contributed to the movements that challenged cultural norms, authority, and power. In this dynamic context, SFHA tenants constructed a political identity around their place and status as tenants. Tenants never spoke with one voice. But they did organize around a vision of government at odds with that of a growing number of middle-income voters, some city leaders, and the Nixon administration and Congress. Indeed, as support for some social programs and federal funds fell around the nation, SFHA tenants and many low-income residents in San Francisco were calling for more public housing, jobs, childcare and health care, civil rights, and art. SFHA tenants even demanded control over SFHA funds, hiring, and policymaking. In the latter demands, their vision of a fully democratic government housing program exceeded the ideas contained in New Deal and Great Society liberalism.

Although tenants never fully democratized San Francisco's public housing, their efforts made policymaking more inclusive. They gained representation on committees and programs and began serving as representatives on the SFHA commission, something many housing authorities across the nation resisted. Their inclusion in SFHA governance often reduced their militancy, but it expanded their knowledge of and voice in SFHA and HUD policymaking.

Their participation unfortunately came at the moment when the federal government cut public housing funding and devolved low-rent housing moneys and social programs to the private sector. At the same time, crime was increasing in low-income neighborhoods, and the standard of living of workers began to decline. The media and public housing critics suggested that government housing in this era had become warehouses for the poor and centers of crime, dependency, and political apathy. Scholars have noted how many voters, especially white voters, lost faith in New Deal–Great Society liberalism and federal programs for the poor by the 1970s. The ideas and actions of San Francisco's tenants, especially those from public housing, demonstrated a continued faith in using government to make housing, urban redevelopment, and employment more democratic and expand the economic security of residents in and out of the city.

In May 1968, at the regional conference of the National Association of Housing and Redevelopment Officials (NAHRO), SFHA Director Eneas Kane presented a talk entitled "The Fabulous Machine Called Public Housing." "Low-rent public housing," Kane told the 500 delegates, was like "a sturdy truck. It steams and sputters up one side of an endless procession of steep hills only to go careening, brakeless down the other side." The local authority was "the driver of this mess," and "he is screaming for help. His truck seems to be coming apart piece by piece. And he can neither stop it nor make it speed up enough to get over the railroad crossing ahead of a freight train racing toward the same intersection." Kane's main point was that "every housing authority today is attempting to carry a 1968 load with a 1937 machine" and that, however "patched and repainted . . . inside—under the hood where the engine snorts and wheezes—it is 30 years old."[3]

That machine, Kane continued, was originally designed to clear slums and meet the housing and employment needs of workers "who were experiencing a hangover from the depression." Since the 1937 Housing Act, Congress had tweaked the program to expand, slightly, the number of units and the number of eligible social groups. But on the whole these periodic adjustments failed to overhaul the machine—or meet the needs of citizens. Public housing authorities continued to operate under federal funding formulas that did not cover maintenance and administration costs of their aging housing or the expanding social services for tenants. In San Francisco from 1961 to 1968, for example, the cost of building maintenance rose 49 percent, administration 39 percent. Across the nation, public housing authorities exhausted their reserves, and some were on the verge of bankruptcy.[4] Kane recommended federal legislation to increase modernization funds, raise maintenance cost ceilings, and create a family subsidy, similar to that given for elderly tenants. He also wanted federal funds to help authorities cover the growing costs of social services addressing the diverse needs of tenants.[5] The stakes were high. Kane said, "TO FAIL IS to add to the turmoil of our cities and to reject our public trust."[6]

Kane's proposal to boost federal funds would help local authorities and the tenants and communities they served, but not solve the national housing problem. The national shortage of affordable housing and continuing racial discrimination required broader measures. Housing activist and scholar Chester Hartman called for new housing policies in this period based on new research and a new set of priorities. At the most basic level, HUD had failed to investigate "how much housing this country would need to provide everyone with a decent place to live." Without such information, Hartman contended, a meaningful national policy was impossible.[7] Moreover, public policies continued to favor private property owners and the wealthy over low-income tenants. One of the first steps to solving the housing crisis, he said, was "to eliminate or reform the totally upside-down nature of the housing subsidies" and restructure "present aids and delivery systems so as to provide assistance to those who need it and take it away from those who don't." Hartman wrote that the federal government needed to "introduce greater equity into the tax system" and reconsider the delivery of public housing. He contended that in cities where local authorities were not meeting the needs of residents, the federal government should restructure the existing housing authority or create a new institution "with broader jurisdiction and powers and greater motivation" than a city-specific authority. Other possibilities included the use of state and even the federal government as a "houser of last resort."[8]

In 1968, a federal overhaul of the kind Kane or Hartman envisioned was not forthcoming, though Congress did pass two pieces of housing legislation that year. In response to continued civil rights organizing and state laws protecting the rights of property owners to discriminate, such as Proposition 14 in California, Congress passed the 1968 Civil Rights Act, which included a ban on discrimination in housing and put HUD in charge of enforcing the act, though low funding, a lack of political will, and the many ways discrimination occurred informally limited the legislation's effectiveness.[9]

The second legislation, the Housing and Urban Redevelopment Act of 1968, authorized more public housing units, but it also signaled an expansion of programs that moved federal low-rent housing assistance funds to private landlords. The act increased Section 23 leased housing, which provided local authorities with funds to lease units directly from landlords in the private sector. The legislation also expanded the "turnkey" program, which had since 1965 provided authorities funds to purchase housing directly from the private sector. Section 235, a new program, provided subsidies and technical assistance to people of modest income so they could purchase a home.

Taken together, the collection of federal housing programs addressed none of the problems outlined by Kane and Hartman and reflected a waning federal commitment to funding permanent public housing. These programs illustrated how the federal government began to use its low-income housing dollars to reward private homeowners and landlords.[10] Through the lens of federal housing policy, this shift to the private sector became part of the debates and policy changes that reduced economic and civil rights, regulations, and social programs, while transferring a growing percentage of wealth and power to elites.

The Nixon administration only hastened this shift. Richard Nixon ran on a racially coded campaign against government social programs for the poor and civil rights and promised to reduce the federal role in cities.[11] Once in office, his New Federalism—the devolution of federal programs to local and state governments and the private sector in spirit and practice—followed through on his campaign pledges, and that worried many city leaders. In San Francisco, Allan Jacobs, director of the Department of City Planning, thought that the federal shift in priorities added to, rather than solved, the problems facing urban governments. He questioned whether state offices were "equipped" for these tasks, and, more importantly, he worried about adding "one more level of government between the applicant (e.g. a city like San Francisco) and the funding source." "What," he asked, "would be achieved by all this?"[12]

San Francisco Mayor Joseph Alioto and other mayors thought the New Federalism generated four problems: too much red tape, too little federal performance, too many federal programs working at cross purposes, and too few federal dollars to make a difference. Without a change of course, Alioto wrote Nixon, federal programs will fail urban residents, and then "the credibility of government goes down the drain."[13] Others worried about the federal shift, too. SFHA Commissioner Reverend Hamilton Boswell thought that any federal "move toward State and local level controls will be a dangerous step backwards." He was concerned "about the encouragement of private interests in federally-funded programs. Poor people," he remarked, "can not compete with private corporations."[14]

Despite these local concerns, the New Federalism began to filter down (and percolate up) through government agencies. California Governor Ronald Reagan (Rep.) and California Assemblyman Pete Wilson (Rep., San Diego) supported new legislation to transfer federal dollars from local agencies to the state government. Wilson introduced, and then helped to pass, a bill that allowed California savings and loan associations to use 1968 Housing Act funds to build and operate low- and moderate-income housing. Wilson also proposed a state agency to handle federal block grants, which HUD officials found "intriguing."[15] In 1969, Governor Reagan created the Intergovernmental Relations Agency to "assume the role of the state clearinghouse for Federal grants-in-aid." To HUD Secretary George Romney, such state offices were "a very important step in the process of improving the effectiveness of State Government."[16] State governors, Romney added, could in these programs "strengthen their own administrative systems" and have more "technical and financial resources."[17] On the other hand, these ideas, if turned into legislation, could also undermine social programs such as public housing by giving state governments more control in the programs and by making local and state governments compete for block grants.

In time, HUD did use block grants to make some of these changes, but instead of using state governments, HUD moved public housing oversight to regional HUD offices. The two policy changes bogged down public housing authorities and urban programs alike. Mayor Alioto explained to Nixon that recent federal modifications produced "so much machinery, so many standards to be met, so many forms to be prepared, such long delays in processing" that public housing and other urban programs suffered. Alioto warned Nixon that the credibility gap between recipients and government would widen further "if we do not reduce the non-productive motions in which we are required to engage."[18]

The Nixon administration also directly undermined the capacity and effectiveness of public housing programs. Secretary Romney reorganized HUD in ways that led to low morale, an exodus of staff, and discouraging delays in public housing work. Kane estimated it took 20 percent longer to move applications through HUD after the reorganization. In the Federal Housing Administration (now housed in HUD), a scandal involving predatory lending in poor neighborhoods hurt the agency's reputation and raised questions about its effectiveness. Romney's commitment to enforcing civil rights legislation also generated problems from above and below. Romney stood out against the growing number of Republicans who used the politics of race to capture white voters from the Democratic Party, for he saw the negative social effects of housing discrimination. When he tried to use HUD's Open Communities to integrate white communities, especially in suburban areas, he encountered tremendous opposition from white residents, local political elites, and Nixon. The Romney–Nixon battle that ensued over fair housing exacerbated HUD's problems, and Romney eventually resigned in 1972.[19]

Although federal housing funding increased in 1968 and 1969, federal programs for the private sector secured the lion's share of funds, while allocations for building and maintenance of public housing did not keep pace with need. And, across the country, urban redevelopment programs often worked at cross purposes in the area of low-rent and public housing supply. Redevelopment agencies, including the San Francisco Redevelopment Agency, continued to demolish more low and moderately priced housing than they produced and in the process displaced mostly poor, nonwhite residents.[20]

Additionally, Nixon pursued political and economic strategies that created financial chaos for public housing authority administrators. Nixon's HUD regularly slowed or stopped funds to housing authorities and continued the untenable maintenance formula that forced authorities to use up their reserves. Kane, as president of the National Association of Housing and Redevelopment Officials and director of one of the nation's largest authorities, understood what Nixon's strategies did to public housing programs. At the 1971 NAHRO conference, Kane said the Nixon "administration has chosen to spend funds for trips to the moon, national defense and many other things rather than to spend the funds for public housing."[21] Responding to a bleak report on federal legislation, SFHA Commissioner Caroline Charles commented, "I have felt for quite some time that we are being driven out of business, and I think it is ultimately going to happen." The core problem, she said, was that HUD officials expected authorities to break even or be "profitable" even though public housing "was established to be a subsidized operation. There is something very different between those two ideas." SFHA Commissioner Walter put it more bluntly: "We all know that housing is being phased out by the Executive Branch of this Government."[22]

During the Nixon administration, Kane said there was much "confusion as to future funding of public housing in the United States. We just have no way of knowing what amount of money is going to be made available to us in San Francisco."[23] Following Nixon's 1972 reelection, the executive branch clarified its attitude toward public housing when it impounded funds for the program—much as it did with the funds of other social and environmental programs with which Nixon disagreed. Housing authorities, including the SFHA, responded with lawsuits that eventually restored their funds, but the eighteen-month impoundment of public housing dollars and general uncertainty constrained housing authorities across the nation.[24]

In addition to the actions of the Nixon administration, changes in the postwar economy also limited the nation's public housing program. By the late 1960s, deindustrialization and inflation eroded the standard of living of workers, including those in San Francisco. In 1969, a San Francisco government report noted that the city's financial, administrative, and entertainment industries added 65,100 jobs, while jobs in manufacturing and wholesale trade declined by roughly 13,000. The report found that employers and many unions continued to limit women and nonwhites to menial jobs that were "temporary, low paying, low prestige and highly vulnerable to shifts in economic activity levels." Female and nonwhite workers often experienced unemployment rates two and even three times higher than the city's average. The report identified discrimination as a key factor in these patterns—but, like so many studies of low-wage workers and the poor, the report suggested that many of these workers lacked the skills demanded by employers, who hired 40 percent of their workers from outside of the city.[25] As was happening in other cities, white-collar careers expanded in this era, and more of these workers commuted to their city jobs, but blue-collar jobs declined in quality and often in number.[26]

Amid these economic and political conditions, San Francisco residents found it challenging to find affordable housing. The city government and citizen groups conducted a number of studies at the end of the 1960s and found that 45,000 of the city's houses were substandard, the vacancy rate for rentals hovered at 1 percent, and rental units made up 70 percent of the city's homes.[27] Many residents turned to the SFHA for assistance—its multiyear waiting list often topped 5,000 applicants, and the agency regularly stopped taking applications. In the worst cases, many applicants, including the elderly, waited more than ten years for a SFHA unit. San Franciscan Kathryn Keeble explained to HUD Secretary Romney the key problem of government-assisted housing in her city and other urban areas: "There are far too few of this type of housing and far too many needing them."[28] The Citizens Emergency Task Force for a Workable Housing Policy, which consisted of an all-star list of civic and religious leaders, echoed Keeble in its report, noting that of all the different program and policy options, "public housing represents San Francisco's best present hope" for meeting the city's low-income housing needs.[29]

The SFHA commissioners and Kane worked within this challenging environment to provide public housing. All were committed to using the SFHA to meet broad housing and social goals. Part of this commitment came from the failure of the private sector to deliver affordable housing and from the recognition that permanent public housing remained the best program for low-income residents. Commissioner Boswell noted that only public housing ensured "real security" to low-income families and that other programs such as Section 23 could be cut, leaving many families "without housing." "Unless we have public housing," he said, "poor people do not stand a chance to remain in the Western Addition, Hunters Point, or anywhere else."[30]

Kane partly blamed past SFHA policies "for the lack of . . . low-rent housing" and for not always delivering high- quality housing, but he knew that public housing was necessary because "the private housing sector has not to date been able to solve the housing problems of San Francisco and other urban areas."[31] San Francisco voters in 1964 and 1968 agreed, approving thousands of future SFHA permanent units, but the long and unstable federal approval process, high costs of land and construction in the city, and Nixon's attacks on public housing delayed building these units.[32]

The SFHA leadership also used their agency for expanding the political capacity of citizens and the social services in and around SFHA projects. Commissioners and Kane directed staff to work with community and tenant organizations to formulate "a city-wide concept of social goals in public housing."[33] The SFHA provided meeting space and resources such as transportation and childcare to facilitate tenant participation. Working with tenants, the SFHA used its contracts and tenant selection to break down racial barriers in unions, government agencies, and neighborhoods. In the area of economic rights, the SFHA's Human Relations Department staff worked to "lead the tenants to social services available or bring services to the tenant." Whether it was Aid to Families with Dependent Children, elderly services, or childcare, SFHA staff tried to make the lives of tenants more economically secure.[34]

The SFHA leadership also responded to demographic changes in its projects: Tenants in the 1960s and 1970s required more services than they had in the 1940s. Seniors, individuals requiring mental health care and drug and alcohol treatment (many displaced from SROs and low-rent housing by redevelopment), and a growing number of very poor tenants (rather than tenants with higher incomes and fewer needs) began to fill public housing projects. These changes in the SFHA tenant population resulted primarily from tenant selection policies, federal legislation, redevelopment, and discrimination in the city's labor and housing markets. SFHA staff often struggled to find the resources for these tenants. A bump in violent crime in the city hit low-income neighborhoods and only heightened these problems. The SFHA never pieced together enough resources and staff to assist all tenants, but as it had done in the past, it provided its tenants and many of their neighbors with programs unmatched by what private landlords did for their tenants—and sometimes unmatched by the nation's welfare state.[35]

SFHA tenants also expanded their political and cultural role in this era, in the process formulating their own version of liberalism. Motivated by the need to find economic security, they sought to counter low wages, rising housing costs, and redevelopment threats, among other concerns. They also sought to expand economic and civil rights. Acting on these motives, SFHA tenants contributed to the burst of tenant organizing underway in the Bay Area. SFHA tenants had more support for organizing than tenants with private sector landlords. The design of government housing, especially projects from the 1940s, aimed to foster tenant community and action. Valencia Gardens in the Mission district, for example, had a serpentine shape that channeled tenants into courtyard gardens where they could sit and discuss the affairs of the day and build social ties, a shared identity, and community. Nearly every SFHA project offered physical space to bring people together in ways apartments and private homes in the private sector often did not. Architecture, in other words, mattered for organizing. The SFHA also provided resources for picnics, holiday parties, childcare, and publications, all of which built the social relations necessary for successful community organizing. Unlike his predecessor John Beard, Kane supported tenant unions philosophically, and he backed up those beliefs by providing tenants with resources and working with their organizations.[36]

Supporting tenant unions was a difficult position for an administrator to take, for it opened up a Pandora's box of competing demands to set SFHA priorities. In San Francisco, those demands regularly focused on the proper role of government, the economic and civil rights of citizens, and the ability of residents to influence their housing and urban space—all matters of intense significance in the context of 1960s liberalism. SFHA tenants organized unions at every permanent project, and the membership of those unions represented the diversity of public housing tenants.

African Americans were the dominant social group at the Hunters Point, Potrero Hill, and Western Addition projects, though their numbers at other SFHA projects were growing by the early 1970s. African Americans made up about 85 percent of all public housing applicants because of the ways they continued to experience housing, job, and union discrimination and have lower incomes and household wealth. Chinatown's unions included a diversity of Asian and Asian American tenants, with those of Chinese ancestry being the largest proportion. At other projects, tenant union membership remained at roughly one-third African American, one-third white, and one-third Asian and Latina/o. SFHA tenants were multilingual. Seniors and tenants with disabilities organized around their needs, as did other groups such as the Samoans for Samoa Association, whose president, Malologa Seuli, led struggles for fair employment and Samoan language services.[37]

Participation rates in tenant unions reached impressive levels. The North Beach Place Chinese Improvement Association, for example, counted sixty-five of sixty-eight resident Chinese families among its members, and it worked with the more racially diverse North Beach Place Neighborhood Improvement Association that had similar levels of tenant participation. Although some friction caused by ethnic and racial differences occurred, the ability of SFHA tenants to work toward common goals showed a high level of solidarity across race and ethnic lines.[38]

Increasingly, the San Francisco tenant unions addressed problems not only in their projects but also in their neighborhoods and even across the nation. In July 1968, the Yerba Buena Tenants Union (YBTU) presented the SFHA commissioners with a list of demands. They called for more favorable rental policies; refunds on excess utility charges collected by the SFHA; improved building maintenance; more police protection; friendlier staff attitudes; tenant involvement in the authority's Modernization-Rehabilitation Program; new admission policies to qualify mothers under 21 years of age for common-law family units and to allow those with less than one year of city residency to be eligible for SFHA units; and stop signs at intersections to improve safety. Although the list had come from the YBTU, Commissioner Boswell found the issues to be "identical to those of other tenant groups throughout the City." Boswell remarked that he "did not want to be 'pressured' into acceding to demands of the tenant groups." But he did instruct staff to begin negotiating immediately with tenants.[39]

SFHA tenant organizing reflected the kinds of actions by tenants around the nation. SFHA tenants worked with the National Tenants Organization (NTO). Led by Jesse Gray and Anthony Henry, the NTO by 1970 was "growing by 'leaps and bounds'" as it assisted tenant groups, lobbied for pro-tenant federal legislation, and contributed to movements for racial and economic justice.[40]

SFHA tenants worked on quality of life issues as well. They continued to assemble hundreds of volunteers to pick up the trash and debris ignored by the city's garbage collectors. In the Chinatown–North Beach area, tenants joined North East Medical Services to increase community-based health care and social services for the recent influx of immigrants, especially from Hong Kong. At the Westside Courts project, tenants created a childcare center open to all, but with a curriculum designed to "increase appreciation of Black Culture." Tenant unions approved bids on SFHA architectural and construction work and made sure SFHA contracts included provisions for employing minorities and tenants, though the enforcement of these employment provisions was spotty at best. Ping Yuen tenants obtained public and private funding for a community center for their building. Tenant union members regularly wrote government officials in support of housing legislation.[41] They joined tenants from private housing in citywide projects, including the city's Economic Opportunity Council (EOC). The EOC, which consisted of elected representatives, reflected the diversity of the city and brought varying educational backgrounds to the problems of low-income residents—some had college degrees, others "street corner degrees," and still others "welfare diplomas." Some came from the LGBT community. Seniors were involved. The EOC Council pressured public agencies to "serve people from the cradle to the grave—these services range from Child Care and Development Center . . . to our Senior Citizens Service Center."[42]

Of the numerous political issues, few triggered political mobilization of the city's residents like redevelopment, and political activists increasingly turned to the SFHA for assistance.[43] Since 1959, San Francisco Redevelopment Agency Director Justin Herman had tirelessly worked to make the goals of city leaders and real estate developers a reality. For city leaders, Herman promised to provide housing for whites inclined to flee from the city, expand the city's economic and tourist capacity, demolish "unattractive" buildings, and raise the city's tax revenues. For developers, Herman promised to clear out people and businesses, obtain federal subsidies, and reorganize massive tracts of land for profit. For the thousands of displaced residents, Herman regularly promised replacement housing that did not exist.[44]

Herman's agency had excluded residents from the decision-making process in the 1950s and, like redevelopment agencies around the nation, displaced poor, mostly nonwhite tenants and small businesses. Throughout the 1960s, Herman pursued his goals with the support of the city's public and private institutions, notably the San Francisco Department of Planning, the San Francisco Planning and Urban Research Association (SPUR, formerly San Francisco Housing and Planning Association), and the Bay Area Council (BAC). Low-income residents complained regularly about the effects of the redevelopment agency. San Francisco resident Cecilia Keough contended the city's residents were "caught in the vicious vise of brutal and heartless 'S.F. style Redevelopment'" because of the difficulty of leaving neighborhood and community to find new housing.[45] Herman was but one of a number of postwar redevelopment officials—such as Robert Moses in New York City and Edward Logue in Boston—who reshaped urban landscapes with similar goals and consequences.[46]

In 1970, the San Francisco Redevelopment Agency had plans for three projects that would directly affect communities with SFHA residents and housing. The agency's Yerba Buena project would build another round of Manhattan-style buildings downtown (South of Market), including high-end hotels and apartments and a convention center. In the Western Addition, the agency wanted to expand

Figure 6.1
Justin Herman (foreground) talking to a packed crowd in 1968. Mayor Joseph Alioto (fingers interlaced) is in the front row.

its existing project with moderate- and high-rent housing as well as commercial buildings. The Hunters Point project was planned for federally subsidized low- and moderate-income housing, though none of it would be public housing. By law, all three redevelopment areas—Yerba Buena, Western Addition, and Hunters Point—required resident participation and a plan to ensure comparable housing for the displaced residents.[47]

The San Francisco Redevelopment Agency's research claimed that existing private rentals, SROs, and SFHA housing provided enough housing to satisfy federal relocation requirements, but this claim largely depended on future (that is, not yet built) housing in the redevelopment projects and on the SFHA having to build the kind of housing the redevelopment agency dictated. For instance, the redevelopment agency assigned tracts of land for the SFHA, but on the condition that the SFHA build high-density towers for elderly tenants without community centers. The agency's insistence on senior-only towers went against the authority's own "standards," "the large consensus of local and national geriatric and social welfare experts," and "the overwhelming support of tenants" who preferred low-density apartments. SFHA officials and tenants also insisted on adding larger apartments for families and including community centers in all new SFHA housing.[48] The

Figure 6.2
Elouise Westbrook speaking at a community meeting in 1972.

different visions slowed plans for both the redevelopment agency and the SFHA; this set the stage for struggles over future development in the Hunters Point, Western Addition, and South of Market (SOMA) districts.

Winning approval of Hunters Point was the easiest of the three projects for the redevelopment agency. The project, which included housing as well as schools, transportation, and cultural and recreation centers, had support from the Chamber of Commerce and the city's political leaders. Hunters Point resident Ruth Williams chaired the Bayview–Hunters Point Joint Housing Committee, and under her direction her committee offered the required community participation while also coordinating plans by five community groups for 1,300 units of low- and moderate-rent housing to be part of the agency's project. The redevelopment agency's plan depended on acquiring SFHA land, which still had temporary wartime housing on it. For its part, the SFHA offered plans for low-rise public housing, but its proposals were rejected by the redevelopment agency. During the process, SFHA commissioners questioned the degree of community support for the plan, the agency's promise of housing for those to be displaced, and HUD's willingness to fund the community-sponsored nonprofit housing projects.

SFHA Commissioner Boswell thought it best to build permanent public housing on the SFHA land. When Ruth Williams stepped down amid growing controversy over the project, Elouise Westbrook, a former Economic Opportunity Council supervisor and one of the most politically active African Americans in the era, became the new point person on the housing committee. Westbrook skillfully secured the committee's endorsement for the redevelopment agency's Hunters Point project and helped overcome some of the public's doubts. After steady pressure from Mayor Joseph Alioto, the SFHA agreed to transfer the land to the redevelopment agency, thus consigning public lands (and potential public housing units) to the private sector and providing a crucial piece for the redevelopment agency proposal.[49]

In contrast to Hunters Point, residents in the Western Addition and South of Market challenged the redevelopment agency. The Western Addition Project Area Committee, which had EOC funding and included dozens of community organizations—including the NAACP, Baptist Minister's Union, Fillmore Youth Organization, ILWU and other labor organizations, the Urban League, and Black Panther Party—came together to fight Herman's plans.[50] The organizations pressed their representatives "on the importance of taking immediate action on this problem" because the "survival of our community depends on it." Two of the coalition members, the Western Addition Community Organization (WACO) and the San Francisco Neighborhood Legal Aid Foundation, filed a lawsuit against the redevelopment agency for excluding residents from the policy process, displacing residents, and exaggerating the amount of available housing stock in the city. WACO's legal offensive aimed to defend "countless neighborhoods that have taken little people many, many years to build."[51]

For Herman, the federal requirement of citizen participation was misguided, especially in redevelopment. "Meaningful and productive involvement can be done only by private citizens who," Herman noted, "have the time and capacity to become thoroughly acquainted with complex problems—otherwise, they are prone to condemn what they do not understand."[52] Yet the ordinary people whose homes and neighborhoods were targeted by redevelopment understood perfectly that the right to participate in the built space around them was crucial to preventing the erosion of economic security and community that had happened to residents in the past.

Residents and a coalition of organizations in the South of Market district responded in similar ways, and for similar reasons, to redevelopment plans. In 1969, the South of Market United Front (SMUF), representing over a dozen organizations, put together a plan to participate in the $250 million Yerba Buena project. SMUF wanted the redevelopment agency to stop all "acquisitions of property," "relocation or displacement of any persons, and demolition in the Yerba Buena Project," until SMUF representatives sat on the committees in charge of redevelopment plans. SMUF also demanded that replacement housing had to be "available at rents that project area residents can afford to pay."[53]

One of the most active SMUF organizations was Tenants and Owners in Opposition to Redevelopment (TOOR). Many in TOOR, including its president George Woolf, were longtime tenants in the district's SROs and often had labor organizing experience dating back to the 1934 General Strike. TOOR, like WACO, worked with the San Francisco Neighborhood Legal Assistance Foundation to file a lawsuit against HUD (*TOOR v. HUD*) claiming that Herman's agency fudged the numbers of available housing and resident participation and was thus out of compliance with federal law.[54]

In this fight, the city's political and economic leaders, including the trade union leadership, rallied to defend Herman's plans and claims of available housing, which included SFHA public housing and Section 23 units. Former San Francisco Mayor George Christopher wrote HUD Secretary George Romney to praise Herman and to express hope that Herman's "relocation assurances can be found to be satisfactory, and that the present legal impediment can be overcome, so that project activities may go forward." But TOOR's case prevailed in the courts and secured an injunction against the San Francisco Redevelopment Agency. Former California Governor Pat Brown intervened as a mediator, and he sided with TOOR and the courts. The settlement required the redevelopment agency to build affordable housing and include resident participation. HUD officials deemed the settlement sufficient for allowing the redevelopment agency to move forward in part because of available SFHA units. With similar negotiations, the Western Addition project was approved, too.[55]

Yet, with the exception of adding some senior housing, the SFHA did not meaningfully increase the quantity of public housing units from the redevelopment agency proposals. In several ways, the redevelopment agency projects highlighted how the SFHA role as the city's main provider of low-income housing was coming under pressure. Redevelopment agency projects did include low- and moderate-income housing and Section 23 units, but these were increasingly run by nonprofit housing organizations. For example, Tenants and Owners Development Corporation (TODCO), a spinoff from TOOR, assumed the role of managing some subsidized homes. Like nonprofit housing, the Section 23 program also shifted resources to the private sector as landlords and investors now captured rent and federal housing funds once earmarked for public housing authorities. The Section 23 program was also much easier to cut than a permanent and physical public housing project. In 1970, for example, HUD proposed cuts threatened 1,000 Section 23 units in the Hunters Point area alone. "We have a right to them," Kane said. "But if they don't give us the money to back up the paper, we are out of luck."[56] The redevelopment agency's projects contributed to and reflected the federal shift in supporting the private sector more than public housing.

In an important contrast, tenants in permanent SFHA housing continued to participate in the decisions that affected their homes and neighborhoods. At a 1970 SFHA commission meeting, SFHA tenants presented a sweeping list of demands. In the administration of federal modernization programs, tenants wanted full consultation on the use of grant monies as well as prompt notification of, and preference for, jobs. Tenants asked for friendlier housing guidelines, especially around evictions, liability, and privacy; lower rent and utility charges; and changes in rental rates, with downward adjustments for "persons with special needs" and upward adjustments to achieve an economic mix of tenants. They wanted written protections for tenants who joined a tenant union or withheld rent for repairs. Tenants requested better security on and near their housing projects and new leases that required the SFHA "to keep the apartments in safe and livable condition."[57]

Other demands suggested a more radical vision of what public housing should do and be. Tenants wanted the right "to review and approve appointments of Project managers, clerks, and similar positions." They requested a grievance board "with elected tenant representatives to hear and decide complaints, including the following: (a) problems with admissions, transfer or eviction; (b) payments of fees or fines; (c) and problems of management, repairs, etc." Tenants wanted to elect tenants to the SFHA commission, a democratic departure from the standard appointment process that too often drew supporters of the mayor rather than advocates for tenants and public housing.[58]

In response to these demands, SFHA commissioners instructed staff to meet "with representatives of all public housing tenant organizations and the San Francisco Neighborhood Legal Assistance Foundation."[59] Five months later in a follow-up meeting, Gloria Davis, who lived in Geneva Towers, said that SFHA communication with tenants and policymaking was improving, but that they were still "concerned that decisions are being made without any consultation with people they are going to affect. We feel there should be some representatives of tenants in negotiations that have to do with where people are going to live."[60]

Throughout 1970, the city's public housing tenant unions continued to work with the SFHA, and their membership grew, especially as tenants saw their power grow through organizing. In January 1971, SFHA tenant union representatives met for a citywide meeting where they decided to gain "tenant control" of the SFHA, make a "Tenant Affairs Board" to handle "complaints and problems," and decide "how millions of dollars of federal fund will be used in public housing."[61]

To accomplish these goals, tenants formed the San Francisco Public Housing Tenants Association (PHTA), which had a steering committee with two representatives from each public housing project. Its first president, Dorothy Tillman, had moved to San Francisco from Alabama, where she had gained valuable organizing experience in the civil rights movement. The PHTA had, as Tillman said, "gotten something together for all the tenants—black, brown, yellow and white." Although a few tenants complained about the direction of the PHTA, Tillman "appealed for unity" so that the tenants could get down to business and have the SFHA recognize "this democratically elected group as the bargaining agent."[62] She enlisted the support of labor, community, and religious leaders such as the Reverend Cecil Williams from Glide Memorial Church—and gained formal SFHA recognition in April 1971. The PHTA also affiliated with the NTO.[63]

Following the recognition of the PHTA, tenant attendance at SFHA commission meetings soared, and in response commissioners moved the meetings to the public library. SFHA commissioners established a grievance board, which handled 223 cases in its first year, and received HUD approval for the SFHA to cover PHTA expenses, including childcare, transportation, lunches, and secretarial and legal services. Eventually, the SFHA funded the PHTA through a formula modeled on labor unions where the PHTA received a per capita payment for every occupied unit in the city.[64] Through their organization, tenants worked with the San Francisco Art Commission and the SFHA to win a Comprehensive Employment and Training Act grant to fund murals and community gardens.[65]

Women such as Tillman were, and would remain, the primary leaders in the tenant movement; the citywide organization greatly expanded tenant resources and influence.

The PHTA leadership improved tenant knowledge of housing policy at the local and national level. Cleo Wallace, whose family had migrated from Texas during World War II, served as the second PHTA president, following her term as president of the Hunters Point Tenants Union. She became a national voice for tenant rights. Wallace and PHTA vice president Donna Billups, who had been president of Sunnydale's tenant union, attended the 1971 National Association of Housing and Redevelopment Officials (NAHRO) conference where they "learned a great deal about NAHRO and HUD operations." Wallace later became the vice president of the NTO. She and Billups regularly attended NAHRO and HUD conferences, and their NTO membership allowed them to network with tenants in public and private housing across the nation.[66] During her time as PHTA president, Wallace increased the number of tenants on SFHA committees, used tenant surveys to shape SFHA policies, and arranged roving seminars to discuss the "various facets of the Housing Authority program."[67] This "marvelous" new learning model, as Commissioner Boswell called Wallace's work, was better than "a one-way street. Our staff needs to learn [about] tenants—tenants need to learn Staff and Housing Authority policies."[68] Although decades-old problems did not disappear, the new model made the policymaking process more responsive to tenants.

To further the goals of SFHA tenants and to continue improving the flow of information to tenants and policymakers, the PHTA pushed for tenant representation on the commission. Since the creation of the SFHA, mayor-appointed commissioners brought various levels of commitment to public housing, and they usually had difficulty understanding the needs and experiences of tenants. For more than a decade, tenants and civic organizations tried to add tenants to the commission, but without success even after a series of protests. After many promises to add tenant commissioners, Mayor Joseph Alioto appointed a non-tenant, Amancio Ergina, to fill a vacant seat on the commission, prompting the PHTA to threaten a rent strike. The Board of Supervisors, the mayor, and SFHA leadership responded in 1973 by expanding the SFHA commission to seven; the two additional commissioners would be tenants elected by their peers but appointed by the mayor.[69] Martin Helpman and Cleo Wallace became the first tenants on the SFHA commission. At their first meeting, Commissioner Ergina welcomed and praised Wallace and Helpman, remarking, "their interest in the community and city is well known. Their record of individual accomplishment is a source of pride to our community and our country."[70]

In theory, the new commissioners represented all the tenants, but in practice Helpman had closer ties to seniors, Wallace to families. The appointments represented an important development for the SFHA. Non-tenant commissioners benefited from the experiences of tenant commissioners, and tenants gained two advocates who understood and identified with the city's public housing community.[71] Although San Francisco was not the first or only city to have tenant commissioners, it was in the minority. A 1970 NAHRO survey found that less than 5 percent of the nation's housing authorities had tenant commissioners.[72]

Tenant commissioners took their position seriously. Wallace and Helpman regularly toured SFHA housing to educate, listen, and organize. They discussed both small and large problems, and tenants turned to Wallace and Helpman for assistance first. This was illustrated in 1973 when redevelopment agency bulldozers were on the verge of destroying 191 permanent public housing units to make way for the Hunters Point redevelopment project. The remaining 155 families refused to leave their homes because they did not believe HUD assurances that housing, public or private, would be available to them. All worried about the impact of redevelopment on their community. SFHA commissioners also did not believe HUD would deliver the Section 23 funding for these tenants, and, even if they did, they knew these tenants had a good chance of not finding housing in the city through this program. Tenants leaned on Wallace for support. At a contentious SFHA commission meeting, she critiqued the redevelopment agency and read a tenant prayer to the crowd entitled "Destiny":

Our father in Heaven, We Pray you save us from Man's evil bulldozers.

The houses you have given the oppressed and poor are being taken the World over by evildoers. H.U.D.

Redevelopment says destruction must come for their own selfish gains.

The politician has let us down for False Gods of money and power. Forgive the politicians, Lord. Redevelopment has confused the world with destruction in our land. Our destiny we do not know with bulldozers coming sooner than we think. Children are asking where are we going? Looking Bewildered. Inspire us, Lord, do not let us loose our Faith.

God speak to man to use their wealth and strength to help mankind, instead of destroying them. Fill the poor and oppressed people with new strength and courage. Let Redevelopment know that God is a builder, not a destroyer.[73]

The commissioners and Kane sided with the Hunters Point families even though HUD, Mayor Alioto's office, and the redevelopment agency told the tenants and the SFHA that they had no choice. Actions by the PHTA and SFHA leadership delayed the evictions and revealed the semiautonomous status of the authority. Yet the SFHA and its tenants did not have the power the next year to stop the San

Francisco Redevelopment Agency from evicting the families and then destroying the housing units to make way for the Hunters Point redevelopment project.[74]

Resident concerns about future housing availability were warranted as new public housing units slowed. By the middle of the 1970s, the SFHA staff increasingly struggled to house applicants and maintain the units under its care. In 1975, the SFHA operated 43 permanent projects with a total of 7,132 units, 28 fewer permanent units than the previous year, and managed roughly 1,300 Section 23 leases. HUD's growing reliance on private solutions such as Section 23 housing led Kane to the conclusion that HUD aimed to turn local housing authorities into a mere "'channel or funnel' through which private enterprise would construct public housing units."[75] Affordable family housing remained particularly tight in the city. Of the SFHA's 1,300 Section 23 units, there were only 2 available five-bedroom units, and the landlords for those two apartments wanted rental rates that were, Kane noted, "too high for Housing Authority applicants."[76]

In a critique of property owners and developers, Kane said, "Not one single unit of new housing had been built in San Francisco by private enterprise in the last 15 to 20 years that our clients could afford." But SFHA construction, too, had ground to a halt in 1973, when the federal government placed a moratorium on new public housing construction. Some older SFHA housing was also in need of major maintenance work, which inflation and HUD formulas made impossible to do. HUD allowed a cost increase of 11.5 percent from 1972 to 1975, for example, while inflation in San Francisco exceeded 34 percent during that period. The budget shortfall led SFHA leadership to eliminate seventy jobs from an already bare-bones maintenance staff and prepared for greater cuts.[77] For residents, there were fewer quality units, especially for families, and in the 1970s labor and housing market, this hurt the housing options of San Francisco's most vulnerable residents—seniors, nonwhites, women, and children. These conditions contributed to two trends. On the one hand, more poor, often African American residents began to leave the city, and on the other hand, the declining quality of SFHA housing contributed to a growing discourse about the failure of federal social programs.

The declining quality of SFHA housing and the economic insecurity of low-income residents in this era ensured an active tenant population. Although rent strikes were less common by the middle of the decade, tenants found that a collective voice and the threat of direct action drew the fastest response from the SFHA staff for small and large matters. When budget cuts slowed modernization repairs at Potrero Terrace, Cleo Wallace told SFHA leadership, "If we do not get the doors we asked for, we do not intend to pay any rent." The commissioners warned HUD officials that there was a "threat of a rent strike, not only at Potrero but in other areas, unless this Housing Authority can deliver its programs to which HUD has agreed." Tenants continued to push for opening more SFHA jobs to tenants, and they worked to defend and expand social services. By 1975, a large majority of the tenants in permanent projects were receiving public assistance, and many depended on the services provided by or through the SFHA.[78] For example, the PHTA worked with a coalition of 100 organizations to turn out residents for a rally on March 1, 1975, to protest a loss of food stamp benefits.[79] Through political work in and out of the SFHA, as they worked together for their common interests, public housing tenants constructed community and a class-based political identity.

At the start of the nation's bicentennial, the Board of Governors of the National Association of Housing and Redevelopment Officials (NAHRO) responded to the nation's urban crisis with a sweeping call for federal action. Their report, "The New American Realism: 'Save and Rebuild America,'" highlighted 200 years of economic, urban, agricultural, and territorial expansion. Acknowledging a heightened environmental awareness and the falling standard of living, the report declared that the nation's resources "are not unlimited, nor our choices of using them. The stark sentinels of inflation and unemployment, energy shortages and housing shortages remind of us of our limitations." Partly to blame were federal policies or the lack thereof. To NAHRO, the lack of federal economic planning and programs harmed not only cities, but the environment and general welfare as well. The report noted, "We are tired of patchwork policies and scattershot programs—often designed to fulfill political slogans." Despite the economic growth in the previous two centuries,

> We know now we have paid a high price. We have abused the land. We have wasted our resources. We have built and abandoned only to build again. There are bleak reminders of abuse and waste—polluted waters, fouled air, abandoned homes, dilapidated neighborhoods, decayed cities. The best place to start saving and rebuilding America is to build upon what we have already built—the homes, the schools, the streets, the hospitals, the factories, stores and office buildings that stand as monuments to our energy and creativeness in every village, town, and city in the country. . . . We must now lay as a cornerstone of domestic policy—the saving and rebuilding of America.[80]

Although NAHRO's proposal called for public housing funding for "the poor, the elderly, and the handicapped," it focused much more on federal programs and subsidies to support neighborhood conservation, redevelopment projects, and leasing or renting privately owned housing (not public housing) for low-income households. It assumed that experts and political and economic elites would determine the shape and scope of these programs.[81] In line with the political realities of the bicentennial, the proposal did not call for programs to expand public housing, the economic or civil rights of citizens, or democratic policymaking. Instead, it was ordinary citizens, like those in the PHTA, who organized for these rights as the United States entered its third century.

In the nation's cities in the 1970s, the affordable housing shortage, weak labor market, and a declining federal commitment to social programs remained the biggest problems facing low- and moderate-income households. In San Francisco, tenants, community organizers, and SFHA leaders understood the housing crisis as a problem resulting from the decisions made by political and economic elites.

To build power, the city's tenants organized to address their vision of what government should do and what housing and redevelopment should look like. In the case of SFHA tenants, their citywide organizing is best understood not in terms of special interest politics but rather as the politics of ordinary people wanting a meaningful voice in the decisions that affected their homes, communities, and economic security. Nonwhite tenants and women especially worked on making urban policies square with political traditions of equality, democracy, and justice. They used the SFHA and Great Society programs to challenge barriers in housing and employment and expand the types of programs available in their neighborhoods. Through the SFHA and their tenant unions, and their struggles over housing and redevelopment, tenants organized around the idea that all people—the elderly, the nonwhite, and the poor—had a right to decent housing, jobs, childcare, and elderly services.[82]

SFHA tenants and their allies offered a vision of government that was very much at odds with the liberalism of local and national politicians who increasingly wanted to scale back the welfare state and the civil and economic rights of citizens.[83] The inclusion of the city's tenants in the policy process and the growth of their power came at a transitional moment in the making and remaking of the nation's welfare state. Within the policy area of housing, tenants entered the decision-making process at a time when government at all levels, but especially at the federal level, began to scale back the support and resources needed to sustain the program.

For local and national elites, the growing power of tenants provided another incentive to dismantle government housing and support private sector alternatives for housing low-income citizens. The legislation, especially from the Nixon administration, clarified this shift and aligned with the broader political shift in liberalism among elites and an increasing number of white voters. In many ways, these politicians and voters were out of step with San Francisco's tenants who organized around a very different vision of the United States at its bicentennial celebration. Those different visions would become more pronounced in the next decade.

CHAPTER 7

ALL HOUSING IS PUBLIC

*Brute money is buying up this town and throwing everybody out
except the very rich and the subsidized poor.*

Kevin Starr[1]

IN AUGUST 1978, a man sexually assaulted and murdered Julia Wong, an 18-year-
old tenant of Ping Yuen, as she walked up the stairs to her apartment. The media
turned the case into a sensational story that reinforced popular stereotypes of public
housing: dangerous and crime-ridden. Less noted in the media was how tenants
responded. Public housing tenants blamed insufficient lighting, a broken elevator,
and security at the building as underlying causes—all problems that their tenant
association had urged the San Francisco Housing Authority to address. They also
blamed the San Francisco Police Department for not protecting and serving their
neighborhood.[2]

The authority's failure to act before and after the tragedy mobilized the tenants
and community behind a rent strike. Tenants met regularly, put their rents in escrow,
and stayed unified. The SFHA eventually responded with security guards, more
bilingual staff, and additional lighting. The strike had succeeded. On February 26,
1979, Ping Yuen tenants threw a Unity Party, inviting tenants from other SFHA
projects to celebrate their gains and plan for the future.[3]

Their success, and the follow-up celebration, encouraged tenants from neighbor-
ing North Beach Place to take similar actions. Asian, white, African American, Native
American, and Latina/o tenants there pressured SFHA Director Carl Williams to
install more lights and add more security at their project. They used the same lawyer who had represented the Ping Yuen tenants and threatened a rent strike if their
demands were not met. Tenants at other SFHA projects framed similar demands
with the threat of a strike. Williams agreed to new lighting but insisted the authority could not continue responding to every tenant threat and action. Williams and
the commissioners worried about the rent strike "syndrome" sweeping the public
housing community and the lack of resources to meet tenant demands.[4]

Williams was right to worry about the lack of SFHA resources. His underfunded agency already did not have enough money to meet its daily expenses, which

increasingly included new services and, as noted above, public safety measures. But two developments made the SFHA's financial situation even more precarious. First, the SFHA did not have the reserves or a realistic chance of winning federal grants to pay for a long list of major repairs at the apartment and project level. The physical decline of some SFHA properties led to uninhabitable units and even entire projects, and these vacancies reduced rental income and SFHA's capacity to house the city's tenants.

The second development was the federal government's continued preferences to fund alternatives to public housing, a trend that continued with the Carter administration and then accelerated under the Reagan administration. HUD programs, in short, funneled more federal housing dollars to private landlords and investors while doing less to assist the nation's public housing program. The shift in federal housing policy was in line with the broader intellectual and political attack on the welfare state, government regulations, taxes, and the poor. This neoliberal philosophy of government produced new legislation and priorities that significantly undermined New Deal and Great Society programs as well as labor and tenant unions.

Within this national political context, San Francisco's tenants remained politically active, though on a smaller scale compared to the previous decade. Public and private housing tenants alike continued to look to the SFHA for help in securing housing and economic and civil rights. In these struggles, tenants continued to support a role of government that was out of step with political and economic elites. SFHA tenants in particular reinforced their identity as tenants and built a strong sense of community through the SFHA program. But in San Francisco, the tenant movement had trouble sustaining its vitality and energy. Federal neoliberal policies drove much of this decline, but so did the increasingly difficult political and economic world of tenants. In some ways, the decline in tenant power matched the decline in the federal commitment to public housing. The image of public housing in and out of the city became more negative, and this, too, damaged political support for the program, contributing to the neoliberal war on the poor that made possible the deep cuts to the welfare state during the Reagan–Bush administrations.[5]

On February 1, 1977, leaders of the National Tenants Organization (NTO) met with Patricia Harris, the new, Carter-appointed HUD secretary, to discuss the future of HUD policies. As with many housing professionals and public housing tenants, the NTO leadership was hopeful that, after years of Republican administrations, HUD might better respond to the needs of tenants who struggled in the declining economy. NTO Chairman Jesse Gray spelled out his organization's priorities for HUD. At the top of the list, the NTO wanted "to see the government get back into the business of building houses" and reverse the trend of subsidizing private property owners. The NTO called "for a mass rehabilitation fund to preserve inner city housing," "the provision of sufficient operating subsidies to bring public housing up to decent and livable standards," and "an increase in public housing utility allowances" for tenants suffering from inflation. The NTO also wanted utility subsidies for all renters, who suffered from "astronomical utility bills." It asked HUD to create "a national tenants leadership training program" and to provide seats for tenants on the HUD policy board to improve communication between HUD staff and tenants. Also, the NTO requested a plan to develop a "national tenants minimum bill of rights" that included protections for tenant activists and tenant preferences for HUD-funded jobs.[6] These proposals were intended to add housing and jobs and expand the political and economic rights of not only the 4 million tenants in the 1 million units of public housing managed by 2,600 local authorities, but of millions of tenants in the private sector as well.[7]

Along with proposals for more tenant resources and rights across the nation, the NTO also wanted to make HUD policymaking more responsive to tenants and more egalitarian. In the past, tenant groups met with HUD, but in informal and nonstructured ways. At the 1977 meeting, NTO representatives urged Harris to give tenants "a say equal to that of housing authority officials, bankers, real estate officials, builders and landlords." To bring this about, Gray proposed "a HUD policy board of tenants to work with the Department in policy development" and HUD assistance to cover the travel costs of tenants who came to Washington for this work.[8]

The NTO formulated these demands after two decades of tenant organizing for economic, civil, and political rights. The NTO demands also reflected the decline in the standard of living in many households. HUD responded with a national tenant task force and committees and conferences for women, disabled, and senior tenants. Yet the agency's priorities remained focused more on redevelopment and private housing than on public housing. HUD left unchanged the operating formula for local public housing authorities, which limited the funding for services to the increasingly diverse tenant populations and repairing aging buildings and infrastructure, some of which dated to the 1940s. As of 1978, the SFHA program, for example, had $45 million worth of deferred work to do on its buildings.[9]

HUD also ramped up its Section 8 program. Created in 1974, the Section 8 program provided housing authorities with rental vouchers that paid 75 percent of HUD's Fair Market Rent calculation for units in newly constructed and rehabilitated housing or in existing housing. Section 8 household recipients paid 25 percent (later 30 percent) of their adjusted family income to the landlord. The program rewarded landlords with market rate rents and became Congress's preferred choice for low-income housing assistance, while taking funding away from local housing authorities.[10]

San Francisco's political and economic leaders envisioned the city's housing and redevelopment much in the same ways as did HUD officials. The election of Mayor George Moscone (1976–1978) and a progressive San Francisco Board of Supervisors (Ella Hill Hutch, Gordon Lau, Harvey Milk) resulted in part from a wave of voter discontent with previous political elites, who put redevelopment and economic growth before the needs and desires of ordinary residents. But early optimism soon gave way to local and national realities. In July 1976, Moscone spoke at the SFHA Commission meeting, where he praised the agency for its decades of service, its awards for senior housing designs, and its provision of housing and social programs to the city. Then he offered several recommendations. The SFHA needed to reduce labor costs and, although it would be challenging in the current budget situation, modernize the 5,500 SFHA family housing units. He recommended improving SFHA–tenant relations, acknowledging that this

> was no easy task. . . . Many complaints by tenants concern the condition of their housing unit and the lack of services. . . . On the other hand, your ability to respond to these complaints is severely limited by inadequate operating funds provided by the Federal Department of Housing and Urban Development.

Moscone commented on national public housing trends and urged the SFHA to ensure "greater involvement of tenants in the management of public housing projects."[11]

If Moscone desired greater tenant involvement in the SFHA, the same was not true of other city agencies. As scholar Chester Hartman noted, Moscone's appointments to the San Francisco Redevelopment Agency did "little immediately or in the long run to alter the city's basic redevelopment activities." After Supervisor Dan White murdered Moscone and Supervisor Harvey Milk, Supervisor Dianne Feinstein became mayor and promptly replaced Moscone's redevelopment agency appointees with officials who maintained a pro-development agenda that did not value the homes or communities that stood in the way of their projects. Under the Moscone and Feinstein administrations, community groups would, to quote Hartman again, "decry, with justification, their exclusion from the decision-making process, and the agency continued to approve projects despite opposition from residents and neighborhoods in its development areas." The Planning Commission, as the other housing-related agency, typically provided the technical and legal legitimacy for redevelopment agency projects.[12]

When Reverend Boswell's seat on the commission became vacant, Mayor Moscone appointed Reverend Jim Jones. A rising political star, Jones had built a large following through his Peoples Temple organization by using a populist, Christian message and by providing social services. A mayor's office biography described Jones "as an uncompromising foe of racism and social injustice" and as someone who created programs "that have rescued many hundreds from extreme poverty, drug addiction and other oppressive conditions."[13] Donald Field, a member of the Peoples Temple, said, "One of our objectives is to communicate the needs and frustrations of the 'little people' who are really the backbone of the community."[14] As commissioner, Jones noted in a discussion about the quality and quantity of public housing that "if this country cannot provide adequate housing for everyone, then it is up to the Commissioners to 'raise a bit of thunder' to see that funding is available to provide 'Cadillac housing' for everyone."[15] When commissioners elected Jones to chair the SFHA Commission, with tenant Cleo Wallace as vice chair, the largely tenant audience gave them a standing ovation. Few at the time imagined, of course, the deadly tragedy in Guyana that Jones and his church would produce.[16]

San Francisco residents in and out of public housing counted on the SFHA for their housing and community needs. The battle over the International Hotel symbolized this relationship. Located at Kearny and Jackson Streets, the International Hotel was home to mostly elderly Chinese and Filipino tenants and was the cornerstone of the Filipino community. After the Hong Kong-based Four Seas Corporation bought the hotel in 1973, the tenants received eviction notices. Rather than give up their homes and community, residents and their allies fought back in a collective rejection of private property rights. A coalition of

Figure 7.1
Anti-eviction protest at the International Hotel.

organizations—including the May First Workers Organization, Ping Yuen Resident Improvement Association, Jones's Peoples Temple, and the Kearny Street Workshop artist collective—launched waves of protests with colorful pickets that stretched for blocks and drew national attention.[17]

Tenants had widespread support from the city government, even from Sheriff Richard Hongisto. When the Four Seas Corporation refused to stop the evictions, residents and city leaders proposed that the SFHA buy and then manage the hotel. At one of many packed SFHA Commission meetings on this proposal, Vernon Baun of the May First Workers Organization said support for these tenants came from the idea that "working people built this country and yet, 'when we are old we are no longer important.'" He said the "matter had become a symbol throughout the country and the Bay Area" and that "we are going to continue to organize. . . . It is our class against parasites like the Four Seas."[18]

The SFHA officials began work on several proposals to buy the hotel. They also made available bilingual staff and housing for some tenants, though the government homes that were provided dispersed elderly tenants across the city and away from the International Hotel community. The SFHA leaders did make an offer to purchase the hotel, but their efforts failed because the offer proved too costly and legally complicated to execute.[19]

Residents fighting another wave of redevelopment in the Western Addition also turned to the SFHA. In 1977, the San Francisco Redevelopment Agency began to relocate small businesses and low-income households from Japantown for its Western Addition project. When residents in two residential buildings on Sutter and Buchanan were served eviction notices, the community mobilized to defend

Figure 7.2
Protest outside the International Hotel, demanding housing as a human right.

the tenants. Unfazed, the redevelopment agency threw tenants out and posted guards at the building's entrance. The Committee Against Nihonmachi Evictions (CANE) and the Kearny Street Workshop artist collective joined the fight against the redevelopment agency; these groups played important roles in defending the district and contributed to the city's Asian American movement. Together, the community asked the SFHA for help. In September 1977, a CANE representative described the urgent situation to the SFHA commission and then requested the authority to "take action in the very near future in order to stop the evictions, stop the destruction and end dispersal of the Japanese community."[20]

At the next meeting, CANE representative Joanne Sheitelman spoke about how the displacement of 2,000 residents from the neighborhood by the redevelopment agency, rising rents, and the long-term effects of World War II internment had reduced the Japanese population and geographic size of Japantown. She noted how the availability of SFHA units had not kept pace with these dislocations and stated that residents would now resist any more evictions.[21]

Redevelopment agency spokesman Gene Suttle then made a presentation. After handing out a package with a history of Western Addition redevelopment, the code violations of the buildings, a list of available housing, and a promise of Section 8 housing to qualifying tenants (not all existing tenants qualified for SFHA housing), he discussed how the elimination of these "dilapidated and decrepit" buildings would improve the district and reduce slums in the city. He observed that the Nihonmachi Community Development Corporation (NCDC) provided the required community participation for the agency's plans. Suttle closed his presentation by stating that the properties in question were under option and that his agency's hands were legally tied on the matter.[22]

The next speaker was Randy Wei of CANE. He pointed out that NCDC membership cost $100, and its members focused on "making money" rather than meeting their "higher moral responsibility to the community." He said "the 'people' had been forced out; that Japantown used to extend for 16 blocks and now it is four blocks." Another speaker, Kris Chen of the Chinese Progressive Association, provided a historical reason why tenants opposed redevelopment. Chen stated that "what was happening in Japantown also happened in Chinatown. They see this as an attempt to disperse the community." The Chinese Progressive Association, Chen concluded, wanted "the armed guards removed because they are not there to protect" the people and promised to resist "whatever eviction attempts or harassment that will come down on the Nihonmachi community."[23]

At the next commission meeting, a CANE representative blasted the SFHA, the redevelopment agency, city government, and corporations for their participation in redevelopment and a "pie-in-the-sky proposal of some vague promises" of Section 8 housing. "We are," the CANE representative noted,

> fighting against the destruction and dispersal of the Historic Japanese community as part of the struggle for full equality for Japanese Americans and all Third World and working people. We are fighting for the people's right to decent low-rent housing in communities that meet their needs. . . . We know that the tenants stand is not just a matter of these two buildings, but like the International Hotel has become a focal point for resisting the city-wide destruction of low-rent housing and dispersal of the communities of Third World and working people.[24]

CANE urged the SFHA to use eminent domain powers to add the two properties to its stock. But the SFHA commissioners did not take over the buildings. As SFHA lawyer Mrs. Harris said, the "agreement between the Redevelopment Agency and the Nihonmachi Development Corporation is a valid, binding contract."[25]

What was striking about the Japantown and the International Hotel struggles was the way that the city's residents made claims for housing rights through the SFHA. After two decades of redevelopment and soaring housing costs, low-income residents had few other options. As one woman told Mayor Moscone at a 1977 community forum in Hunters Point, "You ask us, what do you want? Well, we been fightin' for the last umpteen million years for public housing money, and nobody gives a damn about us."[26] The SFHA never met demand in the city. But the authority's ability to keep some low-rent housing under public control was not lost on residents, as these two cases showed. In this way, the SFHA remained one of the institutions used by the city's residents in their struggle for economic and human rights.

By the 1970s, we should note, the SFHA was a very different institution than it was in the 1940s. Social movements and lawsuits helped to make the institution more diverse and more responsive to residents. To comply with a court settlement, the SFHA printed materials in many languages to "help insure the participation of non-English speaking residents." The SFHA served seniors and individuals with disabilities through building and unit design and social services.[27]

Tenants were involved in hiring and budget decisions, and they often filled commission meetings to overcapacity, leaving many outside and "upset that they can't get in." The San Francisco Public Housing Tenants Association (PHTA) leadership reflected the diversity of its most active members, and PHTA presidents (Dorothy Tillman, Cleo Wallace, Judy McCabe, Lillie Ransom, and Hope Halikias) reflected the high numbers of women in the tenant movement.

As a SFHA commissioner, Cleo Wallace was a whirlwind of activity. She worked closely with tenants, community members, the mayor's office, and progressive politicians John Burton and Phil Burton, and she traveled to conferences around the nation. She represented tenants for the National Tenant Organization, NAHRO, and HUD, and she, like so many other tenants who participated in SFHA decision making, brought a decidedly working-class perspective to her work. As Wallace noted, she didn't have to ask anyone "about being poor. I don't think there is anything you can tell me about it." Internally, SFHA staff also became more diverse from bottom to top. SFHA directors Walter Scott, who replaced Eneas Kane in 1977, and then his successor Carl Williams were the first African Americans to direct the agency. Women began to fill top administrative positions, a shift that Commissioner Wallace said was "long overdue."[28] In 1979, the SFHA added sexual preference to their nondiscrimination policy for their employees and applicants for SFHA housing, thus extending these rights and protections to members of the LGBT community.[29]

For SFHA tenants, the housing program provided several ways to build a shared tenant identity and community. Tenants organized their unions and demands around their specific projects. For example, when Secretary of the Sunnydale Coalition Board Mary Brewer appeared before the SFHA Commission, her list of demands reflected a multiracial and multi-ethnic tenant community at the Sunnydale project. Security needs and maintenance problems plus inadequate staffing topped their priorities. Her presentation was in the first-person plural: "We hope the commissioners with the help of their staff will help us solve our problems." She ended with "We are hoping we may have an answer from the commissioners now or in writing in the next few days."[30] Brewer's use of "we" was similar to that of other tenant union leaders when they discussed themselves and their goals. As social psychologists have found, social groups form around a common experience and shared interests and language, and it was through their group identity, as tenants, that they found the solidarity necessary for community and political action.[31]

Senior tenants were an especially visible part of the public housing community. By 1979, 4,034 seniors lived in SFHA units across the city. These units offered an affordable alternative to the SROs and other low-rent options in the private sector. As one senior noted, "Where else in SF could you get a modern apartment with a gorgeous City view, nice quiet neighbors, well-lit hallways . . . and utilities at an affordable cost based solely on your ability to pay?" Senior projects offered manicured grounds with flowers, gardens, walkways, and benches, and they were near the services seniors needed for independent living.[32]

Beyond the physical amenities and location, SFHA Special Programs Director Effie Robinson ensured a diversity of programs to meet the individual and collective needs of seniors. Meal and transportation programs and friendly pet policies enriched the health and lives of seniors. In these programs, SFHA staff addressed the nation's "shift in emphasis from extended family ties to individual freedom" of children and "a fixated youth culture" that negatively affected many of the nation's elderly. Seniors were also very politically active, not only in the SFHA but also in urban politics. SFHA tenant and retired teacher Ruth Brill, for example, was a board member of the Gray Panthers and contributed to the Gray Power movement locally and nationally.[33]

To bring a few of the good things in life to tenants, SFHA staff coordinated with donors and community groups to offer year-round programming for all ages and backgrounds. Effie Robinson ensured that holiday celebrations were "relevant to our senior population: Christmas, Hanukkah, and Russian Christmas." She noted that these events aimed to reproduce

> cultural traditions which have meaning for the older people . . . [but also] establish new traditions for each building which help to substitute for the loss in their lives. Thus decorations selected by the tenants in the past have been preserved and used each year.[34]

In 1977, Robinson worked with community groups and tenant unions to ensure that 900 seniors and guests from twenty-three developments enjoyed a holiday dinner. Family Tenant Services Director Mel Spriggs worked jointly with tenants and donors to ensure that whether it was a Halloween or Christmas party, SFHA events offered meals with music and singing. Some events even had clowns, jugglers, and acrobats. Combined, SFHA staff estimated 10,000 children and adults participated in the Halloween and Christmas parties in 1977. Public housing youth also participated in summer employment programs, camping trips, and excursions to museums, the zoo, the Exploratorium, and the Sacramento State Fair.[35]

Tenants also had a monthly newsletter, *Update*. The newsletter informed tenants about SFHA and HUD policies and tenant rights; it instructed tenants on how to file grievances against the SFHA; and it ran notices about class action lawsuits by tenants, including cases against the SFHA. The publication listed tenant union meetings and encouraged tenants to stay involved at every level of government. *Update* carried job postings, safety suggestions, and tips for healthy living. News of tenant events also dotted the pages of *Update*. The May 1979 issue highlighted Senior Citizens Month, which featured a jazz festival and an awards ceremony for senior activists that was the "annual tribute to older Americans who have contributed so much to all of our lives." That issue also carried news of annual festivals such as an African American festival: "As with the Chinese Moon Festival, the Japanese Chrysanthemum Festival, and the Hispanic Festival, we will share the music, dance and foods of our Black American friends and neighbors."[36] The newsletter encouraged tenants to attend educational classes because "the larger the group the wider the viewpoints for discussion—the more interesting the classes become." The newsletter along with the range of services and programming helped to build a community of tenants.[37]

Public housing tenants also expressed their identity through art. Building on the SFHA traditions begun in the 1940s with neighborhood-themed murals and Beniamino Bufano's sculptures, tenants continued to make art. Murals brought life to project walls. Bernal Dwellings's mural offered movement and color to reflect "the multitude of races and cultures" in the city; Ping Yuen's had the Eight Immortal Gods in Chinese culture; and North Beach's offered a mix of animals, flowers, and spaceships to "delight the eye and excite the imagination."[38] Art classes, exhibits, and programs were regularly held for tenants of all ages. Holly Courts had a resident artist who directed a citywide summer youth employment program in the housing project's art room, though the artist also led mural projects in many neighborhoods.[39] A regional art festival sponsored by Bay Area public housing authorities and tenant unions drew exhibits from both fine arts and crafts and offered entertainment that "featured gospel singers, Berkeley's New World Ensemble, and Make-a-Circus jugglers." In 1978, the Ping Yuen Children's Art Group and Holly Arts Program from Holly Courts entered their art for the festival's competition, and Louise Yee of the Ping Yuen Tenants Association served as a judge. Tenants, often with SFHA support, wove their artistic expressions into the cultural fabric of their community.[40]

Although the SFHA provided support to improve the daily lives of tenants, by the 1970s the authority, like its counterparts across the nation, had less capacity to address the problems facing government housing. As the tragic case of Julia Wong illustrated, high crime rates and the lack of safety in and around SFHA projects reached deadly levels. Gangs, drug abuse, theft and vandalism, and violent assaults reduced tenants' quality of life, drove up public housing costs, contributing to negative images of public housing and its tenants, even though many of the perpetrators were not public housing tenants. SFHA tenants responded to these issues in different ways. Some retreated; others moved out; still others organized to make improvements. For those who wanted improvements, the SFHA was a natural target of criticism. To be sure, the authority needed to do a better job of providing lighting, working facilities, and security, but the San Francisco Police Department also was not doing its job. SFHA Director Carl Williams noted, in response to requests to improve safety, that the city needed to do more. He said, "Public housing residents are residents of the City and County of San Francisco and the S.F. Police Department has a clear responsibility to provide security for the entire city."[41]

Federal housing policies that moved resources away from public housing presented another challenge to the SFHA program. By the end of the 1970s, HUD dollars flowed to private landlords in a number of ways. Section 8 vouchers, various subsidies for private landlords and developers, and low-income housing tax credits all moved federal money away from public housing. The lack of federal funds necessary to repair aging buildings and infrastructure, some of which dated to the 1940s, and the inability to do repairs added to the social problems caused by poverty and negative images of government housing.[42] Other HUD programs encouraged homeownership over more public housing. When HUD acquired the Navy housing known as Inchon Village in Hunters Point, the federal agency, with support from Supervisor Dianne Feinstein, agreed to transfer the property to the SFHA only if the housing authority refurbished and then sold the homes to low-income residents. HUD Secretary Patricia Harris made a personal visit to endorse the project before the SFHA and San Francisco Redevelopment Agency began turning the property, which was heavily polluted from naval operations, into townhomes known as Mariner's Village.[43]

The SFHA leadership also fended off attempts by San Francisco political leaders who tried to reduce the agency's purpose and even end its existence. In November 1978, just after the murders of Moscone and Milk and the Jonestown mass murder and suicides, Supervisor Dianne Feinstein became mayor. In office, she often favored policies to assist business and redevelopment interests over the rights and desires of residents, and she was willing to reduce social programs and economic rights to align with her budget priorities. After the passage of Proposition 13, a state ballot measure that cut property taxes, Feinstein prepared the SFHA and other city agencies for an era of fiscal constraints. Upon entering office, her motto to the city's administrators became "Do more with less," which included a push to cut wages and benefits and contract out city jobs to the private sector. She also expected SFHA housing to be available for the redevelopment agency in order to meet federal relocation requirements (that is, so that the agency could credibly reference SFHA units as places to which displaced tenants could be moved when they were uprooted by redevelopment projects).[44]

Beyond this, while in office Feinstein revived the idea of merging the SFHA with the redevelopment agency. To justify the merger, she supported a narrative of the SFHA having "real problems" and needing new leadership. The proposed merger would give the San Francisco Redevelopment Agency control of SFHA land and housing as well as the expertise of SFHA staff. It would be a major victory for redevelopment in the city. SFHA commissioners voted against the merger, and SFHA Director Carl Williams worked to prevent it, because they understood the vital role the authority played in providing low-income housing to the city's residents. By 1979, Feinstein gave up on the merger, but even so, her attacks on public housing reflected her belief in a reduced role of government in addressing inequality.[45]

Feinstein belonged to growing number of Democrats in and out of San Francisco who were moving away from the assumptions that had guided the expansion of civil and economic rights during the New Deal and Great Society. These "New Democrats" still believed in government programs and regulations, though now on a smaller scale, and they were influenced in part by the political success of the New Right political movement. New Right politicians captured a growing voter base for the Republican Party through a platform that promised to cut social programs, regulations, and taxes and reverse the gains of the civil rights movement while restoring traditional gender roles and sexuality, military power, and faith in the United States.

The New Right's vision of dismantling the economic and civil rights built up in previous decades and shrinking the public sector—except for military and prison industrial complex spending—was in line with a public philosophy known as neoliberalism. Neoliberalism celebrates individual responsibility and self-sufficiency over the welfare state and a global, free market economy liberated from government restraints. As it evolved in the 1970s, neoliberalism also embodied a belief in tougher criminal sentencing laws and more military spending. In 1980, the election of the New Right presidential candidate Ronald Reagan sharpened and broadened the neoliberal attack on government and the civil and economic rights of citizens. Once in office, Reagan slashed taxes and social programs, particularly urban programs, which he believed created dependency among residents and institutions alike. He deregulated industries, weakened worker rights, and further devolved federal programs to state and local government and the private sector.[46]

Reagan appointees shared his philosophy. To lead HUD, Reagan appointed Samuel Pierce. A former Wall Street lawyer and New York State assistant attorney, Pierce came to the position with little background in or commitment to improving affordable housing. Housing scholar Robert Allen Hays described Pierce as "one of the least aggressive advocates of housing for the poor to be found in the black community." Pierce reduced HUD staff, and he and other high-level appointees pushed to change HUD's institutional culture to match Reagan's vision of smaller government. Housing experts Charles Moore and Patricia Hoban-Moore, who worked and consulted for HUD, noted that Reagan's HUD appointees "were people who were not just inexperienced or bad managers, but they were also ideologically hostile to the very programs they were responsible for managing." And many, including Pierce, were soon associated with corruption and misuse of HUD funds.[47]

Another way the Reagan administration undermined public housing was by producing what was presented as new knowledge to reduce public support for government housing and economic and civil rights. In April 1982, the first of several housing reports came out of the Reagan administration. Written by a committee composed almost entirely of real estate representatives, the 277-page President's Commission on Housing report affirmed "the genius of the market economy, freed of the distortions forced by government housing policies and regulations." As well, it claimed, the private sector "can provide for housing far better than Federal programs." A few months later, HUD's urban policy report similarly emphasized the need to cut urban programs, based on the position that these programs did more harm than good to recipients.[48]

The 1982 federal budget halved the previous year's housing funding, and in 1983 the administration tried to put forward a housing budget that would have authorized no new units and a $2.5 billion reduction from 1982 levels. Congress pushed back, and housing appropriations increased slowly in the following years. Significantly, the allocation of HUD funding favored Section 8 and for-profit and nonprofit housing legislation. The only kind of public housing funding to increase was for seniors and people with disabilities.[49] At a 1985 Urban League conference, few in the audience were likely surprised when a HUD deputy assistant secretary said, "We're basically backing out of the business of housing, period."[50]

This "backing out of the business of housing" meant less federal funding for housing authorities and fewer protections for tenants. HUD, along with state and local governments, increased support for the nonprofit housing sector, which won contracts to provide low-cost housing to tenants who previously would have been in public housing. By 1990, nonprofits built and managed 17 percent of all HUD low-income housing.[51] In the area of fair housing, the Department of Justice and HUD limited the collection of race and gender data necessary for identifying discrimination and segregation, and they did not pursue violations of the fair housing provisions of the 1968 Civil Rights Act with the same vigor as had previous administrations.[52] These policies squared with Reagan's promises to scale back the government's role in the economy and civil rights, and they were part of a larger set of regressive policies that shored up the wealth and power of landlords and bosses. Importantly, his housing policies often built on HUD policies piloted since the 1960s and left housing authorities with even fewer resources to maintain already struggling programs.

In September 1981, the SFHA leadership formed a task force to explore the agency's shrinking options. The group included PHTA president Cleo Wallace and tenant representative Francis Hugunin, Naomi Gray and Donald Tishman from the business sector, SFHA commissioners Joan Byrnes San Jule and Harry Chuck, William Witte from the San Francisco Office of Community Development, SFHA staffer Evert Heynneman, and SFHA Director Carl L. Williams. Their charge was to look at "how to provide the best 'quality of life' for the residents of public housing in the City despite the drastic budget cuts that are being proposed by the federal government." Their work led to the 1982 publication of "Crisis in Public Housing: A Review of Alternatives for Public Housing in San Francisco and Recommendations for the Future." In the area of property management, the report discussed the pros and cons of using private companies to manage public housing. These companies typically replaced a union and government workforce with a cheaper one and received federal subsidies, but, according to the report, these companies had at best a mixed managerial record.[53]

The report also looked at public housing tenant self-management, notably in St. Louis where a long rent strike had won public housing tenants their goal of self-management. Tenant management in St. Louis, as in other parts of the nation, involved extensive technical support from the local housing authority, HUD, consulting companies, and community organizations. Even with substantial support, tenants struggled with managing the daily affairs of their housing. Like housing authorities, tenants too were faced with the consequences of structural problems (higher rates of unemployment, crime, public and private institutional neglect, and so on) in their neighborhoods and the budget realities of running housing programs. The task force report recommended against the tenant self-management option—but it did recommend soliciting proposals from real estate management firms.[54]

The SFHA report discussed other alternatives that were in line with the Reagan administration's housing goals. The "condomania" sweeping urban areas prompted the task force to investigate converting public housing into condominiums, but their report recommended against this option because the cost of such units would be "far above the ability for SFHA residents to pay." The report also discussed converting public housing into cooperatives. When successful, cooperatives allowed individuals to build equity through home ownership, offered a high level of housing democracy, and generally produced a degree of resident stability and security. Although cheaper than condominiums (due to better financing), cooperatives, according to the task force, also proved too expensive.[55]

One last option in the report was for the SFHA to sell properties in order to generate revenue "to ensure the survival of other public housing developments." The Reagan administration had "made it very clear" that it would eliminate the "plethora of regulatory and legal requirements" in the way of selling off public housing assets. The task force report noted that unsolicited proposals from real estate companies already showed "active interest" in SFHA properties. The possible sale of public housing, however, generated concerns for the task force members who wrote that the "emotional trauma involved in displacing a substantial number of public housing residents far outweighs the advantages of any income" from sales. Additionally, the loss of control over this housing by selling it to the private sector "would seriously exacerbate the [dearth of] housing opportunities for low-income persons."[56]

SFHA tenants also opposed the sale of public housing. North Beach tenant Mun Yee Leung was among many who stressed that tenants "are opposed to any sale." The San Francisco Board of Supervisors followed suit with a resolution calling for "no change in the ownership or management of the San Francisco housing projects." The task force report's final recommendation veered from the national trajectory of neoliberal actions, stating that the SFHA should sell off its units only "as a measure of last resort."[57] Too many residents depended on and wanted SFHA housing.

The task force's reluctance to embrace privatization came, in part, from the intensification of the affordable housing crisis. Overall, the city's population had declined in the 1970s, but began rising again in the 1980s (see Table A.1 in appendix). Housing costs had double-digit increases nationally, but in western cities such as San Francisco, rents and housing prices far outpaced national figures and wages adjusted for inflation. The number of single-room occupancy hotels (SROs)—long havens for San Francisco's elderly, immigrants, and poor—dropped from 57,000 to 19,000 between 1975 and 1986, as investors converted SROs into condominiums, office space, and tourist hotels.[58]

The demolition of housing for redevelopment projects also decreased the number of affordable housing units. These losses, which included SROs, meant fewer choices, and a lower standard of living, for low-income households. Nonwhite families struggled the most in the housing market. As SFHA Commissioner A. E. Ubalde noted, "Landlords will not take families with children. . . . If you have children and you're black—that's another strike against you."[59] Director Carl Williams explained, "We should not fool ourselves in assuming that it is something that can be done by the private sector . . . they have all indicated that they could not produce these units within the rent paying ranges of the persons who would be eligible for these units."[60] The cumulative effects of these trends drove many low-income households, especially African Americans, out of the city or onto the streets.

The surge in the city's homeless population became part of a national trend. No longer limited to mostly young and middle-aged male substance abusers, the mentally ill, or hobos living off the grid, the city's homeless population now included workers, veterans, and families.[61] By 1982, San Francisco's city leaders were holding regular conferences on the topic. Fresh from one of these conferences, SFHA Director Carl Williams provided a report, which he concluded by writing that the homeless problem "seems to be quite serious and growing."[62] SFHA Commissioner Elouise Westbrook stated that the agency needed to do more "for the families in San Francisco who are homeless or living in deplorable conditions."[63] During the 1980s, HUD, which had precipitated some of the problem in the first place by shrinking its affordable housing expenditures, responded by opening up Section 8 certificates to homeless applicants, and in 1985, the SFHA began applying for the newly created certificates.[64]

The growing homeless population in the nation prompted federal investigations and legislation. Congressional findings on homelessness found that the nation faced "an immediate and unprecedented crisis due to the lack of shelter for a growing number of individuals and families." "Due to the record increase in homelessness," the report added, "states, units of local government, and private voluntary organizations have been unable to meet the basic human needs of all the homeless." The findings also highlighted the complexity of the problem, since the causes of homelessness and the needs of the homeless did not fit into neat categories. In 1987, the U.S. Congress passed the McKinney–Vento Homeless Assistance Act to expand and coordinate federal programs to better assist the nation's homeless, including the growing number of homeless children. One of the key features of the McKinney–Vento legislation was that it channeled HUD funding through housing authorities, then to private and nonprofit entities that served the homeless.[65]

In San Francisco, Catholic Charities used this HUD funding to rehabilitate thirty-three SRO units and win an annual $190,000 contract for providing housing services. Catholic Charities received other McKinney funds to run the first hotel for AIDS patients in the nation. Other nonprofit housing providers in San Francisco focused on homeless veterans and substance abusers. Taken together, however, these housing solutions still did not have enough rooms and services to meet the needs of the homeless in San Francisco; there, as around the nation, backstreets, parks, and doorways swelled with people without homes.[66]

The SFHA featured prominently in discussions of homelessness, though the agency's capacity to respond to the need was limited by changing tenant demographics and demand. In the 1970s and 1980s, U.S.-backed wars in Southeast Asia

Figure 7.3
Overflow crowds at the San Francisco Housing Authority office in 1981 on the day designated for accepting applications. More than 5,000 applicants applied to join the SFHA's waiting list.

and Central America led to a surge in immigrants from these regions, and some settled in San Francisco. Many became SFHA tenants (the agency had dropped its citizenship requirement). By 1990, roughly 46 percent of the SFHA tenant population was African American, 30 percent Asian, 17 percent white, 1 percent Native American, and 6 percent Latina/o. The waiting list for SFHA housing numbered in the thousands, and in the rare instances when the SFHA accepted new applications, it attracted thousands of applicants who hoped to be added to the list. In these often chaotic scenes, elderly applicants slightly outnumbered family applicants.[67]

Of the 20,000 public housing tenants, 85 percent of SFHA tenant households received some kind of government social insurance program: Aid to Families with Dependent Children, disability insurance, or Social Security. Even though HUD raised the rent of subsidized housing to 30 percent of a tenant's household gross income, the SFHA did not benefit from the higher rent collections because inflation ate up much of that added rental income. The SFHA added new staff and services for seniors, non-English speakers, and tenants with disabilities, none of whose costs were part of the 1937 Housing Act's budget formula.[68]

Inflation and these new services, combined with repair costs, strained the SFHA program. From 1982 to 1992, the SFHA budget climbed from just over $20 million to $35 million, but when adjusted for inflation, that amount actually represented a decline of $16 million in purchasing power. To help offset this loss, the city waived the SFHA's payments in lieu of taxes (PILOTs). By 1992, the SFHA managed roughly 5,400 Section 8 units and about 6,500 permanent units, down from about 7,000 permanent units in 1982. With these two kinds of housing, the agency administered just over 2 percent of the city's rentals.[69]

In this era, the losses in permanent housing units resulted from demolition of family housing in need of repairs. In 1982, the SFHA, with community support, bulldozed ninety-six apartments at the Alice Griffith Homes because, even though everyone agreed that it was unfortunate, the SFHA could no longer wait for HUD funding for needed repairs. The demolition of a project with such an important namesake was a grim example of the consequences of declining federal support and the declining capacity of the SFHA. Vandalism was also to blame for some of the physical decline and subsequent destruction of SFHA housing. Doors, fixtures, lights, wiring, and other materials disappeared or were broken. Pipes and valves necessary for boilers went missing, as did hot water for tenants. Tenants complained of month-long waits to get basic repairs from a decimated SFHA maintenance department whose overworked staff approached work orders like doctors in triage. Not all housing units were falling apart, but there were enough in bad shape to provide evidence of a program in need of assistance.[70] In many ways, this whole situation was predictable. It was the culmination of four decades of structural underfunding to ensure that public housing would not be more attractive than private housing. The situation also provided concrete examples for the neoliberal narrative of ineffective government.[71]

As with the Alice Griffith Homes decision, the SFHA community also had to make a difficult decision about the Yerba Buena Annex project, or the Pink Palace, as it was known. Located in the Western Addition, by 1980 the Pink Palace needed major repairs, some the result of vandalism, and its tenants were often victims of neighborhood crime. It had a national reputation as a high-rise slum. Although the project was not designed for it, many large families crammed themselves into the project's small units. In 1981, Mayor Feinstein asked the SFHA to convert the building into "safe and comfortable senior housing." Her request, which the redevelopment agency supported, assumed that seniors would be less likely than younger family members in the family units to menace others and thus would make safer neighbors in a district targeted for urban redevelopment.[72]

Despite concerns from SFHA Director Carl Williams about the conversion likely not solving the crime problem and taking money from other projects, his staff dutifully assembled a remodel plan based on New York architect Oscar Newman's idea of defensible space. Newman stressed using the built space to create a safer and more stable public housing environment in low-income neighborhoods. To accomplish this defensible turf, projects had to minimize open space—which Newman argued invited criminals in and gave them secure, often hidden places to commit their crimes—and provide physical security through controlled access points, surveillance, and proximity to police substations.[73] The $4.1 million redesign included everything from indoor and outdoor (controlled-access) social spaces and a library to modified bathrooms with showers and grab bars on the walls. In addition to this remodel work, the SFHA would provide onsite staff, social workers, a minibus with driver, and twelve security guards. Plans also called for a service to escort seniors on errands, senior-specific activities, and a tenant-operated cooperative store with fresh produce. HUD Comprehensive Modernization Program funds earmarked for other SFHA projects would finance the remodel. If approved, it would also displace 110 low-income, mostly nonwhite families from the Western Addition.[74]

Residents flooded SFHA Commission meetings to debate the merits of the Pink Palace remodel proposal. Ursula Anderson, president of the Seniors Citywide Council (SCWC), a tenant association that often operated independently of the PHTA, said that seniors did "not want to take from families," but that if the conversion took place, they wanted the increased security, types of architectural changes, and social services proposed in the SFHA plan. Western Addition Project Area Committee (WAPAC) Director Benny Stewart weighed in against the proposal,

stressing the loss of affordable housing in the Western Addition and Hunters Point. He observed that "[f]amily displacement as a means for crime prevention" did not work; instead, it "enhances the problem" of the housing crisis by breaking down the community. Children were, he continued, "being separated from their families because of inadequate housing and they are placed in Juvenile Courts and Foster homes." Steve Nakjo, director of Kimochi, Inc. (a Japanese senior center), and Sandy Mori of the Japan Center commented on the need for family and senior housing, though they wanted to ensure that housing needs of all current Pink Palace tenants were met. Pink Palace tenants opposed the conversion but wanted the proposed material improvements and better security.[75] At the San Francisco Bay Area Baptist Ministers conference, ministers unanimously voted to support the conversion, but only if housing was provided to the displaced. Reverend Amos Brown added that the ministers also wanted the conversion to "insure significant employment for the persons from the area."[76]

The debates highlighted the class divisions over housing in the city. San Francisco's elites continued to push for the conversion in service of redevelopment projects, but residents argued for more public housing. San Francisco Redevelopment Agency's Haig Mardikian said, speaking "as a citizen," the mayor's proposal was "by far the most suitable and appropriate. The conversion to elderly housing will stabilize the occupancy of this project." He further predicted that "if the Yerba Buena Plaza Annex is not converted to senior housing it will inevitable [sic] fall prey to the same fate of the [Pruitt-Igoe] project in St. Louis." His reference to the Pruitt-Igoe public housing project, which had recently been demolished for its social and material problems, was intended to play on negative images of public housing and highlight what opponents of public housing thought should be done to government homes (that is, they should be blown to pieces).[77]

WAPAC representative Mary Rogers critiqued the redevelopment agency for destroying homes in the Western Addition and the SFHA for not yet building the 200 units approved for the district in 1969. She argued that the SFHA should use the HUD Modernization monies to remodel existing units for current residents. Tenant leader Eva Mae Williams thought seniors needed housing, but "families need housing as well." Another tenant leader, Orlando Hall, urged the commissioners to "think about the babies, at a time when there is a housing crisis."[78]

In the end, the SFHA commissioners voted for the conversion and stated that the SFHA "must do everything possible to minimize the impact on the families" being relocated. In September 1982, the Seniors City-Wide Council, a subgroup within the PHTA, proposed Rosa Parks Senior Apartments as the new name for the project. Relocation of families and remodeling commenced, contributing to a further decline in the number of African Americans remaining in the city.[79]

< **Figure 7.4**
The Pink Palace in 1983 exemplified the lack of defensible space, common to older and taller public housing projects. Architect Oscar Newman proposed redesigning such projects for better safety and tenant control.

The Alice Griffith Homes demolition and Rosa Parks conversion highlighted the difficult decisions facing the SFHA community in an era of federal cuts; they also signaled growing divisions among tenants. To be sure, tenants of all ages and family types still worked together on voter registration campaigns and on pressuring local and federal leaders to do more for public housing. And PHTA representatives attended NTO and NAHRO conferences and nominated tenants to the SFHA commission.[80] Tenants still ran a citywide summer food program, which in 1984 operated at 19 SFHA projects, served 2,400 meals a day, and employed 29 SFHA tenants.[81] But the PHTA was losing its unified voice. In 1982, the Hunters View, Westbrook, and Alice Griffith Tenants Associations wrote the SFHA commission to express "their wish to withdraw their participation from PHTA" and asked (unsuccessfully) for their share of PHTA financial allocations. Throughout the decade, other tenant associations asked to leave the PHTA, and tenants voiced their concerns and critiques of the PHTA. PHTA accounting and accountability problems regularly led the SFHA to stop funding the tenant organization and delay PHTA–SFHA contract renewals. PHTA leadership turnover and questionable elections at the project and city level weakened the organization even more.[82] As Commissioner Harry Chuck said, "With the shifts in leadership come shifts in priorities and approaches. It seemed that every two to three months there was a new group of officers coming before the Commission."[83]

In 1983, the Seniors City-Wide Council (SCWC) broke away from the PHTA, a move that would hurt the public housing tenant movement. Made up of seniors and tenants with disabilities, the SCWC had formed because of PHTA problems and because of the different social identities of SCWC members. SCWC representatives attended SFHA meetings, worked on housing legislation, and served on SFHA committees.[84] The SCWC ran its own voter campaigns and remained active at the local and state level because "[a]ll of the senior residents of the San Francisco Housing Authority realize how important it is to be aware of what is happening politically and how it will affect them."[85]

The SCWC tried to leave the PHTA legally and requested a prorated share of PHTA monies (roughly $5,000 per year). The SFHA Commission rejected both proposals.[86] Throughout the 1980s, the SCWC leadership made it clear that the PHTA did not speak for them. In a 1988 letter to SFHA Director James Clay, SCWC President Mary Lou McAllister stated that her group wanted no part of the PHTA, however new and reorganized it might be that month. She noted that each senior building had its own association, which was part of a citywide "umbrella association." McAllister said that there was "100% representation of individual senior tenant associations" at the citywide meetings, a model that represented "seniors in all matters of collective interest to the Authority staff and Commission. Our senior representative on the Housing Authority Commission serves as an appropriate advocate and liaison." She wanted to "continue our current manner of representation" and emphasized that the "PHTA does not now, nor at any time whatsoever, speak for the disabled and senior tenants residing in the Authority's senior housing units."[87]

The PHTA's internal problems strained its relationship with the SFHA. The PHTA leadership had always exercised a degree of autonomy over its affairs and its decisions regarding how to relate to the SFHA—as an adversary, a partner, or an ally. PHTA leaders often reminded the SFHA that "the internal affairs of the PHTA are to be resolved by PHTA and not Authority staff or the Commission."[88] Yet the SFHA supplied staff and resources to the PHTA, including mediators for PHTA internal disputes, funds covering PHTA and senior tenants' travel to NTO and NAHRO conferences, SFHA buses to move tenants around the city for events, and childcare to facilitate tenant participation.

Perhaps the most striking form of support came in 1988 when SFHA commissioners attended a PHTA meeting with the goal to "get PHTA reorganized and on its feet with a set of working by-laws, set of working officers and members committed to providing services to the tenants." Commissioners pledged to assign an SFHA staff person to "help assess what is required in reorganizing the tenant associations and the PHTA" and to "look for outside sources of funding" to pay for an organizer to "work with the tenants to get the organization back on its feet."[89] SFHA staff worked with property managers and tenants to rebuild "strong property organizations" to restore "a strong city wide organization," but the PHTA never recovered the organizational strength it had had in the 1970s.[90]

The decline of the tenant movement can be understood in several ways. Section 8 housing spread tenants across the city's low-income neighborhoods, and this made organizing and including them in the tenant movement more difficult. As the physical quality of SFHA units declined, many tenants lost faith in the SFHA program and their ability to improve their housing and neighborhoods. Some tenant associations prioritized their own project's interests over citywide tenant interests. Incorporated tenant associations, a product of HUD policies, pursued grants for their own projects, creating a political landscape in which one tenant association sometimes competed with another for limited funding. When Ping Yuen tenants won a grant for their project, for example, SFHA Commissioner Elouise Westbrook said that she "did not like to see tenants competing against tenants."[91]

Sometimes local elites encouraged individualistic tenant behavior by promoting neoliberal HUD policies. In 1991, following HUD Secretary Jack Kemp's direction, San Francisco mayoral candidate Frank Jordan (Dem.) penned an open letter to the city's public housing tenants. In it, Jordan blasted the SFHA and pitched the federal Homeownership and Opportunity for People Everywhere (HOPE) program as something "working all across the country." Jordan wrote that HOPE "provides Resident Management Training" so that tenants would have "the skills necessary to eventually manage your own developments" and the "opportunity to own your developments for no more of your incomes than you're currently paying for rent." Jordan's final point drove home the neoliberal message of individualism, choice, and private home ownership—as it offered a dig at his political opponent and current San Francisco Mayor Art Agnos. "Art Agnos opposes H.O.P.E because it takes the power to control your lives away from him and gives it back to you," Jordan wrote, and "I believe you have the talent and energy to make H.O.P.E work. All you need is the chance to do it."[92]

Eight months after Jordan became mayor, tenants at the Alemany project signed an agreement with the SFHA to manage their building and explore private ownership. The Bernal Heights project was the first in the city to be run by tenants, who now had to solve many of the structural problems of an underfunded program on their own rather than collectively across the city.[93] Tenants at Hunters View, Sunnydale, Holly Courts, and Robert B. Pitts projects soon followed their counterparts at Bernal Heights.[94]

Other neoliberal policies disciplined tenants in ways that made tenant organization and solidarity difficult. Instead of using in-house staff to evaluate applicants, the SFHA, like other housing authorities and private landlords, began to use tenant-screening companies that sold reports on an applicant's credit, criminal, and renter performance histories. SFHA commissioners hired the National Tenant Network because, they claimed, an applicant's background, especially in his or her "past performance in the rental market," was helpful in determining if he or she was "a desirable public housing resident."[95] Driven by profit and often unregulated in their behavior, companies such as the National Tenant Network were prone to mistakes and data-driven conclusions that did not account for human or computer errors or moral and ethical outcomes. Consequently, tenants could lose access to low-rent housing they had a right to receive. The contracting out of these kinds of government services often undermined the public sector and fiscal accountability.[96]

The rise of the prison industrial complex and the war on the poor also limited tenant organizing. Starting in the 1970s, a bipartisan push at all levels of government expanded the war on drugs and crime that put more people, especially the poor and nonwhite, in prison. For friends and family members of those charged or convicted of crimes, the financial and psychological burdens made life more difficult and could even impact their access to housing. HUD required housing authorities to evict a family if one of its members, or anyone who visited their home, committed a crime. For SFHA tenants, it meant that the criminal activities of "any tenant, or any member of said tenant's household, or guests of tenant or some other person or persons under tenants control whether adult or minor" triggered an eviction. This one-strike rule aimed to reduce violent crime in communities, but it also expanded state power to discipline tenants who themselves had committed no crimes. The one-strike rule chipped away at the right to housing for members of qualified households.[97]

Federal and state legislation also began using "workfare" to push tenants who received government benefits into the labor market; more often than not, the workfare program ended up punishing tenants more than helping them. In 1992, HUD San Francisco Regional Director Robert De Monte critiqued the workfare program championed by HUD Secretary Jack Kemp. De Monte thought that the "Secretary frequently makes the point that poverty should not be a crime," and HUD "should remove the obstacles and disincentives to self help, schooling and employment." However, De Monte pointed out that workfare programs, while successful in employing tenants, did not always benefit the workers. With the employment of tenants, he said, we "learn on frequent occasions the act of going to work reduces the residents disposable income. The San Francisco PHA has hired over 70 residents who on average lost over $100 per month by working." De Monte thought this was "a case of defeating ourselves."[98] HUD also increased the percentage that tenants had to contribute for HUD housing, from 25 percent to 30 percent of household income.[99] When Great Society community organizing money dried up, tenant organizing work fell on volunteers, who were often pulled in many directions—from dealing with friends and family in jail to having to work more for less. The cumulative effects of these policies took away time and resources from tenants who had trouble volunteering in tenant organizations.

HUD neoliberal policies also targeted public housing authorities. In 1979, HUD began a performance-based evaluation, conducted by regional HUD offices, of the nation's large public housing authorities. Known as the Public Housing Management Assessment Program (PHMAP), the evaluation covered broad areas such as physical quality of housing, financial and management effectiveness, and tenant–authority relations. Poor or failing scores triggered mandatory technical assistance and training, but sustained low scores landed a housing authority on HUD's troubled housing authority list, which increased the likelihood of sanctions, reduced federal funding, and sometimes led to receivership.[100]

In 1984, HUD put the SFHA on the troubled housing authority list. From then to April 1989, the agency limped along with a series of interim directors until the SFHA hired David Gilmore to head the authority. Gilmore came fresh from Boston, where he had helped improve the performance of that city's housing authority. He also served on Congress's National Commission on Severely Distressed Public Housing. Gilmore's main task at the SFHA was to remove the SFHA from the troubled housing authority list. To reach that goal, Gilmore lobbied HUD for monies, wrote grant applications, and addressed the SFHA's most pressing problems: vacancies, unlivable units and uncompleted repairs, and overdue tenant accounts and uncollected rents. He developed a reputation for taking chances, saying "If you play it the safe way all the time and you cloak yourself in overwhelming concern about perception and how it may look, nothing ever happens. You don't get anything done."[101]

Gilmore made a number of changes. He balanced the authority's budget, paid off debt, and dropped the vacancy rate to less than 1 percent. He worked well with the SFHA labor force—hiring tenants and working with labor unions—and continued a legacy of affirmative action in hiring and in contracts.[102] HUD Regional Director Robert De Monte praised Gilmore, stating, "we, at HUD, are frequently in the role of critic of public housing authorities as the monitor. Now, I must say how impressed I am with your [work.] While in the business," De Monte continued, "there are ever changing goals as we all strive to improve the quality of life for our mutual client. You and your staff are due a hearty congratulation. Keep the effort advancing."[103]

In 1992, eighteen months after Gilmore's arrival, HUD took the SFHA off of its troubled housing authority list and awarded a $49.9 million HOPE VI grant to redevelop two aging family projects—Bernal Dwellings and Yerba Buena Plaza East. As with the Rosa Parks project, the redesign of these two projects would be inspired by Newman's defensible space and by New Urbanism's emphasis on small developments within walking distance of people's material and social needs. Drawing on "historic San Francisco Victorian townhouses," designs for the Bernal Dwellings and Yerba Buena Plaza East had homes fronting old streets and even adding new streets that cut through the old super-blocks. The two- and three-story apartments would offer 50 to 300 more square feet per unit, with the total number of units falling from 208 to 160 at Bernal Dwellings and from 276 to 193 at Yerba Buena Plaza East. The designs planned for meeting spaces, youth centers, childcare centers, and even computer labs. At other SFHA projects, Gilmore allocated resources to do repairs, and he worked with the city's police force to improve security.[104]

The future of the SFHA was looking brighter, but institutional and political challenges remained. There were many visible reminders of poor quality housing across the program, and the tenant associations remained fragmented. Many tenants had lost faith in the authority. In January 1992, Mayor Frank Jordan entered office ready to go after the authority and Gilmore. He had campaigned on a neoliberal promise to reduce the role of the SFHA in the city's housing and to give tenants the opportunity for self-management and ownership. To Jordan, Gilmore did not move fast enough in these areas, was using his SFHA post to expand his political power, and was rebuilding the legitimacy of the SFHA. Because the SFHA was not a city agency, Jordan could not oust Gilmore, but he very publicly opposed the renewal of Gilmore's contract in 1992.

Gilmore had the support of many in the SFHA community, including, importantly, the commissioners. Supporters came to Gilmore's aid. At a packed June 11, 1992, SFHA meeting, former SFHA Commissioner Joan Byrnes San Jule commented that she was "awed by the tremendous progress made by the Commission and your very able Executive Director" and supported the extension of Gilmore's contract. Others spoke favorably on his ability to work with tenants, unions, and public and private agencies in the city and in Washington, DC. Commissioners extended Gilmore's contract and praised him, stating that his "stewardship of the Authority has been of the highest quality." Gilmore expressed his gratitude to all in the meeting, saying "that today has been the highlight of my life." He then issued

> an open invitation to all those in attendance (supporters and non-supporters) to join the residents, staff and the rest of the city to work together to preserve public housing, which is "too precious a resource to go down the drain."[105]

By the early 1990s, neoliberal policies made significant inroads in the nation's political culture and public policies. These advances took a heavy toll on tenants, the nation's public housing program, and economic and civil rights more broadly. HUD budget cuts, the trend of shifting public housing resources to the for-profit and nonprofit sectors, and new mechanisms to discipline public housing authorities and their tenants were among the ways public policies shaped how the SFHA operated. The problems of the SFHA, like those of other housing authorities, became more acute and visible, and those problems, from underfunding to rising crime rates, became an important part of the neoliberal narrative about the failure of government social programs. Public housing programs were also strained by inflation, by the increased demand for their low-rent housing, and by rising homelessness.

Yet the SFHA survived. Many of the city's tenants and non-tenants still experienced the SFHA as "their" institution in their struggles for economic and civil rights and for a voice in the decisions that affected their homes, neighborhoods, and communities. Increasingly, local and national forces as well as internal problems in the tenant community reduced the remarkable degree of tenant solidarity that had been a hallmark of the 1960s and 1970s. This, in turn, reduced tenant power in and out of the city, marking the turn toward a more atomistic and individualistic tenant culture. The SFHA did not always meet the needs of tenants or the city's residents; its program suffered from many of the same social, financial, and safety issues as other housing authorities.

The city's residents nevertheless continued to view the SFHA as a vital, if less vibrant, part of their lives. At times, tenants and residents used the authority to exercise power and influence the decisions that affected their lives, housing, and communities. Sometimes they participated in national discussions and tried to influence directly national legislation. And they used the housing program to build a community based on their political interests as well as on their common experiences. In these ways, the SFHA program allowed ordinary people to put the *public* not only into public housing, but also into the workings of city politics itself.

CHAPTER 8

PRIVATIZING THE PUBLIC IN THE DOT-COM ERA

Here's how privatization for profit works: (first) don't maintain anything, let everything deteriorate; (second) throw up your hands in dismay of ever being able to repair anything with the meager public funds available; (third) call in private developers and their bankers to "help out"; (fourth) evict the residents because by now everything has to be torn down; and (fifth) build units to buy, not to rent, that the evicted residents can't afford.

Don Santina[1]

SAN FRANCISCO MAYOR FRANK JORDAN wanted SFHA Director David Gilmore gone. Gilmore had shored up the institution's finances and its relations with tenants and in 1992 helped remove the SFHA from HUD's list of "troubled" housing authorities. Gilmore encouraged "citizens of San Francisco and particularly citizens of public housing" to participate in forums around the city to discuss the good and bad of the program. In just three years, Gilmore had done much to build the agency's goodwill and reputation. Still, Jordan persisted.

In early 1993, Jordan again called for the removal of Gilmore—even more forcefully than the year before. Gilmore's supporters rallied behind the director. In a letter to Jordan and the SFHA commission, Ping Yuan Resident Association President George Lee praised Gilmore for being "better than his predecessors" and recommended that he stay on to head the agency. Lee also demanded "changes in the system itself" so that no matter who ran the SFHA, the public housing program would serve the people in a healthy way, be more democratic, and less prone to "power struggles."[2] President of Clementina Tenants Association Paul Lee said "the process of improvement appears very slow at times," but he and his members expected "to see even more improvement of conditions and service here in the future" and were in "unanimous support of Mr. Gilmore." Again the commissioners agreed and renewed Gilmore's contract. But the pressure from the mayor's office continued. As Jordan searched for more obedient SFHA commissioners and a replacement for Gilmore, he also encouraged willing tenants to mobilize against the director.[3]

While the battle between Gilmore and Jordan took center stage, larger forces were restructuring what the SFHA could and could not do in San Francisco. At the federal level, the administrations of George H. W. Bush, Sr., Bill Clinton, and George W. Bush continued Reagan's social and urban policies that disciplined the poor, reduced economic and civil rights, and devolved government programs to the private sector. Local housing authorities became a crucial institution for the implementation of these policies. For scholars of public housing and the welfare state, the 1992 report by the National Commission on Severely Distressed Public Housing provides an important intellectual framework for understanding these political trends—and the history of the SFHA, like that of other public housing authorities, provides a window into the consequences of these neoliberal policies. HUD's HOPE VI program became the symbol of this new legislation. In San Francisco, HOPE VI projects failed to generate enough low-rent housing for residents and transferred public housing resources to the nonprofit and private sector.

These trends occurred during the 1990s while the expanding economy, fueled in part by Bay Area technology companies, created a severe affordable housing shortage in the city. Although many residents still turned to the SFHA for housing assistance during this era, other residents turned to the nonprofit housing sector or to new organizations as the SFHA lost more of its capacity and its housing. SFHA tenants continued to organize, though significantly more political activity came from tenants in private housing than in SFHA housing. SFHA tenant organizing locally and nationally continued to decrease for the reasons described in chapter 7. As the dot-com economy boomed, affluent households drove San Francisco housing costs to new heights while demand from technology companies for commercial space led landlords to raise rents. Low- and middle-income residents, including many African Americans and Latinas/os, small businesses and artists, were squeezed out of the city. As a result, San Francisco lost some of the diversity that had helped make it one of the world's most admired cities.

While Gilmore was fending off the attacks from the mayor's office, he was also a member of the National Commission on Severely Distressed Public Housing. Formed in 1989 by Congress, the commission included sixteen members from the private and public sector; its mission was to identify the problems in severely distressed public housing projects and propose solutions that might eliminate those problems by 2000.

For the members of the commission, four indicators landed a housing project on the severely distressed list: loss of social control (that is, unstoppable antisocial behavior) of a project and its environment; physical deterioration of units and buildings;

residents having little to no access to jobs and social services; and high rates of serious crime in the neighborhood. The commission's 1992 report found that 6 percent of the nation's public housing fell into the severely distressed housing category, though it warned that without government action many more projects would end up with that classification. All of the projects in the severely distressed category were large developments housing families whose households were "poor and getting poorer." Sounding a moral alarm, the commission emphasized that "as a Nation we must act immediately to eliminate conditions that cause the families—men, women, and children—living in approximately 86,000 units of severely distressed public housing to reside in physical, emotional, social, and economic distress."[4]

To eliminate the causes and conditions of severely distressed housing, the commission identified four broad areas in need of reform. The first area was what passers-by saw: physically rundown projects. These conditions were the result of deferred maintenance and an "era of neglect by the federal government." The report proposed assessing each project for its viability—in other words, have local housing authority staff determine whether a building should be rehabilitated, replaced, or some combination of the two. No matter what route the authority took, the report argued for more federal money to do this vital work and for replacement projects that used defensible space designs to help with crime reduction and tenant safety.

The report's second area requiring reform was the institutional neglect of tenants and residents in these neighborhoods. The report argued that, bearing the brunt of deindustrialization and discrimination from private and public institutions, neighborhoods with severely distressed housing projects harmed tenants (and neighbors), who experienced higher levels of crime, poverty, and unemployment than residents in other neighborhoods. The report also noted that a majority of tenants in family housing in the 1990s, compared to their employed counterparts from the 1940s and 1950s, lived on a declining package of government assistance. It was not just buildings that needed attention. "Traditional approaches to revitalizing severely distressed public housing," the report said, "have too often disproportionately emphasized programs to 'fix' the physical conditions of the developments at the expense or exclusion of the human condition of residents." What was needed was an "integrated, holistic system for delivering human services." But the report also acknowledged the complexity of the problem: Quality jobs, education, and safe and affordable childcare were not going to materialize magically for these neighborhoods.[5]

The third area identified as needing improvement was housing authority management. Many large authorities, according to the report, lacked the managerial expertise to address severely distressed housing. Even with strong and capable leadership, distressed housing was "strikingly different from stable public housing."[6] In the political arena, managers had to oversee HUD applications and harness resources from an array of public and private institutions. Furthermore, the report noted, distressed public housing neighborhoods usually had the poorest residents and the highest rates of violence. In fact, the commission's report argued that housing authorities had lost control over these projects and their surrounding neighborhoods. To regain control of these projects, the commission recommended "intensive, site-based efforts." Conjuring images of military commando missions, they described these efforts as targeting

> a distressed building, in some cases controlled by gangs, drug dealers, and/or illegal squatters, for a sudden, unannounced "sweep" by PHA [public housing authority] operations staff and/or security forces. Physical barriers to unauthorized entry by nonresidents are quickly erected. The condition of units is inspected, and work orders are prepared for maintenance staff follow up; common areas and elevators are cleaned and painted to remove years of graffiti and debris; and broken light fixtures, locks, and windows are replaced. All first floor entries are secured, and security screens and perimeter fencing are installed to maximize security.

Not all housing authority leaders possessed the skills to pull off such martial actions or to move forward with a comprehensive plan once a project was under control. The commission recommended boosting HUD training capacity so public housing administrators could more effectively eliminate severely distressed housing.[7]

The fourth area the report identified for reform was HUD public housing regulations. Too often, HUD treated all public housing equally—both stable and severely distressed—in terms of regulations and funding, and this limited how local authorities approached distressed housing. HUD rules on household income still required authorities to place only the poorest families in projects, a practice that reinforced class and, by extension, racial segregation, and it defied what housing experts and nonexperts believed to be best for public housing tenant populations—that is, to have mixed-income populations. The HUD operating subsidy continued to fall short of the actual costs of maintaining and updating the nation's public housing. New formulas were needed to adjust for local conditions—a necessary change for high-cost cities such as San Francisco. Finally, the report proposed replacing HUD's "performance standards" with an evaluation system modeled on the quasi-independent accreditation system used in higher education and health care. As noted earlier, when a housing authority landed on the troubled list, it was punished with greater oversight and less funding. The accreditation model would instead "emphasize continuous improvement" through reviews every three to five years followed by targeted initiatives to work on specific problems.

The report's analysis and solutions clearly revealed the evolution of thinking among housing professionals and political leaders of that era about the role of the federal public housing program and federal social policy. During the 1930s, under pressure from social movements, Congress recognized the failure in the private sector to provide economic security for the nation's citizens, and it responded with New Deal programs and regulations to expand the economic rights and protections for many citizens. Public housing fit into the New Deal vision by providing jobs, affordable housing, and rational economic planning during the economic crisis. In the 1960s—another period of social movements for political and cultural change—Great Society legislation targeted many issues, from poverty and housing to expanding the economic and civil rights of citizens. Public housing continued to be an important site for addressing urban problems and expanding the rights and protections of citizens; federal legislation funded and supported the political organizing in and around public housing, though congressional public housing funding remained below what housing officials and urban residents thought was needed to end poverty and inequality.

In contrast, the 1992 commission report, written at a moment when the economy was expanding, did acknowledge poverty as a problem, but the report's main focus was on burdensome HUD regulations and the shortcomings of housing authorities, the poor, and low-income neighborhoods. It criticized government officials for not having the expertise to oversee severely distressed projects, the political know-how to win federal grants (basically, compete and survive), and the community organizing skills to empower tenants. The report did not discuss the economic and civil rights attached to citizenship, nor did it offer meaningful recommendations for addressing the low wages, unemployment, and affordable housing shortages in these communities. The report's focus on the best methods to lock down neighborhoods suffering from high levels of crime coincided with tough-on-crime narratives, longer and mandatory sentencing, and the growth of the prison industrial complex. The report also proposed selling distressed public housing properties to the private sector. In all of these ways, the 1992 report's analysis of problems and recommendations for solving them reflected the impact of the New Right movement, Reagan, and neoliberalism on the body politic. The commission's report in turn influenced HUD policies and actions. In fact, 94 percent of the nation's public housing was *not* classified as severely distressed, demonstrating that government housing remained a viable low-rent housing solution.[8]

Yet politicians and the media alike highlighted a public housing "crisis" and used the report to reinforce the popular narrative about the failure of social programs and the welfare state. HUD drew on the 1992 report to implement Homeownership and Opportunity for People Everywhere grants. Also known as HOPE VI, this program had three goals: improve the physical environment of public housing, mainly through demolition and replacement of buildings in and near distressed projects; decrease the concentration of very low-income tenants in projects; and provide opportunities for financial independence of tenants and economic development. In practice, the program provided one-time funding to replace aging public housing with a mix of public and private housing units and to move management and services away from the public sector.[9] HOPE VI had the support of New Democrats who joined Republicans in scaling back social programs such as the 1996 welfare reform act (Personal Responsibility and Work Opportunity Reconciliation Act, PRWORA), in cutting government regulations, and in passing tougher sentencing laws.

Although President Clinton had better relations with urban leaders than his Republican predecessors, he and his HUD Secretary Henry Cisneros did not fundamentally alter the neoliberal trajectory of federal urban programs. If anything, New Democrats accelerated it. Cisneros, a former San Antonio mayor and financial consultant, blended a critique of individual and urban agency dependency (on federal programs) with support for private sector solutions to city problems. HOPE VI fit nicely into this belief system. As Cisneros put it, "a chief goal of the Clinton Administration is to allow residents of public housing projects to buy the homes in which they live." Cisneros incorporated "enterprise zones/communities" into HUD's work, legislation that provided investors with subsidies, tax credits, and fewer regulatory constraints for creating businesses in poor neighborhoods. Cisneros also incorporated much of the repressive legislation, including tougher work rules and punishment of tenants associated with crime, into HUD policies.[10]

During the 1990s, the SFHA underwent a period of transition and instability. San Francisco Mayor Jordan, still obsessed with removing Gilmore, appointed Barbara Meskunas and public housing tenants Jan Allen and Karen Huggins to the SFHA commission based in part on their opposition to Gilmore. The appointments—coupled with the resignation of SFHA Commissioner Lewis Lillian over Jordan's interference in SFHA affairs—paved the way for a majority to replace Gilmore with someone more likely to carry out the mayor's desire to privatize the city's public housing. When the new commission stalled Gilmore's contract negotiations, he responded by taking a position with the Seattle Housing Authority.[11]

The search for his replacement revealed an increasingly divided SFHA leadership and disenfranchised tenant population. In a February 1994 commission meeting, tenants voiced their preference for Paul Fletcher, an African American candidate, over the mayor's choice, Felipe Floresca, who had Filipino roots. Tenants and SFHA Commissioner Robert Boileau raised questions about the process and claimed that the selection of the "Director had been made prior to the formal vote." Commissioner Boileau wanted to hire someone local and with more experience, and he urged a "vote against the selection of Floresca." Even SFHA Commissioner Jan Allen, a recent Jordan appointee, agreed. Reverend Amos Brown, a civil rights leader who later served on the San Francisco Board of Supervisors and as San Francisco NAACP president and SFHA commissioner, spoke in favor of Paul Fletcher and criticized what he saw as a selection process flawed by racism and a lack of transparency. The most recent Jordan appointee, Commissioner Richard Carpeneti, advocated for Floresca. After considerable debate and public comment, commissioners voted five to two in favor of Floresca.[12] Much of the tension behind this decision came from what many in the SFHA community considered excess meddling from Jordan's office and the deepening divisions among those in the SFHA community.

The SFHA's troubles only worsened under the Jordan administration. Floresca barely lasted a year. Jordan's continued meddling in SFHA policies and shoddily assembled commissions contributed to the agency's problems. SFHA commissioners as a group were better known for bickering and policy paralysis than leadership.[13] In an era when housing authorities competed against one another for increasingly limited HUD and foundation grants, the weak SFHA leadership hurt the authority's chances for public housing funding.

SFHA problems were felt at the local level and noticed at the national level. "Nothing gets done," commented SFHA tenant Faye Lacy. "If I see something (in my mailbox) with the word 'commission' on it, I throw it out."[14] Tenants complained about the lack of transparency in SFHA budgets, and they filed lawsuits to force the SFHA to comply with its own and HUD policies.[15] Former Director Gilmore, who continued to follow SFHA developments, was pointed in his criticism of Jordan's SFHA:

> In less than two years, you [Jordan] and the inept commission you appointed have managed to bring this agency to its knees. . . . Your appeal to the federal government not only speaks volumes of your ineptitude, it represents a shameful abdication of your mayoral responsibility.[16]

After several interim directors, Jordan handpicked Shirley Thornton as the next permanent SFHA director. Thornton was former deputy state superintendent of California's Department of Public Education and a retired army colonel—and she had no housing experience.[17] She struggled to move the agency forward, and the SFHA landed on HUD's troubled list again. To his critics, Jordan caused many of the SFHA's internal problems by making the agency "a political football." The same causes of leadership problems at the SFHA, and their effects, dogged other city agencies in this era, a factor that contributed to Jordan's reelection loss to Willie Brown in 1995.[18]

In March 1996, the new San Francisco mayor, with HUD Secretary Cisneros by his side, offered a stinging condemnation of the SFHA. Brown announced that he was firing SFHA Director Shirley Thornton and all seven commissioners. Calling the condition of the SFHA "worse than expected," Cisneros pledged hundreds of millions of HUD dollars and technical assistance to help the troubled SFHA recover.[19] His recovery team arrived on March 4 and included HUD Assistant Secretary Kevin Marchman, who had had a successful three-year stint at the Denver Housing Authority, and former West Coast Regional HUD Director and UCLA Associate Professor of Architecture and Urban Planning Emma McFarland.[20]

In July 1997, Mayor Brown appointed a new slate of commissioners who, after being trained by HUD videos and staff, began managing the SFHA. For day-to-day operations, HUD borrowed Ronnie Davis from the Cuyahoga Metropolitan Housing Authority in Cleveland, where he was a popular administrator who helped remove the agency from HUD's troubled authority list. Davis, who had grown up in public housing in New Orleans, quickly garnered the same kind of positive support in San Francisco. After the HUD receivership ended, Brown recruited Davis to head the SFHA, making the former public housing tenant the tenth SFHA director in five years. Davis championed the authority and its residents. As he stated, "I am here to empower the tenants, the residents of public housing."[21] He lived in the SFHA JFK

Figure 8.1

Protests over the firing of low-paid staff and the hiring of higher-paid management at the main office of the SFHA on August 25, 1994. Lawanna Preston addresses the crowd and asks for answers.

housing project and then the Ping Yuen project.[22] Two years after his arrival, HUD removed the SFHA from its troubled list, and Davis was soon traveling the nation to share his best practices with other housing administrators.[23]

From Gilmore to Davis, SFHA directors implemented neoliberal policies. Directors reduced SFHA worker rights, fostered competition (not solidary) among tenants through self-management initiatives, and applied HUD measures designed to be tough on crime and the poor.[24] Floresca, one of the SFHA directors in this period, eliminated the Office of Resident Services, which had improved tenant services and relations, and replaced some SFHA staff with private contractors and SFHA tenants, who often were hired on a part-time basis. After two months at the job, Floresca told SFHA commissioners that despite "some resistance to his reorganization efforts" and protests from staff and tenants, he would continue with the cuts. He also requested a new personnel policy to start a mandatory drug-testing program for SFHA employees and "enhance the authority of the Executive Director" to be able to fire any nonunion worker without cause.[25]

After Floresca and under the HUD receivership, Kevin Marchman in 1996 immediately laid off 138 of 526 SFHA staff positions, with only one of those positions coming from the executive office, and he planned more cuts to the construction, office, and management personnel at the project level.[26] When authority work needed to be done, SFHA directors often had little choice but to hire contractors. In many ways, these employment changes followed the bipartisan efforts at all levels during this period to "reinvent government" by reducing its size and scope; these reductions also followed broader attacks on the rights, security, and compensation of workers taking place in the private and public sectors.[27]

Another initiative during the reinventing government years was the push by HUD and the SFHA to foster tenants' economic self-sufficiency. To increase tenant employment, Floresca negotiated with the painters union to relax initiation fees and union dues for SFHA tenants who "wished to join the Union." As the national economy and demand for labor expanded, a HUD pilot program in six cities, including San Francisco, subsidized the placement of public housing tenants into apprenticeship programs in the building trades, especially for painters, carpenters, and joiners. Under this program, all public housing jobs required one tenant apprentice for every three journey-level workers employed from the hiring hall. Many of the first job assignments for SFHA tenants involved lead and asbestos removal. In addition to expanding union apprenticeship opportunities, the SHFA continued to employ tenants, though usually in part-time, apprenticeship, or temporary positions and in blue-collar work rather than full-time positions in the main office. Importantly, these tenant workers often did the work that full-time SFHA staff had once done under a union contract.[28]

Under Ronnie Davis, a few SFHA tenants supervised prison laborers from the Garden Project, which was a San Francisco Sheriff Work Alternative Program (SWAP). At SFHA projects, SWAP workers did landscaping and cleaning. The SFHA spent $200,000 a year for tenant supervisor salaries but got the work gangs for free—a labor savings, Davis noted, of almost $800,000. Yet demand for SFHA jobs, whether to supervise prisoners or to remove lead, outstripped supply, and when their SFHA stints were done, comparable jobs in the public or private sector proved difficult to land.[29]

HUD and local authorities tried other ways to move low-income tenants into the labor market. HUD adjusted its ceiling rent policy so that households with a rising income did not automatically trigger a rent increase, eviction, or loss of other social programs. The new policy capped rents, as a percentage of household income and benefits, so that tenants were less penalized for wage work. The new rent policy aimed to accomplish different (sometimes contradictory) goals: "encourage more working families to remain in our developments and set examples for other residents," "diversify our developments by reflecting a greater income mix," and "make public housing transitional housing, a stepping stone into the private housing stock." The assumption behind this new policy was that the previous "Federal and State Welfare system fosters dependency." For many tenants, the rent policy, like a SFHA job or union apprenticeship or workfare, did not always lead to financial independence.[30]

The policies that incentivized wage work did contribute to a larger policy framework for the implementation of the welfare act of 1996 (PRWORA). When Congress and President Clinton ended "welfare as we know it" by replacing Aid to Families with Dependent Children (AFDC) with Temporary Assistance for Needy Families (TANF), the government stripped families of an economic right in place since 1935. The legislation also moved many TANF recipients into the labor market, reducing benefits and lowering their standard of living, and increased work requirements and government surveillance of recipients. Housing authorities, which had access to household data and information, sometimes took on the role of monitoring their tenants for TANF violations.[31]

Surveillance and discipline of tenants took other forms in this era. Section 8 recipients, who by the 1990s outnumbered public housing tenants in San Francisco, had to pay higher deposits and more of their income to landlords.[32] The SFHA continued to use National Tenant Network services to screen prospective tenants and report tenants for violations. Tenants with a negative NTN record, criminal backgrounds, and poor credit increasingly became ineligible for any public housing in the nation. Under Clinton, HUD instructed authorities to enforce a revised 1986 HUD Admissions and Continued Occupancy Policy (ACOP). ACOP established the rules for local authorities in their management of tenants, including everything from pet ownership and the number of occupants per unit to the ways authorities verified and recertified tenant income. In 1997, HUD revised ACOP rules to give authorities more power to transfer tenants to other projects, conduct home visits, and evict tenants. HOPE VI projects, which relocated tenants during construction, offered the SFHA another opportunity to screen tenants—before they returned to their former projects—and this process of recertification often rendered tenants ineligible for projects they once occupied.[33]

In 1996, Clinton pushed HUD to enforce the one-strike policy more vigorously than it had in the past. On the books since 1988, but selectively followed by housing officials, HUD's one-strike policy allowed housing authorities to evict a tenant if anyone in or near his or her house committed a crime. Importantly, tenants charged with violating the one-strike rule did not have access to federal legal aid and thus had a difficult time fighting wrongful evictions.[34] As Kevin Marchman framed the culmination of these new policies and the greater willingness to enforce them when he took over the SFHA, "It's going to be stricter getting in (to public housing) and if you do act up, it's going to be quicker getting you out."[35]

The SFHA became more aggressive on evictions in general, not just for one-strike violations but also for late rent and other ACOP violations.[36] SFHA evictions, which the authority by that point was contracting out to the private sector, increased in the decade, jumping 25 percent from 1994–1995 alone. Tenants fought back, but the one-strike policy became legal with the *HUD v. Rucker* (2001) ruling and handed authorities more power to evict.[37] These expanded efforts of surveillance and discipline ostensibly aimed to restore control over these neighborhoods, cut agency costs, and improve the safety of residents—but they also contributed to the economic insecurity of the poor; to the growing population of poor, often nonwhite men and women in prison; and to the vast number of former inmates whose records severely limited their post-prison employment opportunities and political and economic rights.[38] They also contributed to pushing people out of federal housing programs.

HUD's Operation Safe Home program and anticrime grants also contributed to greater surveillance and discipline of the poor. Operation Safe Home drew from the 1992 report on severely distressed public housing and provided law enforcement with broad powers to conduct warrantless searches and sweeps in low-income neighborhoods. When the program came to San Francisco, SFHA Director Floresca supported it, but some SFHA commissioners—Larry Lee, who was in the plumbers union, and Jan Allen, a tenant—opposed the sweeps. Allen hoped that "this HA, this Commission and tenants do not become encumbered by them, enamoured by them or even to help them; it will hurt the children."[39]

As a tenant, Allen knew firsthand the ways police sweeps and obsession with crime and arrest statistics produced more misery and injustice than assistance for low-income communities. According to a 2001 Government Accountability Office report, Operation Safe Home suffered from a range of problems from juking the numbers to a lack of financial accountability.[40] HUD anticrime grants helped the SFHA pay the San Francisco Police Department for extra services, especially for community policing details, and to contract with private security firms to supplement the SFHA police force. By 2000, the SFHA and HUD were spending millions of dollars every year for such services.[41]

HUD also influenced the SFHA program by supporting tenants who wanted to manage and own their housing. Using technical, financial, and legal support from their housing authority and HUD, tenants across the nation established resident management corporations (RMCs) at their projects. RMCs allowed tenants to manage their project, apply for grants, and ultimately convert their public housing units into individually owned units. The local authority enforced HUD guidelines and paid many of the bills associated with RMCs.

Mayor Jordan regularly leaned on the SFHA to "move in an orderly way to greater resident responsibility for management" and to find ways to foster tenant ownership. For SFHA Director Floresca, RMCs allowed tenants to "embark on a road to self-sufficiency. Resident management," he emphasized, "translates into resident empowerment." And he supported the creation of the Council of Resident Management Corporations (CORMC), which would coordinate the citywide efforts and activities of the individual RMCs.[42]

Not all tenants took the road to self-management, but many did. Encouraged and supported from above, the formation of RMCs facilitated competition among projects and the privatization of SFHA jobs and public housing; however, it also contributed to divisiveness among tenants who had in the past exhibited the kind of cohesion necessary for collective political action for the general welfare of its members and the city's residents. For private consultants willing to navigate HUD rules, the move to tenant self-management was lucrative. As management consultant Bill Higgins noted,

> For property management companies, the public housing arena represents the single best opportunity for new business. If you get on board with HUD, it's a very big new potential market.[43]

With the rise of the dot-com economy in the 1990s, the cumulative effects of HUD and SFHA policies made it difficult for many low- and middle-income residents to remain in the city. Fueled by technological advances in the Internet and personal computers and by speculation in the stock market, the dot-com boom produced a flood of affluent residents in the San Francisco Bay Area. Drawn by jobs and the attractions of the city, high-tech workers gentrified San Francisco's working-class and nonwhite neighborhoods, and companies drove up the cost of commercial space. Landlords skirted city laws and tenant rights, from rent control to clearly defined procedures for no fault evictions. Many residents struggled to keep or secure housing as the cost of living in the city went up. The housing crisis remained—though this time in an era of economic expansion, gentrification, and shifting labor markets that rewarded white-collar workers much more than service and blue-collar workers.[44]

The city's South of Market and eastern neighborhoods attracted many of the affluent workers and new technology companies. For example, David Talbot, founder of Salon.com, moved into Bernal Heights in 1993. Amid the occasional sounds of gunshots, Talbot recalled, the district in the 1990s remained "a glorious urban mix of deeply rooted blue-collar families, underground artists, radical activists, and lesbian settlers." Within a decade, he noted that the gentrification of Bernal Heights diminished both the gunshots and the diversity of the neighborhood. Another resident and community and housing activist, Buck Bagot, also recalled the neighborhood's diversity. "There were Latinos, blacks, American Indians, Samoans, Filipinos. They had good union jobs, and they could raise their families here. Now they're all gone."[45]

Just to the north and east of Bernal Heights, neighborhoods long known for light industry and multicultural, working-class communities (South of Market, Mission, Potrero Hill, Mission Bay, Central Waterfront/Dogpatch) followed the demographic trends in Bernal Heights. A 2002 study by the San Francisco Planning Department found that between 1980 and 2000, the population of one section of South of Market had tripled, from less than 5,400 to 13,500. But this growth came from newer affluent residents while soaring rents and real estate costs drove out some of the existing artists, blue-collar workers, and businesses. Employment in the printing and publishing sector, to give one example, fell from 1,700 workers in 140 shops in 1998 to 660 workers in 80 shops in 2001. Demographically, the number of white households rose from 42 to 48 percent, while Latina/o households went from 7 to 10 percent; other nonwhite numbers fell: Asian households dropped from 31 to 25 percent, and African American households went from 19 to 12 percent.[46]

Of all of the districts, the Mission's residents organized the most resistance to gentrification. In the 1990s, the Mission district remained one of the most diverse districts in the city and had the highest Latina/o population in the city. The area's small businesses reflected the diversity of the residents, especially Latinas/os, and the art community thrived with artists, dancers, photographers, and writers. Dance studios, colorful murals depicting indigenous culture and protests against

United States intervention in Central America, and the annual Carnival parade reflected the creative energy and politics of the district's residents. When affluent professionals and technology workers began moving into the area, landlords raised rents on homes. Commercial rents also rose as technology companies moved to the area. Developers responded by creating new live/work lofts and high-end condominiums and commercial office space. From 1994 to 1998, rents for housing rose more than 56 percent in the district. In 1998, a one-bedroom apartment averaged $1,245 a month, and almost three-quarters of all low-income tenants in the district (and San Francisco and Oakland in general) spent more than 50 percent of their income on housing. No-fault evictions skyrocketed to the highest levels in the nation, garnering attention from around the globe, as landlords evicted tenants whose rent-controlled units were below market rates. The evictions hit the city's Latina/o community hard. In fact, San Francisco's Latina/o population declined in the decade—the only major U.S. city to experience this demographic trend.[47]

The social and economic look and feel of the district began to change. The number of white residents increased, and establishments that catered to affluent customers replaced existing neighborhood and ethnic businesses and art and dance studies. While many saw progress in these changes, others understood the injustice that was occurring. "By focusing on the new restaurants, bars, the dot-com parties, and the new work/live lofts," scholar Nancy Mirabal noted, "it was easy for those moving into the neighborhood to rationalize the large numbers of evictions, the displacement of long-term residents, the uprooting of families, and the end of community agencies and organizations as simply a necessary part of the economic (r)evolution of the Mission District."[48]

Figure 8.2
"Resist the Dot Con" billboard in the Mission district illustrates antigentrification public art and protest.

Organizing for tenant rights and community control in the Mission district took several forms. Some individuals and organizations targeted the sources and visible manifestations of gentrification. Tenant activist Kevin Keating, who moved to the Mission in 1988, formed the Yuppie Eradication Project, which, while few in number, plastered the district with posters that advocated the destruction of property likely owned by the affluent. Directly inspired by the CIA sabotage manual used in 1980s counterinsurgency campaigns in Central America, one poster, entitled "Here Are a Few Ways to Welcome Rich People to the Mission," encouraged residents to add water to gasoline tanks, use keys to scratch cars, and clog plumbing in high-end restaurants. A fair amount of damage to expensive cars and businesses happened. The police arrested Keating, though he was never convicted. The Yuppie Eradication Project drew national attention for its violent message, but it also raised awareness of the effects of gentrification.[49]

In addition to YEP's agitprop efforts, artists and grassroots community organizations also launched a campaign against evictions and changes in the Mission district. Graffiti, posters, and billboards appeared through the district. In 2000, artists Jaime Cortez, René García, John Jota Leaños, Gerardo Pérez, and Monica Praba Pilar created a public art and street performance with the billboard mural "Ese, the Last Mexican in the Mission" on Bryant and 24th Street to critique the ethnic displacement happening in the district. Parodying the story of Ishi, the last member of the California Yahi tribe made famous by University of California anthropologist Alfred Kroeber at the turn of the twentieth century, the artists created a narrative about an elusive Mexican who lost his studio and was now living and hiding in Dolores Park. When authorities captured "Ese," they took him to the UC Department of Cultural Anthropology for observation, giving researchers an opportunity to learn more about "pre-digital behavior" from the last Mexican in the Mission.[50]

The Mission Anti-Displacement Coalition (MAC) brought together individuals, artists, and community groups that targeted particular landlords and developers for public shaming and held rallies and marches with hundreds of people participating. MAC also became involved in community discussions about the future of the SFHA's Valencia Gardens, which became a possible HOPE VI project. Latina/o residents played a vital role in this collective resistance and were able to maintain many of their institutions and even housing. According to urban geographer Brian J. Godfrey, their ability to defend against gentrification in this era was based on their social and cultural bonds, a shared identity and history connected to place, and a sense of "being under siege [that] heightened the feelings of ethnic and social solidarity."[51]

Across the city, similar housing pressures produced a decline in the African American population, especially in the Western Addition and Hunters Point districts. The changing labor market and persistence of racial discrimination left many

African Americans at a disadvantage in the 1990s. Many struggled to stay in the city. One Western Addition resident, Shanika Long, noted that her income as a clerk at Labor Ready was insufficient for economic security in the city. She wanted to "live where black people can afford to buy houses and rear children" and felt that she was "being pushed out of San Francisco. . . . The community now is, like, dead."[52] Edna Cooper was forced out of her Fillmore apartment in 1998, and after a year of hunting for Section 8 housing she failed to find a unit in the Western Addition or in Hunters Point.[53] African American businesses and institutions from bookstores to churches began to decline in number and influence in the district. In the area of affordable housing, neither the SFHA nor the city's expanding nonprofit housing sector produced enough homes to keep many African American families in the city. As the city's homeless newspaper *Street Sheet* predicted in 1996, the

> loss of public housing units represents a new effort towards gentrification. In a few years, there will only be a vestige of the African American community left in San Francisco. For a city that prides itself on diversity, this forced displacement of low-income African Americans is not only hypocritical, it is racist.[54]

Although more SFHA housing would have helped stem the outflow of African Americans, the rising cost of private sector housing drove their exodus. In 1996, the median family home in the Bayview district cost $129,000, but by 2008, even after a year of declining prices, it had risen to $570,000. From 1992 to 2008, the Western Addition and Bayview–Hunters Point districts became more diverse, but African American homeowners and renters alike found it more difficult to stay.

Figure 8.3
"Ese, the Last Mexican in the Mission," a performance and public art project in 2000 to protest gentrification by Los Uber-Locos.

Some African Americans moved to the East Bay, where housing costs were cheaper, but in San Mateo, Santa Clara, and Alameda counties, as in San Francisco, inequality and housing costs caused an overall decline in the African American population. The number of African Americans in San Francisco dropped from 79,039 in 1990 to 60,515 in 2000 and to 48,870 in 2010.[55]

This out-migration was so great that in 2007 Mayor Gavin Newsom created a task force to study why so many African Americans were leaving the city and what could be done to reverse the trend. The heart of the problem, according to the report, was insufficient household income, with African Americans earning half as much as whites in the city. The report also found that African Americans worried about their children's education, public safety (related to the dangers of crime as well as the police themselves), the effects of redevelopment projects, and, as Shanika Long noted above, the loss of community caused by out-migration. In contrast to the direct actions and social and cultural bonds used by residents of the Mission district to fight displacement, African Americans often tried to work within the city's political structures and with politicians to find ways to end the out-migration.[56]

Across the city, residents organized for greater housing rights and control over the direction of their neighborhoods. Compared to the 1960s and 1970s, this mobilization came more from tenants in private housing than in public housing, and their solutions focused more on private and nonprofit sector programs than on the SFHA. The San Francisco Tenants Union, in operation since 1970, continued to inform tenants about how to fight against landlords who wanted to convert apartments into condominiums, sidestep rent control, and conduct no-cause evictions. In 1996, a coalition of organizations created the Eviction Defense Collaborative because members of those organizations believed that "the poor and vulnerable of our community deserve equal access before the law."[57]

In 2003, housing activists created the San Francisco Community Land Trust as a membership organization to marshal public and private funds to turn apartments into tenant-run cooperatives free from the speculative marketplace. The first of a growing number of their projects opened in 2009 in Chinatown. The Community Land Trust also became a resource for residents interested in affordable housing options.[58] Across the city, Hunters Point activists organized around two neighborhood issues. They participated in development plans, especially the Lennar Corporation's 702-acre project, with the goal of increasing the number of affordable housing units there. They also pressured government agencies to ensure a proper cleanup of the superfund site at the Hunters Point shipyard.[59]

In addition to organizational, individual, and artistic efforts to push against gentrification, tenants and their allies also tried to expand tenant rights and affordable housing at the ballot box. The 1999 mayoral race was infused with tenant and neighborhood concerns. Willie Brown was up for reelection. Just weeks before the November election, San Francisco Supervisor Tom Ammiano joined the race as the champion of tenant rights and progressive politics and hammered away at Brown for catering to big business, landlords, and developers at the expense of ordinary residents. As San Francisco author Rebecca Solnit wrote, the election "was a war of sorts about what kind of a city San Francisco should be, and for whom." Ammiano obtained enough write-in votes to force a runoff, but lost the election to Brown, who spent millions of dollars to win 58 percent of the vote. Ammiano carried the South of Market districts hit hardest by gentrification, the Upper Market–Eureka Valley area whose residents supported the gay candidate, and the younger voters, especially renters. He also got the progressive vote. Brown did well with Asian and African Americans and Republicans, maintained AFL-CIO backing, and carried the homeowner vote on the west side of the city by portraying Ammiano as a radical.[60]

The election symbolized the complexity of working-class politics and struggles in the city. Just one year later, in the 2000 election, tenants again organized against the pro-development Proposition K, which had the support of property owners, the Chamber of Commerce, and Mayor Willie Brown. Tenants and their allies supported Proposition L, which would close development loopholes and restrict property rights. Unlike the Ammiano loss in 1999, the pro-tenant coalition helped to sway voters to reject Proposition K and vote in Proposition L, two legislative victories for tenants and evidence of political support for government action in the area of economic rights.[61]

During the era, public housing tenants continued to engage with political issues, but they lacked the organizational strength of the past. SFHA tenants worked on voter registration and get-out-the-vote campaigns, receiving assistance from the San Francisco League of Women Voters, A. Philip Randolph Institute, San Francisco, and the SFHA. In 2006, the precarious financial state of public housing and proposed HUD cuts prompted SFHA commissioners to try to mobilize tenants. Commissioner Reverend George Woodruff thought a voter registration campaign needed to commence and the SFHA should "get our residents as educated as possible" so they could "vote for those that have the best interests of public housing at heart." Commissioner Reverend Amos Brown suggested a national political campaign "with other public housing authorities." He said, "we need to be just as astute, sophisticated, and determined as our adversaries are." Generally, SFHA senior tenants answered such calls or took the initiative for political action more often than younger tenants. By the twenty-first century the PHTA, once a political force locally and nationally, had lost much of its political power. Project level tenant associations remained active in shaping the direction of their homes and neighborhoods but had a mixed record of acting in solidarity with other tenants.[62]

Discussions of a senior housing project in the South of Market area illustrated the complexity of SFHA tenant politics. When the SFHA proposed adding eighty-five units to its Clementina Senior project, residents weighed in on the benefits and problems of the proposal. Planned to be built over an SFHA-owned parking lot, the development would make the SFHA a partner with the nonprofit housing organization Tenants and Owners Development Agency (TODCO, formerly Tenants and Owners in Opposition to Redevelopment or TOOR). TODCO would own and manage the building, provide tenant services and landscaping, and lease the land from the SFHA.

The project had HUD and mayoral support, but Clementina tenants and neighbors offered mixed reactions. At an October 25, 2001, SFHA Commission meeting, Clementina resident Clara Nesca said that the project would have "a negative effect on residents" because the building would decrease natural light and ventilation in units and obstruct views. Jim Berk, a neighbor, thought the area was "overcrowded already." Clementina Tenant Association President Abdul Kadir said his members were against the proposal because of the ways it would inconvenience tenants. Samuel Kwok, Clementina resident and former president of the Clementina Tenant Association, spoke in favor of the proposal and said we in Clementina should appreciate our "good fortune and not forget the thousands of other people who are still waiting and are not so fortunate." The crowd booed him.[63]

Other SFHA tenants and community groups supported the TODCO–SFHA project. Lydia Garcia of the Senior Action Network reminded the audience about the ten-year waiting list for SFHA senior housing and urged people to "not be selfish." San Le Chu from the Ping Yuen Resident Association stated

> Ten years ago there was the same situation of using the parking lot to build senior housing at Ping Yuen. The residents opposed that project too but 10 years later, everyone is happy and living in harmony in Chinatown. . . . [We must show compassion to] people who have no place to live.

Tenant activist Bao Yen Chen said she "has been lobbying for over 10 years," and there was a need "to be solidly together to fight for and preserve more housing. It is not necessary for those who have housing to be selfish—others need a place to live."[64]

In December 2001, the SFHA approved the project, and it was named the Eugene Coleman House after the tireless advocate for the rights of the poor in the city. It opened in 2006 under the control of TODCO, and, although it expanded affordable housing units in the city, the project offered another example of a housing authority giving up ownership and management of housing units.[65]

San Francisco's HOPE VI projects had many similarities with the SFHA–TODCO partnership but on a larger scale. HUD awarded the SFHA five HOPE

VI projects: North Beach Place in North Beach, Hayes Valley (in Hayes Valley), Plaza East in the Western Addition, Bernal Dwellings in Bernal Heights, and Valencia Gardens in the Mission. HOPE VI funds did not provide for the full replacement of all existing units, so the SFHA used creative financing for the projects. In the case of North Beach Place, HUD provided $23.2 million of the $106 million total budget. The rest of the funding came from bonds, nonprofit builders, and for-profit investors and contractors who would receive residential and commercial rental income, tax credits, building contracts, and management and consulting fees.[66] The other SFHA HOPE VI projects had similar kinds of financing and structuring. Significantly, the five projects resulted in a net loss of 18 percent of public housing units, though if the figures included the number of bedrooms (many family units were lost in these projects), the losses were greater (see Table 8.1). But San Francisco did keep more of its public housing units than other cities, whose housing authorities lost on average about 50 percent of their housing from HOPE VI projects.[67]

Perhaps no SFHA–HOPE VI project captured the city's perception and misperception of public housing better than Valencia Gardens. The wrecking crews demolished the Mission district project in 2001 amid almost as much public fanfare as the demolition of the infamous Pruitt-Igoe public housing project in St. Louis. Valencia Garden tenants like their counterparts in the other HOPE VI projects worked in the construction, relocation, and support services that were needed for the project. When Valencia Gardens reopened in 2006, the project offered townhome-style units influenced by Oscar Newman's defensible space concept, a tenant association office, a community room, and learning and daycare centers. The new units were larger than previous ones. The project also reinstalled eight beloved animal sculptures created by Beniamino Bufano during the 1940s in the lobby and plaza.

Table 8.1
Data from SFHA, *Minutes,* and Ilene Lelchuk, "They Don't Call the Project Outta Control Anymore: Success of Renewal Using HOPE VI Is Evident All Around," *San Francisco Chronicle* (March 28, 2005).

HOPE VI Projects in San Francisco

HOPE VI Projects	Year Built	Original No. of Units	HOPE VI Grant (in millions)	Total Cost (in millions)	Reopened	Post–HOPE VI No. of Units	Lost Units
Valencia Gardens	1942	260	$23.2	$71.7	2006	260	0
North Beach Place	1952	229	$23.0	$106.3	2004	229	0
Bernal Dwellings	1953	208	$29.8	$39.4	2001	160	48
Plaza East	1956	276	$20.2	$43.1	2002	193	83
Hayes Valley	1962	294	$22.0	$42.5	1998–99	195	99
Total		1,267	$131.2	$303.0		1,037	230

To fund and manage the project, the SFHA partnered with the nonprofit and private sectors. The Mission Housing Development Corporation (an expanding nonprofit housing organization with projects across the city) and the John Stewart Company (a San Francisco-based property management company) developed and managed the new building. Although Valencia Gardens did not sport thousands of feet of commercial rental properties, as did the renovated North Beach Place, it too had turned management and services over to the nonprofit and private sectors. Many residents and the media praised Valencia Gardens for the flowerpots resting on front stoops, indoor washing machines and dryers, and moms walking hand in hand with their children by newly planted trees—all sights in stark contrast to the old days when the project was known for its "institutional design" and "decrepit block structure, drug dealing, violence, rodent infestation, and obsolete plumbing and sewage system."[68]

The new Valencia Gardens was also important for other reasons. Roughly 50 percent of previous Valencia Gardens tenants returned to the new project, though in the case of families the figure was lower. The physical improvements to the project were welcomed by the tenants, community, and city, but they also helped affluent residents and businesses feel more comfortable settling in the neighborhood. As was happening in other working-class districts, these changes associated with the new Valencia Gardens advanced the process of gentrification in the Mission. For tenants, the spirit of community at the project and city level, as well as their activism, decreased. Half of the original tenants did not return. The open courtyards that fostered social interactions were replaced with smaller highly regulated spaces

Figure 8.4
The new Valencia Gardens project, with defensible space, was part of the HOPE VI program and contributed to the gentrification process in the Mission district.

by the John Stewart company. Tenants also increasingly worried about punishment and eviction by the company. Tenants were divided by the kinds of housing they were in (public or low income), and they no longer had the same landlord (the SFHA) as did other public housing tenants in the city.[69]

Although HOPE VI projects were popular with the media, the public, politicians, and some tenants, the HUD program lost its luster under President George W. Bush, and this prompted San Francisco leaders to create new affordable housing programs. By 2006, the Bush administration had reduced HOPE VI funding by more than 90 percent from its peak in 1994 ($755 million for twenty-six projects across the nation in 1994 versus $72 million for four projects in 2006).[70] Public housing authority subsidies were also reduced in this period. Reflecting on the recent federal housing allocations, SFHA Commissioner George Brown noted that HUD policy changes seemed to be "another ploy to do away with all public housing authorities in the country."[71] Some of Brown's concern related to the mounting maintenance costs for SFHA projects and the thousands of applicants on the SFHA waiting list as much as to the neoliberal dismantling of the welfare state.

With federal funds disappearing and private sector development in mind, San Francisco Mayor Gavin Newsom floated the idea of HOPE SF, a city-led program that would combine city funding, private investment, and nonprofit providers to take over the remaining SFHA family projects. Newsom justified HOPE SF with a critique of the SFHA program and the promise of reducing crime, providing jobs, improved housing, and creating opportunities and self-sufficiency for tenants. HOPE SF would focus on Potrero Terrace, Sunnydale, Westside Courts, and Alice Griffith—all, for sure, in need of major renovations or replacement. Once completed, the SFHA would still own the land but HUD funds and the project management of the buildings would be turned over to nonprofits, management companies, or resident management corporations, showing how federal policies became local policies in terms of neoliberal models of "revitalizing" public housing and providing residents with affordable housing. Few in the city seemed concerned that the SFHA had lost its position in overseeing the city's affordable housing.[72]

From the perspective of the city's political leadership, Hunters Point was the most pressing target for HOPE SF projects, in part because public housing upgrades there were crucial to a massive development planned by the Lennar Corporation in the district. The Lennar Corporation's project had the backing of Mayor Newsom, Dianne Feinstein (her husband Richard Blum was a Lennar partner), Congresswoman Nancy Pelosi (Dem., San Francisco), and the local press. After a massive lobbying and political campaign, voters also got behind the multibillion-dollar project, which included not only commercial and retail space but also parks, trails, a new stadium for the San Francisco 49ers football team, and up to 12,000 homes. In this redevelopment project, Lennar and city officials promised the community jobs, low-income housing, and a commitment to not displace current residents. There was also a commitment to clean up the toxic mess left by the Navy's operations.[73]

But African American residents in the district were skeptical. Community organizer Dr. Espanola Jackson drew on decades of experience in civil rights, housing, and social justice work when she analyzed the Lennar proposal. She critiqued Lennar for its history of corruption and its abysmal record of cleaning up the toxic waste in the early stages of the project. She also slammed the company's plan, and the city government's support of it, because the project did not take into account global warming or the ability of African Americans to remain there. She said, "Because of global warming, that entire area is going to be underwater," but before that happens, she continued, "only white folks will be able to afford" the Lennar homes. When thinking about Lennar's plans for the area, Bayview–Hunters Point resident Charlie Walker stated, "Redevelopment destroyed the Western Addition. And now they're destroying Bayview–Hunters Point. Black people are not leaving San Francisco—we are being driven out."[74]

In 2006, the San Francisco Housing Authority owned 6,400 public housing units spread over 53 sites. When combined with Section 8 housing, the SFHA served 35,000 low-income tenants, including a handful of displaced tenants from Hurricane Katrina in New Orleans in 2005. The SFHA expanded its programs and services for those displaced from Katrina and for veterans returning from the wars in Afghanistan and Iraq, showing some of the ways the authority tried to do good.[75]

Demand for SFHA housing remained high. In 2006, the waiting list still numbered in the thousands; four-person households were eligible for HUD housing with household incomes as high as $90,500.[76] Poor and middle-income households continued to quietly leave San Francisco—family by family, individual by individual—as the city's employers, landlords, government, and nonprofit programs failed to find a formula to keep a diverse population in the city. The transfer of SFHA housing to the private and nonprofit sectors meant not only the erosion of public control over some housing and jobs, but the erosion of a seventy-year experiment to make housing, however imperfect, part of the economic and civil rights of citizenship. At the start of the twenty-first century—at the convergence of work, housing, and redevelopment—those rights, and in many ways the heart and soul of the city, were further eroded.

In 2006, 100 years after the great earthquake and fire and on the eve of the Great Recession and massive collapse of the housing industry, the SFHA had lost much of its political support and capacity to provide and manage low-cost housing to the residents of San Francisco. Presidential appointments, new HUD policies, and local elites had contributed to the diminished power and resources of the city's housing authority. The SFHA, like other local housing authorities in the nation, had fewer public housing units to offer residents; instead, the authority oversaw the transfer and administration of HUD funds to resident management corporations and nonprofit and for-profit housing operations. Many SFHA housing projects continued to suffer from maintenance problems, declining quality, and neighborhoods marked by crime and inequality. More broadly, neoliberal policies unrelentingly diminished social programs and disciplined the poor—from HOPE VI and TANF to one-strike penalties for public housing tenants.

Not surprisingly, as the reputation and power of the SFHA declined, fewer and fewer residents and local elites turned to the housing authority to address the city's affordable housing shortage and crumbling economic and civil rights. The loss of effective SFHA tenant organizations reduced tenant power to participate meaningfully at the city level, though seniors and tenants at some projects did contribute to the decisions that affected their homes and communities. In meaningful ways, housing activists turned to the vote, community organizations, and nonprofits to expand affordable housing for housing. In the case of the Mission district, residents drew on a shared identity and used direct actions to push back against gentrification with some success.

Low- and middle-income residents struggled to live in the city, and more and more, people, especially nonwhites, left San Francisco. The lack of affordable housing and the financial struggles of many residents reflected the structural problems of an economy that since the 1970s saw wealth and income inequality grow and housing costs outpace wages.[77] The decline of the SFHA program reflected those trends and curtailed the SFHA's ability to house residents in the City by the Bay.

CONCLUSION

LIKE MANY URBAN AREAS, San Francisco has always had an affordable housing short-age. In 2017, the median home price in the city hovered around $1.3 million, and median rent for a two-bedroom apartment averaged $4,200 a month. Boosted by another high-tech housing bubble, the higher-than-average cost of housing in the City by the Bay has spurred lively discussions of the housing problem and its consequences, as well as the idea of housing as a right. But for more than a century, landlords (the SFHA included) and developers in the city have failed to provide enough housing, especially for the city's workers and low-income families, as well as the elderly, the disabled, the poor, and nonwhite households.

There are many social costs of unaffordable housing markets. When individuals and families lack access to affordable housing, many double or triple up with friends or relatives; others sacrifice food, health care and childcare, leisure, education, and other necessities to make rent payments; still others must live in dangerous dwell-ings, temporary shelters, their cars, squats, or on the streets. The 2017 San Francisco "Homeless Census" found that of the 7,499 individuals without homes that year, 69 percent had housing in the city *before* losing their homes. In eviction cases, individuals in and out of San Francisco lose their shelter and personal belongings, and they suffer both financially and emotionally. High housing costs also force many to leave their neighborhoods and even their cities.

San Francisco's shortage of affordable housing is not unique, as national and in-ternational urban housing costs have outpaced wages in past decades. In 2017, Joseph Chamie, former director of the United Nations Population Division, estimated that 150 million individuals, about 2 percent of the world's population, were without a home, and 1.6 billion lived in substandard housing in urban areas alone.[1]

From its origins in progressive and New Deal era reforms to its shrinking role in the twenty-first century, the history of San Francisco's public housing offers important lessons for understanding the challenges of making—and keeping—af-fordable housing in a capitalist economy. This history also offers ways to relate the struggles for economic and civil rights to the rise and decline of the welfare state and to competing liberal ideas about the proper role of government. During the progressive era, proponents of the "new liberalism" favored government intervention in the economy as the solution to the labor question; this growing political group included housing reformers who crusaded for safe, affordable housing. Later, housing reformers, workers, and tenants sought an expanded state role through the New Deal and Great Society. Such efforts consistently evoked an anti-statist response that backed smaller government, individual responsibility, and volunteer efforts as the best way to address housing and other forms of inequality. By the start of the twenty-first century, neoliberal ideas about reducing the welfare state and the government's role in the economy had significant influence on both housing policy discussions and actual policies as evidenced in the case of the SFHA.

Housing the City by the Bay has examined the arc of urban liberalism over a century of U.S. history as its development and changes influenced housing activism. During the progressive era, the labor question drove discussions in the Atlantic World about the best way to ensure the economic security and political rights of citizens while increasing reform efforts. Housing reformers, often affluent and highly educated, were influenced by their sympathy for the working poor as well as by their interest in successful models of large-scale European housing and planning experiments. In San Francisco, these reformers advocated for a range of government regulations and programs to improve the city's housing and planning, though—like many progressives seeking other reforms—they failed to address the issue of racial discrimination. Nor did they meaningfully invite workers and tenants to join their housing efforts. That failure to mobilize the city's workers and their organizations meant that no meaningful pressure was exerted on landlords and their government allies, and as a result few reforms came to fruition. But the discussions about, and to some extent the frustration with, the housing reform efforts provided valuable experience and knowledge for many in the city who would soon push for federal housing programs during the New Deal, when government homes became a reality with the SFHA.

The New Deal drove two important developments in how citizens understood the government's role in the housing market and the rights of citizens. First, in light of the failure of private and corporate efforts to bring meaningful recovery prior to Franklin Roosevelt's election, more and more people throughout the nation accepted the view that government should promote recovery by seeking full (or fuller) employment through funding public works programs such as the Civilian Conservation Corps, Works Progress Administration, and Tennessee Valley Authority. In his second inaugural address, Franklin Roosevelt memorably reported that he saw around him one-third of the nation ill-housed, ill-clad, and ill-nourished. New Dealers and their constituencies shared these concerns, and together they sought a range of legislation aimed to provide recognition for a set of economic rights—among them, steady employment, adequate housing, income security for children and the elderly, and workplace protections, when the private sector failed to do so. Mostly enacted into law, these New Deal legislative efforts, which included public housing, represented a distinct transition in policy thinking about economic rights from previous classical liberalism (or laissez-faire) and Hoover's associative liberalism during his role at the Commerce Department and in the White House. As the New Deal gained momentum, the U.S. government began to build a welfare state, though not with the degree of protection and provision that European welfare states provided.

Second, and in line with these new initiatives, the New Deal's attention to the public housing program motivated ordinary residents to organize around class interests and identities. Compared to private sector housing, where property owners make decisions about housing and development in their own interests and where tenants are rarely organized politically, the SFHA offered an institution through which the wider public participated in shaping housing, urban development, and economic and civil rights. Women, nonwhites, and workers seized this opportunity, and, however imperfect the policy process was, their participation marked a turning point in how decisions were made in areas such as low-income housing, civil rights, employment, and even public planning. The federal government's legislative and political support of the SFHA was vital to these new, disruptive ways of thinking about, participating in, and shaping policies related to housing, civil rights, planning, and the welfare state.

From World War II to the 1970s, the SFHA program was a political target for city residents on all sides of the major issues of the period. SFHA elites and organized political groups greatly impacted how the SFHA and other city institutions either reinforced or chipped away at inequality. When John Beard took the SFHA helm in 1943, his appointment signaled a victory for many of the city's whites who wanted SFHA projects to maintain segregation in the city. For the next twenty-two years, civil rights activists and tenant groups struggled to oust Beard and pushed commissioners to end discriminatory practices in tenant selection and hiring practices. In the area of participatory policy making, the most promising movement to emerge was the San Francisco Public Housing Tenants Association, which emboldened poor, propertyless tenants and their allies to pursue policies that would improve their housing, broaden their civil and economic rights, and influence government at the city and national level.

For SFHA tenants, the public housing program offered a source of economic security, community, and a vehicle to address economic and racial inequality. To sustain these gains, their mobilization ensured that the SFHA remained a powerful force for responsive government. By the 1960s, their actions also revealed that ordinary people desired a fuller set of government programs to ensure economic security, a desire that sharply contrasted with the views of most of the local and national political and economic elites who had risen to power in the decades following World War II.

This growing political gap was connected to broader struggles over the future of the U.S. welfare state. By the 1970s, a bipartisan turn reduced social and urban programs—partly due to the rise of the New Right and partly due to a backlash against the federal government's attempts to assist the poor, nonwhites, women, and the environment. The full expression of this shift, and the acceleration of neoliberal values and policies, happened with the 1980 election of Ronald Reagan. Building on earlier cuts to social programs from local and national legislation, many of Reagan's policies aimed to further dismantle public housing and social programs. In pursuit of neoliberal policies, Congress moved more resources from public housing authorities to private and nonprofit institutions.

In San Francisco, the upsurge in tenant participation and power coincided with these federal efforts to weaken the nation's public housing program, including the transfer of public housing to the private market. As a result, the city's public housing tenants had to wrestle with federal funding cuts and new legislation that moved SFHA control of resources to the private sector. HUD's neoliberal policies that facilitated the leased housing programs, resident management corporations, nonprofit housing providers, and HOPE VI and HOPE SF projects were all examples of this private sector shift. With every such program, the SFHA lost more control of the city's nonspeculative housing, while its influence on the city's social, political, and built landscape diminished. These changes also scattered tenants across the city in different kinds of housing and with different landlords, a development that made launching and maintaining class-based organizing more difficult than when tenants were all housed in SFHA permanent projects.

The history of the SFHA and the political activism it inspired offers insight into past attempts at solving the housing problem that continues to afflict cities in the United States. For a good portion of the twentieth century, the idea that all residents had a right to a home and to a voice in their housing and communities drove discussions about alternatives to private housing. The existence and public nature of the SFHA was crucial to those discussions and to meeting the needs of at least some of the city's residents.

But for more than forty years now, political leaders in and out of San Francisco have abandoned public housing as the option to meet the nation's housing needs. Instead, government officials have subsidized mortgages and socialized the risk of building, selling, and financing private homes, farms, and commercial properties.

HUD resources favor non-public housing programs for low-income housing assistance. Landlords have been allowed to skirt rent control and anti-eviction laws, transgressions that have contributed to poverty and inequality. When tenants hand over a part of their income to their landlords, a powerful class of propertied individuals and capitalist institutions benefit, and their interests often clash with the goal of ensuring housing for all.

This transfer of income and wealth has contributed to structures of racial, economic, and gender inequality—in and out of the United States. Political leaders have long sided more closely with landlords than with tenants. In 1965, an astute San Francisco tenant, Mildred Van Reed, complained to President Lyndon Johnson about the ways "outlandish rents" and "landlords are placing everyone in the 'Poverty Group.'" She urged Johnson to take action, but she was skeptical because our "Congressmen, Mayor, Governor, etc., hesitate to do anything regarding this rent deal as they themselves are landlords and own most of the property concerned." She wondered "what they would do if the shoe were on the other foot."[2]

Rather than wait for political leaders to act, citizens will have to organize to change the ways our homes are built, owned, and managed. To do this, tenants will need to organize a broad-based movement, redirect the dominant political culture to discussions and policies geared around economic and civil rights, and make housing and urban development democratic. As demonstrated in this book, residents in one city imagined ways to use their housing authority to make housing more responsive, accessible, and compatible with democratic traditions. The history of the SFHA suggests that with more funding, more tenant participation, and a greater federal commitment to public housing, local and regional housing authorities could be used once again not only to improve housing, boost community-based urban development, and achieve full employment, but also to foster democratic principles and practices in communities around the nation.

APPENDIX

SAN FRANCISCO BAY AREA COUNTY POPULATIONS, 1890–2010

	Alameda	Contra Costa	Marin	Napa	San Francisco	San Mateo	Santa Clara	Solano	Sonoma	Total Bay Area	Total Calif.	Total U.S.
1890	93,864	13,515	13,072	16,411	298,997	10,087	48,005	20,946	32,721	547,618	1,213,398	62,947,714
1900	130,197	18,046	15,702	16,451	342,782	12,094	60,216	24,143	38,480	658,111	1,48,5053	75,994,575
1910	246,131	31,674	25,114	19,800	416,912	26,585	83,539	27,559	48,394	925,708	2,377,549	91,972,266
1920	344,177	53,889	27,342	20,678	506,676	36,781	100,676	40,602	52,090	1,182,911	3,426,861	105,710,620
1930	474,883	78,608	41,648	22,897	634,394	77,405	145,118	40,834	62,222	1,578,009	5,677,251	122,775,046
1940	513,011	100,450	52,907	28,503	634,536	111,782	174,949	49,118	69,052	1,734,308	6,907,387	131,669,275
1950	740,315	298,984	85,619	46,603	775,357	235,659	290,547	104,833	103,405	2,681,322	10,586,223	150,697,361
1960	908,209	409,030	146,820	65,890	740,316	444,387	642,315	134,597	147,375	3,638,939	15,717,204	179,323,175
1970	1,071,446	556,116	208,652	79,140	715,674	557,361	1,065,313	171,989	204,885	4,630,576	19,953,134	203,302,031
1980	1,105,379	656,380	222,568	99,199	678,974	587,329	1,295,071	235,203	299,681	5,179,784	23,667,902	226,545,805
1990	1,279,182	803,732	230,096	110,765	723,959	649,623	1,497,577	340,421	388,222	6,023,577	29,760,021	248,718,000
2000	1,443,741	948,816	247,289	124,279	776,733	707,161	1,682,585	394,542	458,614	6,783,760	33,871,648	281,421,906
2010	1,510,271	1,049,025	252,409	136,484	805,235	718,451	1,781,642	413,344	483,878	7,150,739	37,253,956	308,745,538

Data from U.S. Census Bureau;
http://www.dof.ca.gov;
http://www.bayareacensus.ca.gov/index.html

STATE POPULATION GROWTH, 1900–2010

	Washington	Oregon	California	Total U.S.
1900	518,103	413,536	1,485,053	75,994,575
1910	1,141,990	672,765	2,377,549	91,972,266
1920	1,356,621	783,389	3,426,861	105,710,620
1930	1,563,396	953,786	5,677,251	122,775,046
1940	1,736,191	1,089,684	6,907,387	131,669,275
1950	2,378,963	1,521,341	10,586,223	150,697,361
1960	2,853,214	1,768,687	15,717,204	179,323,175
1970	3,409,169	2,091,385	19,953,134	203,302,031
1980	4,132,156	2,633,105	23,667,902	226,545,805
1990	4,866,692	2,842,321	29,760,021	248,718,000
2000	5,894,121	3,421,399	33,871,648	281,421,906
2010	6,724,540	3,831,074	37,253,956	308,745,538

Data from U.S. Census Bureau;
ca.gov;
access.wa.gov;
https://www.pdx.edu/prc/about-prc

Appendix A.3

WEST COAST MAJOR CITY/COUNTY POPULATIONS, 1900–2010

	Seattle (King County)	Portland (Multnomah County)	Los Angeles County	San Francisco County
1900	110,053	103,167	170,298	342,782
1910	284,638	226,261	504,131	416,912
1920	389,273	275,898	936,455	506,676
1930	463,517	338,241	2,208,492	634,394
1940	504,980	355,099	2,785,643	634,536
1950	732,992	471,537	4,151,687	775,357
1960	935,014	522,813	6,038,771	740,316
1970	1,159,375	556,667	7,041,980	715,674
1980	1,269,898	562,640	7,477,238	678,974
1990	1,507,305	583,887	8,863,164	723,959
2000	1,737,046	660,486	9,519,338	776,733
2010	1,931,249	735,334	9,818,605	805,235

Data from U.S. Census Bureau;
ca.gov;
access.wa.gov;
https://www.pdx.edu/prc/about-prc

Appendix A.4

ABSORPTION OF VACANT LAND IN THE COMMUNITY AREAS OF SAN FRANCISCO, 1921–1948

(EXCLUDES TIDELAND)

District	Vacant Land (Acres)		Percent of Vacant Land Lost Between 1921–1948
	1921	1948	
(1) Park-Presidio	513	39	92.4
(2) Richmond	107	50	53.3
(3) Marina	269	28	89.3
(4) Russian Hill-N. Beach	167	37	87.8
(5) Western Addition	108	53	50.9
(6) Buena Vista	631	495	21.6
(7) Mission	457	317	30.6
(8) Potrero-Bernal	324	133	59.0
(9) Bayview (Hunters Point)	990	469	52.6
(10) Outer Mission	786	196	73.1
(11) West of Twin Peaks	2,272	830	73.5
(12) Sunset	1,763	315	82.1
Total	*8,397*	*2,962*	*64.7*

Data from Department of City Planning, San Francisco, *Planning 1*, 3 (March 1951).

ARCHIVAL SOURCES AND ABBREVIATIONS

BANC: Bancroft Library, University of California, Berkeley

- × Alice Griffith Papers
- × California Federation for Civic Unity Papers
- × Catherine Bauer Wurster Papers
- × C. L. Dellums Papers
- × Commonwealth Club of California and San Francisco
- × Department of Industrial Relations, Housing and Immigration Division
- × Mel Scott Papers
- × National Association for the Advancement of Colored People Papers
- × Patrick McDonough Papers
- × Robert W. Kenny Papers
- × Patrick William McDonough Papers
- × San Francisco Labor Council Records
- × Simon Julius Lubin Papers
- × T. J. Kent Papers
- × William Byron Rumford Papers

CHS: California Historical Society, San Francisco

- × American Civil Liberties Union Papers
- × Cow Hollow Improvement Club
- × League of Women Voters of San Francisco (MS 1270)
- × League of Women Voters of California (MS 1268)
- × Marshall Dill Papers
- × Roger D. Lapham Papers, 1917–1971
- × San Francisco Chamber of Commerce
- × San Francisco Planning and Urban Research Association, 1960–1978

CSA: California State Archives, Sacramento

- × California Commission of Immigration and Housing

CSHS: California State Historical Society, Sacramento

- × Earl Warren Papers

CU: Cornell University Library, Division of Rare and Manuscript Collections

- × San Francisco Planning and Urban Research Association

EDL: Environmental Design Library, University of California, Berkeley

- × Henry Temple Howard Collection
- × Frederick H. Meyer Collection
- × William Wurster Papers

ESL: Ethnic Studies Library, University of California, Berkeley

- × Chinese Historical Society of America
- × Him Mark Lai Papers

FDRL: Franklin D. Roosevelt Presidential Library and Museum, New York

- × Franklin D. Roosevelt Papers, the President's Official File

GLBTHS: GLBT Historical Society, San Francisco, California

- × Donald Stewart Lucas Papers

MSRC: Moorland-Spingarn Research Center, Howard University, Washington, DC

- × Stewart-Flippin Collection

NARA/CP: National Archives, College Park, Maryland

- × Department of Housing and Urban Development, RG 207
- × Federal Public Housing Administration, RG 196
- × National Resource Planning Board, RG 187

NARA/SB: National Archives, San Bruno, California

- × Department of Housing and Urban Redevelopment, RG 207
- × National Resource Planning Board, RG 187
- × Public Housing Administration, RG 196
- × Records of the Community Services Administration, RG 381

SFLA: San Francisco Labor Archives, San Francisco, California

- × San Francisco Labor Council Meeting Notes

SFPL: San Francisco Public Library History Center, San Francisco, California

- Elmer E. Robinson Papers
- George Christopher Papers
- Joseph L. Alioto Papers
- Subject Files

UCLA/DSC: Department of Special Collections, University of California, Los Angeles

- Carey McWilliams Papers
- John Randolph Haynes Papers

NOTES

INTRODUCTION

1. When Kihagi failed to pay, the city required her tenants to pay their rent to the city. See J. K. Dineen, "Court Says Landlord Must Pay SF $2.4 Million for Bad Evictions," *SFGate* (May 2, 2017); Joe Eskenazi, "SF Goes After City's Cruelest Landlord, Snatching Away Her Rent Payments," *Mission Local* (February 5, 2018).

2. For images of public housing, see Nicholas Dagen Bloom, Fritz Umbach, and Lawrence J. Vale, eds., *Public Housing Myths: Perception, Reality, and Social Policy* (Ithaca, NY: Cornell University Press, 2015); R. Allen Hays, *The Federal Government and Urban Housing* (New York: SUNY Press, 2012); Alex F. Schwartz, *Housing Policy in the United States*, 3rd ed. (New York: Routledge, 2014). For earlier images of government housing, see Nathan Straus, *The Seven Myths of Housing* (New York: Arno Press, 1974 [1944]).

3. Novels featuring public housing include Ayn Rand's *The Fountainhead* (1943) and several by Richard Price: *Freedomland* (1998), *Clockers* (1992), and *Samaritan* (2003). For movies and documentaries, see *Candyman* (1992), *Losing Isaiah* (1995), *Clockers* (1995), *Public Housing* (1997), *He Got Game* (1998), *Bringing Out the Dead* (1999), and *Girlfight* (2000). For television, see *The Wire* (2002–2008). Although the 1970s television classic *Good Times* (1974–1979) offered a hardworking, politicized, and creative family in the Chicago projects, the story of the building and neighborhood reflected the prevailing images of government housing. Joseph Godlewski, "The Tragicomic Televisual Ghetto: Popular Representations of Race and Space at Chicago's Cabrini-Green," *Berkeley Planning Journal* 22, 1 (2009): 115–25.

4. Gwendolyn Wright, *Building the Dream: A Social History of Housing in America* (Cambridge, MA: MIT Press, 1983); Hays, *The Federal Government and Urban Housing*; Lawrence J. Vale, *Purging the Poorest: Public Housing and the Design Politics of Twice-Cleared Communities* (Chicago: University of Chicago Press, 2013); Michael B. Katz, *The Undeserving Poor: America's Enduring Confrontation with Poverty* (Oxford: Oxford University Press, 2013).

5. Arnold R. Hirsch, *Making the Second Ghetto: Race and Housing in Chicago, 1940–1960* (New York: Cambridge University Press, 1983); John F. Bauman, *Public Housing, Race, and Renewal: Urban Planning in Philadelphia, 1920–1974* (Philadelphia: Temple University Press, 1987); Robert B. Fairbanks, *Making Better Citizens: Housing Reform and the Community Development Strategy in Cincinnati, 1890–1960* (Urbana: University of Illinois Press, 1988); Gail Radford, *Modern Housing for America: Policy Struggles in the New Deal Era* (Chicago: University of Chicago Press, 1996); Sudhir Venkatesh, *American Project: The Rise and Fall of a Modern Ghetto* (Cambridge, MA: Harvard University Press, 2000). For recent works that often expand the location, time period, and impact of public housing, see Rhonda Y. Williams, *The Politics of Public Housing: Black Women's Struggles Against Urban Inequality* (New York: Oxford University Press, 2004); Donald Craig Parson, *Making a Better World: Public*

Housing, the Red Scare, and the Direction of Modern Los Angeles (Minneapolis: University of Minnesota Press, 2005); Nicholas Dagen Bloom, *Public Housing That Worked: New York in the Twentieth Century* (Philadelphia: University of Pennsylvania Press, 2008); D. Bradford Hunt, *Blueprint for Disaster: The Unraveling of Chicago Public Housing* (Chicago: University of Chicago Press, 2009); John Arena, *Driven from New Orleans: How Nonprofits Betray Public Housing and Promote Privatization* (Minneapolis: University of Minnesota Press, 2012); Edward G. Goetz, *New Deal Ruins: Race, Economic Justice, and Public Housing Policy* (Ithaca, NY: Cornell University Press, 2013); Amy Lynne Howard, *More Than Shelter: Activism and Community in San Francisco Public Housing* (Minneapolis: University of Minnesota Press, 2014); Vale, *Purging the Poorest.*

6. The Pew Charitable Trusts, "Connecting Public Housing and Health: A Health Impact Assessment of HUD's Designated Housing Rule," *Health Impact Project* (June 16, 2015).

7. On the relationship of political engagement, neighborhood, and identity, see Ocean Howell, *Making the Mission: Planning and Ethnicity in San Francisco* (Chicago: University of Chicago Press, 2015).

8. "New Designs for Living," *San Francisco News* (March 19, 1940); Catherine Bauer, *A Citizen's Guide to Public Housing* (Poughkeepsie, NY: Vassar College, 1940), 44–45; rent cost is from SFHA, *Third Annual Report* (1941).

9. I use the term "citizenship" broadly. To be sure, there are incidents in the book when residents of the city connected their housing ideas and actions to the modern nation-state model of citizenship, but at other times residents—immigrants and citizens alike—constructed a model of citizenship grounded in basic human rights and participatory decision making that transcended national (and nation-state) boundaries. For the classic study of citizenship and the modern nation-state, see T. H. Marshall, *Class, Citizenship, and Social Development* (New York: Doubleday, 1964). See also Alan Dawley, *Struggles for Justice: Social Responsibility and the Liberal State* (Cambridge, MA: Harvard University Press, 1993); Daniel T. Rodgers, *Atlantic Crossings: Social Politics in a Progressive Age* (Cambridge, MA: Harvard University Press, 2000); Thomas J. Sugrue, *Sweet Land of Liberty: The Forgotten Struggle for Civil Rights in the North* (New York: Random House, 2008); Michael B. Katz, *The Price of Citizenship: Redefining the American Welfare State* (Philadelphia: University of Pennsylvania Press, 2008).

10. See Vale, *Purging the Poorest*, chapter 1. David Harvey's work has also examined the relationship of individuals, communities, power, and built space in *Social Justice and the City* (Athens: University of Georgia Press, 2008).

11. The competing visions of liberalism and, by extension, government and the market that emerged in the 1870s to 1940s are often described like this. Advocates of "new liberalism" moved away from classical economic liberalism, sometimes referred to in shorthand as laissez-faire economics, and argued for a greater role for government in the economy and civic life, with the aim of bringing about greater equality and justice not only in the United States but in other parts of the industrialized world. This new liberalism stood in contrast to a corporate or volunteer model of liberalism that advocated minimal government and increased voluntary activity to address poverty and social inequality. New liberalism would take hold in the United States with the New Deal and then the Great Society but become less popular among voters by the 1970s. Steve Fraser and Gary Gerstle, eds., *The Rise and Fall of the New Deal Order, 1930–1980* (Princeton, NJ: Princeton University

Press, 1990); Mary O. Furner and Barry Supple, eds., *The State and Economic Knowledge: The American and British Experiences* (Cambridge: Cambridge University Press, 1990); Michael J. Lacey and Mary O. Furner, eds., *The State and Social Investigation in Britain and the United States* (Cambridge: Cambridge University Press, 1993); Rodgers, *Atlantic Crossings*; Alice O'Connor, *Poverty Knowledge: Social Science, Social Policy, and the Poor in Twentieth-Century U.S. History* (Princeton, NJ: Princeton University Press, 2001); Alice Kessler-Harris, *In Pursuit of Equity: Women, Men, and the Quest for Economic Citizenship in 20th-Century America* (New York: Oxford University Press, 2001); Robert O. Self, *American Babylon: Race and the Struggle for Postwar Oakland* (Princeton, NJ: Princeton University Press, 2005); David Harvey, *A Brief History of Neoliberalism* (Oxford: Oxford University Press, 2007); Edward J. Balleisen and David A. Moss, eds., *Government and Markets: Toward a New Theory of Regulation* (Cambridge: Cambridge University Press, 2010); Katz, *The Undeserving Poor* and *The Price of Citizenship*; Gail Radford, *The Rise of the Public Authority: Statebuilding and Economic Development in Twentieth-Century America* (Chicago: University of Chicago Press, 2013).

12. Radford, *Rise of Public Authority* and *Modern Housing for America*; Thomas J. Sugrue, *The Origins of the Urban Crisis: Race and Inequality in Postwar Detroit* (Princeton, NJ: Princeton University Press, 2005); Arena, *Driven from New Orleans*; Vale, *Purging the Poorest*.

13. Chester Hartman, *City for Sale: The Transformation of San Francisco* (Berkeley: University of California Press, 2002); Self, *American Babylon*; Rebecca Solnit and Susan Schwartzenberg, *Hollow City: The Siege of San Francisco and the Crisis of American Urbanism* (New York: Verso, 2001); Christopher Lowen Agee, *The Streets of San Francisco: Policing and the Creation of a Cosmopolitan Liberal Politics, 1950–1972* (Chicago: University of Chicago Press, 2014), chapters 6–7; William Issel, "Liberalism and Urban Policy in San Francisco from the 1930s to the 1960s," *Western Historical Quarterly* 22, 4 (1991): 431–50, and *Church and State in the City: Catholics and Politics in Twentieth-Century San Francisco* (Philadelphia: Temple University Press, 2012).

14. See Tomás Almaguer, *Racial Fault Lines: The Historical Origins of White Supremacy in California* (Berkeley: University of California Press, 1994); Albert S. Broussard, *Black San Francisco: The Struggle for Racial Equality in the West, 1900–1954* (Lawrence: University Press of Kansas, 1993); Judy Yung, *Unbound Feet: A Social History of Chinese Women in San Francisco* (Berkeley: University of California Press, 1995); Nayan Shah, *Contagious Divides: Epidemics and Race in San Francisco's Chinatown* (Berkeley: University of California Press, 2001); Tomás F. Summers Sandoval, *Latinos at the Golden Gate: Creating Community and Identity in San Francisco* (Chapel Hill: University of North Carolina Press, 2013).

15. William Issel and Robert W. Cherny, *San Francisco, 1865–1932: Politics, Power, and Urban Development* (Berkeley: University of California Press, 1986); Michael Kazin, *Barons of Labor: The San Francisco Building Trades and Union Power in the Progressive Era* (Urbana: University of Illinois Press, 1987); Philip J. Ethington, *The Public City: The Political Construction of Urban Life in San Francisco, 1850–1900* (Cambridge: Cambridge University Press, 1994); Hartman, *City for Sale*; Barbara Berglund, *Making San Francisco American: Cultural Frontiers in the Urban West, 1846–1906* (Lawrence: University Press of Kansas, 2007); Estella Habal, *San Francisco's International Hotel: Mobilizing the Filipino American Community in the Anti-Eviction Movement* (Philadelphia: Temple University Press, 2007); Jessica Ellen Sewell, *Women and the Everyday City: Public Space in San Francisco, 1890–1915*

(Minneapolis: University of Minnesota Press, 2011); Issel, *Church and State in the City*; Karl Beitel, *Local Protests, Global Movements: Capital, Community, and State in San Francisco* (Philadelphia: Temple University Press, 2013); Howard, *More Than Shelter*; Agee, *The Streets of San Francisco*, chapters 6–7.

CHAPTER 1

1. Lawrence Veiller, *A Model Housing Law* (New York: Russell Sage Foundation, 1914 [1909]), quote on 77.

2. Frank W. Aitken and Edward Hilton, *A History of the Earthquake and Fire in San Francisco: An Account of the Disaster of April* 18, 1906 (San Francisco: The Edward Hilton Co., 1906); Judd Kahn, *Imperial San Francisco: Politics and Planning in an American City, 1897–1906* (Lincoln: University of Nebraska Press, 1979); Andrea Rees Davies, *Saving San Francisco: Relief and Recovery After the* 1906 *Disaster* (Philadelphia: Temple University Press, 2012). Scholars have debated the precise number of deaths, putting it as high as 3,000 when indirect casualties are included. See Gladys Hansen and Emmet Condon, *Denial of Disaster: The Untold Story and Photographs of the San Francisco Earthquake of* 1906 (San Francisco: Cameron and Company, 1989), 152–53; Philip J. Dreyfus, *Our Better Nature: Environment and the Making of San Francisco* (Norman: University of Oklahoma Press, 2008), chapter 5. For a comparative study of opportunities and constraints from urban fires, see Greg Bankoff, Uwe Lübken, and Jordan Sand, eds., *Flammable Cities: Urban Conflagration and the Making of the Modern World* (Madison: University of Wisconsin Press, 2012).

3. Ernest S. Simpson, "The Wisdom of the Dogs," *San Francisco Chronicle* (May 6, 1906); Kahn, *Imperial San Francisco*; Hansen and Condon, *Denial of Disaster*.

4. The American National Red Cross staff expressed such common ideas about deserving and undeserving charity cases. See *Sixth Annual Report* (1910), and Jean Burton, *Katherine Felton and Her Social Work in San Francisco* (Stanford, CA: Stanford University Press, 1947), quote on 69; Kahn, *Imperial San Francisco*, chapter 6; Davies, *Saving San Francisco*. For historical debates on charity and distinctions between deserving and undeserving recipients, see Robyn Muncy, *Creating a Female Dominion in American Reform, 1890–1935* (New York: Oxford University Press, 1991); Alice O'Connor, *Poverty Knowledge: Social Science, Social Policy, and the Poor in Twentieth-Century U.S. History* (Princeton, NJ: Princeton University Press, 2001); Michael B. Katz, *In the Shadow of the Poorhouse: A Social History of Welfare in America* (New York: Basic Books, 1996).

5. American National Red Cross, *Sixth Annual Report*; Kahn, *Imperial San Francisco*, chapter 6; Daniel T. Rodgers, *Atlantic Crossings: Social Politics in a Progressive Age* (Cambridge, MA: Harvard University Press, 1998).

6. Kahn, *Imperial San Francisco*, chapter 6, quote on 148–49; American National Red Cross, *Sixth Annual Report*; Rodgers, *Atlantic Crossings*.

7. American National Red Cross, *Sixth Annual Report*, quote on 157; Kahn, *Imperial San Francisco*, chapter 6.

8. Telegraph Hill Neighborhood Association, *Annual Reports* (1907 and 1911); Mrs. Eric Cochran (Adelaide Griffith) Interview (April 7, 1969), BANC. For studies on settlement houses, see Muncy, *Creating a Female Dominion in American Reform*; Mina Carson, *Settlement Folk: Social Thought and the American Settlement Movement, 1885–1930* (Chicago: University of Chicago Press, 1990); O'Connor, *Poverty Knowledge*, chapter 1; Christina A. Ziegler-McPherson,

Americanization in the States: Immigrant Social Welfare Policy, Citizenship, and National Identity in the United States, 1908–1929 (University Press of Florida, 2009).

9. American National Red Cross, *Sixth Annual Report,* quote on 157; Telegraph Hill Neighborhood Association, *Annual Reports* (1907 and 1911); Burton, *Katherine Felton,* chapter 5; Kahn, *Imperial San Francisco,* chapter 6; Davies, *Saving San Francisco.*

10. Kahn, *Imperial San Francisco*; William Issel and Robert W. Cherny, *San Francisco, 1865–1932: Politics, Power, and Urban Development* (Berkeley: University of California Press, 1986), 109–11; Michael Kazin, *Barons of Labor: The San Francisco Building Trades and Union Power in the Progressive Era* (Urbana: University of Illinois Press, 1987); William H. Wilson, *The City Beautiful Movement* (Baltimore: Johns Hopkins University Press, 1989); Gray Brechin, *Imperial San Francisco: Urban Power, Earthly Ruin* (Berkeley: University of California Press, 1999); Rodgers, *Atlantic Crossings,* especially chapter 5; Robert Fishman, ed., *The American Planning Tradition: Culture and Policy* (Washington, DC: Woodrow Wilson Center Press, 2000).

11. Quote in Issel and Cherny, *San Francisco,* 110. Ocean Howell argues that a key source of opposition came from the Mission Promotion Association, which had become a political power in urban planning in and out of the Mission district. See his *Making the Mission: Planning and Ethnicity in San Francisco* (Chicago: University of Chicago Press, 2015).

12. Quote in Telegraph Hill Neighborhood Association, *Annual Report* (1907).

13. For housing reformers, large-scale projects offered the most hope for addressing the housing problem and eradicating slum conditions, but these kinds of projects generally lacked government support and financing. Here are some definitions of various housing types, used in this discussion: (1) Limited-dividend housing offers investors a legal structure for a fixed return on their investment; the housing is affordable for tenants, of adequate quality, and allows the government a way to regulate the housing itself. (2) Public housing agencies build, own, and manage low-cost housing. (3) Cooperative housing creates a corporation that is run by occupant-owners, who act as a collective landlord under the guidelines of the corporation. See Rodgers, *Atlantic Crossings.*

14. Veiller's idea of a gradualist legislative reform approach would focus on building codes (unexciting and technical but easiest to pass); the Tenement House Laws (better for dealing with light and ventilation and plumbing issues); and housing legislation (best for outlawing all substandard housing, whether owned or rented). Veiller, *A Model Housing Law,* especially preface and chapter 1, quotes on 11. For biographical information on Veiller, see Robert Bruce Fairbanks, "From Better Dwellings to Better Neighborhoods: The Rise and Fall of the First National Housing Movement," in John F. Bauman, Roger Biles, and Kristin M. Szylvian, eds., *From Tenements to the Taylor Homes: In Search of an Urban Housing Policy in Twentieth- Century America* (University Park: Pennsylvania State University Press, 2000).

15. San Francisco Housing Association, *Annual Reports* (1911, 1912, and 1913). See Veiller, *A Model Housing Law.*

16. San Francisco Housing Association, *Annual Reports* (1911, 1912, and 1913); Telegraph Hill Neighborhood Association, *Annual Reports* (1907 and 1911).

17. Quote in Telegraph Hill Neighborhood Association, *Annual Report* (1911). For low-income housing conditions, also see Telegraph Hill Neighborhood Association, *Annual Report* (1907); San Francisco Housing Association, *Annual Reports* (1911, 1912, and 1913); SFHA, 1939 *Real Property Survey* (1940). The social survey became a reform tool in an era

marked by the dramatic social dislocations and conflicts of industrialization and urbanization. Mary and Charles Booth, W. E. B. Du Bois, and Jane Addams produced studies of London, Philadelphia, and Chicago. For studies of social surveys, see Mary O. Furner, "Knowing Capitalism: Public Investigation and the Labor Question in the Long Progressive Era," in Mary O. Furner and Barry Supple, eds., *The State and Economic Knowledge: The American and British Experience* (New York: Cambridge University Press, 1990); Martin Bulmer, Kevin Bales, and Kathryn Kish Sklar, eds., *The Social Survey in Historical Perspective, 1880–1940* (New York: Cambridge University Press, 1992); Mary O. Furner, "The Republican Tradition and the New Liberalism: Social Investigation, State Building, and Social Learning in the Gilded Age," in Michael J. Lacey and Mary O. Furner, eds., *The State and Social Investigation in Britain and the United States* (New York and Cambridge: Cambridge University Press, 1993); Maurine W. Greenwald and Margo Anderson, eds., *Pittsburgh Surveyed: Social Science and Social Reform in the Early Twentieth Century* (Pittsburgh: University of Pittsburgh Press, 1996); Rodgers, *Atlantic Crossings*; Shelton Stromquist, *Re-Inventing "The People": The Progressive Movement, the Class Problem, and the Origins of Modern Liberalism* (Champaign: University of Illinois Press, 2006).

18. San Francisco Housing Association, *Annual Report (1911)*; John F. Bauman, *Public Housing, Race, and Renewal: Urban Planning in Philadelphia, 1920–1974* (Philadelphia: Temple University Press, 1987); Robert B. Fairbanks, *Making Better Citizens: Housing Reform and the Community Development Strategy in Cincinnati, 1890–1960* (Urbana: University of Illinois Press, 1988); Rodgers, *Atlantic Crossings*.

19. San Francisco Housing Association, *Annual Reports* (1911, 1912, and 1913). Porter quote in 1911 *Annual Report*, 7.

20. See NHA publications in Folder "Housing (1–3)," Box 76 "Housing," John Randolph Haynes Papers Collection 1241, UCLA/DSC; San Francisco Housing Association, *Annual Reports* (1911, 1912, and 1913); Fairbanks, "From Better Dwellings to Better Neighborhoods." Benedict Anderson's concept of imagined communities is helpful for understanding how reformers, who often did not know one another personally, understood their collective identity and work, largely through printed materials. See his *Imagined Communities: Reflections on the Origin and Spread of Nationalism* (New York: Verso, 1996).

21. San Francisco Housing Association, *Annual Reports* (1911, 1912, and 1913); Telegraph Hill Neighborhood Association, *Annual Report* (1911); CCIH, *First Annual Report* (1915); Issel and Cherny, *San Francisco*; Ziegler-McPherson, *Americanization in the States*.

22. See Griffith's correspondence in San Francisco Housing Association, *Annual Report* (1911).

23. San Francisco Housing Association, *Annual Report* (1913).

24. San Francisco Housing Association, *Annual Reports* (1911 and 1913); Telegraph Hill Neighborhood Association, *Annual Report* (1911); CCIH, *First Annual Report*, especially 10–12. Griffith quote in San Francisco Housing Association, *Annual Report* (1911).

25. San Francisco Housing Association, *Annual Reports* (1911, 1912, and 1913); Telegraph Hill Neighborhood Association, *Annual Reports* (1907 and 1911); Burton, *Katherine Felton*; Rogers, *Atlantic Crossings*; Ziegler-McPherson, *Americanization in the States*.

26. Quote on 6 in San Francisco Housing Association, *Annual Report* (1911).

27. The West's social and urban problems, and the health of the republic in general, had "frontier thesis" overtones. See Frederick Jackson Turner, *The Frontier in American History*

(Tucson: University of Arizona Press, 1997); Robert W. Rydell, *All the World's a Fair: Visions of Empire at American International Expositions, 1876–1916* (Chicago: University of Chicago Press, 1984); Brechin, *Imperial San Francisco.*

28. Catherine Bauer, *Modern Housing* (Boston: Houghton Mifflin, 1934); Gail Radford, *Modern Housing for America: Policy Struggles in the New Deal Era* (Chicago: University of Chicago Press, 1996); Marc A. Weiss, *The Rise of the Community Builders: The American Real Estate Industry and Urban Land Planning* (New York: Columbia University Press, 1987); Rodgers, *Atlantic Crossings.*

29. Ibid.

30. CCIH, *First Annual Report*; Ziegler-McPherson, *Americanization in the States*; George J. Sanchez, *Becoming Mexican American: Ethnicity, Culture, and Identity in Chicano Los Angeles, 1900–1945* (New York: Oxford University Press, 1993). For progressive reform in California, see William Deverell and Tom Sitton, eds., *California Progressivism Revisited* (Berkeley: University of California Press, 1994).

31. Katherine Felton to Simon Lubin (November 25, 1912, and December 16, 1912), Folder "Felton, Katherine," Box 2, Simon Lubin Papers, BANC. Quote in November 25, 1912, letter. Also see Ziegler-McPherson, *Americanization in the States.*

32. CCIH, *First Annual Report*, *An A-B-C of Housing* (1915), and *A Plan for a Housing Survey* (1916); Simon Lubin Papers, especially Box 3, BANC; Ziegler-McPherson, *Americanization in the States*; Deverell and Sitton, *California Progressivism Revisited*; Sanchez, *Becoming Mexican American.* Johnson also created California's Industrial Accident Commission and the Industrial Welfare Commission.

33. CCIH, *First Annual Report*, *An A-B-C of Housing*, and *A Plan for a Housing Survey*; Ziegler-McPherson, *Americanization in the States*; Deverell and Sitton, *California Progressivism Revisited.* Lubin led the investigation into a 1913 IWW strike waged for better food, housing, and wages at Durst Ranch in Wheatland, California that turned violent when local authorities arrived. See Ziegler-McPherson, *Americanization in the States*; Melvyn Dubofsky, *We Shall Be All: A History of the Industrial Workers of the World* (Chicago: Quadrangle Books, 1969); 294–302; Dino Cinel, *From Italy to San Francisco: The Immigrant Experience* (Stanford: Stanford University Press, 1982), 243–45; Simon Lubin Papers, especially Box 3, BANC.

34. In 1923, the CCIH director thought Los Angeles needed thirty inspectors. State Director to Mr. A. S. Hoff, President of SF Local Painters Union #19 (April 6, 1923), Folder "General Correspondence H, 1923–24," Carton 40, CA Department of Industrial Relations, BANC. CCIH, *First Annual Report*; Ziegler-McPherson, *Americanization in the States*; Stephanie S. Pincetl, *Transforming California: A Political History of Land Use and Development* (Baltimore: Johns Hopkins University Press, 1999), chapters 2–3.

35. Chicago leaders used the 1893 World's Fair to show how their city came back after the 1871 fire. *The Improver: The Monthly Magazine for the Advancement of San Francisco* (August 1912), CHS; Pamphlets in Folder "Materials Concerning Exhibits, Grounds, and Services," Panama– Pacific International Exposition, BANC; Frank Morton Todd, *The Story of the Exposition*, vol. II (New York: G. P. Putnam's Sons, Knickerbocker Press, 1921); Issel and Cherny, *San Francisco*, 166–69; Abigail M. Markwyn, *Empress San Francisco: The Pacific Rim, the Great West, and California at the Panama–Pacific International Exposition* (Lincoln: University of Nebraska Press, 2014).

36. *The Improver: The Monthly Magazine for the Advancement of San Francisco* (August 1912); Pamphlets in Folder "Materials Concerning Exhibits, Grounds, and Services," Panama–Pacific International Exposition, BANC; Issel and Cherny, *San Francisco*; Markwyn, *Empress San Francisco.*

37. See Folder "Public Ownership Association," Carton 14, San Francisco Labor Council Records, BANC; Anthony Perles, *The People's Railway: The History of the Municipal Railway of San Francisco* (Glendale: Interurban Press, 1981); Issel and Cherny, *San Francisco*, 176–79, 210.

38. Dubofsky, *We Shall Be All*; Rodgers, *Atlantic Crossings*, chapter 7; Edith Elmer Wood, *Recent Trends in American Housing* (New York: Macmillan Company, 1931), chapter 1; Mel Scott, *American City Planning Since 1890* (Berkeley: University of California Press, 1969), 170–74; Eric Karolak, "'No Idea of Doing Anything Wonderful': The Labor-Crisis Origins of National Housing Policy and the Reconstruction of the Working-Class Community, 1917–1919," in John F. Bauman, Roger Biles, and Kristin M. Szylvian, eds., *From Tenements to the Taylor Homes: In Search of an Urban Housing Policy in Twentieth-Century America* (University Park: Penn State University Press, 2000).

39. Karolak, "'No Idea of Doing Anything Wonderful'"; quote in Wood, *Recent Trends*, 77.

40. Elizabeth H. Ashe, *Intimate Letters from France and Extracts from the Diary of Elizabeth Ashe, 1917–1919* (San Francisco: Bruce Brough Press, 1931); Burton, *Katherine Felton*; Oscar Lewis, *San Francisco: Mission to Metropolis* (Berkeley: Howell-North Books, 1966), 227; Howard A. DeWitt, *Images of Ethnic and Radical Violence in California Politics, 1917–1930: A Survey* (San Francisco: R and E Research Associates, 1975), chapter 3; Roger W. Lotchin, *Fortress California 1910–1961: From Warfare to Welfare* (New York: Oxford University Press, 1992); Issel and Cherny, *San Francisco.*

41. CCIH, *A Report on Relief of Destitute Unemployed, 1914–15,* and *Americanization: A Program for California*; Robert Porter to Simon Lubin (May 16, 1919), Folder "Misc. I–P," Box 1, Simon Julius Lubin Papers, BANC; Dorothy Shaffter, *State Housing Agencies* (New York: Columbia University Press, 1942), 94–105; NHA publications in Folder "Housing (1–3)," Box 76 "Housing," John Randolph Haynes Papers Collection 1241, UCLA/DSC.

42. San Francisco Housing Association, *Minutes* (November 10, 1933), Folder 16, Box 3, SPUR, CU; Weiss, *The Rise of the Community Builders*; Fairbanks, "From Better Dwellings to Better Neighborhoods"; O'Connor, *Poverty Knowledge*, 42–44. For San Francisco's politically active residents, see Kazin, *Barons of Labor*; Issel and Cherny, *San Francisco*; Philip J. Ethington, *The Public City: The Political Construction of Urban Life in San Francisco, 1850–1900* (Cambridge: Cambridge University Press, 1994); Barbara Berglund, *Making San Francisco American: Cultural Frontiers in the Urban West, 1846–1906* (Lawrence: University Press of Kansas, 2007).

43. CCIH, *A Report on Housing Shortage* (1923); SFHA, 1939 *Real Property Survey* (1940); Works Projects Administration in Northern California, *San Francisco: The Bay and Its Cities* (New York: Hastings House, 1947), 220–28; Issel and Cherny, *San Francisco*, chapters 1–3; Cinel, *From Italy to San Francisco*, chapter 5; Tomás F. Summers Sandoval, *Latinos at the Golden Gate: Creating Community and Identity in San Francisco* (Chapel Hill: University of North Carolina Press, 2013); Frank R. Quinn, *Growing Up in the Mission District* (San Francisco Archives, 1985); Howell, *Making the Mission.*

44. Grievance Committee Report of San Francisco Branch, NAACP, March, c. 1925, Folder 423, Box 97–21, Stewart-Flippin Collection, MSRC; Charles Spurgeon Johnson,

The Negro War Worker in San Francisco: A Local Self-Study (San Francisco: Y.W.C.A and American Missionary Association, 1944); Katherine Stewart-Flippin, Transcripts of Oral Interview 1977–78, Black Women Oral History Project, Radcliffe College, 68; Albert S. Broussard, *Black San Francisco: The Struggle for Racial Equality in the West, 1900–1954* (Lawrence: University Press of Kansas, 1993); Quintard Taylor, *The Forging of a Black Community: Seattle's Central District from 1870 Through the Civil Rights Era* (Seattle: University of Washington Press, 1994).

45. Edward Mabson to Robert Bagnall (April 9, 1923), Folder 389, Box 97–20, Stewart-Flippin Collection, MSRC; Johnson, *The Negro War Worker*; Stewart-Flippin, Oral Interview 1977–78; for Mabson biographical information, and attempts by whites to prevent integration in housing and employment, see Broussard, *Black San Francisco*, chapter 1.

46. "State in the Union" quote on 285 from Works Project Administration, *San Francisco: The Bay and Its Cities*, 282–303; Issel and Cherney, *San Francisco*, 66–70, 188–90.

47. Quote in School of Social Studies, San Francisco College, *Living Conditions in Chinatown* (1939), Folder "Hogan—Living in Chinatown," Box 2, Records of the Central Office: Records of the Office of the Central Historian, Records Relating to the History of the Agency ("Historical File"), 1934–48, PHA, RG 196, NARA/CP; Judy Yung, *Unbound Feet: A Social History of Chinese Women in San Francisco* (Berkeley: University of California Press, 1995); Nayan Shah, *Contagious Divides: Epidemics and Race in San Francisco's Chinatown* (Berkeley: University of California Press, 2001).

48. Ibid. Quote in *Living Conditions in Chinatown*. For the relationship between racial stereotypes and urban reform, see Shah, *Contagious Divides*; Tera W. Hunter, *To 'Joy My Freedom: Southern Black Women's Lives and Labors After the Civil War* (Cambridge, MA: Harvard University Press, 1997), especially chapters 6 and 9.

49. San Francisco Housing Association, *Annual Reports* (1911 and 1913); "Commission Talks of Building Laws," *San Francisco Call* (April 25, 1911); Lawrence J. Vale, *Purging the Poorest: Public Housing and the Design Politics of Twice-Cleared Communities* (Chicago: University of Chicago Press, 2013).

50. Bauer, *Modern Housing*; Radford, *Modern Housing for America*; Rodgers, *Atlantic Crossings*.

51. Wood, *Recent Trends*; Weiss, *The Rise of the Community Builders*; Kenneth T. Jackson, *Crabgrass Frontier: The Suburbanization of the United States* (New York: Oxford University Press, 1985); Rodgers, *Atlantic Crossings*, 382; Janet Hutchison, "Shaping Housing and Enhancing Consumption: Hoover's Interwar Housing Policy," in Bauman, Biles, and Szylvian, *From Tenements to the Taylor Homes*; Ellis W. Hawley, "Herbert Hoover, the Commerce Secretariat, and the Vision of an 'Associative State,' 1921–1928," *Journal of American History* 61, 1 (June 1974): 116–40; Guy Alchon, *The Invisible Hand of Planning: Capitalism, Social Science, and the State in the 1920s* (Princeton, NJ: Princeton University Press, 1985); Radford, *Modern Housing*, 12–57; Mark Hendrickson, *American Labor and Economic Citizenship: New Capitalism from World War I to the Great Depression* (New York: Cambridge University Press, 2013).

52. Ibid. Loula Lasker "Uncle Sam—Landlord," *Survey Graphic* (March 1934): 124–28, 141–42; quote on 124.

53. Report of the President's Conference on Home Building and Home Ownership (1932); Jackson, *Crabgrass Frontier*, 192–95; Radford, *Modern Housing*, 85–89.

54. Issel and Cherny, *San Francisco*, 49–51.

55. Burton, *Katherine Felton*, 224–27, quote on 226.

56. Kernan Robson to Senator Huey Long (March 24, 1934), Folder 4500.09, Box 297 Project 4402, Project 4600, Project Files (1933–1937), RG 196, NARA/CP.

57. Wood, *Recent Trends*, 297.

58. Ibid., 11.

CHAPTER 2

1. SFHA, 1939 *Real Property Survey* (1940).

2. Catherine Bauer, *Modern Housing* (Boston: Houghton Mifflin, 1934), quote on 237; H. Peter Oberlander and Eva Newbrun, *Houser: The Life and Work of Catherine Bauer* (Vancouver: University of British Columbia Press, 1999); Report (January 2, 1942), Western Addition Housing Council, Folder 3, Box 3, SPUR, CU; Gwendolyn Wright, *Building the Dream: A Social History of Housing in America* (Cambridge, MA: MIT Press, 1983); Daniel T. Rodgers, *Atlantic Crossings: Social Politics in a Progressive Age* (Cambridge, MA: Harvard University Press, 1998).

3. Bauer, *Modern Housing*; Gail Radford, *Modern Housing for America: Policy Struggles in the New Deal Era* (Chicago: University of Chicago Press, 1996), 59–89; Oberlander and Newbrun, *Houser*, chapters 4 and 5.

4. Frank R. Quinn, *Growing Up in the Mission District* (San Francisco Archives, 1985), 46–47.

5. Mrs. Earl Treadwell [known as Anne deGruchy Dettner after her divorce from Earl], President of the League of Women Voters of San Francisco, to Mayor Rossi (February 13, 1933), Folder 28 "1932 Sept. to 1933 August," Box 7, League of Women Voters of San Francisco, MS 1270, CHS. For Great Depression San Francisco, see Jean Burton, *Katherine Felton and Her Social Work in San Francisco* (Stanford, CA: Stanford University Press, 1947); Albert S. Broussard, *Black San Francisco: The Struggle for Racial Equality in the West, 1900–1954* (Lawrence: University Press of Kansas, 1993), chapter 6; Judy Yung, *Unbound Feet: A Social History of Chinese Women in San Francisco* (Berkeley: University of California Press, 1995), chapter 4; William Issel, *Church and State in the City: Catholics and Politics in Twentieth-Century San Francisco* (Philadelphia: Temple University Press, 2012).

6. Theda Skocpol, "Political Response to Capitalist Crisis: Neo-Marxist Theories of the State and the Case of the New Deal," *Politics and Society* 10, 2 (1980): 155–201; Christopher Tomlins, *The State and the Unions: Labor Relations, Law, and the Organized Labor Movement in America, 1880–1960* (New York: Cambridge University Press, 1985); Frances Fox Piven and Richard A. Cloward, *Regulating the Poor: The Functions of Public Welfare* (New York: Vintage Books, 1993); Lizabeth Cohen, *Making a New Deal: Industrial Workers in Chicago, 1919–1939* (Cambridge: Cambridge University Press, 1990); Gwendolyn Mink, *The Wages of Motherhood: Inequality in the Welfare State, 1917–1942* (Ithaca, NY: Cornell University Press, 1995); Steve Fraser and Gary Gerstle, eds., *The Rise and Fall of the New Deal Order, 1930–1980* (Princeton, NJ: Princeton University Press, 1989); Rodgers, *Atlantic Crossings*; Jason Scott Smith, *Building New Deal Liberalism: The Political Economy of Public Works, 1933–1956* (New York: Cambridge University Press, 2006).

7. Radford, *Modern Housing for America*, chapter 4; Oberlander and Newbrun, *Houser*, chapters 4 and 5; Rodgers, *Atlantic Crossings*, 465–68.

8. Kohn believed in Modern Housing. All quotes are from his "A National Programme for Housing in the United States" in the excellent collection of essays edited by Carol Aronovici, *America Can't Have Housing* (New York: Committee on the Housing Exhibition by the Museum of Modern Art, 1934), 11–14.

9. Quotes in San Francisco Housing Association, *Minutes* (November 10, 1933, and December 5, 1933) and *Report of Committee on Investigations and Statistics* (January 19, 1934), Folder 16, Box 3, SPUR, CU; Correspondence in Folder 4500, Box 297, "Series Project Files (1933–1937)," RG 196, NARA/CP. Also see Louis Mooser to Vincent Brown, Chief of California Dept. of Industrial Relations, Division of Immigration and Housing (December 18, 1933), Folder "16 Limited Dividend Housing, Aug–Dec. 1933," Carton 40, CA Department of Industrial Relations, BANC.

10. Rossi appointed Griffith to run the Public Emergency Housing Corporation research. San Francisco Housing Association, *Minutes* (November 10, 1933, and December 5, 1933) and *Report of Committee on Investigations and Statistics* (January 19, 1934), Folder 16, Box 3, SPUR, CU; Correspondence in Folder 4500, Box 297, "Series Project Files (1933–1937)," RG 196, NARA/CP; *San Francisco Chronicle* (August 24, 1934).

11. Correspondence in Folder 4500, Box 297, "Series Project Files (1933–1937)," RG 196, NARA/CP; Radford, *Modern Housing*, 85–109.

12. Robert Kohn to Eugene Glaber (March 9, 1934), Folder 4500, Box 297, "Series Project Files (1933–1937)," RG 196, NARA/CP. Also, see Nicholas Dagen Bloom, *Public Housing That Worked: New York in the Twentieth Century* (Philadelphia: University of Pennsylvania Press, 2008), chapter 1. On clearing out poor residents in the name of urban progress, see Lawrence J. Vale, *Purging the Poorest: Public Housing and the Design Politics of Twice-Cleared Communities* (Chicago: University of Chicago Press, 2013).

13. Correspondence and maps in Folder 4500–02, Box 297, Project H4402–4600, "Project Files (1933–1937)," RG 196, NARA/CP; Application, Folder "Jefferson Park Housing Project SF, 1938," Box 1, Frederick Meyer Collections, EDL.

14. Correspondence and maps in Folder 4500–02, Box 297, Project H4402–4600, "Project Files (1933–1937)," RG 196, NARA/CP; Report of Committee on Investigations and Statistics (January 19, 1934), Folder 16, Box 3, SPUR, CU.

15. Upton Sinclair, *I, Candidate for Governor: And How I Got Licked* (Berkeley: University of California Press, 1994); William Issel, "Liberalism and Urban Policy in San Francisco from the 1930s to the 1960s," *Western Historical Quarterly* 22, 4 (November 1991): 431–50; Frances Fox Piven and Richard A. Cloward, *Poor People's Movements: Why They Succeed, How They Fail* (New York: Vintage Books, 1979); Chris Carlsson, "The Progress Club: 1934 and Class Memory," in James Brook, Chris Carlsson, and Nancy J. Peters, eds., *Reclaiming San Francisco: History, Politics, Culture* (San Francisco: City Lights Books, 1998); Issel, *Church and State in the City.*

16. Ibid.

17. Radford, *Modern Housing*, 93–101.

18. Correspondence in Folder 4500, Box 297, Project H4402–4600, "Series Project Files (1933–1937)," RG 196, NARA/CP; U.S. Government, *Legal Problems in the Housing Field: A Technical Monograph on One Phase of Housing Prepared for the Industrial Committee of the National Resources Committee* (1939); William Ebenstein, *The Law of Public Housing*

(Madison: University of Wisconsin Press, 1940); Robert A. Kagan, "Adversarial Legalism and American Government," *Journal of Policy Analysis and Management* 10, 3 (1991): 369–406; Rodgers, *Atlantic Crossings*, chapter 10.

19. Housing Legislation Information Office pamphlet, Folder 50, "San Francisco Housing Authority," Carton 1, Chinese Historical Society of America, ESL; Radford, *Modern Housing*; Oberlander and Newbrun, *Houser*, chapters 4 and 5.

20. Philip Selznick, *TVA and the Grass Roots: A Study of Politics in the Sociology of Formal Organization* (New York: Harper & Row, 1966); Joseph Arnold, *The New Deal in the Suburbs: A History of the Greenbelt Town Program, 1935–1954* (Columbus: Ohio State University Press, 1971); Mark Gelfand, *A Nation of Cities: The Federal Government and Urban America, 1933–1965* (New York: Oxford University Press, 1975); Donald Worster, *Dust Bowl: The Southern Plains in the 1930s* (New York: Oxford University Press, 1979); Rodgers, *Atlantic Crossings*; Michael A. Bernstein, *A Perilous Progress: Economists and Public Purpose in Twentieth-Century America* (Princeton, NJ: Princeton University Press, 2001), chapter 3. For the National Planning Board history, and agency name changes, see Marion Clawson, *New Deal Planning: The National Resources Planning Board* (Baltimore: Johns Hopkins University Press, 1981).

21. Catherine Bauer to F.J. (April 17, 1948), Folder "April–May 1948," Box 3, Catherine Bauer Papers, BANC.

22. Housing Legislation Information Office Pamphlet (no date), Folder 50 "San Francisco Housing Authority," Carton 1, Chinese Historical Society, ESL.

23. Ethel Johnson, "Public Attitudes Towards Housing in San Francisco with Particular Emphasis on the Activities of the San Francisco Housing Association" (December 5, 1940), paper for Catherine Bauer; Sara Jenkins to Mrs. M. P. Hagin, Director of Projects, WPA (May 6, 1940), Folder 339, Box 97–17, Stewart-Flippin Papers, MSRC.

24. Speech (May 31, 1936), Alice Griffith Papers, BANC.

25. The best work on San Francisco's political culture in the 1930s is by William Issel. See his "Business Power and Political Culture in San Francisco, 1900–1940," *Journal of Urban History* (1989): 52–77; and "Liberalism and Urban Policy in San Francisco"; and *Church and State in the City*. See also Fred Rosenbaum, *Cosmopolitans: A Social and Cultural History of the Jews of the San Francisco Bay Area* (Berkeley: University of California Press, 2009).

26. Ibid.; Sinclair, *I, Candidate for Governor*; Cohen, *Making a New Deal*; Michael Denning, *The Cultural Front: The Laboring of American Culture in the Twentieth Century* (New York: Verso, 1996).

27. Langdon W. Post to the President (March 13, 1936), Folder January to March 1936, Box 2, "Official Files, Housing," Franklin Roosevelt Papers, FDR.

28. Gelfand, *A Nation of Cities*; Radford, *Modern Housing*, 188–89; Oberlander and Newbrun, *Houser*, chapter 5.

29. Langdon W. Post, *The Challenge of Housing* (Farrar & Rinehart, 1938), chapter 7; Robert Moore Fisher, *Twenty Years of Public Housing: Economic Aspects of the Federal Program* (New York: Harper, 1959), chapter 1; Radford, *Modern Housing*, 180–91; John F. Bauman, *Public Housing, Race, and Renewal: Urban Planning in Philadelphia, 1920–1974* (Philadelphia: Temple University Press, 1987), 40–48; R. Allen Hays, *The Federal Government and Urban Housing* (New York: SUNY Press, 2012).

30. See the series of letters, especially from the Los Angeles Chamber of Commerce on December 8, 1937, and the California Real Estate Association on February 1, 1938, in Folder

"2 of 2 Housing Low Cost (Assembly Interim Committee) 1937," Box 77, John Randolph Haynes Papers Collection 1241, UCLA/DSC.

31. "State Housing Act Enactment Urged by Rossi," *San Francisco Chronicle* (December 15, 1937), "Labor Lines Up for Low Cost Homes Statute," *San Francisco Chronicle* (January 12, 1938), and "Mayor Speeds Action on S.F. Housing Plan," *San Francisco Chronicle* (January 26, 1938); Professor of Architecture Howard Moise, University of California, Berkeley, to Mayor Rossi (March 21, 1938), and Mrs. Lovell Langstroth, President of the San Francisco League of Women Voters, to Mayor Rossi (March 15, 1938), Folder 77B "Project Housing, General 1938–1942," Box 17, MS 1270, League of Women Voters of San Francisco, CHS. Quote is from Langstroth letter.

32. Alice Griffith, "A Review of the Proceedings of the Housing Authority of San Francisco" (April 18, 1938–August 17, 1943), Folder 377, Box 97–19, Stewart-Flippin Papers, MSRC; Leon Keyserling, "Legal Aspects of Public Housing," in Horace Russell and Leon Keyserling, *Legal Problems in the Housing Field* (Washington, DC: U.S. Government Printing Office, 1939); Shaffter, *State Housing Agencies*, 115–21.

33. SFHA, *Minutes* (March 2, 1939); Ethel Johnson, "Public Attitudes Towards Housing in San Francisco"; SFHA, *First Annual Report* (1939).

34. Issel, "Liberalism and Urban Policy in San Francisco"; Letter to Herman Boxer (April 29, 1940), Folder 5, Box 1, Catherine Bauer Wurster Papers, BANC.

35. SFHA, *Minutes* (April 22, 1938); "Many States Need Housing Authority Laws," *The American City* 53, 1 (January 1938): 5. San Francisco has a city/county government structure, with the Board of Supervisors in charge of the combined city and county government. For simplicity, this book will use city government. Also, the San Francisco Housing Association remained active after the formation of the SFHA.

36. SFHA, *Minutes* (April, May, and June 1938). From here forward, "Director" will be used for "Executive Secretary Director."

37. SFHA, *Minutes* (June 16, 1938). Resolution No. 12 made this informal cooperation agreement formal policy. SFHA, *Minutes* (January 12, 1939).

38. SFHA, *Minutes* (April, May, and June 1938, especially April 22, 1938, and June 16, 1938); SFHA, *Eighth Annual Report* (no date). For public authorities, see Keyserling, "Legal Aspects of Public Housing"; Gail Radford, *The Rise of the Public Authority, Statebuilding and Economic Development in Twentieth-Century America* (Chicago: University of Chicago Press, 2013). For PILOTs, see Fisher, *Twenty Years of Public Housing.* The Commission of Parks and the Commission of Recreation were separate bodies at the time, which meant that the SFHA worked with two separate agencies until 1950.

39. Radford, *The Rise of the Public Authority.*

40. In his study of Philadelphia's public housing, John Bauman detected two competing discourses that existed in New Deal housing circles: that of housing reformers who clung to progressive era ideas that stressed sanitation and regulation, and that of communitarian housing reformers who, influenced by the Modern Housing movement, championed public housing as a way to build vibrant communities and as part of urban and regional planning. Robert Fairbanks, in his study of Cincinnati's public housing and planning, found that by the New Deal the communitarian housing reformers were the dominant force. Bauman, *Public Housing*; Robert B. Fairbanks, *Making Better Citizens: Housing Reform and the Community Development Strategy in Cincinnati, 1890–1960* (Urbana: University of Illinois Press, 1988),

chapter 8 and fn. 2, 210; Howard Gillette, Jr., "The Evolution of Neighborhood Planning from the Progressive Era to the 1949 Housing Act," *Journal of Urban History* 9 (1983): 421–44. Also, see Griffith, *"A Review of the Proceedings of the Housing Authority of San Francisco";* Catherine Bauer, *A Citizen's Guide to Public Housing* (Poughkeepsie, NY: Vassar College, 1940).

41. Quote in SFHA, *Minutes* (October 6, 1938). SFHA, 1939 *Real Property Survey* (1940).

42. Quote in SFHA, *Minutes* (May 26, 1938); SFHA, *First Annual Report* (1939).

43. SFHA, *Minutes* (September 1, 1938, and June 9, 23, and 30, 1938). Fairbanks, *Making Better Citizens*, chapter 9.

44. SFHA, *Minutes* (June 23, 1938).

45. SFHA, *Minutes* (September 1, 1938); Griffith, "A Review of the Proceedings of the Housing Authority of San Francisco."

46. UCB Professor of Architecture Howard Moise to Mayor Rossi (March 21, 1938), Folder 77B "Project Housing, General 1938–1942," Box 17, MS 1270, League of Women Voters of San Francisco, CHS.

47. SFHA, *Minutes* (September 8, 1938).

48. SFHA, *Minutes* (October 6, 1938).

49. SFHA, *Minutes* (May 26, 1938, and September 8, 1938). SFHA, 1939 *Real Property Survey* (1940).

50. "S.F. Prepared to Aid Housing Plan, Says Rossi," *San Francisco Chronicle* (January 12, 1938). Rossi missed what the 1939 *Real Property Survey* investigators found the next year when they conservatively estimated that 20 percent, or 46,000 units, of the city's housing stock was substandard. The SFHA *Second Annual Report* (1940) put the number closer to 73,000 units. SFHA, 1939 *Real Property Survey* (1940).

51. Nathan Straus, *The Seven Myths of Housing* (New York: Arno Press, 1974 [1944]), chapter 1. For one of the best discussions of slum narratives, see Lawrence J. Vale, *Purging the Poorest: Public Housing and the Design Politics of Twice-Cleared Communities* (Chicago: University of Chicago Press, 2013).

52. SFHA, *Minutes* (October 17, 1938).

53. SFHA, *Second Annual Report* (1940) and *Eighth Annual Report* (no date); SFHA, *Minutes* (May and June 1938; October 17, 1938; November 10, 1938; December 15, 1938; and March 23, 1939); and "New Designs for Living," *San Francisco News* (five-part series, March 18–23, 1940). On the USHA preference for large projects, see SFHA, *Minutes* (1938–39).

54. Johnson, "Public Attitudes Towards Housing in San Francisco"; SFHA, *First Annual Report* (1939) and *Second Annual Report* (1940); "New Designs for Living" (March 18–23, 1940). Quote in SFHA, *Second Annual Report* (1940).

55. Quote in SFHA, *Minutes* (March 30, 1939). See SFHA, *Minutes* (June 29, 1939, and February 8, 1940).

56. "New Designs for Living" (March 22, 1940).

57. For opposition in San Francisco, see Johnson, "Public Attitudes Towards Housing in San Francisco"; Griffith, "A Review of the Proceedings of the Housing Authority of San Francisco"; SFHA, *Minutes* (1940–42). For national level opposition, see Fisher, *Twenty Years of Public Housing*, 21–22; Bauman, *Public Housing*, 30; Wright, *Building the Dream*; Gelfand, *A Nation of Cities*.

58. Bauman, *Public Housing*, 44–45, Fairbanks, *Making Better Citizens*, 117–20; Fisher, *Twenty Years of Public Housing*, 183–214. Historian Robert Fisher determined that PILOTs

had to be reviewed on a case-by-case basis. On the whole, however, he found that localities had gained more in PILOTs than they had lost from property taxes. Public housing projects were denser and of higher value than the substandard housing or vacant land they typically replaced, thus producing payments higher than the taxes previously collected. He also noted that many properties on which public housing were built had been delinquent on their taxes and that PILOTs assured localities "income similar to taxes without involving the usual expense connected with tax-assessment and collection procedures." Fisher, *Twenty Years of Public Housing*, 197.

59. For firsthand accounts of attacks on the New Deal in California, see Sinclair, *I, Candidate for Governor*, and Ernest Besig, ACLU Director, to Hon. Maury Maverick (January 16, 1940), Folder 108 "General Correspondence, (Jan.–March 1940), ACLU, CHS. Attacks of the New Deal varied from industry to industry, region to region. Robert Collins, *The Business Response to Keynes, 1929–1964* (New York: Columbia University Press, 1981); Devra Weber, *Dark Sweat, White Gold: California Farm Workers, Cotton, and the New Deal* (Berkeley: University of California Press, 1994); Nelson Lichtenstein, *State of the Union: A Century of American Labor* (Princeton, NJ: Princeton University Press, 2001), especially chapter 3; Ira Katznelson, *Fear Itself: The New Deal and the Origins of Our Time* (New York: Liveright, 2013).

60. SFHA, *Minutes* (June 22, 1939).

61. SFHA, *Minutes* (March 9, 1939; September 21 and 28, 1939; November 30, 1939; and December 14, 1939).

62. The two films went through title changes, from *San Francisco Sees the Light* and *More Than Shelter* to *Our City* and *Housing in Our Time* (available at www.archive.org/details/housing_in_our_time). SFHA, *Minutes* (March 21 and 28, 1940; May 15 and 29, 1941; June 26, 1941; and July 10, 1941); SFHA, *Third Annual Report* (1941); 1940 Program Report, Folder 1 "Annual Program Report," Box 10, MS 1270, League of Women Voters of San Francisco, CHS.

63. Johnson, "Public Attitudes Towards Housing in San Francisco"; Griffith, "A Review of the Proceedings of the Housing Authority of San Francisco"; SFHA, *Second Annual Report* (1940) and *Third Annual Report* (1941). On positive media coverage, see "New Designs for Living" (March 18–23, 1940). On the SFHA not abusing its social power, see "New Designs for Living" (March 19, 1940).

64. SFHA, 1939 *Real Property Survey* (1940); President of San Francisco Junior Chamber of Commerce Arthur Dolan to Civic Clubs of San Francisco (November 10, 1939), Folder 50 "SF Housing Authority," Carton 1, Reference Files, Chinese Historical Society of America, ESL; School of Social Studies, San Francisco College, *Living Conditions in Chinatown* (1939), Folder "Hogan—Living in Chinatown," Box 2, Records of the Central Office: Records of the Office of the Central Historian, Records Relating to the History of the Agency ("Historical File"), 1934–48, RG 196, NARA/CP. Nayan Shah detailed the informal and formal mechanisms that San Francisco whites used to contain the Chinese to Chinatown in his *Contagious Divides: Epidemics and Race in San Francisco's Chinatown* (Berkeley: University of California Press, 2001).

65. Quote in SFHA, *Minutes* (July 21, 1938). Emily Fong usually appears as Mrs. B. S. Fong in historical records. Yung, *Unbound Feet*.

66. SFHA, *Minutes* (October 26, 1939).

67. SFHA, *Minutes* (February 8, 1940); SFHA, *Second Annual Report* (1940) and *Third Annual Report* (1941). Shah, *Contagious Divides*, chapter 8.

68. See Friends of China material in Folder 34 "1937 Jan to Dec.," Box 8, League of Women Voters of San Francisco, MS 1270, CHS. Historian William Issel argues that in the 1930s and 1940s, race relations improved in San Francisco, though customs were slow to change especially in housing. Issel, "Liberalism and Urban Policy in San Francisco." On change and continuity in white stereotypes of Chinese and Chinese Americans within the context of New Deal programs, see Yung, *Unbound Feet*; Shah, *Contagious Divides*.

69. Three-quarters of property owners in Chinatown were of Chinese descent. "New Designs for Living" (March 23, 1940); Shah, *Contagious Divides*, 234–37.

70. SFHA, *Minutes* (October 19, 1939).

71. SFHA, *Minutes* (December 14, 1939).

72. SFHA, *Minutes* (February 1, 1940; February 29, 1940); "New Designs for Living" (March 23, 1940).

73. SFHA, *Minutes* (June 13, 1940, and July 25, 1940); SFHA, *Minutes* (June 20, 1940).

74. Folders 5 and 6, "Ping Yuen Housing Project, Correspondence," Box 1, Henry Temple Howard Papers, EDL; SFHA, *Twenty-Seventh Annual Report* (1964–65); "New Designs for Living" (March 23, 1940); Shah, *Contagious Divides*, chapter 8.

75. SFHA, *Minutes* (May 26, 1938, and June 2, 1938). Quote in May 26, 1938, *Minutes*.

76. SFHA, *Minutes* (January 4, February 8, and February 15, 1940); Sara Jenkins to Mildred Andrews Letter (April 27, 1940), Folder 339, Box 97–17, Stewart-Flippin Papers, MSRL. Evers quote in SFHA, *Minutes* (January 4, 1940).

77. Sara Jenkins to Mildred Andrews Letter (April 27, 1940), Folder 339, Box 97–17, Stewart-Flippin Papers, MSRL.

78. "Social evils" quote in Jenkins letter to Mrs. M. P. Hagin, WPA (May 6, 1940). Jenkins's letter, the WPA application, and related documents are in Folder 339, Box 97–17, Stewart-Flippin Papers, MSRL. Although the WPA did not approve Jenkins's application, in the 1930s the federal government did fund such research on intergroup relations with the goal of reducing racial discrimination. The Public Housing Administration formed an "Intergroup Relations Branch" in 1936 to study race relations. See materials in "Records of the Intergroup Relations Branch, 1936–1963," RG 196, NARA/CP.

79. SFHA, *Minutes* (March 28, 1940). The political pressure leading up to the advisory committee is in SFHA *Minutes* from January to March, 1940.

80. Western Addition Housing Council Report (January 2, 1942), Folder 3, Box 3, SPUR, CU; Alice Griffith to Mayor Elmer Robinson (January 26, 1950), Folder "O. A. Correspondences," Carton 14, NAACP West Coast Papers, BANC; Broussard, *Black San Francisco*, chapter 13; Thomas J. Sugrue, *Sweet Land of Liberty: The Forgotten Struggle for Civil Rights in the North* (New York: Random House, 2008).

81. Aronovici, *America Can't Have Housing*; Bauer, *Modern Housing*.

82. SFHA, *Minutes* (June 6, 1940).

83. SFHA, *Minutes* (September 12, September 19, and June 6, 1940); SFHA, *Eighth Annual Report* (no date).

84. The SFHA first named this site Jefferson Park but changed it to Westside Courts, which I use throughout to prevent confusion. For support of the project, see SFHA *Minutes*

(especially September 19, 1940), and the "New Designs for Living" series in the *San Francisco News* (March 18–23, 1940).

85. SFHA, *Minutes* (October 10, 1940, and March 27, 1941).

86. Quotes in SFHA, *Minutes* (April 10, 1941). Katherine Stewart-Flippin, Transcripts of Oral Interview 1977–78, Black Women Oral History Project, Radcliffe College, 68.

87. SFHA, *Minutes* (March 20, 1941).

88. SFHA, *Minutes* (April 10 and April 18, 1941).

89. SFHA, *Minutes* (April 24, 1941).

90. Quotes from undated poster "Housing Authority Act Un-American" and editorial "S.F. Housing Job: Agreed on Principle But Not on Method" in "Scrapbook, 1939–1943," Marshall Dill Papers, CHS. See also "New Designs for Living" (March 22, 1940); "New Fight Looms on Low Rental Projects," *San Francisco Call* (May 3, 1940). Series of letters (especially June 8, 1940), from Nathan Straus to Mrs. John Flick, President of California League of Women Voters, Folder 77B "Project Housing General, 1938–1942," Box 17, League of Women Voters of San Francisco, MS 1270, CHS.

91. "New Designs for Living" (March 22, 1940); SFHA, *Minutes* (March 7, 1940).

92. Grace McCann Morley, "Architects in an Exhibition," *California Arts and Architecture* (March 1942); Sally Carrighar, "Valencia Gardens—A Prelude to Mass Housing," *Architect and Engineer* (March 1943): 20–23, 32; "Valencia Gardens," *Pencil Points* (January 1944): 26–36. Quote by both architects in *Pencil Points*. Wurster would lose government work during the McCarthy era for his New Deal activities. See his and Catherine Bauer's files at UC Berkeley and Bauer's biography by Oberlander and Newbrun, *Houser*.

93. Carrighar, "Valencia Gardens—A Prelude to Mass Housing"; "Valencia Gardens," *Pencil Points*. Quote in "Valencia Gardens," 22.

94. SFHA, *Minutes* (August 29, 1940).

95. SFHA, 1939 *Real Property Survey* (1940), 24–26.

96. SFHA, *Minutes* (September 26, 1940; February 20, 1941; April 10, 1941).

97. The Glen Park Property Owners Association had almost 400 members. For the Glen Crags–SFHA legal battle, see SFHA, *Minutes* (September 26, 1940; February 20, 1941; April 10, 1941; June 12, 1941; July 10, 1941; August 7 and August 21, 1941; September 11 and September 25, 1941; and October 25, 1941). Alice Griffith to Mayor Elmer Robinson (January 26, 1950), Folder "O. A. Correspondences," Carton 14, NAACP West Coast Papers, BANC.

98. See chapter 4.

99. Catherine Bauer to Nathan Straus (July 25, 1940), Folder 5, Box 1, Catherine Bauer Wurster Papers, BANC.

100. Evers noted later that Straus and his staff "agreed on most of the principles" to cut the red tape, but federal procedures did not effectively change. SFHA, *Minutes* (December 12, 1940).

101. "New Designs for Living" (March 21, 1940); "Community of Living Units in the West," *California Arts and Architecture* (January 1942); SFHA, *Eighth Annual Report* (no date).

102. SFHA, *Sixth Annual Report*(1944).

103. "New Designs for Living" (March 19, 1940).

104. "New Designs for Living" (March 19, 1940); Bauer, *A Citizen's Guide to Public Housing*, 44–45; SFPHA, *San Francisco's Public Housing: A Citizen's Guide* (San Francisco

Planning and Housing Association, 1946). Rent and income data from SFHA, *Third Annual Report* (1941). Amy Lynne Howard, *More Than Shelter: Activism and Community in San Francisco Public Housing* (Minneapolis: University of Minnesota Press, 2014), chapter 1.

105. Else Reisner, "Home Making and Family Adjustment Services in Public Housing: The Experience at Holly Courts, the First Western Housing Project" (San Francisco: SFHA, 1942); Bauer, *A Citizen's Guide to Public Housing*, 44–45; SFPHA, *San Francisco's Public Housing: A Citizen's Guide*.

106. Reisner, "Home Making and Family Adjustment Services in Public Housing." Reisner's report reflected the gendered and sometimes awkward transition from the moral reform impulse of the progressive era to the economic reform impulse of the New Deal. That political and cultural transition, put simply, attempted to recast social benefits—such as housing, social insurance programs, and relief—as social rights, not charity, and shift responsibility from private institutions to public institutions.

107. Bauer, *A Citizen's Guide to Public Housing*; SFHA, *Eighth Annual Report* (no date).

108. Reisner, "Home Making and Family Adjustment Services in Public Housing," 14–17.

109. SFHA, *Eighth Annual Report* (no date); Reisner, "Home Making and Family Adjustment Services in Public Housing."

110. SFHA, 1939 *Real Property Survey* (1940).

111. The evolution of economic and civil rights of citizens can be examined in the following works: T. H. Marshall, *Class, Citizenship, and Social Development* (New York: Doubleday, 1964); Rodgers, *Atlantic Crossings*; Michael B. Katz, *The Price of Citizenship: Redefining the American Welfare State* (Philadelphia: University of Pennsylvania Press, 2008); Alice Kessler-Harris, *In Pursuit of Equity: Women, Men, and the Quest for Economic Citizenship in 20th-Century America* (New York: Oxford University Press, 2003); Sugrue, *Sweet Land of Liberty*; Issel, *Church and State in the City*; Mark Hendrickson, *American Labor and Economic Citizenship: New Capitalism from World War I to the Great Depression* (Cambridge: Cambridge University Press, 2013).

112. SFHA, *Second Annual Report* (1940).

113. Letter (February 22, 1940), Folder 5, Box 1, Catherine Bauer Wurster Papers, BANC.

114. Griffith, "A Review of the Proceedings of the Housing Authority of San Francisco."

CHAPTER 3

1. Nathan Straus, *The Seven Myths of Housing* (New York: Arno Press, 1974 [1944]), 11.

2. For federal commitments, see "War Housing Week: Ceremonies at Center to Mark Opening of New Campaign," *San Francisco Chronicle* (January 24, 1943); "War Housing Week Starts with S.F. Rally," *San Francisco Chronicle* (January 26, 1943); and a special housing section in the January 27, 1943, issue of the *San Francisco Chronicle*. Marilynn S. Johnson, "Urban Arsenals: War Housing and Social Change in Richmond and Oakland, California, 1941–1945," *Pacific Historical Review* (1991): 283–308; Shirley Ann Wilson Moore, *To Place Our Deeds: The African American Community in Richmond, California, 1910–1963* (Berkeley: University of California Press, 2000), chapter 3. Quote in "Why Not Convert Your Attic or Basement into an Apartment," *San Francisco Chronicle* (January 27, 1943).

3. Special housing section, *San Francisco Chronicle* (January 27, 1943); "Exodus of 10,000 from S.F. Suggested as Housing Aid," *San Francisco Chronicle* (August 5, 1943).

4. Johnson, "Urban Arsenals," 290.

5. Vicki L. Ruiz, *Cannery Women, Cannery Lives: Mexican Women, Unionization, and the California Food Processing Industry,* 1930–1950 (University of New Mexico Press, 1987); Roger W. Lotchin, *Fortress California* 1910–1961: *From Warfare to Welfare* (New York: Oxford University Press, 1991), 131–69, and *The Bad City in the Good War: San Francisco, Los Angeles, Oakland, and San Diego* (Bloomington: Indiana University Press, 2003); Roger W. Lotchin, ed., *The Way We Really Were: The Golden State in the Second Great War* (Chicago: University of Illinois Press, 2000); Moore, *To Place Our Deeds,* chapter 3; William Issel, *Church and State in the City: Catholics and Politics in Twentieth Century San Francisco* (Philadelphia: Temple University Press, 2012).

6. Charles Spurgeon Johnson, *The Negro War Worker in San Francisco: A Local Self-Study* (San Francisco: Y.W.C.A and American Missionary Association, May 1944), 10–16; Bruce J. Schulman, *From Cotton Belt to Sunbelt: Federal Policy, Economic Development, and the Transformation of the South,* 1938–1980 (Durham: Duke University Press, 1991); Albert S. Broussard, *Black San Francisco: The Struggle for Racial Equality in the West,* 1900–1940 (Lawrence: University Press of Kansas, 1993), 24; Moore, *To Place Our Deeds,* chapter 3.

7. SFHA, *Minutes* (1941–1945); Johnson, *The Negro War Worker,* 10–16; Department of Commerce and Bureau of Census, "Population," Folder III CA, San Francisco, Box 2, Labor Records, "Record of the Intergroup Relations Branch, 1936–63," RG 196, NARA/CP; Broussard, *Black San Francisco,* 24, 133–36.

8. SFHA, *Minutes* (August 21, 1941, and December 4, 1941).

9. SFHA, *Minutes* (December 18, 1941).

10. Western Addition Housing Council Report (January 2, 1942), Folder 3, Box 3, SPUR, CU; SFHA, 1939 *San Francisco Real Property Survey* (1940); Johnson, *The Negro War Worker;* Leo Katcher, *Earl Warren: A Political Biography* (New York: McGraw-Hill, 1967), chapters 18 and 19; Broussard, *Black San Francisco,* 171–74, quote on 173.

11. SFHA *Minutes* (February 19, 1942); SFHA, *Eighth Annual Report* (no date).

12. Copper wiring was one of the most needed materials. SFHA, *Minutes* (October 22, 1942).

13. "Testimony of Nathan Straus, Before the Special Committee Investigating the National Defense Program, United States Senate, October 29, 1941," Folder "California State Counsel of Defense, Housing," Box 21, "General Correspondence, 1936 to 1943," RG 187, NARA/SB; SFHA, *Minutes* (October 22, 1942).

14. SFHA, *Minutes* (December 27, 1942).

15. SFHA, *Minutes* (August 27, 1942, and April 16, 1942); SFHA, *Eighth Annual Report* (no date); SFPHA, *San Francisco's Public Housing: A Citizen's Guide* (San Francisco Planning and Housing Association, 1946); "Valencia Gardens," *Pencil Points* (January 1944): 26–36; Alexander von Hoffman, "The Curse of Durability: Why Housing for the Poor Was Built to Last," *Journal of Housing and Community Development* 55, 5 (September/October: 1998): 34–38. On Bufano, see Tommy Lott, "Black Consciousness in the Art of Sargent Johnson," in James Brook, Chris Carlsson, and Nancy J. Peters, eds., *Reclaiming San Francisco: History, Politics, and Culture* (San Francisco: City Lights Books, 1998); Amy Lynne Howard, *More Than Shelter: Activism and Community in San Francisco Public Housing* (Minneapolis: University of Minnesota Press, 2014), chapter 5.

16. SFHA, *Minutes* (August 27, 1942, and April 16, 1942); SFHA, *Eighth Annual Report* (no date); SFPHA, *San Francisco's Public Housing;* "Valencia Gardens"; von Hoffman, "The Curse of Durability."

17. "Testimony of Nathan Straus, Before the Special Committee Investigating the National Defense Program, United States Senate, October 29, 1941," Folder "California State Counsel of Defense, Housing," Box 21, "General Correspondence, 1936 to 1943," RG 187, NARA/SB; Robert B. Fairbanks, *Making Better Citizens: Housing Reform and the Community Development Strategy in Cincinnati, 1890–1960* (Urbana: Illinois University Press, 1988), 136–38; Robert Moore Fisher, *Twenty Years of Public Housing: Economic Aspects of Public Housing* (New York: Harper, 1959), 104–06; J. Paul Mitchell, ed., *Federal Housing Policy and Programs: Past and Present* (New Brunswick, NJ: Rutgers University Press, 1985), 194–95; Ruth G. Weintraub and Rosalind Tough, "Federal Housing and World War II," *Journal of Land and Public Utility Economics* 18, 2 (May 1942): 155–62; Kristin M. Szylvian, "The Federal Housing Program During World War II," in John F. Bauman, Roger Biles, and Kristin M. Szylvian, eds., *From Tenements to the Taylor Homes: In Search of an Urban Housing Policy in Twentieth-Century America* (University Park: Penn State University Press, 2000). Public housing supporters also lobbied for the USHA to run the program. See CHPA Newsletter, Folder "CHPA," Box 19, "General Correspondence," RG 187, NARA/CP; Catherine Bauer to Senator Wagner (December 18, 1941), Folder 6, "1941," Box 1 Correspondence, Catherine Bauer Wurster Papers, BANC.

18. SFHA, *Seventh Annual Report* (1945) and *Eighth Annual Report* (no date); Los Angeles Housing Authority, "The Housing Authority of the City of Los Angeles Presents a Solution," *California Arts and Architecture* (May 1943); Johnson, "Urban Arsenals."

19. George H. Thomas, Jr., "Appraisal," Folder "Hunters Point," Box 9, RG 196, NARA/SB.

20. SFHA, *Seventh Annual Report* (1945) and *Eighth Annual Report* (no date); SFHA, *Minutes* (October 19, 1944); Lawrence J. Vale, *Purging the Poorest: Public Housing and the Design Politics of Twice-Cleared Communities* (Chicago: University of Chicago Press, 2013).

21. SFHA, *Minutes* (May 6, June 10, July 15, November 4, and November 18, 1943; March 23, 1944; and August 2, 1945).

22. Spalding replaced the labor representative Alexander Watchman on the SFHA in 1943. Quote in SFHA, *Minutes* (May 24, 1944). A Public Housing Administration bulletin noted that the temporary units had a "substandard design, size and composition." See Federal Public Housing Administration, *Bulletin* 2, 4 (September 1, 1944), Folder "FPHA Bulletins, (1946–1944)," Box 9 Senate and House Bills, 1945–46, Records Relating to the History of the Agency, 1934–48, RG 196, NARA/CP.

23. Johnson, "Urban Arsenals"; SFHA, *Minutes* (1944–45); SFHA, *Seventh Annual Report* (1945) and *Eighth Annual Report* (no date).

24. Maurice Harrison, "Report of the Mayor's Committee on Civic Unity of San Francisco" (March 15, 1945), Stewart-Flippin Papers, Folder 377, Box 97–19, MSRC; special housing section, *San Francisco Chronicle* (January 27, 1943; Mel Scott to V. B. Stanbery (February 5, 1943), "Letters Sent Jan. 1936–43, Folder S-Index Copies," Box 9, Series Letters Sent Jan. 1936–43, RG 187, NARA/SB. During war, the SFHA commissioners and staff were in constant negotiations with businesses. SFHA, *Minutes* (especially January 6, 1944) and *Sixth Annual Report* (1944), *Seventh Annual Report* (1945), and *Eighth Annual Report* (no date) for range of services provided to tenants.

25. Ibid. "City within a city" quote in SFHA, *Sixth Annual Report* (1944).

26. SFHA, *Minutes* (January 2, 1947); SFHA, *Sixth Annual Report* (1944), *Seventh Annual*

Report (1945), and *Eighth Annual Report* (no date); "City Hits Tax Jackpot: SFHA Tax Payment of $407,449.61," *San Francisco Housing* 4, 1 (January 1947).

27. See discussions in SFHA, *Minutes* (1941–1945); San Francisco Home Builders Forum, Associated Home Builders of San Francisco (July 1945), Folder 34, Box 1, 3199, SPUR, CU.

28. Ibid.

29. SFPHA, *San Francisco's Public Housing*; special housing section, *San Francisco Chronicle* (January 27, 1943); Johnson, "Urban Arsenals"; Los Angeles Housing Authority, "The Housing Authority of the City of Los Angeles."

30. Some scholars have explained the underdeveloped nature of the U.S. welfare state by pointing to the lack of institutional capacity; public housing authorities in the 1940s offer a counterargument. See Margaret Weir, Ann Shola Orlof, and Theda Skocpol, eds., *The Politics of Social Policy in the United States* (Princeton, NJ: Princeton University Press, 1988); Theda Skocpol, "Political Responses to Capitalist Crisis: Neo-Marxist Theories of the State and the Case of the New Deal," *Politics and Society* 10, 2 (1980): 155–201.

31. See letters (especially January 22, January 29, and February 6, 1942), Folder "Urban Redevelopment," Box 94, "General Correspondence, 1936–1943," RG 187, NARA/SB. Quotes in Albert Evers letter to Earl Draper(January 22, 1942).

32. Ibid. Draper quote is in response to Evers's proposal but in a letter to Morse Erskine (February 6, 1942). Gail Radford, *The Rise of the Public Authority: Statebuilding and Economic Development in Twentieth-Century America* (Chicago: University of Chicago Press, 2013).

33. The California housing and planning community joined the national campaign to keep the NRPB open. See letters and documents, especially CHPA, Confidential (February 23, 1943), Folder "V. B. Stanbery—Confidential," Box 89, "General Correspondence, 1936–1943," RG 187, NARA/SB. Marion Clawson, *New Deal Planning: The National Resource Planning Board* (Baltimore: Johns Hopkins University Press, 1981); Radford, *The Rise of the Public Authority*.

34. Ibid.

35. See CHPA Memorandum No. 2 (March 5, 1943), which reviewed California bills related to housing and planning. Assembly Bills 1441 and 1443 would have expanded housing authority power along the lines Albert Evers and Earl Draper discussed. Memorandum (March 5, 1943), Folder "State Planning CA," Box 89, "General Correspondence, 1936–1943," RG 189, NARA/SB. National Association of Housing Officials, *Housing for the United States After the War*, Publication No. N193 (May 1944); Mark I. Gelfand, *A Nation of Cities: The Federal Government and Urban America, 1933–1965* (New York: Oxford University Press, 1975).

36. Quotes in the Commonwealth Club of California, *The Commonwealth* 19, 48 (November 29, 1943). For the public and private policies that produced the flow of capital and whites to the suburbs, see Kenneth Jackson, *Crabgrass Frontier: The Suburbanization of the United States* (New York: Oxford University Press, 1985), chapters 10–12.

37. Smith's critique of state-sponsored integration drew on popular ideas about race relations. Quotes from Commonwealth Club of California, *The Commonwealth*. Another argument against public housing was that increasing low-rent housing supply reduced the profits and power of landlords. See the February 1941 issue of *Apartment Houses and Management* monthly, Folder "San Francisco Housing Reports," Special Collections,

SFPL. On the growing civil rights movement outside of the U.S. South, see Thomas J. Sugrue, *Sweet Land of Liberty: The Forgotten Struggle for Civil Rights in the North* (New York: Random House, 2008).

38. W. K. Granger to Mr. A. S. Brown, Chairman of Department of Publicity and Industrial Development (February 16, 1943), Folder "V. B. Stanbery—Confidential," Box 89, Series "General Correspondence, 1936–1943," RG 187, NARA/SB; Commonwealth Club of California, *The Commonwealth*; Straus, *Seven Myths of Housing*; Gelfand, *A Nation of Cities*, chapter 6; Donald Craig Parson, *Making a Better World: Public Housing, the Red Scare, and the Direction of Modern Los Angeles* (Minneapolis: University of Minnesota Press, 2005).

39. Ibid.

40. Broussard, *Black San Francisco*, 133–36, 172–73; Johnson, *The Negro War Worker*, 28–33; Clement E. Vose, *Caucasians Only: The Supreme Court, the NAACP, and the Restrictive Covenant Cases* (Berkeley: University of California Press, 1959); Jackson, *Crabgrass Frontier*, chapters 10–12.

41. Scholars have examined discriminatory public policies and their connection to assessments of deserving social groups and political and economic power. Anne Larason Schneider and Helen Ingram, *Policy Design for Democracy* (Lawrence: University Press of Kansas, 1997), and Vale, *Purging the Poorest*. For SFHA tenant selection practices, see SFHA, *Minutes*; Western Addition Housing Council Report (January 2, 1942), Folder 3, Box 3, SPUR, CU; Broussard, *Black San Francisco*; Howard, *More Than Shelter*.

42. See SFHA, *Minutes* (February and March, 1942).

43. For the concerned citizens, see SFHA, *Minutes* (March 5, 1942). The tensions leading up to the 1943 Detroit race riots are described in Thomas J. Sugrue, *The Origins of the Urban Crisis: Race and Inequality in Postwar Detroit* (Princeton, NJ: Princeton University Press, 2005), 28–30.

44. Broussard, *Black San Francisco*, 194–200; SFHA, *Minutes* (April and May 1942). Quote in SFHA, *Minutes* (May 21, 1942).

45. *CHPA Newsletter* 1, 7 (December 9, 1942); CHPA Memorandum No. 2 (March 5, 1943), Folder CHPA, Box 19, "General Correspondence, 1936 to 1943," RG 187, NARA/SB; document entitled "San Francisco" (no date), Folder 39, Box 2, 3199 SPUR, CU; Broussard, *Black San Francisco*.

46. SFHA, *Minutes* (March, April, and May 1942).

47. Resolution in SFHA, *Minutes* (May 21, 1942).

48. *CHPA Newsletter*; CHPA Memorandum No. 2; "San Francisco"; Katcher, *Earl Warren*, chapters 17–25; Jack Harrison Pollack, *Earl Warren: The Judge Who Changed America* (Upper Saddle River, NJ: Prentice-Hall, 1979), chapters 3–4; Broussard, *Black San Francisco*. Quote in Augustus Hawkins to Robert Flippin (February 1, 1943), Folder 225, Box 97–17, Stewart-Flippin Papers, MSRC.

49. Mario García, *Mexican Americans: Leadership, Ideology, and Identity, 1930–1960* (New Haven, CT: Yale University Press, 1991); George Lipsitz, *Rainbow at Midnight: Labor and Culture in the 1940s* (Chicago: University of Illinois Press, 1994), chapter 4; K. Scott Wong, "War Comes to Chinatown: Social Transformation and the Chinese of California," in Lotchin, *The Way We Really Were*; Judy Yung, *Unbound Feet: A Social History of Chinese Women in San Francisco* (Berkeley: University of California Press, 1995); Nayan Shah, *Contagious Divides: Epidemics and Race in San Francisco's Chinatown* (Berkeley: University of California

Press, 2001), chapter 8; Darlene Clark Hine, "Black Professionals and Race Consciousness: Origins of the Civil Rights Movement, 1890–1950," *Journal of American History* 89 (March 2003): 1279–94; Sugrue, *Sweet Land of Liberty*; Ira Katznelson, *Fear Itself: The New Deal and the Origins of Our Time* (New York: Liveright, 2013).

50. Social science research on intergroup relations can be traced to Du Bois's work in Philadelphia, but it accelerated in the first half of the twentieth century. See W. E. B. Du Bois, *The Philadelphia Negro: A Social Study* (Philadelphia: University of Pennsylvania Press, 1899); Gunnar Myrdal, *An American Dilemma: The Negro Problem and Modern Democracy* (New York: Harper & Row, 1944); St. Clair Drake and Horace R. Cayton, *Black Metropolis: A Study of Negro Life in a Northern City* (Chicago: University of Chicago Press, 1945); Alice O'Connor, *Poverty Knowledge: Social Science, Social Policy, and the Poor in Twentieth-Century U.S. History* (Princeton, NJ: Princeton University Press, 2001), chapter 3. African American writers also explained racial discrimination in this era. See Richard Wright, *Native Son* (New York: Harper & Row, 1940); Chester Himes, *If He Hollers Let Him Go* (New York: Signet, 1945); Ralph Ellison, *Invisible Man* (New York: Random House, 1947).

51. Johnson, *The Negro War Worker*; O'Connor, *Poverty Knowledge*, chapter 3. On Johnson's significance in national race relations discussions, see Patrick J. Gilpin and Marybeth Gasman, *Charles S. Johnson: Leadership Beyond the Veil in the Age of Jim Crow* (Albany: SUNY Press, 2003); Richard Robbins, *Sidelines Activist: Charles S. Johnson and the Struggle for Civil Rights* (Jackson: University Press of Mississippi, 2010).

52. Katherine Flippin, Black Women Oral History Project, Radcliffe College, 1977–1978 (oral interview). Some established African Americans offered classes on "charm" and "proper public deportment." *Historical Souvenir Booklet: Black History Week* (Feb. 12–14, 1978), SF African American Historical and Cultural Society, Folder 515, Box 97–28, Stewart-Flippin Papers, MSRC.

53. Quote in Johnson, "Urban Arsenals," 301; Johnson, *The Negro War Worker*.

54. Broussard, *Black San Francisco*, 133–36, 172–73; Johnson, *The Negro War Worker*.

55. Report of the Interim Steering Committee of the Johnson Survey (June 30, 1944), "Other Organizations," Box 17, ACLU, CHS. The tensions existed in other cities, too. See Keith E. Collins, *Black Los Angeles: The Maturing of the Ghetto, 1940–1950* (Saratoga, CA: Century Twenty One Publishing, 1980); Sugrue, *The Origins of the Urban Crisis*; Moore, *To Place Our Deeds*.

56. Eileen Kulchar, President of YWCA, to Morse Erskine, San Francisco Planning and Housing Association (August 20, 1943), Folder 12, Box 3, 3199, SPUR, CU. Quotes in Johnson, *The Negro War Worker*.

57. Johnson, *The Negro War Worker*; Broussard, *Black San Francisco*. Although usually applied to worker struggles, especially as it hurt cross-racial solidarity, the concept of whiteness complements older intergroup research that explains white resistance to integration and racial equality. David R. Roediger, *The Wages of Whiteness: Race and the Making of the American Working Class* (New York: Verso, 1993); Peter Kolchin, "Whiteness Studies: The New History of Race in America," *Journal of American History* 89, 1 (June 2002), 154–73. For older research, see Oliver Cromwell Cox, *Caste, Class, and Race: A Study in Social Dynamics* (New York: Doubleday, 1948), 640–705; John Dollard, *Caste and Class in a Southern Town* (New York: Doubleday Anchor, 1937); Myrdal, *An American Dilemma*; Drake and Cayton, *Black Metropolis*.

58. Johnson, *The Negro War Worker*; Johnson, "Urban Arsenals," 301; Moore, *To Place Our Deeds*; Shah, *Contagious Divides*.

59. SFHA, *Minutes* (August 17 and August 19, 1943); "Housing Board Fight," *San Francisco Chronicle* (October 19, 1943); Alice Griffith, "A Review of the Proceedings of the Housing Authority of San Francisco" (April 18, 1938 to August 17, 1943), Folder 377, Box 97–19, Stewart-Flippin Papers, MSRC.

60. "Unfair practices" quote in Griffith, "A Review of the Proceedings." Dill quote is in his letter to Rossi (August 18, 1943), Folder 34, Box 3, Dill Papers MS3357, CHS.

61. Edgar Zook to Albert Evers Letter (August 19, 1943), Folder 34, Box 3, Marshall Dill Papers, CHS.

62. For support of Griffith, Evers, and Dill, see 1943 and 1944 letters in Box 1 and Box 2, Catherine Bauer Wurster Papers, BANC, and clippings and letters in Folder 34, Box 3, Marshall Dill Papers, CHS. For Post's views, see *San Francisco Examiner* (August 19, 1943); Bauer quote in letter to Martha (November 30, 1943), Folder 1, Box 2, Catherine Bauer Wurster Papers, BANC.

63. Alice Griffith to Catherine Bauer (August 29, 1943), Folder 15, Box 18, Catherine Bauer Wurster Papers, BANC; Bauer to Martha (November 30, 1943); "Housing Board Fight" *San Francisco Chronicle* (October 19, 1943).

64. "Housing Board Fight" (October 19, 1943); Griffith, "A Review of the Proceedings of the Housing Authority."

65. SFHA, *Minutes* (November 4, 1943); SFHA, *Fourth Annual Report* (1942), *Fifth Annual Report* (1943), and *Eighth Annual Report* (no date). For discrimination in AFL unions in the Bay Area, see School of Social Studies, San Francisco College, *Living Conditions in Chinatown* (1939), Folder "Hogan—Living in Chinatown," Box 2, Records of the Central Office: Records of the Office of the Central Historian, Records Relating to the History of the Agency ("Historical File"), 1934–48, RG 196, NARA/CP; Broussard, *Black San Francisco*; Yung, *Unbound Feet*.

66. SFHA, *Minutes* (June 8, 1944).

67. Quotes in SFHA, *Minutes* (June 8, 1944, and November 15, 1945). The CIO and International Longshore and Warehouse Union (ILWU), in contrast to the San Francisco Board of Supervisors, requested an expansion of 20,000 permanent public housing units for San Francisco. See ILWU to G. H. Hembold (February 3, 1945), Folder 376, Box 97–19, Stewart-Flippin Papers, MSRC. On the ways local elites used and misused public authorities, see Philip Selznick, *TVA and the Grass Roots: A Study in the Sociology of Formal Organization* (New York Harper & Row, 1966); Radford, *The Rise of the Public Authority*. For liberalism, see William Issel, "New Deal and Wartime Origins of San Francisco's Postwar Political Culture: The Case of Growth and Policy," in Lotchin, *The Way We Really Were*; Issel, "Liberalism and Urban Policy in San Francisco from the 1930s to the 1960s," *Western Historical Quarterly* 22, 4 (November 1991): 431–50; and Issel, *Church and State in the City*.

68. Beard quote in Broussard, *Black San Francisco*, 177–78; SFHA, *Minutes* (November 16, 1944).

69. Johnson, *The Negro War Worker*; SFHA, *Minutes* (August 6, 1945); SFHA, *Fourth Annual Report* (1942), *Fifth Annual Report* (1943), and *Eighth Annual Report* (no date).

70. Andrews commented on everything from refrigerators and strange odors to race relations. SFHA, *Minutes* (February 15, 1945).

71. See CCU and Mayor's Committee on Civic Unity of San Francisco meeting minutes and reports in Folders 375–381, Box 97–19, Stewart-Flippin Papers, MSRC; Broussard, *Black San Francisco*, chapter 11.

72. The CCU replaced the defunct BACAD. Quotes in Gibson letters to Flippin (February 15, 1945) and Council Member (May 8, 1945), Folder 375, Box 97–19, Stewart-Flippin Papers, MSRC. Also see Broussard, *Black San Francisco*, chapter 11; Issel, *Church and State in the City*.

73. For overlap of members of CCU and the Mayor's Committee on Civic Unity, see minutes of both groups in Folders 37–381, Box 97–19, Stewart-Flippin Papers, MSRC.

74. Quote in Harrison, "Report of the Mayor's Committee on Civic Unity of San Francisco."

75. Beard's statements are in Mayor's Committee on Civic Unity, *Minutes* (November 15, 1944), Folder 380, Box 97–19, Stewart-Flippin Papers, MSRC.

76. Quote in Mayor's Committee on Civic Unity, *Minutes* (November 15, 1944). For the findings of the CCU and the Mayor's Committee on Civic Unity, see meeting notes of both groups in Folders 37–381, Box 97–19, Stewart-Flippin Papers, MSRC.

77. Quote in Lucy McWilliams's report to Harold Boyd (February 28, 1945), Folder 376, Box 97–19, Stewart-Flippin Papers, MSRC.

78. CCU Meeting Notes, Folders 37–381, Box 97–19, Stewart-Flippin Papers, MSRC. For Dunleavy's recommendation and quotes, see CCU Meeting Notes (January 11, 1945), Folder 381, Box 97–19, Stewart-Flippin Papers, MSRC.

79. National Housing Agency, FPHA (December 31, 1945), "Tenant Organizations, Activities and Services in War and Low-Rent Housing," Folder "S-640 Statistics Division," Box 140, Reports Containing Statistics on Public Housing Operations, 1939–1969, RG 196, NARA/CP.

80. Quote in Mayor's Committee on Civic Unity "Questions and Answers" with John Beard (January 17, 1945), Folder 377, Box 97–19, Stewart-Flippin Papers, MSRC. Beard's managerial style was that of an authoritarian. See chapter 4, and Donald Canter, "Housing Head Defends His Regime," *San Francisco Chronicle* (October 10, 1965).

81. Harrison, "Report of the Mayor's Committee on Civic Unity of San Francisco."

82. On Beard, see chapter 4, and Canter, "Housing Head Defends His Regime." For the Richmond rent strike, see *U.N.A. Rent Strike Bulletin* (February 15, 1945), Folder "Discrimination, Racial—General Housing, 1940–1950," #566, ACLU, CHS; Questions and Answers (January 17, 1945), Folder 377, Box 97–19, Stewart-Flippin Papers, MSRC; Wilson Wyatt, FPHA Commissioner, "Weekly Report No. 20," Folder "Weekly Report to Administrator [Sept. 47–July 1946] (1 of 2), Box 12, Records of the Central Office: Records of the Office of the Central Historian, "Records Relating to the History of the Agency ("Historical File"), 1934–1948, RG 196, NARA/CP. For the two years of negotiations between tenants, African American leaders, and city officials in Richmond, see Moore, *To Place Our Deeds*, chapter 3.

83. For tenant–landlord relations, see Elizabeth Blackmar, *Manhattan For Rent, 1785–1850* (Ithaca, NY: Cornell University Press, 1989); Charles W. McCurdy, *The Anti-Rent Era in New York Law and Politics, 1839–1865* (Chapel Hill: University of North Carolina Press, 2001). For parallels with the evolution of management rights in labor–capital relations, see Christopher L. Tomlins, *The State and the Unions* (Cambridge: Cambridge University Press, 1985); Edna Bonacich, "A Theory of Ethnic Antagonism: The Split Labor Market," *American*

Sociological Review 37, 5 (October 1987): 547–59; David Roediger and Elizabeth D. Esch, *The Production of Difference: Race and the Management of Labor in U.S. History* (New York: Oxford University Press, 2012).

84. "Authority Warns of S.F. Harlem," *San Francisco Chronicle* (September 19, 1945). Charles Johnson had suggested the same in his *The Negro War Worker.*

85. SFHA, *Minutes* (November 15, 1945). For similar left–labor–civil rights coalitions, see Martha Biondi, *To Stand and Fight: The Struggle for Civil Rights in Postwar New York City* (Cambridge, MA: Harvard University Press, 2006).

86. Quote in CCU Meeting Notes (January 11, 1945), Folder 381, Box 97–19, Stewart-Flippin Papers, MSRC. Johnson, "Urban Arsenals," 301; Johnson, *The Negro War Worker.*

87. See Kenny's speeches in Boxes 12 and 14, Robert W. Kenny Papers, BANC. Quote in "The Proceedings of Statewide Emergency Legislative Conference, Sacramento, CA (January 5 and 6, 1946)," Folder "Attorney General's Office—Postwar Planning and Reconversion," Box 14, Robert W. Kenny Papers, BANC. For conference coverage, see *Los Angeles Times* (January 6–7, 1946). Some scholars see the end of New Deal planning in the 1940s as a result of New Deal liberals putting their energies into civil rights and Keynesian economic policies. See Steve Fraser and Gary Gerstle, eds., *The Rise and Fall of the New Deal Order, 1930–1980* (Princeton, NJ: Princeton University Press, 1990); Alan Brinkley, *Liberalism and Its Discontents* (Cambridge, MA: Harvard University Press, 2000); Nelson Lichtenstein, *Walter Reuther: The Most Dangerous Man in Detroit* (Urbana: University of Illinois Press, 1995); Sugrue, *The Origins of the Urban Crisis.* But those in the California housing and planning community continued to believe that the state should do economic planning, end discrimination, and provide economic security. See Catherine Bauer Papers, BANC; Bauer, SFPHA, *San Francisco Public Housing*; Postwar Speeches and Materials, Boxes 12 and 14, Robert Kenny Papers, BANC; SFHA, *Minutes*; Shah, *Contagious Divides*, chapter 9; Issel, *Church and State in the City.*

88. Philip Klutznick to Orvil Olmsted, Confidential (February 21, 1946), Folder "Monthly Letters to the Regions by Klutznick to Myer [1947–1944]," Box 12, Records of the Central Office: Records of the Office of the Historian, Series "Records Relating to the History of the Agency (Historical File), 1934–1948," RG 196, NARA/CP.

89. See Folders 38 and 39, Box 2, SPUR, CU; "Third Graders Read About City Planning," *San Francisco Chronicle* (September 20, 1948).

90. Katcher, *Earl Warren*, chapters 22–23.

91. Gelfand, *A City of Nations*; Lipsitz, *Rainbow at Midnight*; Michael James Lacey, ed., *The Truman Presidency* (New York: Cambridge University Press, 1991).

92. SFHA, *Minutes* (April 18, 1946); Broussard, *Black San Francisco*, chapters 10 and 12.

93. *San Francisco Housing* 3, 4 (May 1946) [published by SFHA]; Broussard, *Black San Francisco*, chapters 10 and 12.

94. Quote in "City Asked to End Jim Crow Vet Housing," *San Francisco Chronicle* (June 6, 1946); "Supervisors Meeting: Policy Against Vet Segregation in Housing Units Urged by Board," *San Francisco Chronicle* (July 16, 1946).

95. "City Asked to End Jim Crow Vet Housing."

96. Quote in SFPHA, *San Francisco Public Housing: A Citizen's Guide*, 21.

97. Although FPHA policy did not require the integration of public housing programs, FPHA regional director Langdon Post did pressure authorities in the West to eliminate "seg-

regation and discrimination." Langdon Post to San Francisco Board of Supervisors, FPHA Policy on Segregation (May 3, 1946), Folder 13, SPUR, CU; CCU (October 24, 1949), Folder "Discrimination, Racial—General Housing, 1940–1950," #566, ACLU, CHS.

98. SFHA, *Minutes* (November 26, 1947); Marion Howden to Catherine Bauer (January 5, 1949?), Folder "Marion Howden," Box 23, Catherine Bauer Wurster, BANC.

99. Catherine Bauer to Edward Weeks, Editor of *Atlantic Monthly* (May 13, 1945), Folder 5, Box 2, Catherine Bauer Wurster Papers, BANC.

100. Johnson, *The Negro War Worker*, 33.

101. SFPHA, *San Francisco Public Housing: A Citizen's Guide*. "Policy Statement on Planning and Housing, 1946–47," Folder 31, Box 1, California League of Women Voters, MS 1275, CHS; Mayor's Committee on Civic Unity, Meeting Notes, Folders 376–81, Box 97–19, Stewart-Flippin Papers, MSRC; Catherine Bauer, "Report of the Interim Steering Committee of the Johnson Survey" (June 30, 1944), Folder "Other Organizations," Box 17, ACLU, CHS; Secretary of Los Angeles Housing Authority Howard Holtzendorff to Eneas Kane Letter (February 1, 1945), Folder 376, Box 97–19, Stewart-Flippin Papers, MSRC; Langdon Post, Monthly Report (June 4, 1945), to Philip Klutznick, Folder Region I, Monthly Reports, Box 4 Monthly Reports, Series: Records Relating to the History of the Agency (History File), 1934–1948, RG 196, NARA/CP.

102. "Occupancy Reaches New High of 99.25% in January," *San Francisco Housing* 3, 1 (January 1946). Quote in Elmer Robinson, Radio Address, Folder "Reelection Speeches, 1951," Box 2, Elmer Robinson Papers, SFPL.

103. San Francisco Attorney General (May 1, 1947), "Survey of Housing Conditions in San Francisco," Folder "SF Housing Reports 1947," Subject Files, SFPL.

104. San Francisco Home Builders Forum, Associated Home Builders of San Francisco (July 1945), Folder 34, Box 1, 3199, SPUR, CU. SFHA, *Minutes* (May 3, 1946).

105. SFHA Commissioner Thomas proposed eliminating all restrictions for applicants, and despite a second from Commissioner Bullard, his motion did not pass. SFHA, *Minutes* (February 6, 1947; August 7, 1947; March 17, 1949). FPHA Commissioner Raymond Foley, Report No. 43 (June 2, 1947), Folder "Weekly Report to Administrator [Sept 47–July 1946] (1 of 2)," Box 12, Records Relating to the History of the Agency (Historical File, 1934–48), Records of the Central Office: Records of the Office of the Central Historian, RG 196, NARA/CP.

106. SFHA, *Minutes* (February 14, 1948; October 21, 1948; and January 6, 1949).

107. SFHA, *Minutes* (August 21, 1947).

108. Sydney Williams, Chief, Master Plan Division, to Catherine Bauer (December 31, 1948), Folder, "SF Dept. of Planning," Box 36, Catherine Bauer Papers, BANC.

109. Catherine Bauer to Sydney Williams (March 7, 1949), Folder, "Jan.–June 1949," Box 3, Catherine Bauer Papers, BANC. The management of the New York City Housing Authority reduced the problems associated with concentrating the poorest tenants in high-density housing through tenant selection. Nicholas Dagen Bloom, *Public Housing That Worked: New York in the Twentieth Century* (Philadelphia: University of Pennsylvania Press, 2008).

110. Sydney Williams, Chief, Master Plan Division, to Catherine Bauer (April 4, 1949), Folder, "SF Dept. of Planning," Box 36, Catherine Bauer Papers, BANC.

111. SFHA, *Minutes* (September 4, 1947); Gelfand, *A Nation of Cities*; Lawrence J. Vale,

From the Puritans to the Projects: Public Housing and Public Neighbors (Cambridge, MA: Harvard University Press, 2000), chapter 3.

112. Katherine Gray, Housing Report 1946/47, Folder 2, Box 10, League of Women Voters of San Francisco, MS 1270, CHS.

113. SFHA, *Minutes* (December 18, 1947).

114. Ibid.

115. Quotes in Vale, *From the Puritans to the Projects*, 238–39.

116. Gelfand, *A Nation of Cities*, 142–48; Don Parson, "Los Angeles' 'Headline-Happy Public Housing War," *Southern California Quarterly* 65 (Fall 1983): 251–85.

117. Gelfand, *A Nation of Cities*; Lacey, *The Truman Presidency*.

118. Richard O. Davies, *Housing Reform During the Truman Administration* (Columbia: University of Missouri Press, 1966), chapters 8 and 9; preamble quote in Gelfand, *A Nation of Cities*, 153.

119. Gelfand, *A Nation of Cities,* 145–56.

120. Broussard, *Black San Francisco*, 143–77, quote on 169.

CHAPTER 4

1. Proceedings and Debates of the 81st Congress, First Session, *Congressional Record* (June 7, 1949).

2. Edward Howden, CCU, "Housing a Giant: Memorandum of the Willie Mays Incident" (November 27, 1957), Folder "Willie Mays—Discrimination re SF Home Buying," Carton 39, BANC, West Coast NAACP, BANC.

3. SFHA, *Minutes* (August 2, 1951, and January 23, 1952). Keds quote in Nate Hall, "5000 See Dedication of Ping Yuen Housing," *San Francisco Chronicle* (October 22, 1951).

4. Quotes in SFHA, *Fourteenth Annual Report* (1951). SFHA, *Minutes* (October 18, 1951); "New Face for S.F. Chinatown," editorial, *San Francisco Chronicle* (October 20, 1951); "Chinatown's Ping Yuen Dedication Today," *San Francisco Chronicle* (October 21, 1951); and "5000 See Dedication of Ping Yuen Housing," *San Francisco Chronicle* (October 22, 1951); Nayan Shah, *Contagious Divides: Epidemics and Race in San Francisco's Chinatown* (Berkeley: University of California Press, 2001), chapter 9.

5. Quotes in SFHA, *Fourteenth Annual Report* (1951). SFHA, *Minutes* (October 18, 1951); "New Face for S.F. Chinatown"; "Chinatown's Ping Yuen Dedication Today"; "5000 See Dedication of Ping Yuen Housing"; Shah, *Contagious Divides*, chapter 9. On Anna Lee, see SFHA resolution commending her twenty-six years of service. SFHA, *Minutes* (August 18, 1977).

6. An October 3, 1951, *San Francisco Chronicle* editorial, for example, said Ping Yuen would help fight the horrors of the slum. "The disgraceful tenement living which has for so long characterized Chinatown amounts not merely to discomfort to those who must live there. In its dark interiors are rooted the crime and vice and other festering social organisms that bring a measure of economic and cultural loss to us all." On the narrative of Chinatown slums and race, see Shah, *Contagious Divides*.

7. The literature on postwar U.S. social policy emphasizes the ways support for expanding the welfare state ebbed in fits and starts, eventually moving from public planning and welfare state building to macroeconomic policies, employer-provided benefits, and civil rights. See Steve Fraser and Gary Gerstle, eds., *The Rise and Fall of the New Deal Order,*

1930–1980 (Princeton, NJ: Princeton University Press, 1990); Alan Brinkley, *Liberalism and Its Discontents* (Cambridge, MA: Harvard University Press, 2000); Michael James Lacey, ed., *The Truman Presidency* (New York: Cambridge University Press, 1991); Nelson Lichtenstein, *Walter Reuther: The Most Dangerous Man in Detroit* (Urbana: University of Illinois Press, 1995); Thomas J. Sugrue, *The Origins of the Urban Crisis: Race and Inequality in Postwar Detroit* (New Jersey, NJ: Princeton University Press, 2005); Jennifer Klein, *For All These Rights: Business, Labor, and the Shaping of America's Public–Private Welfare State* (Princeton, NJ: Princeton University Press, 2006); Ira Katznelson, *Fear Itself: The New Deal and the Origins of Our Time* (New York: Liveright, 2013).

8. The SFHA used its housing program to show foreign dignitaries how the United States was culturally tolerant during the Cold War. The roster of groups that toured SFHA housing was a who's who of CIA targets and U.S. aid recipients, including Greece, Japan, Guatemala, Burma, Indonesia, and Thailand, to name just a few. SFHA, *Minutes* (October 1, 1953; November 19, 1953; April 5, 1955; and June 2, 1955). Mary L. Dudziak, *Cold War Civil Rights: Race and the Image of American Democracy* (Princeton, NJ: Princeton University Press, 2011).

9. Poll cited in "Urban Redevelopment Meetings Notes" (February 17, 1950), Folder 77A, "Project Housing Authority, 1949–1952," Box 17, League of Women Voters of San Francisco, MS 1270, CHS.

10. For the suburban boom in the San Francisco Bay Area, see "Boom with Sense: Making Dreams Come True in Golden Gate Area," *Newsweek* (December 13, 1954); U.S. Department of Labor, "Bay Area Homebuilding Reached All Time High Peak During 1950" (February 6, 1951), Folder "III California, San Francisco," Box 2 Labor Records, Records of the Intergroup Relations Branch, 1936–63, RG 196, NARA/CP. For suburban development especially in the West, see Roger W. Lotchin, *Fortress California 1910–1961: From Warfare to Welfare* (New York: Oxford University Press, 1991); Becky M. Nicolaides, *My Blue Heaven: Life and Politics in the Working-Class Suburbs of Los Angeles, 1920–1965* (Chicago: University of Chicago Press, 2002); Robert O. Self, *American Babylon: Race and the Struggle for Postwar Oakland* (Princeton, NJ: Princeton University Press, 2005).

11. "Boom with Sense"; Donald Foley, *The Suburbanization of Administrative Offices in the San Francisco Bay Area* (Berkeley: Real Estate Research Program, Bureau of Business and Economic Research, University of California, 1957); Keith E. Collins, *Black Los Angeles: The Maturing of the Ghetto, 1940–1950* (Saratoga, CA: Century Twenty One Publishing, 1980); Arnold R. Hirsch, *Making the Second Ghetto: Race and Housing in Chicago, 1940–1960* (New York: Cambridge University Press, 1983); John F. Bauman, *Public Housing, Race, and Renewal: Urban Planning in Philadelphia, 1920–1974* (Philadelphia: Temple University Press, 1987); Donald Craig Parson, *Making a Better World: Public Housing, the Red Scare, and the Direction of Modern Los Angeles* (Minneapolis: University of Minnesota Press, 2005); Douglas S. Massey and Nancy A. Denton, *American Apartheid: Segregation and the Making of the Underclass* (Cambridge, MA: Harvard University Press, 1994); Sugrue, *The Origins of the Urban Crisis*; Self, *American Babylon*; Nicolaides, *My Blue Heaven*; Richard Rothstein, *The Color of Law: A Forgotten History of How Our Government Segregated America* (New York: Liveright, 2017).

12. Roper quoted in statement by John F. Kennedy in Proceedings and Debates of the 81st Congress. In 1948, housing had ranked first in a Gallop poll. See SFHA, *Minutes* (May 20, 1948).

13. *San Francisco News* (July 2, 1949, and February 7, 1951). Playland was on the decline by the mid-1950s. For these San Francisco districts, see http://www.foundsf.org and http://www.outsidelands.org

14. The Cow Hollow and League of Women Voters collections at the CHS are filled with grassroots efforts by white property owners to maintain racial and class homogeneity in their neighborhoods. See exchange of letters by T. J. Kent, Director of City Planning Commission; Mrs. James Lawry, Chairman of Cow Hollow Improvement Club Zoning Committee; and Alfred Ghirardelli (of chocolate family fame) in Folder 3, Box 1, Cow Hollow MS 3161, CHS; Selah Chamberlain, President of San Francisco Planning and Housing Association, to John Beard, Director of SFHA, Folder 77D "Project Housing, 1949–50," Box 17, League of Women Voters of San Francisco, MS 1270, CHS. "Civic Unity Federation Hits Public Housing Referendum," *San Francisco News* (June 12, 1950).

15. Some 3,000 acres came from tidal reclamation and 160 acres from cemetery relocation. San Francisco Department of City Planning, *Planning* 1, 3 (March 1951), Folder "California—San Francisco #2," Carton 6, Catherine Bauer Papers, BANC; San Francisco Department of City Planning, *San Francisco Population and Housing* (March 1962), BANC. For postwar Chinatown housing trends, see Community Design Center, *Chinatown—An Analysis of Population and Housing* (San Francisco, June 1969). By the 1950s, some thought filling the bay was a solution for adding new land. See the U.S. Army Corps of Engineers (1959), "Future Development of the San Francisco Bay Area, 1960–2020."

16. "Census Has Bad News on S.F. Housing," *San Francisco Chronicle* (November 3, 1950), and "25,000 Homes Are Found Substandard," *San Francisco Chronicle* (June 16, 1952). Quote in "Census Has Bad News on S.F. Housing."

17. Quotes in "Slum Experiment," *San Francisco Chronicle* (May 17, 1950). This local effort by public health mirrored what was happening around the nation. See Andrew Biemiller remarks in Proceedings and Debates of the 81st Congress. For tenant problems with private housing in San Francisco, see 1950 correspondence in Folder "Shelly, John F. (California)," Box 31 Saylor, John to Sikes, Robert, Congressional Correspondence Files, 1942–1962, Special Assistant to the Commissioner for Congressional Liaison, RG 196, NARA/CP.

18. Two years later, the same conditions existed. One landlord was arrested eleven times before fixing his units. "City Officials Plan Attack on Slums," *San Francisco Chronicle* (July 18, 1952). The Public Housing Administration in 1947 allowed the SFHA to spend $1,000 to assist the city's Planning Department to research redevelopment. SFHA Commissioner Edgar Ayer was on the Advisory Committee. See SFHA, *Minutes* (August 7, 1947). By the 1950s, numerous texts about slums existed to support redevelopment in poor communities. See "Slum Clearance Plan for South of Market Region," *San Francisco Chronicle* (June 30, 1952); San Francisco Department of City Planning's report *Modernizing Downtown San Francisco* (January 1955), HUD Library, Washington, DC; HHFA, *How Localities Can Develop a Workable Program for Urban Renewal* (1956), in Folder "Administrator's Advisory Committee on Housing and Community Development 1959, Box 13 Correspondence of the Commissioner of Public Housing, 1952–67," RG 196, NARA/CP.

19. Quote in Catherine Bauer to Max Lerner (December 7, 1955), Folder "October–December, 1955," Box 5, Catherine Bauer Papers, BANC. On the federal role in cities, see Mark H. Rose, *Interstate: Express Highway Politics, 1941–1956* (Lawrence: University Press of Kansas, 1979); Mark Gelfand, *A Nation of Cities: The Federal Government and Urban*

America, 1933–1965 (New York: Oxford University Press, 1975); Kenneth Jackson, *Crabgrass Frontier: The Suburbanization of the United State*s (New York: Oxford University Press, 1985); Lotchin, *Fortress California* 1910–1961; Marc Reisner, *Cadillac Desert: The American West and Its Disappearing Water* (New York: Penguin Books, 1995); Roger Biles, *The Fate of Cities: Urban America and the Federal Government,* 1945–2000 (Lawrence: University Press of Kansas, 2011); Rothstein, *The Color of Law.*

20. On the continuation of U.S. housing advocates looking to Europe for nonspeculative housing, see Catherine Bauer to Honorable Ralph Flanders (February 27, 1950), Folder "January to June 1950," Box 3, Catherine Bauer Papers, BANC; Catherine Bauer, "The Middle Class Needs Houses Too," *New Republic* (August 29, 1949). On the lack of popular support for cooperative housing, see Richard O. Davies, *Housing Reform During the Truman Administration* (Columbia: University of Missouri Press, 1966); quote on anti-cooperative housing on 145 in Roger Biles, "Public Housing and the Postwar Urban Renaissance, 1949–1973," in John F. Bauman, Roger Biles, and Kristin M. Szylvian, eds., *From Tenements to the Taylor Homes: In Search of an Urban Housing Policy in Twentieth- Century America* (University Park: Pennsylvania State University Press, 2000).

21. SFHA, *Minutes* (August 1 and August 15, 1950); "It Would Kill Public Housing!" *San Francisco News* (October 6, 1950). Quote in SFHA, *Minutes* (August 15, 1950).

22. Newsletter of the SFPHA (*P & H*), volume 4, number 5, Folder 17, Box 3, 3199, SPUR, CU; Minutes of Northern California Meeting, CHPA (August 5, 1950), Folder 1, Box 1, 3199, SPUR, CU; Catherine Bauer to William (September 18, 1950), Folder "July to December 1950," Box 3, Catherine Bauer Papers, BANC.

23. Catherine Bauer to Mary and Leon [Keyserling] (June 21, 1950), Folder "January to June 1950," Box 3, Catherine Bauer Papers, BANC.

24. Lacey, *The Truman Presidency*; Robert Moore Fisher, *Twenty Years of Public Housing: Economic Aspects of Public Housing* (New York: Harper, 1959); Don Parson, "Los Angeles' Headline-Happy Public Housing War," *Southern California Quarterly* 65 (Fall 1983): 251–85; Biles, *The Fate of Cities.*

25. "S.F. Housing Authority Issues Report," *San Francisco Chronicle* (April 20, 1951). The SFHA generated more operating income than most authorities, but Robert Fisher found that PILOTs from a majority of public housing authorities were more than the city services they received. See his *Twenty Years of Public Housing.*

26. San Francisco Mayor Elmer Robinson and the Board of Supervisors showed continual support for public housing as long as it did not threaten racial segregation or the interests of organized homeowners and developers. See SFHA, *Minutes* (especially March 17, 1949); William Issel, "Liberalism and Urban Policy in San Francisco from the 1930s to the 1960s," *Western Historical Quarterly* 22, 4 (November 1991): 431–50. For public housing troubles in other parts of the country, see Davies, *Housing Reform During the Truman Administration*; Don Parson, *Making a Better World*; Hirsch, *Making the Second Ghetto*; Sugrue, *The Origins of the Urban Crisis*; D. Bradford Hunt, *Blueprint for Disaster: The Unraveling of Chicago Public Housing* (Chicago: University of Chicago Press, 2009).

27. See correspondence in Folder "Ping Yuen Housing Project, Correspondence, Notes, etc., 1949," and in Folder 6 "Ping Yuen Housing Project—Project Notes and Correspondence," Box 1, Henry Temple Howard Collection, 1999–1, EDL; SFHA, *Minutes* (November 17, 1949; and May 4, 1950).

28. SFHA, *Minutes* (May 4, 1950); "Glen Park Home Project Is Killed," *San Francisco Chronicle* (March 10, 1950). Quote in Miriam Weber to Mrs. Charles (October 30, 1949), Folder 77D "Project Housing, 1949–1951," Box 7, League of Women Voters of San Francisco, MS 1270, CHS.

29. Miriam Weber to Mrs. Charles (October 30, 1949), Folder 77D "Project Housing, 1949–1951," Box 7, League of Women Voters of San Francisco, MS 1270, CHS; SFHA, *Minutes* (May 4, 1950). Quote in "Glen Park Home Project Is Killed."

30. SFHA, *Minutes* (August 2, 1949; June 1 and June 27, 1950); Louis Schalk, SFHA Technical Director, to Mark Daniels and Henry Howard, architects (August 22, 1949), Folder 6 "Ping Yuen Housing Project, notes c. 1949," Box 1, Henry T. Howard Collection, EDL. Quote in SFHA, *Minutes* (August 2, 1949).

31. Quote in "Report on Recreation Facilities in Chinatown and North Beach Areas, May 1949," Mrs. George Kulchar, Community Chest of San Francisco, to Alice Griffith (April 19, 1950), and June 5, 1950 Press Release by Carroll Pebbles, Jr., San Francisco Youth Council. Both documents are in Folder 29, Box 2, SPUR, CU.

32. SFHA, *Minutes* (August 18, 1949, and April 20, 1950).

33. The Chinese Housing Committee, which shepherded Ping Yuen through the political process, likely approved the original mural. SFHA, *Minutes* (June 19 and October 2, 1952). Quote in SFHA, *Minutes* (June 19, 1952). See Amy Lynne Howard, *More Than Shelter: Activism and Community in San Francisco Public Housing* (Minneapolis: University of Minnesota Press, 2014), 114–16. On white anti-Chinese sentiment, Workingmen's Party, and Pick-Handle Brigade, see William Issel and Robert W. Cherny, *San Francisco, 1865–1932: Politics, Power, and Urban Development* (Berkeley: University of California Press, 1986), 125–30. On 1950s Cold War pluralism, see Kevin M. Shultz, *Tri-Faith America: How Catholics and Jews Held Postwar America to Its Protestant Promise* (Oxford: Oxford University Press, 2011); William Issel, *Church and State in the City: Catholics and Politics in Twentieth Century San Francisco* (Philadelphia: Temple University Press, 2012); Dudziak, *Cold War Civil Rights*.

34. SFHA commissioner meeting minutes are filled with examples of tenant appreciation for items such as new handrails and stoves; interview with Ms. Bea McQuaid, conducted by author in 1999 and 2000; interview with Darryl Cox, conducted by author in 2004. Tenant quote in "Public Housing—Godsend or Vote-Getter," *San Francisco Chronicle* (September 20, 1950).

35. SFHA adjustments to tenant eligibility consumed almost as much time as planning and building public housing. See SFHA, *Minutes* (especially July 17 and October 2, 1952; January 8, 1957; March 3, 1960; and August 2, 1962). Tenant control also guided some tenant decisions. "Housing Head Defends His Regime," *San Francisco Chronicle* (October 10, 1965). For attempts at tenant control in other authorities, see Rhonda Y. Williams, *The Politics of Public Housing: Black Women's Struggles Against Urban Inequality* (New York: Oxford University Press, 2004); Lisa Levenstein, *A Movement Without Marches: African American Women and the Politics of Poverty in Postwar Philadelphia* (Chapel Hill: University of North Carolina Press, 2010); Nicholas Dagen Bloom, *Public Housing That Worked: New York in the Twentieth Century* (Philadelphia: University of Pennsylvania Press, 2008); Lawrence J. Vale, *Purging the Poorest: Public Housing and the Design Politics of Twice-Cleared Communities* (Chicago: University of Chicago Press, 2013).

36. Theme of ILWU forum in SFHA, *Minutes* (October 2, 1952). SFHA, *Minutes* (No-

vember 3, 1955; August 2, 1956; and January 3, 1957). The 1952 Gwinn Amendment aimed to weed out subversives in the nation's public housing. Tenants, including a Molly Thorner in San Francisco, challenged the amendment, which was ruled unconstitutional in 1956.

37. Catherine Bauer to Leo Johnson (October 25, 1951), Folder 3 "July to December 1951," Box 4, Catherine Bauer Papers, BANC.

38. By 1960, San Francisco's elderly population (65 or older) reached 12.6 percent of its total population of 740,316. SFHA, *Seventeenth Annual Report* (1954); SFHA, *Minutes* (August 2, 1956). For a discussion of housing, planning, and the elderly in public policy, see Jerome Kaufman, prepared for the American Society of Planning Officials, "Planning and an Aging Population," Information Report No. 148 (Chicago, July 1961). In Canada and the United States, single-room occupancy hotels are also called single-resident occupancy hotels. For this study, I use single-room occupancy hotels (SROs).

39. Broussard, *Black San Francisco*, chapters 11 and 12.

40. Catherine Bauer to Robert Weaver (March 17, 1953), Folder "March to June 1953," Box 4, Catherine Bauer Papers, BANC. Broussard, *Black San Francisco*; Issel, *Church and State in the City*.

41. See December 12, 1949, document and Howden's attached letter in *San Francisco News* (October 29, 1949), Folder "Discrimination, Racial-General Housing, 1940–1950," #566, ACLU, CHS. The narrative that San Francisco was "different" on race relations did not square with customs, especially in housing. See Broussard, *Black San Francisco*; Shah, *Contagious Divides*; Issel, *Church and State in the City*.

42. Edward Howden, Director of CCU, and Ralph Reynolds, President of CCU, to Board of Supervisors (October 24, 1949), Folder "Discrimination, Racial-General Housing, 1940–1950," #566, ACLU, CHS; "Housing Body Rules on Segregation," *San Francisco Chronicle* (December 12, 1949), and "Segregation and S.F. Housing," *San Francisco Chronicle* (January 15, 1950); Broussard, *Black San Francisco*, chapter 13. Two months later, however, the Board of Supervisors did not support a fair employment measure, claiming insufficient evidence of employment discrimination. "Setback for Local FEPC," *San Francisco Chronicle* (January 6, 1950).

43. In the *San Francisco Chronicle*, "Housing Body Rules on Segregation" (December 12, 1949), "Segregation and S.F. Housing" (January 15, 1950), and "Housing Officials Agree to Nonsegregation in Projects" (February 21, 1950); "Deadlock Blocking Public Housing Here Must Be Broken at Once," *San Francisco News* (February 14, 1950); William Thomas Telegram to E. N. Ayer in SFHA, *Minutes* (February 16, 1950); Issel, "Liberalism and Urban Policy in San Francisco." Arnold Hirsch found a similar reliance on public housing by Chicago's redevelopment agency in his *Making the Second Ghetto*, chapter 4.

44. "Segregation and S.F. Housing," *San Francisco Chronicle* (January 15, 1950).

45. Ibid. Christopher, a Republican, did become mayor.

46. Alice Griffith, Honorary President of the SFPHA, to Elmer Robinson (January 26, 1950), Folder "O. A. Correspondence 'S,'" Carton 14, NAACP West Coast Papers, BANC.

47. Selah Chamberlain, President of SFPHA, to John Beard (December 23, 1949), Folder "77D Project Housing, 1949–51," Box 17, League of Women Voters of San Francisco, MS 1270, CHS.

48. Quote in "Segregation and S.F. Housing"; "Deadlock Blocking Public Housing Here Must Be Broken at Once"; SFHA, *Minutes* (January 19, 1950).

49. "Housing Body Rules on Segregation"; "Housing Officials Agree to Nonsegregation in Projects"; "Segregation and S.F. Housing." Quote in "Deadlock Blocking Public Housing Here Must Be Broken at Once."

50. "Segregation and S.F. Housing."

51. "Housing Officials Agree to Nonsegregation in Projects."

52. Quotes in SFHA, *Fourteenth Annual Report* (1951). "North Beach Housing," *San Francisco Chronicle* (March 10, 1950); Howard, *More Than Shelter*.

53. Broussard, *Black San Francisco*, chapter 13, quotes on 224. "S.F. Segregation in Housing to End" *San Francisco Chronicle* (May 25, 1954), and "Housing Board Bows to Ruling," *San Francisco Chronicle* (May 25, 1954); SFHA, *Minutes* (August 21 and November 6, 1952); Howard, *More Than Shelter*.

54. "S.F. Segregation in Housing to End" and "Housing Board Bows to Ruling." Quote in Broussard, *Black San Francisco*, on 224.

55. On the commission vote, see SFHA, *Minutes* (September 17, 1953); "S.F. Segregation in Housing to End" and "Housing Board Bows to Ruling"; Loren Miller, *The Petitioners: The Story of the Supreme Court of the United States and the Negro* (New York: Pantheon Books, 1966), chapter 22; Broussard, *Black San Francisco*, chapter 13.

56. Quote in "S.F. Segregation in Housing to End." Also see "Housing Board Bows to Ruling" and SFHA, *Minutes* (May 27, 1954). Jordan D. Luttrell, "The Public Housing Administration and Discrimination in Federally Assisted Low-Rent Housing," *Michigan Law Review* 64, 5 (1966), 871–90.

57. Howden noted how the press delayed, much to the relief of the State Department, breaking this story. That week, San Francisco was hosting a four-day UNESCO conference on Asian–U.S. relations, and this would have been a major embarrassment. News of the story got out anyway. Edward Howden, CCU, "Housing a Giant: Memorandum of the Willie Mays Incident, November 27, 1957," Folder "Willie Mays—Discrimination re SF Home Buying," Carton 39, BANC, West Coast NAACP, BANC.

58. Community Design Center, *Chinatown—An Analysis of Population and Housing*.

59. Mr. Theodore Lee, President of San Francisco Lodge, Chinese American Citizens Alliance, to William Mailliard, House of Representative (October 6, 1956), and Mildred Oulicky, Secretary for Mailliard, to Charles Slusser, Public Housing Administration, Administrator, in Folder "Mailliard, William (California)," Box 22 Magnuson, Warren to May, Edwin, Congressional Correspondence File, 1942–1962, Special Assistant to the Commissioner for Congressional Liaison, RG 196, NARA/CP; Community Design Center, *Chinatown—An Analysis of Population and Housing*; Tomás F. Summers Sandoval, *Latinos at the Golden Gate: Creating Community and Identity in San Francisco* (Chapel Hill: University of North Carolina Press, 2013), chapter 2. SFHA, *Twentieth Annual Report* (1958); SFHA, *Twenty-Second Annual Report* (1960).

60. Community Design Center, *Chinatown—An Analysis of Population and Housing*; Patricia Guthrie and Janis Hutchinson, "The Impact of Perceptions on Interpersonal Interactions in an African American/Asian American Housing Project," *Journal of Black Studies* 25, 3 (January 1995): 377–95; Howard, *More Than Shelter*, chapter 4.

61. Irving Kriegsfeld, Director of Mission Neighborhood Centers, Inc., to Walter Steilborg (April 23, 1962), Folder "Districts: Mission, 1960–1963," Box 3, Christopher Papers, SFPL; Mission Neighborhood Centers, Inc., *A Self Portrait of the Greater Mission District*

in Southeastern San Francisco (November 21, 1960), Folder "Districts: Mission, 1960–1963," Box 3, Christopher Papers, SFPL; San Francisco Department of City Planning, *San Francisco Population and Housing*, March 1962, BANC; Arthur D. Little, Inc., *San Francisco Community Renewal Program: Final Report to City Planning Commission, City and County of San Francisco, California* (October 1965); Sandoval, *Latinos at the Golden Gate*, chapter 2; Ocean Howell, *Making the Mission: Planning and Ethnicity in San Francisco* (Chicago: University of Chicago Press, 2015).

62. "Slum Clearance South of Market" and "Contract for Mission Housing Unit," *San Francisco Chronicle* (June 20, 1952); *San Francisco News* (June 25, 1956); Chester Hartman, *City for Sale: The Transformation of San Francisco* (Berkeley: University of California, 2002), chapter 4; Frederick Wirt, *Power in the City: Decision Making in San Francisco* (Berkeley: University of California Press, 1974), chapter 2; Arthur D. Little, Inc., *San Francisco Community Renewal Program*.

63. For SFHA housing data, see SFHA, *Minutes* (April 2, 1953; January 21, 1954; March 17, 1956; and October 11, 1956). Hunters Point Boys' Club in SFHA, *Minutes* (July 21 and August 9, 1960). Herbert Hoover, as president of the Boys' Club of America, spoke at the dedication. SFHA, *Minutes* (August 9, 1960). For demographic patterns, see San Francisco Dept. of City Planning, "Population and Housing," (San Francisco, 1962) at the BANC, UC Berkeley; Broussard, *Black San Francisco*; Christopher Lowen Agee, *The Streets of San Francisco: Policing and the Creation of a Cosmopolitan Liberal Politics, 1950–1972* (Chicago: University of Chicago Press, 2014).

64. "To Be Black and Live in S.F.," *San Francisco News* (June 25, 1956); "A Mourning Figure Walks," *San Francisco News* (June 30, 1956); David DeMarche to John Beard (December 1, 1962), Memorandum, Folder "Districts: Western Addition, Beyond Project Areas, 1962," Box 4, Christopher Papers, SFPL; "1950 Black Business Directory 1950," Folder 18, Box 2, Frederick Haynes Papers, MS 3355A, CHS; James Baldwin's "Take This Hammer" (1963), produced by KQED; Broussard, *Black San Francisco*.

65. See series in *San Francisco News* (June 25–30, 1956); see series in *San Francisco Chronicle* (January 12–15, 1959). The "children" quote in "'I Lived with S.F.'s Negroes,'" *San Francisco Chronicle* (January 15, 1959).

66. *San Francisco News* (June 25, 1956).

67. *San Francisco News* (June 25, 1956).

68. *San Francisco News* (June 25–30, 1956). Quotes in "S.F. Unions and Job Bias," (June 29, 1956).

69. "Negro Housing Woe Told," *San Francisco News* (June 28, 1956).

70. Hartman, *City for Sale*; Biles, *The Fate of Cities*; Vale, *Purging the Poorest*.

71. "Community Redevelopment Act of California" (September 1, 1949), Folder 99 "Project Urban Development, 1949–1951," Box 18, League of Women Voters of San Francisco, MS 1270, CHS; *San Francisco Chronicle* (May 22, 1956); Hartman, *City for Sale*, chapters 1–2.

72. The Bay Area Council (BAC) hired researchers and contracted with organizations to gather information for private and public projects. Bay Area Council, prepared by Van Buren Stanbery, *Regional Planning Needs of the San Francisco Bay Area* (1954); Bay Area Council, *A Program of Progress* (1950?); Bay Area Council, *A Guide to Industrial Locations in the San Francisco Bay Area* (1956). Hartman, *City for Sale*, chapters 1–3; Wirt, *Power in the City*, 190.

73. The redevelopment agency relied heavily on reports by BAC, the San Francisco Planning Commission, and later Arthur D. Little, Inc. SFPHA, *Minutes* (November 7, 1951), Folder 11, Box 1, 3199, SPUR, CU; Morse Erskine, Chairman Urban Redevelopment Committee, SFPHA, to SF Redevelopment Agency (January 14, 1952), Folder 27, Box 2, SPUR 3199, CU; Marion Mahony to Mr. Bolles (October 6, 1952), Folder 2, and Herbert Bartholomew, SFPHA President, to SF Redevelopment Agency (March 23, 1953), Folder 2, in Box 1, 3199, SPUR, CU. Bay Area Council, prepared by Van Buren Stanbery, *Regional Planning Needs of the San Francisco Bay Area* (1954); Bay Area Council, *A Program of Progress*; Bay Area Council, *A Guide to Industrial Locations in the San Francisco Bay Area*; Arthur D. Little, Inc., *San Francisco Community Renewal Program*; and Arthur D. Little, Inc., *Community Renewal Programming: A San Francisco Case Study* (New York: Praeger, 1966). Also see Issel, *Church and State in the City*, chapter 8; Howell, *Making the Mission*.

74. Ibid.

75. SFPHA, *Minutes* (November 7, 1951), Folder 11, Box 1, 3199, SPUR, CU; Morse Erskine, Chairman Urban Redevelopment Committee, SFPHA to San Francisco Redevelopment Agency (January 14, 1952), Folder 27, Box 2, SPUR 3199, CU; Marion Mahony to Mr. Bolles (October 6, 1952), Folder 2, and SFPHA President Herbert Bartholomew to San Francisco Redevelopment Agency (March 23, 1953), Folder 2, in Box 1, 3199, SPUR, CU. See Bauer Papers, BANC, and H. Peter Oberlander and Eva Newbrun, *Houser: The Life and Work of Catherine Bauer* (Vancouver: University of British Columbia Press, 1999). Cold War politics influenced these individuals, too. The red scare led to investigations of New Deal housing and planning advocates, and some nearly lost their academic appointments for not signing loyalty oaths. See Catherine Bauer letters, especially Catherine Bauer to William [no last name] (September 18, 1950), Folder "July to Dec. 1950," Box 3; Catherine Bauer to Coleman [Woodbury] (June 15, 1951), Folder "March to June 1951," Box 4; Catherine Bauer to Clark Kerr (April 26, 1955), Folder "April–June 1955," Box 5; November 11, 1957, Folder "Oct.–Dec. 1957," Box 6. All in Catherine Bauer Papers, BANC. Mel Scott, *American City Planning Since 1890: A History Commemorating the Fiftieth Anniversary of the American Institute of Planners* (Berkeley: University of Press, 1969).

76. Catherine Bauer, "The Increasing Social Responsibility of the City Planner," speech at Canadian and American City Planners Convention, Niagara Falls (1950), Folder "The Increasing Social Responsibility," Box 2, Catherine Bauer Papers, BANC; Scott, *American City Planning*, chapter 7.

77. Quote in Scott, *American City Planning*, 477; Jane Jacobs, *The Death and Life of Great American Cities* (New York: Vintage Books, 1961); Herbert J. Gans, *The Urban Villagers: Group and Class in the Life of Italian-Americans* (New York: Free Press of Glencoe, 1962).

78. Quote in Catherine Bauer to Bruce [Bliven?] (May 8, 1955), Folder "April–June 1955," Box 5, Catherine Bauer Papers, BANC. For the Bay Area housing and planning community, see the collections of Mel Scott, Catherine Bauer, and T. J. Kent at the Bancroft Library, UC Berkeley. See Albert Lepawsky, *State Planning and Economic Development in the South* (Washington, DC: National Planning Association, 1949); Bauer, "The Increasing Social Responsibility of the City Planner"; and Bauer, "The Patterns of Economic and

Urban Development: Social Implications," *Annals of the American Academy of Political and Social Science* (May 1956); Mel Scott, *The San Francisco Bay Area: A Metropolis in Perspective* (Berkeley: University of California Press, 1959), and Scott, *American City Planning*, preface, chapters 6–8; Philip J. Dreyfus, *Our Better Nature: Environment and the Making of San Francisco* (Norman: University of Oklahoma Press, 2008).

79. Catherine Bauer to Paul [Taylor] (December 7, 1959), Folder "September to December 1959," Box 6, Catherine Bauer Papers, BANC.

80. Alison Isenberg, *Designing San Francisco: Art, Land, and Urban Renewal in the City by the Bay* (Princeton, NJ: Princeton University Press, 2017).

81. "Community Redevelopment Act of California" (September 1, 1949), Folder 99 "Project Urban Development, 1949–1951," Box 18, League of Women Voters of San Francisco, MS 1270, CHS; Oscar Lewis, *San Francisco: Mission to Metropolis* (Berkeley: Howell-North Books, 1966), 250–55; Richard Brandi, "San Francisco's Diamond Heights: Urban Renewal and the Modernist City," *Journal of Planning History* 12, 2 (May 2013): 133–53.

82. "Slum Clearance South of Market" and "Contract for Mission Housing Unit," *San Francisco Chronicle* (June 20, 1952); Lewis, *San Francisco*, 250–55; Hartman, *City for Sale*, chapter 4.

83. "Slum Clearance South of Market"; "Contract for Mission Housing Unit"; San Francisco Redevelopment Agency, *The Effects of Redevelopment on Residents and Property Owners: Western Addition Project Area No. 1* (October 10, 1952); Everett Griffin, Chairman of San Francisco Redevelopment Agency, to George Christopher (January 3, 1961), Folder "Districts: Western Addition, Japanese Center, 1 of 2, 1961–1962," Box 4, Christopher Papers, SFPL; Lewis, *San Francisco*, 250–55; Hartman, *City for Sale*, chapter 4.

84. Ibid. Quotes in San Francisco Redevelopment Agency, *The Effects of Redevelopment on Residents and Property Owners*.

85. SFHA, *Minutes* (August 21, 1958).

86. SFHA, *Minutes* (May 2, 1957; and November 7, 1959).

87. Quotes in SFHA, *Minutes* (November 19, 1959).

88. SFHA, *Minutes* (November 19, 1959). Support for San Francisco redevelopment came primarily from the economic, labor, and political leaders who put profit, jobs, and economic development before the rights of residents. This pro-growth liberal agenda was popular in cities across the nation. See Wirt, *Power in the City*; Hartman, *City for Sale*; Issel, "Liberalism and Urban Policy in San Francisco from the 1930s to the 1960s" and *Church and State in the City*; John H. Mollenkopf, *The Contested City* (Princeton, NJ: Princeton University Press, 1983); Biles, *The Fate of Cities*.

89. SFHA, *Minutes* (March 21, 1957; January 7 and December 4, 1958). SFHA, 1960 *Annual Report*; transcript of interview with Stephen Walter [SFHA commissioner], Folder 17, Box 3, California League of Women Voters, MS 1272, CHS.

90. SFHA, *Minutes* (November 6, 1958); California League of Women Voters, "Low and Moderate Income Housing in San Francisco," Folder 8 "1969 A Report to Members," Box 7, League of Women Voters, 1271, CHS; quote in PHA News Release (December 30, 1959), Folder "Speeches—Slusser, Commissioner," Box 10 "Commissioner's Staff, Records of the Intergroup Relations Branch, 1936–1963," RG 196, PHA, NARA/CP.

91. SFHA, *Minutes* (November 7, 1957); quote in SFHA, *Minutes* (August 15, 1957).

CHAPTER 5

1. Governor Edmund Brown to Robert Weaver (October 26, 1956), Folder "400 Programming Nov.," Box 11, Subject Correspondence, 1966–78, RG 207, NARA/CP.

2. Helen O. Little to Rev. Hamilton Boswell, Chair of the SFHA Commission (June 2, 1967), in SFHA, *Minutes* (June 7, 1967).

3. In 1961, the SFHA collected about $350,000 a month in rents. SFHA, *Twenty-Third Annual Report* (1961); quote in "Records Saved," *San Francisco Chronicle* (January 6, 1961). The San Francisco Fire Department excluded women before 1976; it took a lawsuit to open the hiring process to women and nonwhites.

4. SFHA, *Twenty-Third Annual Report* (1961).

5. The SFHA requested 500 units of Section 23 housing. SFHA, *Minutes* (October 6, 1966). Lawrence M. Friedman and James E. Krier, "A New Lease on Life: Section 23 Housing and the Poor," *University of Pennsylvania Law Review* 116, 4 (January 1968): 611–47; R. Allen Hays, *The Federal Government and Urban Housing* (New York: SUNY Press, 2012), 4; William J. Collins, "The Housing Market Impact of State-Level Anti-Discrimination Laws, 1960–1970" (Cambridge, MA: National Bureau of Economic Research, March 2003); Roger Biles, *The Fate of Cities: Urban America and the Federal Government, 1945–2000* (Lawrence: University Press of Kansas, 2011); Alex F. Schwartz, *Housing Policy in the United States* (New York: Routledge, 2014).

6. Donald Canter, "Housing Head Defends His Regime," *San Francisco Chronicle* (October 10, 1965); Transcript of Interview with Stephen Walter [SFHA commissioner], Folder 17, Box 3, California League of Women Voters, MS 1272, CHS. SFHA, *Minutes* (October 17, 1960; December 14, 1960; January 5, 1960; and January 26, 1961); Bruce Savage, Commissioner PHA (November 16, 1960), Folder "Press Releases 1960 (2), Box 22, Correspondence of the Commissioner of Public Housing, 1952–1967," RG 196, NARA/CP.

7. Quotes in SFHA, *Minutes* (October 17 and December 14, 1960; January 5, 1960; and January 26, 1961). On New York City housing, see Nicholas Dagen Bloom, *Public Housing That Worked: New York in the Twentieth Century* (Philadelphia: University of Pennsylvania Press, 2008).

8. As per the 1950 state law passed by California's voters, all public housing authorities had to win local voter approval for additional public housing allocations. See chapter 4. SFHA, *Minutes* (October 17 and December 14, 1960; January 5, 1960; January 26, 1961; and June 7, 1962); Bruce Savage, Commissioner PHA (November 16, 1960), Folder "Press Releases 1960 (2), Box 22, Correspondence of the Commissioner of Public Housing, 1952–1967," RG 196, NARA/CP.

9. Quote in "Unit Opened for Elderly," *San Francisco Examiner* (September 15, 1961); "Yerba Buena Annex, Newest S.F. Housing Project, Dedicated," *San Francisco News-Call* (September 14, 1961); SFHA, *Twenty-Third Annual Report* (1961). For senior housing in San Francisco, see Marie McGuire to William Mailliard (August 29, 1961), Folder "Maillard, William S. (California), Box 22 Magnuson, Warren to May, Edwin, Congressional Correspondence Files, 1924–1962, Special Assistant to the Commissioner for Congressional Liaison," RG 196, NARA/CP.

10. SFHA, *Minutes* (January 18, 1962).

11. SFHA, *Minutes* (October 5, 1961).

12. SFHA, *Minutes* (September 15, 1960); SFHA, *Twenty-Third Annual Report* (1961); Community Design Center, *Chinatown: An Analysis of Population and Housing* (June 1969, San Francisco).

13. SFHA, *Minutes* (October 5, 1961, and February 2, 1961); Community Design Center, *Chinatown: An Analysis of Population and Housing*.

14. H. J. Hickox to Representative William Mailliard (August 9, 1961), and Marie McGuire to William Mailliard (August 29, 1961), Folder "Maillard, William S. (California), Box 22 Magnuson, Warren to May, Edwin, Congressional Correspondence Files, 1924–1962, Special Assistant to the Commissioner for Congressional Liaison," RG 196, NARA/CP.

15. The SFHA even purchased tickets to the show. SFHA, *Minutes* (May 3, 1962).

16. Quote in SFHA, *Minutes* (April 7, 1960). SFHA, *Minutes* (April 7 and October 6, 1960). Boys Club membership was 450 in 1961 (January 26, 1961). James Gilbert, *A Cycle of Outrage: America's Reaction to the Juvenile Delinquent in the 1950s* (New York: Oxford University Press, 1986).

17. Quote in SFHA, *Minutes* (February 2, 1961); "'Programs' Stifle a Lofty Ghetto," *Washington Post* (August 28, 1966).

18. SFHA, *Minutes* (November 7, 1963); "'Programs' Stifle a Lofty Ghetto"; Alice O'Connor, "Community Action, Urban Reform, and the Fight Against Poverty: The Ford Foundation's Gray Areas Program," *Journal of Urban History* 22, 5 (July 1996): 586–625. More men than women landed these positions. SFHA, *Minutes* (June 7, 1962).

19. Greenstone stated he "would vote against any housing that did not have services in connection with it." SFHA, *Minutes* (February 16, 1961).

20. John Kenneth Galbraith, *The Affluent Society* (Boston: Houghton Mifflin, 1958); Michael Harrington, *The Other America: Poverty in the United States* (New York: Simon & Schuster, 1997 [1962]); Judith Russell, *Economics, Bureaucracy, and Race: How Keynesians Misguided the War on Poverty* (New York: Columbia University Press, 2004); Alice O'Connor, *Poverty Knowledge: Social Science, Social Policy, and the Poor in Twentieth-Century U.S. History* (Princeton, NJ: Princeton University Press, 2001), chapter 6.

21. The CSES, California's public employment agency, trained workers, delivered workers to employers, and conducted research for government officials and employers. It assisted disadvantaged workers such as parolees and the disabled, and it administered the unemployment insurance program. Under Governor Pat Brown, it also worked on ending racial discrimination in employment. See California State Employment Services, *Objectives and Functions of the California State Employment Service* (1964) and *The Economic Status of Negroes in the San Francisco-Oakland Bay Area* (May 1963). Quotes are from the 1963 report, *The Economic Status of Negroes in the San Francisco-Oakland Bay Area*. For African American employment in other urban areas, see Keith E. Collins, *Black Los Angeles: The Maturing of the Ghetto, 1940–1950* (Saratoga, CA: Century Twenty One Publishing, 1980); Quintard Taylor, *The Forging of a Black Community: Seattle's Central District from 1870 Through the Civil Rights Era* (Seattle: University of Washington Press, 1994); Thomas J. Sugrue, *The Origins of the Urban Crisis: Race and Inequality in Postwar Detroit* (Princeton, NJ: Princeton University Press, 2005), and *Sweet Land of Liberty: The Forgotten Struggle for Civil Rights in the North* (New York: Random House, 2008); Shirley Ann Wilson Moore, *To Place Our Deeds: The African American Community in Richmond, California, 1910–1963* (Berkeley: University of

California Press, 2000); Robert O. Self, *American Babylon: Race and the Struggle for Postwar Oakland* (Princeton, NJ: Princeton University Press, 2005).

22. James Richardson, *Willie Brown: A Biography* (Berkeley: University of California Press, 1996), 73.

23. "Real Estate 'Sit-in' at S.F. Tract," *San Francisco Chronicle* (May 29, 1961), "Full-Scale 'Sit-In Drive Opens in S.F.," *San Francisco Chronicle* (May 30, 1961), "Full-Scale 'Sit-In' at S.F. Home," *San Francisco Chronicle* (May 31, 1961), "Tract Owner Says Negro May Look," *San Francisco Chronicle* (June 3, 1961); Richardson, *Willie Brown*, chapter 8.

24. Quote in "S.F. Realtors Fight Bill on Housing Bias," *San Francisco Chronicle* (April 11, 1961). Edward Rutledge, Director of National Committee Against Discrimination in Housing, *A Report on California Proposition 14*, Folder 450 "CA Legislation, Rumford Act," ACLU, CHS. For the rise in postwar housing discrimination in California and the West, see Tarea Hall Pittman, Secretary West Coast Region, NAACP, to United States Commission on Civil Rights (January 27, 1960), Folder "Statement on Housing, Tarea Hall Pittman," Carton 39, NAACP, BANC; "SF Lauded, Rapped at Racial Quiz," *San Francisco Examiner* (January 28, 1960); "Expert Says Housing Bias in Bay Area Is Increasing," *San Francisco Chronicle* (March 16, 1961); Sugrue, *Sweet Land of Liberty*; William Issel, *Church and State in the City: Catholics and Politics in Twentieth Century San Francisco* (Philadelphia: Temple University Press, 2012), chapter 7.

25. Frank Quinn, Coordinator, San Francisco Committee for Fair Housing Practices to Sponsors (February 7, 1964), Folder 582 "Discrimination, Racial Blacks, Housing, 1964," ACLU, CHS; "Housing Bill Signed—No Money," *San Francisco Chronicle* (July 18, 1963); Rutledge, *A Report on California Proposition 14*; Jill Quadagno, *The Color of Welfare: How Racism Undermined the War on Poverty* (Oxford: Oxford University Press, 1994), 95–100. See Collins, "The Housing Market Impact of State-Level Anti-Discrimination Laws."

26. "'Housing Project Segregation': Bitter Blast at Beard," *San Francisco Chronicle* (February 18, 1965); "Low and Moderate Income Housing in San Francisco," Folder 6 "1969 A Report to Members," Box 7, League of Women Voters MS 1271, CHS. Quote in SFHA, *Minutes* (December 20, 1962). Issel, *Church and State in the City*.

27. SFHA, *Minutes* (July 16, 1964). Statistics of SFHA employment of African Americans in SFHA, *Minutes* (June 16, 1964).

28. "Shelley Assails Housing Body Again," *San Francisco Chronicle* (April 23, 1964). SFHA, *Minutes* (April 2, 1964). Brotsky quote in SFHA, *Minutes* (June 16, 1964).

29. For an account of the attempted removal, see "Shelley Assails Housing Body Again." Also see SFHA, *Minutes* (April 2 and June 18, 1964); "NAACP 'Action' Threat to Housing Authority," *San Francisco Chronicle* (February 11, 1965). Lee ran an import-export business, was president of the Chinese Chamber of Commerce and the Kong Chow Association, and was a director of the Downtown Association. See SFHA, *Minutes* (February 18, 1965).

30. All quotes in SFHA, *Minutes* (July 16, 1964).

31. SFHA, *Minutes* (September 24, 1964). See Robinson obituary in *Sonoma West Times and News* (June 11, 2003).

32. Quotes in SFHA, *Minutes* (October 15, 1964). For a sensationalized view of white images of San Francisco's African Americans, see "'I Lived with S.F.'s Negroes'" series in the *San Francisco Chronicle* (July 15–18, 1963).

33. SFHA, *Minutes* (April 16, September 24, and October 15, 1964); Effie Robinson, SFHA Director of Human Relations, "Critical and Urgent Need for Services for Relocates from South of Market" (June 29, 1970), Folder "HUD, Yerba Buena Center, 1 of 3, 1970–1973," Box 10, Alioto Papers, SFPL. Other city departments also created positions for intergroup relations officers. SFHA, *Minutes* (February 7, 1963). "Be good citizens" quote in job description in SFHA, *Minutes* (March 19, 1964); "deputized" quote in SFHA, *Minutes* (October 15, 1964).

34. SFHA, *Minutes* (July 16, 1964).

35. During the 1960s, city officials repeatedly threatened to put the SFHA under redevelopment agency control. SFHA, *Minutes* (November 23, 1963; June 4, July 16, August 7, and October 1, 1964); "Shelley Assails Housing Body Again"; Statement by Mayor John F. Shelley on Western Addition Area 2 (September 3, 1964), Folder "California—San Francisco, #3," Carton 6, Catherine Bauer Papers, BANC.

36. SFHA, *Minutes* (July 16, 1964).

37. SFHA, *Minutes* (August 7, 1964).

38. SFHA, *Minutes* (August 27 and November 5, 1964).

39. Rutledge, *A Report on California Proposition* 14; SFHA, *Minutes* (August 27 and October 1, 1964). Quote in Joseph Mazzola letter to Mayor John Shelley (May 18, 1965), in SFHA, *Minutes* (May 20, 1965).

40. Frank Quinn, Coordinator, San Francisco Committee for Fair Housing Practices to Sponsors (February 7, 1964), Folder 582 "Discrimination, Racial Blacks, Housing, 1964," ACLU, CHS; Rutledge, *A Report on California Proposition* 14; Quadagno, *The Color of Welfare*, 95–100; Lisa McGirr, *Suburban Warriors: The Origins of the New American Right* (Princeton, NJ: Princeton University Press, 2001); Self, *American Babylon*; Issel, *Church and State in the City*.

41. Louella Hayes, president of All Neighborhoods Improvement Club, to League of Women Voters (August 13, 1964), Folder 32, Box 1, California League of Women Voters MS 1275, CHS.

42. Eason Monroe, ACLU of Southern California, to ACLU Board of Directors (national) (August 3, 1964), Folder 449 "California Legislation, Rumford Act, 1964 Correspondence," ACLU, CHS. Quotes from poster, Folder "Proposition 14–NAACP Suit 1964," Carton 40, NACCP, BANC.

43. Frank Quinn, Coordinator San Francisco Committee for Fair Housing Practices to Sponsors (February 7, 1964), Folder 582 "Discrimination, Racial Blacks, Housing, 1964," ACLU, CHS.

44. Lou Jones Newsletter (August 1, 1964), Folder 449 "California Legislation, Rumford Act, 1964 Correspondence, ACLU, CHS; Latinas/os in the Mission District worked with others across the Bay Area. See Tomás F. Summers Sandoval, *Latinos at the Golden Gate: Creating Community and Identity in San Francisco* (Chapel Hill: University of North Carolina Press, 2013), chapter 4.

45. See Memorandum "California Proposed Initiative Constitutional Measure—Discrimination in Housing," and following general correspondence and opinions by J. E. Prisin-Zano, San Francisco Regional Office of the PHA, to Joseph Burstein, PHA General Counsel, Folder "Equal Opportunity in Housing (Executive Order 11063)" (Jan. 1963–March 1964),

Box 3, Equal Opportunity in Housing (Executive Order 11063) (Jan. 1964–March 3, 1964), General Legal Files (1936–1970), RG 196, NARA/CP. Quote in Milton Semar to Charles Bosley (March 10, 1964).

46. Oral interview with M. Justin Herman conducted by League of Women Voters (September 7, 1966), Folder 18, Box 3, California League of Women Voters MS 1272, CHS.

47. Frank Quinn, Coordinator San Francisco Committee for Fair Housing Practices to Sponsors (February 7, 1964), Folder 582 "Discrimination, Racial Blacks, Housing, 1964," ACLU, CHS.

48. Quote and data in Rutledge, *A Report on California Proposition* 14; SFHA, *Minutes* (December 3, 1964; January 7, 1965). Also, see "Realtors' Measure Now Is the Law," *San Francisco Chronicle* (November 4, 1964) and "A Quick Test of Prop. 14 in the Courts," *San Francisco Chronicle* (November 5, 1964).

49. Mendenhall quote in "Realtor Chief Hails Passage of Prop. 14," and Brown quote in "Change of Tactics in Anti-14 Fight." Both articles in *San Francisco Chronicle* (November 11, 1964).

50. "A Quick Test of Prop. 14 in the Courts" and "More Funds Cut Off by Prop. 14."

51. SFHA, *Minutes* (December 3, 1964); Robert Weaver, HUD Secretary, to Ella Seabrook, San Francisco NAACP (May 19, 1966), Folder "133 Proposition 14 in California," Box 3 1966, Subject Correspondence, 1966–78, RG 207, NARA/CP; Quadagno, *The Color of Welfare*, 95–103. "Property" quote in Rutledge, *A Report on California Proposition* 14.

52. "A Quick Test of Prop. 14 in the Courts" and "More Funds Cut Off by Prop. 14." For an analysis of the legal case against Proposition 14, see League of Women Voters of California, "Current Review of California Continuing Responsibilities," No. 7 (May 1966), Folder 90 "Continuing Responsibility—Fair Housing 1966," Box 6, League of Women Voters, MS 3585, CHS. For the rise of the New Right in California, see McGirr, *Suburban Warriors*.

53. From the start, Great Society programs caused tensions between organizers and local elites in San Francisco. See "Poor Win Command in Poverty War," *San Francisco Chronicle* (September 9, 1965); Frederick Wirt, *Power in the City: Decision Making in San Francisco* (Berkeley: University of California Press, 1974); Chester Hartman, *City for Sale: The Transformation of San Francisco* (Berkeley: University of California, 2002); Issel, *Church and State in the City.* Also see Frances Fox Piven and Richard A. Cloward, *Poor People's Movements: Why They Succeed, How They Fail* (New York: Vintage Books, 1979); Quadagno, *The Color of Welfare*; Rhonda Y. Williams, *The Politics of Public Housing: Black Women's Struggles Against Urban Inequality* (New York: Oxford University Press, 2004), chapters 5 and 6; Alice O'Connor, "Swimming Against the Tide: A Brief History of Federal Policy in Poor Communities," in Ronald Ferguson and William Dickens, eds., *Urban Problems and Community Development* (Washington DC: Brookings Institute Press, 1999), and O'Connor, *Poverty Knowledge*, chapter 7; Frank Stricker, *Why America Lost the War on Poverty—And How to Win It* (Chapel Hill: University of North Carolina Press, 2007); Gordon K. Mantler, *Power to the Poor: Black-Brown Coalition and the Fight for Economic Justice, 1960–1974* (Chapel Hill: University of North Carolina Press, 2013).

54. "Now, U.S. Subsidies for Rents—Who Gets Them . . . How Much," *U.S. News & World Report* (August 2, 1965); Mark Gelfand, *A Nation of Cities: The Federal Government and Urban America, 1933–1965* (New York: Oxford University Press, 1975), chapters 9–11; Hays, *The Federal Government and Urban Housing*, 105; Biles, *The Fate of Cities*, chapters 1–3. For

Weaver's ideas on urban problems, see his *The Negro Ghetto* (New York: Harcourt Brace, 1948), *Dilemmas of Urban America* (Cambridge, MA: Harvard University Press, 1965), and *Urban Complex: Human Values in Urban Life* (New York: Anchor Books, 1966).

55. SFHA, *Minutes* (February 4, 1965). Westbrook had migrated from the South to San Francisco during the war years. See Rachel Brahinsky, "Race and the Making of Southeast San Francisco: Towards a Theory of Race-Class," *Antipode*, 46, 5 (2014): 1258–76.

56. SFHA, *Minutes* (March 4, 1965).

57. Quote in SFHA, *Minutes* (January 21, 1965); SFHA, *Minutes* (March 4, 1965; and December 17, 1964); "'Programs' Stifle a Lofty Ghetto."

58. SFHA, *Minutes* (December 3, 1964). Arthur Hippler noted that Beard regularly punished tenants, sometimes with evictions. See his *Hunters Point: A Black Ghetto* (New York: Basic Books, 1974). On tenant organizing, see Ronald Lawson, ed., *The Tenant Movement in New York City*, 1904–1984 (New Brunswick, NJ: Rutgers University Press, 1986); Ronald Brooks, "Tenant Intervention in Los Angeles' Public Housing Program," Ph.D. dissertation (University of California, Los Angeles, 1993); Lisa Levenstein, *A Movement Without Marches: African American Women and the Politics of Poverty in Postwar Philadelphia* (Chapel Hill: University of North Carolina Press, 2010); Williams, *The Politics of Public Housing*; Michael Karp, "The St. Louis Rent Strike of 1969: Transforming Black Activism and American Low-Income Housing," *Journal of Urban History* 40, 4 (July 2014): 648–70. Roberta Gold, *When Tenants Claimed the City: The Struggle for Citizenship in New York City Housing* (Champaign: University of Illinois Press, 2014).

59. SFHA, *Minutes* (May 20, 1965). At North Beach Place, the tenants convinced the SFHA to convert storage space into community space. SFHA, *Minutes* (August 5, 1965).

60. "NAACP 'Action' Threat to Housing Authority," *San Francisco Chronicle* (February 11, 1965).

61. "'Housing Project Segregation': Bitter Blast at Beard."

62. "An Orderly Protest on S.F. Housing," *San Francisco Chronicle* (February 20, 1965).

63. Quote in "NAACP 'Action' Threat to Housing Authority," *San Francisco Chronicle* (February 11, 1965); SFHA, *Minutes* (February 18 and March 4, 1965); "New Housing Delayed by Charge," *San Francisco Chronicle* (February 10, 1965) and "'Housing Project Segregation': Bitter Blast at Beard."

64. SFHA, *Minutes* (February 18, 1965); "'Housing Project Segregation': Bitter Blast at Beard."

65. Ibid.

66. Joseph Mazzola to Mayor John Shelley (May 18, 1965), in SFHA, *Minutes* (May 20, 1965). And SFHA, *Minutes* (May 6, 1965).

67. SFHA, *Minutes* (July 1, 1965). In 1967, Commissioner Bigarani resigned after lying under oath in a FEPC investigation of discrimination on a Golden Gate Bridge job. "Shelley Ignoring NAACP Charge," *San Francisco Chronicle* (June 8, 1967); "Accused City Aide Resigns," *San Francisco Chronicle* (June 9, 1967).

68. SFHA, *Minutes* (October 7, 1965).

69. Quotes and Burton telegram in SFHA, *Minutes* (October 7, 1965). Donald Canter, "Housing Head Defends His Regime," *San Francisco Chronicle* (October 10, 1965); "Housing Chief Out: Kane Gets Job," *San Francisco Chronicle* (October 23, 1965).

70. *San Francisco Chronicle* (October 10 and October 23, 1965); Oral Interview of Eneas Kane Conducted by League of Women Voters (September 8, 1966), Folder 18, Box 3, California League of Women Voters MS 1272, CHS.

71. "Housing Chief Out: Kane Gets Job."

72. SFHA, *Minutes* (May 19, 1966).

73. Kane quote in SFHA, *Twenty-Ninth Annual Report* (1966); SFHA, *Minutes* (August 4, 1966).

74. SFHA, *Twenty-Ninth Annual Report* (1966); SFHA, *Minutes* (August 4, 1966); Eneas Kane, "The Fabulous Machine Called Public Housing," Confidential, Folder "Housing Authority, 1967–1969," Box 16, Alioto Papers, SFPL; SFHA, *Minutes* (August 4, 1966).

75. SFHA, *Minutes* (November 4, 1965; May 19, 1966; and May 18, 1967). For SFHA Section 23 housing, see SFHA, *Minutes* (October 6, 1966; and August 17, 1967).

76. Quote in Harry Bigarani to Mayor John Shelley (June 8, 1967) in SFHA, *Minutes* (July 20, 1967). SFHA, *Twenty-Ninth Annual Report* (1966).

77. SFHA, *Twenty-Ninth Annual Report* (1966).

78. SFHA, *Minutes* (April 21, 1966). Quote in SFHA, *Twenty-Ninth Annual Report* (1966).

79. Quote in SFHA, *Minutes* (June 16, 1966); SFHA, *Minutes* (January 5 and September 1, 1966). HUD Circulars (November 11, 1967; April 4, 1968; and March 22, 1968), Folder "Poor People's March 1968," Box 6, Secretary Weaver's Subject Files, 1960–69, RG 207, NARA/CP.

80. "'Programs' Stifle a Lofty Ghetto"; SFHA, *Minutes* (October 6, 1966); Hippler, *Hunters Point*. For the riot and its causes, see Agee, *The Streets of San Francisco*, chapter 5.

81. SFHA, *Minutes* (October 20, 1966).

82. Ibid.

83. The HEW grant was done through the Economic Opportunity Act. SFHA, *Minutes* (November 17, 1966; and January 5, 1967); SFHA Counsel John Sullivan report in SFHA, *Minutes* (February 2, 1967). George Earl to Robert Weaver (October 19, 1966), Marie McGuire, Acting Deputy Assistant Secretary HUD, to George Earl (November 17, 1966), and Louis Ambler, Jr., HAO, Reg. VI to Abner Silverman, Director Management Division, HAA (November 14, 1966), all in Folder "480 Housing Assistance Admin, Aug.–Nov.," Box 16 1966, General Correspondence, RG 207, NARA/CP.

84. Quote in SFHA, *Minutes* (January 19, 1967).

85. SFHA, *Minutes* (January 19, March 16, and April 20, 1967). Earl to Weaver, McGuire to Earl, and Ambler to Silverman, Folder "480 Housing Assistance Admin." Quote in SFHA, *Minutes* (June 7, 1967). For Alioto's work in Hunters Point, see Agee, *The Streets of San Francisco*, chapter 5.

86. On Reagan's rise in politics, see "Ronald Reagan: Rising Star in the West," *Newsweek* (May 22, 1967); Lou Cannon, *Ronnie & Jesse: A Political Odyssey* (New York: Doubleday, 1969); Jules Tygiel, *Ronald Reagan and the Triumph of American Conservatism* (New York: Pearson, 2006). The influence of social movements of the 1960s on liberalism, social policy, and party politics have received much scholarly attention. A few examples include Steve Fraser and Gary Gerstle, eds., *The Rise and Fall of the New Deal Order, 1930–1980* (Princeton, NJ: Princeton University Press, 1990); William C. Berman, *America's Right Turn: From Nixon*

to Bush (Baltimore: John Hopkins University Press, 1994); O'Connor, *Poverty Knowledge*; McGirr, *Suburban Warriors*; Self, *American Babylon*; Doug McAdam and Karina Kloos, *Deeply Divided: Racial Politics and Social Movements in Postwar America* (Oxford: Oxford University Press, 2014).

87. By 1967, the SFHA had leased 133 Section 23 units and was in talks with landlords for another 663 units. SFHA, *Minutes* (August 17, 1967).

88. Mr. L. George to President Lyndon Johnson (December 2, 1965), Folder "480 PHA," Box 17 1966, Subject Correspondence, 1966–1978, RG 207, NARA/CP.

CHAPTER 6

1. SFHRC (May 14, 1970), Folder "Housing-Human Rights Commission, 1970–1973," Box 8, Alioto Papers, SFPL.

2. Quotes in "Tenants Union," *San Francisco Bay Guardian* (December 16, 1969), and "Roaches, Rents, and Repairs: Tenants Are Striking All Over . . . They Won't Be Pushed," *San Francisco Bay Guardian* (April 17, 1970). For tenant organizing, see A. E. Rosfeld, Acting Deputy Asst. Secretary, HUD, to William Burton, St. Louis Rent Strike Leaders (April 19, 1969), Folder "PRO 7 Low-Rent Public Housing April 3–24," Box 59–1969, Subject Correspondence, 1966–1978, RG 207, NARA/CP; Ronald Brooks, "Tenant Intervention in Los Angeles' Public Housing Program," Ph.D. dissertation (University of California, Los Angeles, 1993); Peter Marcuse, "Housing Movements in the USA," *Housing, Theory, and Society* 16, 2 (1999): 67–86; Rhonda Y. Williams, *The Politics of Public Housing: Black Women's Struggles Against Urban Inequality* (New York: Oxford University Press, 2004), chapters 5 and 6; see special edition of *Journal of Urban History* that focuses on public housing tenants: *Journal of Urban History* 33, 3 (March 2007); Amy L. Howard, *More Than Shelter: Activism and Community in San Francisco Public Housing* (Minneapolis: University of Minnesota Press, 2014); Michael Karp, "The St. Louis Rent Strike of 1969: Transforming Black Activism and American Low-Income Housing," *Journal of Urban History* 40, 4 (July 2014): 648–70; Roberta Gold, *When Tenants Claimed the City: The Struggle for Citizenship in New York City Housing* (Champaign: University of Illinois Press, 2014).

3. Eneas Kane, "The Fabulous Machine Called Public Housing," Confidential, Folder "Housing Authority, 1967–1969," Box 16, Alioto Papers, SFPL; "Kane Asks 'Overhaul' of Public Housing," *San Francisco Examiner* (May 27, 1968); "New Laws on Housing Advocated," *The Phoenix Gazette* (May 27, 1968). The talk went over well with the audience and housing officials who read it. See Marie McGuire to Eneas Kane (June 10, 1968), Folder "SA–SH 1968," Box 19–1968, Subject Correspondence 1966–1978, RG 207, NARA/CP.

4. Kane, "The Fabulous Machine Called Public Housing."

5. Ibid.; "New Laws on Housing Advocated"; Lawrence J. Vale, *From the Puritans to the Projects: Public Housing and Public Neighbors* (Cambridge, MA: Harvard University Press, 2000), chapter 4.

6. Kane, "The Fabulous Machine Called Public Housing."

7. Chester Hartman, *Housing and Social Policy* (Englewood Cliffs, NJ: Prentice-Hall, 1975), 170. Also, see letters in General Correspondence Files in RG 207, NARA/CP.

8. Quotes in Hartman, *Housing and Social Policy*, 160–62. HUD General Counsel Sherman Unger and the San Francisco League of Women Voters agreed with nearly every

point made by Hartman and thought alternative delivery methods (state or federal) might also be effective for ending segregation. See Unger's letter to George Romney (October 30, 1969), Folder "Rel 6–2 Equal Opportunity in Housing, Sept. 9–Dec. 31," Box 68–1969, Subject Correspondence, 1966–1978, RG 207, NARA/CP, and SF League of Women Voters, "Housing Unit-Resource" Report (November 1969), Folder 23 "Action Public Housing," LWV Box 3, MS 1273, CHS.

9. California's Proposition 14 encouraged thirteen other states to pass similar legislation. Jill Quadagno, *The Color of Welfare: How Racism Undermined the War on Poverty* (Oxford: Oxford University Press, 1994), 95–103. For the ways the 1968 act was not enforced in San Francisco, see SFHRC, "Sorry, It's Just Been Rented: Twelve Cases of Discrimination in San Francisco" (June 1973), Folder "Fair Housing Committee, 1972–1973," Box 8, Joseph Alioto Papers, SFPL.

10. Hartman, *Housing and Social Policy*; Quadagno, *The Color of Welfare*, chapter 4; Vale, *From the Puritans to the Projects*, 234–38; R. Allen Hays, *The Federal Government and Urban Housing* (New York: SUNY Press, 2012); Alexander von Hoffman, "Calling Upon the Genius of Private Enterprise: The Housing and Urban Development Act of 1968 and the Liberal Turn to Public-Private Partnerships," *Studies in American Political Development* 27, 2 (October 2013), 165–94; Roger Biles, *The Fate of Cities: Urban America and the Federal Government, 1945–2000* (Lawrence: University Press of Kansas, 2011).

11. Bruce J. Schulman, *The Seventies: The Great Shift in American Culture, Society, and Politics* (New York: Free Press, 2001), chapter 1; Hays, *The Federal Government and Urban Housing*.

12. Quote in Allan Jacobs to Lawrence Cox, HUD (March 13, 1969), Folder "REL 8 Recommendations, Suggestions and Views from the Public, March 18–25," Box 70–1969, Subject Correspondence, 1966–1978, RG 207, NARA/CP. Schulman, *The Seventies*; Hays, *The Federal Government and Urban Housing*; Steve Fraser and Gary Gerstle, eds., *The Rise and Fall of the New Deal Order, 1930–1980* (Princeton, NJ: Princeton University Press, 1990); Thomas Byrne Edsall and Mary D. Edsall, *Chain Reaction: The Impact of Race, Rights, and Taxes on American Politics* (New York: Norton, 1992).

13. Joseph Alioto to Richard Nixon (April 18, 1969), Folder "US President, 1969–1971," Box 7, Alioto Papers, SFPL. Housing expert Charles Abrams, according to historian A. Scott Henderson, argued that "the mismatch between local needs and federal programs was a . . . serious problem in American state-building." Henderson, *Housing and the Democratic Ideal: The Life and Thought of Charles Abrams* (New York: Columbia University Press, 2000), 206–07; Alice O'Connor, "Swimming Against the Tide: A Brief History of Federal Policy in Poor Communities," in Ronald Ferguson and William Dickens, eds., Urban Problems and Community Development (Washington DC: Brookings Institute Press, 1999); Biles, *The Fate of Cities*.

14. SFHA, *Minutes* (October 23, 1969).

15. See Ronald Reagan's press release and the correspondence among Pete Wilson, James Hall (California State Banking Department), George Romney (HUD), and Norman Roettger (HUD), Folder "PRO 3 Federal Housing Administration, August 13–15," Box 53 1969, Subject Correspondence, 1966–78, RG 207, NARA/CP.

16. Ronald Reagan and George Romney correspondence, (June 9 and June 23, 1969),

Folder "REL Governmental Relations and Liaison, June 21–December," Box 66–1969, Subject Correspondence, 1966–1978, RG 207, NARA/CP.

17. George Romney to Ronald Reagan (June 24, 1969), Folder "PRO 5 Model Cities July," Box 57–1969, Subject Correspondence, 1966–1978, RG 207, NARA/CP. See analysis of 701 Comprehensive Planning Assistance program in California in "Administration of the HUD-701 Comprehensive Planning Assistance Grant Program by the State of California" (August 1974) done by the Commission on California State Government Organization and Economy.

18. Mayor Alioto to President Nixon (April 18, 1969), Folder "U.S. President, 1969–1971," Box 7, Alioto Papers, SFPL.

19. For Kane's analysis, see Eneas Kane to Joseph Alioto (June 29, 1972), "Departments under Mayor—Housing Authority, 1972," Box 12, Alioto Papers, SFPL. For HUD's problems in the 1970s and insight into Nixon and Romney, see Chris Bonastia, "Why Did Affirmative Action in Housing Fail During the Nixon Era? Exploring the 'Institutional Homes' of Social Policies," *Social Problems* 47, 4 (2000), 523–42; Kenneth Jackson, *Crabgrass Frontier: The Suburbanization of the United States* (New York: Oxford University Press, 1985); Charles M. Lamb, *Housing Segregation in Suburban America Since 1960: Presidential and Judicial Politics* (New York: Cambridge University Press, 2009); Biles, *The Fate of Cities*.

20. A 1970 report by the U.S. Comptroller General reported that urban redevelopment in 324 cities demolished "88,000 more units than had been constructed under all other HUD programs." Quote and description of report in Hartman, *Housing and Social Policy*, 170. Brian Godfrey, "Urban Development and Redevelopment in San Francisco," *The Geographical Review* 87, 3 (July 1997): 309–33; John H. Mollenkopf, *The Contested City* (Princeton, NJ: Princeton University Press, 1983); Biles, *The Fate of Cities*.

21. Kane quote in SFHA, *Minutes* (October 14, 1971). The breakdown of federal housing spending is in Hays, *The Federal Government and Urban Housing*, 154.

22. Charles and Walter quotes in SFHA, *Minutes* (September 28, 1972).

23. Kane quote in SFHA, *Minutes* (October 26, 1972). On SFHA problems created by HUD funding, see SFHA, *Minutes* (February 25, 1970; August 12, 1971; September 28 and October 26, 1972).

24. For Nixon cuts and impoundment, see Hays, *The Federal Government and Urban Housing*, chapter 4; Neil Soltman, "The Limits of Executive Power: Impoundment of Funds," *Catholic University Law Review* 23, 2 (Winter 1973): 359–74; Lamb, *Housing Segregation in Suburban America Since 1960*; Biles, *The Fate of Cities*. On the rising use of the courts to make policy, see Robert A. Kagan, "Adversarial Legalism and American Government," *Journal of Policy Analysis and Management* 19 (1991): 369–406.

25. All San Francisco data, quotes, and information are from Interagency Committee on Urban Renewal, "October 1969 Report," Folder "Interagency Committee on Urban Renewal," 2 of 2, Box 10, Alioto Papers, SFPL. See also Community Design Center, "Chinatown—An Analysis of Population and Housing" (San Francisco, June 1969); Stephen Weissman, "The Limits of Citizen Participation: Lessons from San Francisco's Model Cities Program," *Western Political Quarterly* 31, 1 (March 1978). For Bay Area trends, see Robert O. Self, *American Babylon: Race and the Struggle for Postwar Oakland* (Princeton, NJ: Princeton University Press, 2005).

26. The San Francisco Mission Coalition noted that discrimination, not lack of skills, led to these employment patterns in its critique of the 1969 report. See Weissman, "The Limits of Citizen Participation." For deindustrialization, see Thomas J. Sugrue, *The Origins of the Urban Crisis: Race and Inequality in Postwar Detroit* (Princeton, NJ: Princeton University Press, 2005); Self, *American Babylon*; Jefferson Cowie and Joseph Heathcott, *Beyond the Ruins: The Meanings of Deindustrialization* (Ithaca, NY: Cornell University Press, 2003).

27. Citizens Emergency Task Force for a Workable Housing Policy, *The Shame of San Francisco*, Folder "The Shame of San Francisco," Box 11, Alioto Papers, SFPL; San Francisco League of Women Voters, *Low and Moderate Income Housing in San Francisco*, Folder 8 "1969 A Report to Members," Box 7, LWV 1271, CHS; "Housing: October 1969 Report," Folder "Interagency Committee on Urban Renewal," 2 of 2, Box 10, Alioto Papers, SFPL; San Francisco Department of City Planning, *Residence Strategy and Programs* (December 1973), SFSU Government Documents.

28. Kathryn Keeble to George Romney (January 27, 1969), Folder "Pro 7 Low-rent Public Housing, Feb. 1–18," Box 59–1969, Subject Correspondence 1966–1978, RG 207, NARA/CP.

29. Reverend Cecil Williams, Herman Gallegos, and Victor Honig, to name a few, were on the task force. Citizens Emergency Task Force, *The Shame of San Francisco*.

30. Quote in SFHA, *Minutes* (May 9, 1968). SFHA, *Minutes* (1967–1970, especially March 21, 1968); Caroline Charles, "The Action and Passion of Our Times," interview conducted by Gabrielle Morris (1974–1978), ROHO, UCB.

31. Eneas Kane to Mayor Joseph Alioto (July 7, 1969), "HUD Workable Program Correspondence, 1968–1969," 1 of 2, Box 11, Alioto Papers, SFPL. Quotes in SFHA, *Minutes* (September 12, 1968).

32. Interagency Committee on Urban Renewal, "October 1969 Report," Folder "Interagency Committee on Urban Renewal," 2 of 2, Box 10, Alioto Papers, SFPL. A 1950 state law required voter approval for all new public housing. See chapter 4.

33. SFHA, *Minutes* (December 12, 1968). Quote in SFHA, *Minutes* (March 27, 1969).

34. SFHA, *Minutes* (especially July 11 and February 2, 1968). Quote in SFHA, *Minutes* (February 2, 1968). Also see, Effie Robinson, Director of Human Relations, SFHA, *Critical and Urgent Need for Services for Relocatees from South of Market* (June 1970), Folder "HUD, Yerba Buena Center," 1 of 3, 1970–1973, Box 10, Alioto Papers, SFPL.

35. SFHA, *Minutes* (July 11 and February 2, 1968). Also see Robinson, *Critical and Urgent Need for Services for Relocatees from South of Market*; David A. Rochefort, *From Poorhouses to Homelessness: Policy Analysis and Mental Health Care* (Westport, CT: Greenwood, 1997), chapters 3 and 4. On social service politics, see Frances Fox Piven and Richard A. Cloward, *Poor People's Movements: Why They Succeed, How They Fail* (New York: Vintage Books, 1979); Williams, *The Politics of Public Housing*; Lisa Levenstein, *A Movement Without Marches: African American Women and the Politics of Poverty in Postwar Philadelphia* (Chapel Hill: University of North Carolina Press, 2010); Self, *American Babylon*; Gold, *When Tenants Claimed the City*. Self's study emphasizes how in Oakland, mostly African American residents organized for both quality jobs and social services, but political elites were more willing to provide services instead of ensuring jobs. On elderly political organizing in San Francisco, and specifically displaced tenants who moved to SFHA housing, see Paul Kley-

man, *Senior Power: Growing Old Rebelliously* (San Francisco: Glide Publications, 1974), chapters 7 and 8. Lawrence Vale shows how the selection of the poorest tenants in public housing in Chicago and Atlanta—in contrast to New York City, which maintained a mixed economic tenant population—helped to undermine the program politically and ultimately led to the purging of these tenants from their housing and communities. See Lawrence J. Vale, *Purging the Poorest: Public Housing and the Design Politics of Twice-Cleared Communities* (Chicago: University of Chicago Press, 2013) and Nicholas Dagen Bloom, *Public Housing That Worked: New York in the Twentieth Century* (Philadelphia: University of Pennsylvania Press, 2008). The SFHA program leaned more toward housing poorer tenants. For the bump in crime, see Christopher Lowen Agee, *The Streets of San Francisco: Policing and the Creation of a Cosmopolitan Liberal Politics, 1950–1972* (Chicago: University of Chicago Press, 2014).

36. The SFHA *Minutes* highlight Kane's support of tenants.

37. San Francisco League of Women Voters, *Low and Moderate Income Housing in San Francisco*, Folder 8 "1969: A Report to Members," Box 7, LWV 1271, CHS; San Francisco Department of City Planning, *Residence Strategy and Programs* (December 1973), SFSU Government Documents; SFHA, *Minutes* (November 9, 1972; and May 10, 1973); Interview with Darryl Cox, conducted by author in 2004. For Sunnydale Coalition, see SFHA, *Minutes* (May 12, 1977).

38. Numbers in SFHA, *Minutes* (March 27, 1969). For her study, Amy Howard conducted interviews with tenants at North Beach and found the tensions surmountable, though previous scholars had found that residents' differences were obstacles to tenant organizing. At least for this period, my research confirms Howard's research. See Howard, *More Than Shelter* and Patricia Guthrie and Janis Hutchinson, "The Impact of Perceptions on Interpersonal Interactions in an African American/Asian American Housing Project," *Journal of Black Studies* 25 (January 1995): 377–95. Also see Gordon K. Mantler, *Power to the Poor: Black-Brown Coalition and the Fight for Economic Justice, 1960–1974* (Chapel Hill: University of North Carolina Press, 2013).

39. SFHA, *Minutes* (July 11, 1968).

40. Quote in SFHA, *Minutes* (February 26, 1970). For the NTO, see Williams, *The Politics of Public Housing;* Thomas J. Sugrue, *Sweet Land of Liberty: The Forgotten Struggle for Civil Rights in the North* (New York: Random House, 2008), chapter 12.

41. Quote in SFHA, *Minutes* (March 26, 1970). For a sample of services, see SFHA, *Minutes* (May 23, 1968; March 26 and December 10, 1970; and February 11, 1971); Thomas Hum, M.D., Chairman North East Medical Services to George Romney (May 29, 1969), Folder "PRO Programs Administration, June 17–27," Box 49–1969, Subject Correspondence, 1966–78, RG 207, NARA/CP. The SFHA funded the PHTA (Public Housing Tenants Association) with a $3 a month per unit formula modeled on labor union dues. Tenants had full control over this money. See SFHA, *Minutes* (October 7, 1976).

42. Quotes in Western Addition Area Community Action Program of the EOC, Annual Report (March 1968–February 1969), Folder "Western Addition Area Annual Report, Feb. 1969," Box 4, Donald Lucas Papers, GLBT. The EOC did much to encourage diverse representation. In the Western Addition, a 27-member board was elected from a pool of 94 candidates representing 1,300 residents, and this board sent 5 individuals to serve on the citywide EOC. For discussions of community organizing, see Piven and Cloward, *Poor*

People's Movements; Williams, *The Politics of Public Housing*; Self, *American Babylon;* Gold, *When Tenants Claimed the City.*

43. Federally subsidized redevelopment is a major theme in urban history because it highlights the power of policymaking to reinforce inequality. See Jane Jacobs, *The Death and Life of Great American Cities* (New York: Vintage Books, 1961); John F. Bauman, *Public Housing, Race, and Renewal: Urban Planning in Philadelphia, 1920–1974* (Philadelphia: Temple University Press, 1987); Raymond A. Mohl, "Making the Second Ghetto in Metropolitan Miami, 1940–1960," *Journal of Urban History* 21, 3 (March 1995): 395–427; Arnold R. Hirsch, *Making the Second Ghetto: Race and Housing in Chicago, 1940–1960* (New York: Cambridge University Press, 1983); Sugrue, *The Origins of the Urban Crisis*; Mollenkopf, *Contested City*; Mike Davis, *City of Quartz: Excavating the Future in Los Angeles* (New York: Verso, 2006) and *Ecology of Fear: Los Angeles and the Imagination of Disaster* (New York: Vintage Books, 1999); Chester Hartman, *City for Sale: The Transformation of San Francisco* (Berkeley: University of California, 2002); Self, *American Babylon*; Samuel Zipp, *Manhattan Projects: The Rise and Fall of Urban Renewal in Cold War New York* (New York: Oxford University Press, 2011); Biles, *The Fate of Cities*; Ocean Howell, *Making the Mission: Planning and Ethnicity in San Francisco* (Chicago: University of Chicago Press, 2015).

44. Mollenkopf, *Contested City*, 178–79.

45. Cecilia Keough to George Romney (January 30, 1969), Folder "PRO 8 Urban Renewal and Development, Feb. 1–10," Box 61–1969, Subject Correspondence, 1966–78, RG 207 NARA/CP.

46. Zipp, *Manhattan Projects*; Biles, *The Fate of Cities*.

47. *San Francisco Bay Guardian* (April 17, 1970); San Francisco League of Women Voters, *Low and Moderate Income Housing in San Francisco*, Folder 8 "1969 A Report to Members," Box 7, LWV 1271, CHS; Hartman, *City for Sale*; Mollenkopf, *The Contested City*.

48. SFHA *Minutes* are filled with negotiations with the San Francisco Redevelopment Agency, which repeatedly tried to gain control over all SFHA housing stock, personnel, and resources. See SFHA, *Minutes* (May 23, October 8, and October 10, 1968). Quote in SFHA, *Minutes* (October 10, 1968). George Christopher and George Romney correspondence, Folder "PRO 8–1 Relocation, January–July," Box 61–1969, Subject Correspondence, 1966–1978, RG 207, NARA/CP.

49. Ruth Williams to Don Hummel, HUD (May 7, 1968), Folder "MGT 2 Committees Conferences, and Meetings, May 20–Aug. 22," Box 2 1968, Subject Correspondence, 1966–78, RG 207, NARA/CP; San Francisco Redevelopment Agency, "Bayview–Hunters Point Joint Housing Committee Residents and Redevelopment Build a New Hunters Point Community," Folder "SF Hunters Point Bayview, May–August 1967, Carton 17, NAACP, BANC; SFHA, *Minutes* (December 12, 1968); David Yamakawa, Special Assistant for Model Neighborhoods, to Victor Cary, HUD (June 12, 1969), Folder "Correspondence for Tolan, Anderson, and Slade, 1969," 1 of 2, Box 8, Alioto Papers, SFPL; Rachel Brahinsky, "Race and the Making of Southeast San Francisco: Towards a Theory of Race-Class," *Antipode* 46, 5 (2014): 1258–76; John Arena, *Driven from New Orleans: How Nonprofits Betray Public Housing and Promote Privatization* (Minneapolis: University of Minnesota Press, 2012).

50. "Roaches, Rents, and Repairs." Quote in William Middleton, Director of Western Addition Project Area Committee (WAPAC), to Congressman Phillip Burton (January 26,

1970), Folder "PRO 15 Urban Renewal and Redevelopment March 3–17," Box 96–1970, Subject Correspondence, 1966–78, NARA/CP.

51. Quote in WACO to Robert Weaver (no date), "Correspondence, n.d., EOC Administration," Box 4, Don Lucas Papers, GLBT. Also see San Francisco Neighborhood Legal Assistance Foundation to George Romney (January 24, 1969), Folder "LEG Litigation and Claims Jan. 1–June 6," Box 46 1969, Subject Correspondence, 1966–78, RG 207, NARA/CP; Hartman, *City for Sale*.

52. Justin Herman to Richard Ludwig, (July 17, 1970), "HUD Workable Program, 1971, Midterm Review," 1 of 2, Box 11, Alioto Papers, SFPL.

53. Richard Park to M. Justin Herman (November 11, 1969), Folder "HUD Workable Program Correspondence, 1968–1969," Box 11, Alioto Papers, SFPL; SFHA, *Minutes* (April 23, 1970).

54. George Christopher and George Romney correspondence (no date), Folder "PRO 8–1 Relocation, January–July," Box 61–1969, Subject Correspondence, 1966–1978, RG 207, NARA/CP; see materials in Folder "HUD Workable Program, 1971, Recertification, Jackson Letter, 1971," Box 11, Alioto Papers, SFPL; Hartman, *City for Sale*.

55. Ibid. Quote in George Christopher and George Romney correspondence.

56. Kane quote in SFHA, *Minutes* (January 8, 1970). Hartman, *City for Sale*.

57. SFHA, *Minutes* (March 12, 1970).

58. Ibid.

59. Ibid.

60. SFHA, *Minutes* (August 13, 1970).

61. The SFHA staff edited some flyers for the meeting to emphasize "tenant involvement" and a joint approach (tenants/SFHA staff) to the SFHA's budget. SFHA, *Minutes* (January 14, 1971).

62. SFHA, *Minutes* (April 8, 1971). Women were crucial to tenant organizing in and out of San Francisco. For comparison, see Williams, *The Politics of Public Housing*; Levenstein, *A Movement Without Marches*; Gold, *When Tenants Claimed the City*.

63. SFHA, *Minutes* (April 8, April 22, and November 9, 1971). The level of community organizing and political engagement by tenants in this era counters the images of an underclass. For discussions of the underclass and public housing, see Lee Rainwater, *Behind Ghetto Walls: Black Families in a Federal Slum* (Chicago: Aldine, 1970); William Julius Wilson, *The Truly Disadvantaged: The Inner City, the Underclass, and Public Policy* (Chicago: University of Chicago Press, 1987); Bauman, *Public Housing, Race, and Renewal*; Michael B. Katz, ed., *The Underclass Debate: Views from History* (Princeton, NJ: Princeton University Press, 1993); Alice O'Connor, *Poverty Knowledge: Social Science, Social Policy, and the Poor in Twentieth-Century U.S. History* (Princeton, NJ: Princeton University Press, 2001); Sudhir Venkatesh, *American Project: The Rise and Fall of a Modern Ghetto* (Cambridge, MA: Harvard University Press, 2000).

64. SFHA, *Minutes* (April 8, April 22, and November 9, 1971). In 1976, the SFHA funded the PHTA with a $3 a month per unit formula modeled on labor union dues. See SFHA, *Minutes* (October 7, 1976).

65. The CETA grant led to a National Endowment for the Arts grant to film those who worked on the murals and gardens. SFHA, *Minutes* (October 9, 1973).

66. Quote in SFHA, *Minutes* (May 27, 1971). SFHA, *Minutes* (October 28, 1971; and January 13, 1977).

67. SFHA, *Minutes* (August 12, 1971).

68. Ibid.; SFHA, *Minutes* (August 27, 1970).

69. See SFHA, *Minutes*.

70. SFHA, *Minutes* (August 23, 1973).

71. One example of this social distance between non-tenant commissioners and tenants occurred when Commissioner Charles (non-tenant) doubted poor tenants wanted to integrate with higher-income tenants, stating that "low-income people, because of their timidity and degradation, might not want to venture into an 'unfamiliar' world and will need help and guidance to introduce them to off-project facilities." SFHA, *Minutes* (July 11, 1968).

72. For public housing tenant participation on housing authority commissions, see "Tenant-Management Issues," *Journal of Housing* 27 (1970): 534–43; Edward White, "Tenant Participation in Public Housing Management," *Journal of Housing* 26 (1969): 416–19. In "Tenant-Management Issues," the author cites a survey based on 891 respondents (out of the 2,700 housing authorities in the nation) and how 42 had tenant commissioners; another 58 were in the process of adding tenants. Also see Williams, *The Politics of Public Housing*, and Howard, *More Than Shelter*.

73. SFHA, *Minutes* (January 10, 1974).

74. SFHA, *Minutes* (December 20, 1973; January 10 and February 2, 1974); Correspondence among Elouise Westbrook, James Lynn, and Cleo Wallace (no date), Folder "PRO 8 Low Rent Public Housing, January," Box 14 Subject Correspondence, 1975, Subject Correspondence, 1966–1978, RG 207, NARA/CP.

75. Quote in SFHA, *Minutes* (February 14, 1974). For a discussion of HUD's programs, see Hays, *The Federal Government and Urban Housing*; Chester Hartman, ed., *America's Housing Crisis: What Is to Be Done?* (New York: Routledge & Kegan Paul, 1983).

76. Kane's quote in SFHA, *Minutes* (October 25, 1973). Also, see Eneas Kane to Joseph Alioto (June 29, 1972), "Departments under Mayor—Housing Authority, 1972," Box 12, Alioto Papers, SFPL; SFHA Commissioner George Evankovich to Carla Hill, HUD Secretary (July 16, 1975), Folder "PRO 8–Low Rent Public Housing Sept.–October," Box 14 Subject Correspondence, 1975, Subject Correspondence, 1966–1978, RG 207, NARA/CP.

77. Those seventy SFHA jobs were 29 percent of the staff. Kane to Alioto, "Departments under Mayor—Housing Authority, 1972"; Evankovich to Hill, "PRO 8–Low Rent Public Housing Sept-October"; Kane's quote in SFHA, *Minutes* (October 25, 1973); Alexander von Hoffman, "The Curse of Durability: Why Housing for the Poor Was Built to Last," *Journal of Housing and Community Development* 55 (September/October: 1998): 34–38.

78. Quote on strike threat in SFHA, *Minutes* (September 14, 1972). Evankovich to Hill, "PRO 8–Low Rent Public Housing Sept-October."

79. SFHA, *Minutes* (February 13, 1975).

80. Board of Governors, National Association of Housing and Redevelopment Officials, "The New American Realism: 'Save and Rebuild America,'" (1976).

81. SFHA, *Minutes* (February 26, 1976).

82. Frederick M. Wirt, *Alioto and the Politics of Hyperpluralism* (Berkeley: University of California, Institute of Governmental Studies, no. 36, April 1970); William Issel, "Liberalism and Urban Policy in San Francisco from the 1930s to the 1960s," *Western Historical Quarterly*

22, 4 (November 1991): 431–50, and Issel's *Church and State in the City*. For discussions of pluralism and policymaking, see Theodore J. Lowi, *The End of Liberalism* (New York: Norton, 1979); Anne L. Schneider and Helen M. Ingram, *Policy Design for Democracy* (Lawrence: University Press of Kansas, 1997).

83. For the shift in liberalism in this period, see Fraser and Gerstle, *The Rise and Fall of the New Deal Order*; Edsall and Edsall, *Chain Reaction*; Allen Brinkley, *Liberalism and Its Discontents* (Cambridge, MA: Harvard University Press, 2000); Schulman, *The Seventies*; Alice Kessler-Harris, *In Pursuit of Equity: Women, Men and the Quest for Economic Citizenship in 20th-Century America* (New York: Oxford University Press, 2003); Heather Ann Thompson, *Whose Detroit: Politics, Labor, and Race in a Modern American City* (Ithaca, NY: Cornell University Press, 2004); Self, *American Babylon*; Sugrue, *Sweet Land of Liberty*.

CHAPTER 7

1. Kevin Starr, "Speculations," *San Francisco Examiner* (February 13, 1979).

2. "A Celebration by Project's Tenants," *San Francisco Chronicle* (February 22, 1979); *Neighborhood Improvement Update*, 1, 8 (January 1979), Folder "Chinatown Neighborhood Improvement Resource Center," Box 1, MS 1647 SPUR, CHS.

3. Ibid.

4. North Beach household demographics broke down in the following way: ninety-five Asian, fifty-four white, forty-seven African American, one Native American, four Latinas/os, and nine other. "Fed-Up Tenants Fight City Hall," *San Francisco Chronicle* (February 26, 1979). Amy Lynne Howard, *More Than Shelter: Activism and Community in San Francisco Public Housing* (Minneapolis: University of Minnesota Press, 2014).

5. Herbert J. Gans, *The War Against the Poor: The Underclass and Antipoverty Policy* (New York: Basic Books, 1995).

6. Jesse Gray to Patricia Harris, letter (February 2, 1977), Folder "Rel 8 Suggestions and Views from the Public," Box 38 1977, Subject Correspondence, 1966–78, RG 207, NARA/CP. On the initial "guarded optimism" among housing professionals and tenants, see SFHA commissioner reports from the National Housing Conference and NAHRO's conferences in SFHA, *Minutes* (March 10, 1977). R. Allen Hays, *The Federal Government and Urban Housing* (New York: SUNY Press, 2012); Roger Biles, *The Fate of Cities: Urban America and the Federal Government, 1945–2000* (Lawrence: University Press of Kansas, 2011).

7. Patricia Harris to Director of OMB Bert Lance, letter (August 9, 1977), Folder "PRO 8 Low Rent Public Housing, Jan.–May," Box 35 1977, Subject Correspondence, 1966–78, RG 207, NARA/CP.

8. Gray to Harris (February 2, 1977).

9. Harris to Lance (August 9, 1977). On national priorities, see Hays, *The Federal Government and Urban Housing*; Chester Hartman, *City for Sale: The Transformation of San Francisco* (Berkeley: University of California Press, 2002); SFHA, *Minutes* (February 23 and March 9, 1978).

10. Other HUD programs included tax credits for low-income housing investors and subsidies for privately built and owned (for profit and nonprofit) housing. These programs also drained money from the public housing program. For Section 8, see Hays, *The Federal Government*; Alex F. Schwartz, *Housing Policy in the United States* (New York: Routledge, 2014).

11. SFHA, *Minutes* (July 29, 1976).

12. Hartman, *City for Sale*, chapter 11. Quotes on 277. Also see Ocean Howell, *Making the Mission: Planning and Ethnicity in San Francisco* (Chicago: University of Chicago Press, 2015).

13. "Housing Authority picks Rev. Jones as Chairman," *San Francisco Examiner* (February 25, 1977).

14. "Peoples Temple," Donald Field letter to editor, *San Francisco Examiner* (June 20, 1977).

15. SFHA, *Minutes* (January 27, 1977).

16. Moscone had lobbied to make Jones chair. "Housing Authority Picks Rev. Jones as Chairman," *San Francisco Examiner* (February 25, 1977). For Jones's life, see David Chidester, *Salvation and Suicide: Jim Jones, the Peoples Temple, and Jonestown* (Bloomington: Indiana University Press, 2004).

17. Estella Habal, *San Francisco's International Hotel: Mobilizing the Filipino American Community in the Anti-Eviction Movement* (Philadelphia: Temple University Press, 2007).

18. Ibid.; quote in SFHA, *Minutes* (December 23, 1976).

19. SFHA leaders and nearly all tenants favored buying the International Hotel, though a few tenants noted that this would take resources from their projects. See SFHA, *Minutes* (1974–1978). In 1994, HUD and the mayor's office funded low-income senior housing and a Manilatown Center on the former International Hotel land. See Habal, *San Francisco's International Hotel*. For the senior movement, see Paul Kleyman, *Senior Power: Growing Old Rebelliously* (San Francisco: Glide Publications, 1974); Roger Sanjek, *Gray Panthers* (Philadelphia: University of Pennsylvania Press, 2011).

20. Quote in SFHA, *Minutes* (September 22, 1977). For CANE and Western Addition redevelopment, see Donna Graves and Page & Turnbull, Inc., "Japantown: San Francisco, California: Historical Context Statement," prepared for the City and County of San Francisco Planning Department (San Francisco, May 2011).

21. SFHA, *Minutes* (October 13, 1977); Hartman, *City for Sale*, 277.

22. Ibid.; "Gene Suttle—Community Leader," *San Francisco Chronicle* (September 21, 1995).

23. Quotes in SFHA, *Minutes* (October 13, 1977). Even Dianne Feinstein worried about insufficient funding for relocating businesses. Letters Between Dianne Feinstein and Carla Hills (June 4 and June 28, 1976), Folder "PRO 16 Relocation," Box 25 1976, Subject Correspondence, 1966–78, RG 207, NARA/CP.

24. SFHA, *Minutes* (October 27, 1977).

25. SFHA, *Minutes* (October 13 and October 27, 1977).

26. Quote in Walter Blum, "Voices from a Forgotten Land," *California Living* (magazine of the *San Francisco Chronicle* and *Examiner*) (March 20, 1977).

27. SFHA, *Minutes* (June 29, 1978).

28. For "overflow crowds" see SFHA, *Minutes* (January 1, 1977). On Kane resignation and Scott and Williams, see SFHA, *Minutes* (December 23, 1976) and "New Housing Chief Starts Making Reforms," *San Francisco Examiner* (August 25, 1978). Cleo Wallace quote on women in SFHA, *Minutes* (May 25, 1978); and her quote on being poor in SFHA, *Minutes* (December 23, 1976). For a great study of women tenant activism in Baltimore, see Rhonda Y. Williams, *The Politics of Public Housing: Black Women's Struggles Against Urban Inequality* (New York: Oxford University Press, 2004).

29. SFHA, *Minutes* (July 12, 1979).

30. SFHA, *Minutes* (April 13, 1978).

31. Henri Tajfel and John C. Turner, "The Social Identity Theory of Intergroup Behavior," in Stephen Worchel and William G. Austin, eds., *Psychology of Intergroup Relations* (Chicago: Nelson-Hall, 1986), and Richard D. Ashmore and Frances K. Del Boca, "Conceptual Approaches to Stereotypes and Stereotyping," in David L. Hamilton, ed., *Cognitive Processes in Stereotyping and Intergroup Behavior* (Hillsdale, NJ: Erlbaum, 1981). For class identity, see E. P. Thompson, *The Making of the English Working Class* (New York: Vintage Books, 1963). For community building in public housing, see Williams, *The Politics of Public Housing*; Howard, *More Than Shelter*.

32. Quote in *Update* (November 1979). Monthly issues of *Update* (1978–1988), which was published by the SFHA for tenants, can be found in the SFPL.

33. Pet policy in *Update* (March 1982). Nearly every *Update* issue reported on senior public housing tenant activities and lives. Brill in *Update* (April 1983). Kleyman, *Senior Power*. For analysis of senior housing, see Galen Cranz, David Christensen, and Sam Dyer, "A User-Oriented Evaluation of San Francisco's Public Housing for the Elderly," sponsored by the Departments of Senior Citizen Social Services, SFHA, and Center for Planning and Development Research, UC Berkeley, 1977 (located at the SFPL).

34. Quote in SFHA, *Minutes* (January 12, 1978). Also see *Update* (1978–1988).

35. SFHA, *Minutes* (September 22, 1977).

36. Quotes in May 1979 *Update*.

37. Quote in July 1978 *Update*. On the importance of print media to building community, see Benedict Anderson, *Imagined Communities: Reflections on the Origin and Spread of Nationalism* (New York: Verso, 1996).

38. *Update* (November 1978). Also see Howard, *More Than Shelter*.

39. See *Update* (July 1979); SFHA, *Minutes* (September 22, 1977).

40. SFHA, *Minutes* (April 13, 1978).

41. Quote in SFHA, *Minutes* (January 11, 1979). For problems of crime surrounding public housing, see Nicholas Dagen Bloom, Fritz Umbach, and Lawrence J. Vale, eds., *Public Housing Myths: Perception, Reality, and Social Policy* (Ithaca, NY: Cornell University Press, 2015; Howard, *More Than Shelter*.

42. SFHA, *Minutes* (February 23 and March 9, 1978). For Carter's urban policies, see Raymond Mohl, "Jimmy Carter, Patricia Roberts Harris, and Housing Policy in the Age of Limits," in John F. Bauman, Roger Biles, and Kristin M. Szylvian, eds., *From Tenements to the Taylor Homes: In Search of an Urban Housing Policy in Twentieth-Century America* (University Park: Penn State University Press, 2000); Hays, *The Federal Government and Urban Housing*; Biles, *The Fate of Cities*; Schwartz, *Housing Policy in the United States*.

43. SFHA, *Minutes*, (August 18, 1977; and May 25, 1978); for Harris visit, see SFHA, *Minutes* (April 13 and April 27, 1978). Also see "San Francisco Redevelopment Program: Summary of Project Data and Key Elements, 1981" [copy located at HUD library, Washington, DC]; Lisa Davis, "Diseaseville," *San Francisco Weekly* (August 27, 2003).

44. Quotes in "Feinstein Tells the City's Chiefs: 'Do More for Less,'" *San Francisco Examiner* (December 13, 1977). Also see SFHA, *Minutes* (July 27, 1978), and Dianne Feinstein to Ronald Pelosi letter (November 28, 1979) in SFHA, *Minutes* (December 13, 1979). Hartman, *City for Sale*; Brian J. Godfrey, "Urban Development and Redevelopment in San Francisco," *Geographical Review* 87, 3 (July 1997): 309–33.

45. Quotes in "Feinstein Tells the City's Chiefs: 'Do More for Less.'" SFHA, *Minutes* (July 27, 1978); Feinstein to Pelosi (November 28, 1979).

46. Biles, *The Fate of Cities*, chapter 8. Hays, *The Federal Government and Urban Housing*; Schwartz, *Housing Policy in the United States*. For a sample of New Right scholarship, see Jon F. Hale, "The Making of the New Democrats," *Political Science Quarterly* 110, 2 (January 1995): 207–32; Margaret Weir, ed., *The Social Divide: Political Parties and the Future of Activist Government* (Washington, DC: Brookings Institution Press, 1998); Lisa McGirr, *Suburban Warriors: The Origins of the New American Right* (Princeton, NJ: Princeton University Press, 2001); Sean Wilentz, *The Age of Reagan: A History, 1974–2008* (New York: HarperCollins, 2008); Bruce J. Schulman and Julian E. Zelizer, eds., *Rightward Bound: Making Conservative America in the 1970s* (Cambridge, MA: Harvard University Press, 2008); David Harvey, *A Brief History of Neoliberalism* (Oxford: Oxford University Press, 2007); John Arena, *Driven from New Orleans: How Nonprofits Betray Public Housing and Promote Privatization* (Minneapolis: University of Minnesota Press, 2012).

47. Hays quote on Pierce in his *The Federal Government and Urban Housing*, chapter 8, on 234. Chester Hartman, "Housing Policies Under the Reagan Administration," in Rachel G. Bratt, Chester Hartman, and Ann Meyerson, eds., *Critical Perspectives on Housing* (Philadelphia: Temple University Press, 1986); Charles Moore and Patricia Hoban-Moore, "Some Lessons from Reagan's HUD: Housing Policy and Public Service," *Political Science and Politics* 23, 1 (March 1990): 13–18.

48. Quote in Biles, *The Fate of Cities*, 259. The President's Commission on Housing, the Report of the President's Commission on Housing (Washington, DC, 1982); Hartman, "Housing Policies Under the Reagan Administration."

49. Hartman, "Housing Policies Under the Reagan Administration"; Hays, *The Federal Government and Urban Housing*; Moore and Hoban-Moore, "Some Lessons from Reagan's HUD"; *Update* (December 1982).

50. Quoted in Hartman, "Housing Policies Under the Reagan Administration," 384.

51. The largest HUD non-public housing programs from 1960 to 1990 were Section 8, Section 202, Section 236, Section 502, Section 515, and community development block grants. Katherine O'Regan and John Quigley, "Federal Policy and the Rise of Nonprofit Housing Providers," *Journal of Housing Research* 11, 2 (2000): 297–317; Schwartz, *Housing Policy in the United States*, chapter 9.

52. SFHA, *Crisis in Public Housing: A Review of Alternatives for Public Housing in San Francisco and Recommendations for the Future* (April 1982); Hartman, "Housing Policies Under the Reagan Administration"; Julee H. Kryder-Coe, Lester M. Salamon, and Janice M. Molnar, eds., *Homeless Children and Youth: A New American Dilemma* (New Brunswick, NJ: Transaction, 1992), 208; Biles, *The Fate of Cities*; Lawrence J. Vale, *Purging the Poorest: Public Housing and the Design Politics of Twice-Cleared Communities* (Chicago: University of Chicago Press, 2013); Arena, *Driven from New Orleans*.

53. SFHA Public Housing Task Force, "Crisis in Public Housing: A Review of Alternatives for Public Housing in San Francisco and Recommendations for the Future" (1982). Contracting services out, or what became known as "reinventing government," expanded rapidly in the 1970s and 1980s. Municipal governments alone tripled their service contract values with the private sector from $22 billion in 1972 to $66 billion in 1980. See Stephen

Moore, "Contracting Out: A Painless Alternative to the Budget Cutter's Knife," *Proceedings of the Academy of Political Science* 36, 3 (1987): 60–73. Also see Daphne T. Greenwood, "The Decision to Contract Out: Understanding the Full Economic and Social Impacts" (Colorado Springs: Colorado Center for Policy Studies, March 2014); Arena, *Driven from New Orleans*.

54. SFHA Public Housing Task Force, "Crisis in Public Housing." For tenant management, see Robert Kolodny, "What Happens When Tenants Manage Their Own Public Housing," (Washington, DC: Office of Policy Development and Research, HUD, August 1983).

55. Quotes in SFHA Public Housing Task Force, "Crisis in Public Housing."

56. Quotes in SFHA Public Housing Task Force, "Crisis in Public Housing."

57. SFHA Public Housing Task Force, "Crisis in Public Housing." For developer interests in SFHA properties, see report and SFHA, *Minutes* (April 8, 1982). Leung quote in SFHA, *Minutes* (April 8, 1982).

58. Godfrey, "Urban Development and Redevelopment in San Francisco"; Randy Shaw, "Tenant Power in San Francisco," in James Brook, Chris Carlsson, and Nancy J. Peters, eds., *Reclaiming San Francisco: History, Politics, and Culture* (San Francisco: City Lights Books, 1998). In 1978, housing costs rose 12 to 14 percent around the nation—17 percent on the West Coast. SFHA, *Minutes* (March 22, 1979). Sharon M. Keigher, *Housing Risks and Homelessness Among the Urban Elderly* (New York: Haworth Press, 1991), 78–87.

59. Quote in SFHA, *Minutes* (September 12, 1977).

60. SFHA, *Minutes* (September 11, 1980).

61. Hays, *The Federal Government and Urban Housing*, chapter 8. See also Bratt, Hartman, and Meyerson, *Critical Perspectives on Housing*; Kay Young McChesney, "Family Homelessness: A Systemic Problem," *Journal of Social Issues* 46, 4 (1990): 191–205; John M. Quigley, Steven Raphael, and Eugene Smolensky, "Homeless in America, Homeless in California," *Review of Economics and Statistics* 83, 1 (February 2001): 37–51; Teresa Gowan, *Hobos, Hustlers, and Backsliders: Homeless in San Francisco* (Minneapolis: University of Minnesota Press, 2010).

62. SFHA, *Minutes* (November 24, 1982).

63. SFHA, *Minutes* (December 27, 1984).

64. SFHA, *Minutes* (April 25, 1985). For national homeless trends, see Martha R. Burt, *Over the Edge: The Growth of Homelessness in the 1980s* (New York: Russell Sage Foundation, 1993); Quigley, Raphael, and Smolensky, "Homeless in America, Homeless in California."

65. SFHA, *Minutes* (April 25, 1985; December 10, 1987; and February 11, 1988). For congressional findings and language of the act, see https://www.govtrack.us/congress/bills/100/hr558/text

66. SFHA, *Minutes* (April 25, 1985; December 10, 1987; and February 11, 1988). Gowan, *Hobos, Hustlers, and Backsliders*.

67. Data from SFHA Public Housing Task Force, "Crisis in Public Housing," and Carl Williams, "Public Housing Discussion Paper for the Mayor's Housing Policy Group" (April 23, 1981). Both documents are in SFHA, *Minutes* (June 24, 1982). See SFHA, *Minutes* (August 26, 1982; and April 25, 1985). For 1990s data, see Memo to City Services Committee (May 22, 1990), "Operations of the SFHA, Board of Supervisors Budget Analysis" (1990) and Report to the Board of Supervisors "Management Audit of the SF Housing Authority" (November 1993).

68. Ibid.

69. Available SFHA housing stock changed daily as units and buildings came on or off line. From 1982–1992, the SFHA added 137 senior/disability units while demolishing 705 family units. Data from SFHA Public Housing Task Force, "Crisis in Public Housing," and Williams, "Public Housing Discussion Paper for the Mayor's Housing Policy Group," both in SFHA, *Minutes* (June 24, 1982). And SFHA, *Minutes* (August 26, 1982; and April 25, 1985). For 1990s data, see Memo to City Services Committee and "Management Audit of the SF Housing Authority."

70. Ibid.; for Alice Griffith Homes, see SFHA, *Minutes* (May 13 and July 22, 1982). For comparison, see Atlanta Housing Authority, "HOPE: Atlanta Housing Authority 15 Year Progress Report, 1995–2010."

71. Rachel G. Bratt, "Public Housing: The Controversy and Contribution" in Bratt, Hartman, and Meyerson, *Critical Perspectives on Housing*, 335–61. Also see D. Bradford Hunt, *Blueprint for Disaster: The Unraveling of Chicago Public Housing* (Chicago: University of Chicago Press, 2009); Vale, *Purging the Poorest*; Howard, *More Than Shelter*; Bloom, Umbach, and Vale, *Public Housing Myths*.

72. The Pink Palace was not originally built for large families, but many lived there. Seniors already lived there when Feinstein put in her request. SFHA, *Minutes* (July 17, 1981). For the Pink Palace's national reputation as a high-rise slum and as contributing to crime, see Wallace Turner, "San Francisco Tackling 'Den of Thieves' Project," *New York Times* (July 30, 1981).

73. SFHA, *Minutes* (June 11, 1981). See Oscar Newman, *Defensible Space: Crime Prevention Through Urban Design* (New York: Macmillan, 1972). The idea of senior tenants being less of a menace than family tenants justified a national trend to support more senior housing (public and Section 8) in the 1970s. See Hays, *The Federal Government and Urban Housing*, chapter 5.

74. SFHA, *Minutes* (July 17, 1981) and *Update* (July 1984).

75. SFHA, *Minutes* (July 17, 1981).

76. SFHA, *Minutes* (August 13, 1981).

77. Public comments and Mardikian quote in SFHA, *Minutes* (August 13, 1981). For Pruitt-Igoe, see Alexander von Hoffman, "Why They Built Pruitt-Igoe," in Bauman, Biles, and Szylvian, *From Tenements to the Taylor Homes*, 180–206.

78. SFHA, *Minutes* (August 13, 1981).

79. Quote in SFHA, *Minutes* (August 27, 1981). SFHA, *Minutes* (September 23, 1982); Allan Temko, "Old Pink Palace Wiped Out by New Color, Life," *San Francisco Chronicle* (April 15, 1985).

80. SFHA, *Minutes*, (November 10 and November 23, 1983; and October 23, 1986); *Update* (July 1984).

81. SFHA, *Minutes* (June 14, 1984); *Update* (July 1984).

82. Quote in SFHA, *Minutes* (October 14, 1982). For PHTA problems, see SFHA *Minutes* in the 1980s. In 1983, the SFHA took over the bill-paying duties for the PHTA. SFHA, *Minutes* (February 10, 1983). For a sample PHTA–SFHA contract, which had many of the same provisions as a labor union contract, see SFHA, *Minutes* (October 13, 1983).

83. SFHA, *Minutes* (October 22, 1987).

84. SFHA, *Minutes* (March 10, 1983).

85. Quote in *Update* (July 1982). *Update* and the SFHA *Minutes* document senior tenant activities.

86. SFHA, *Minutes* (October 28, 1982).

87. Quotes in SFHA, *Minutes* (March 24, 1988).

88. SFHA, *Minutes* (January 26, 1984).

89. SFHA, *Minutes* (February 25, 1988).

90. SFHA, *Minutes* (April 28, 1988).

91. SFHA, *Minutes* (February 28, 1985).

92. Robert De Monte to Frank Jordan, letter (December 19, 1991), Folder "1992 Corres," Box 1, Program Subject Files, R. J. De Monte, Regional Administrator, 1988–1992, NARA/SB, RG 207. A Feinstein appointee, SFHA Commissioner Preston Cook pushed for private sector and tenant management in 1980. See SFHA, *Minutes* (September 25, 1980).

93. The Alemany Resident Management Council took over SFHA services too, including childcare, employment training and counseling, literacy training, landscaping, co-op store, laundry, and recreation center. See Memorandum of Understanding (MOU) between the Alemany RMC and SFHA in SFHA, *Minutes* (August 27, 1992).

94. SFHA, *Minutes* (August 8, 1991).

95. Quote in SFHA, *Minutes* (December 12, 1991). See exchange of letters between HUD San Francisco Regional Administrator Robert J. De Monte and others about tenant databases, Folder "1989 Chron File, R. J. De Monte," Box 1, RH De Monte Reg. Administrator-RHC, 1988–1991, Program Files, RG 207, NARA/SB.

96. For a summary of problems resulting from contracting out, see Greenwood, "The Decision to Contract Out."

97. SFHA, *Minutes* (March 22, 1990). The discipline even extended to SFHA employees with the Drug-Free Workplace Act of 1988. For the prison industrial complex, see Christian Perenti, *Lockdown America: Police and Prisons in the Age of Crisis* (New York: Verso, 2009); Michelle Alexander, *The New Jim Crow: Mass Incarceration in the Age of Colorblindness* (New York: New Press, 2012).

98. Robert De Monte email to Jack Kemp, William Dal, and Linda Marston (May 18, 1992), Folder "1992 Corres," Box 1, Program Subject Files, R. H. De Monte, Regional Administrator, 1988–1992, NARA/SB, RG 207.

99. The rent increase happened over a five-year period for existing tenants, hitting 30 percent in 1985. All new tenants paid 30 percent after 1982.

100. U.S. General Accounting Office, "Information on Receiverships at Public Housing Authorities, GAO 303–363 a Report to Subcommittee on Housing, Committee on Banking, Housing and Urban Affairs, U.S. Senate" (February 1983); U.S. General Accounting Office, "HUD Should Improve the Usefulness and Accuracy of Its Management Assessment Program, GAO 303–363 a Report to Chairman, Subcommittee on Housing, Committee on Banking and Financial Services, House of Representatives" (January 1997); SFHA, *Minutes* (January 23, 1992).

101. For Gilmore background, see "Official Is a Player But Skirts the Rules—Housing Chief Cuts It Perilously Close to the Edge, Critics Say," *Seattle Times* (November 3, 1994), and SFHA, *Minutes* (April 27, 1989). Quote in "Official Is a Player." For the performance issues addressed by Gilmore, see SFHA, *Minutes* (January 23, 1992).

102. SFHA, *Minutes* (January 23 and June 11, 1992).

103. Quote in SFHA, *Minutes* (July 11, 1991). For optimism with Gilmore, see SFHA *Minutes* in 1991 and early 1992.

104. For an excellent account of these projects, see Larry Buron and Michael Baker, Abt Associates, Inc., "Interim Assessment of HOPE VI Program: Case Study of Bernal Dwellings and Plaza East in San Francisco, California, Final Report: Vol. 1" (March 2003), prepared for U.S. Department of HUD.

105. All quotes in SFHA, *Minutes* (June 11, 1992). SFHA, *Minutes* (January 23, 1992). For Jordan's ideas, see his letter to SFHA Commissioner Barbara Meskunas (April 12, 1995), in SFHA, *Minutes* (April 13, 1995), and De Monte to Jordan (December 19, 1991).

CHAPTER 8

1. Don Santina, "Gentrification Rears Its Racist Head: Ethnic Cleansing in San Francisco," *Counterpunch.org* (September 29, 2007).

2. SFHA, *Minutes* (September 10, 1992). Quote in SFHA, *Minutes* (February 11, 1993).

3. Rachel Gordon, "Jordan Struggles with Public Housing Mess," *San Francisco Examiner* (June 6, 1995). SFHA, *Minutes* (January 23, 1992). Gilmore left the SFHA in 1993 for the Seattle Housing Authority and then later the District of Columbia Housing Authority. He formed the consulting firm Gilmore Kean, LLC, that won a 2009 contract to administer the Housing Authority of New Orleans, which was on HUD's troubled authority list. Lee quote in SFHA, *Minutes* (April 8, 1993).

4. "The Final Report of the National Commission on Severely Distressed Public Housing: A Report to the Congress and the Secretary of Housing and Urban Development," Washington, DC. (August 1992). Quotes (in order) on 46 and xiii. Also see "Techniques for Revitalizing Severely Distressed Public Housing," Hearing Before the Subcommittee on Housing and Urban Affairs of the Committee on Banking, Housing, and Urban Affairs, 103rd Congress (May 11, 1993).

5. "The Final Report," quotes in this and previous paragraph on 46, 49 and 75.

6. "The Final Report," quote on 21.

7. "The Final Report," quote on 65.

8. "The Final Report."

9. Susan J. Popkin, et al., "A Decade of Hope VI: Research Findings and Policy Challenges" (Washington, DC: Urban Institute and Brookings Institution, May 2004). Property managers, if they could learn HUD rules, stood to profit handsomely from HUD changes. Mariwyn Evans, "Privatization of Public Housing," *Journal of Property Management* 62, 2 (March–April 1998): 25–30. John Arena, *Driven from New Orleans: How Nonprofits Betray Public Housing and Promote Privatization* (Minneapolis: University of Minnesota Press, 2012); Lawrence J. Vale, *Purging the Poorest: Public Housing and the Design Politics of Twice-Cleared Communities* (Chicago: University of Chicago Press, 2013).

10. Cisneros quote in SFHA, *Minutes* (November 15, 1993). Roger Biles notes how the Republican Party proposed "enterprise zones" ten years earlier. Roger Biles, *The Fate of Cities: Urban America and the Federal Government, 1945–2000* (Lawrence: University Press of Kansas, 2011), chapter 10. For Clinton's neoliberal policies, see Chester Hartman interview with Joseph Shuldiner, HUD assistant secretary for Public and Indian Housing (July 21, 1994), *Shelterforce Magazine*, 77 (September/October 1994); Margaret Weir, ed., *The Social*

NOTES TO CHAPTER 8   283

Divide: Political Parties and the Future of Activist Government (Washington, DC: Brookings Institution Press, 1998); Alice O'Connor, *Poverty Knowledge: Social Science, Social Policy, and the Poor in Twentieth-Century U.S. History* (Princeton, NJ: Princeton University Press, 2001), chapters 10 and 11; Gwendolyn Mink, *Welfare's End* (Ithaca, NY: Cornell University Press, 2002 rev. ed.); Arena, *Driven from New Orleans*; Vale, *Purging the Poorest*.

11. Allen and Meskunas worked on Jordan's mayoral campaign, and Meskunas became the director of the San Francisco Taxpayers Union, which lobbied for smaller government. Memo to Michael Janis, General Deputy, Assistant Secretary, from Robert De Monte, Regional Administrator-Regional Housing Commissioner, 9S (October 9, 1990), "Folder "RH De Monte-Chron File—1991," Box 1, Program Files RH De Monte, Reg. Administrator, RHC, 1988–1992, RG 207, NARA/SB. Catherine Bowman, "Housing Authority as Albatross?" *San Francisco Chronicle* (May 1, 1995); April Lynch, "Tenants Tell Jordan Housing Chief Must Go," *San Francisco Chronicle* (February 4, 1993); April Lynch, "Jordan Stymied: Housing Chief Stays," *San Francisco Chronicle* (February 3, 1993); Marc Sandalow, "S.F. Housing Director Is Quitting," *San Francisco Chronicle* (June 16, 1993).

12. SFHA, *Minutes* (March 10, 1994).

13. Bowman, "Housing Authority as Albatross?"; Gordon, "Jordan Struggles with Public Housing Mess."

14. Quote in Catherine Bowman, "The View from S.F.'s Public Housing: Tenants See Daily Indications of Commission's Turmoil," *San Francisco Chronicle* (June 5, 1995).

15. See SFHA, *Minutes* (1993–1996); Catherine Bowman, "S.F. Housing Authority Sued by Angry Tenants," *San Francisco Chronicle* (January 4, 1995); George Cothran, "Rooms with a View: Hunters View Residents Stand Up to the Housing Authority in the Name of Self-Governance," *SF Weekly* (October 25, 1995).

16. Rachel Gordon, "Jordan Struggles with Public Housing Mess," *San Francisco Examiner* (June 6, 1995).

17. Leslie Goldberg, "S.F. Housing Chief Stakes Claim," *San Francisco Examiner* (July 18, 1995). For Jordan's push to hire Thornton, see SFHA, *Minutes* (July 13 and July 17, 1995).

18. Kandace Bender, "Leadership on Trial: Achtenberg, Brown Lay Housing Problem at Jordan's Doorstep," *San Francisco Examiner* (October 29, 1995). Other housing authorities (NYC's excepted) also experienced similar internal and external challenges in this period. Nicholas Dagen Bloom, *Public Housing That Worked: New York in the Twentieth Century* (Philadelphia: University of Pennsylvania Press, 2008); D. Bradford Hunt, *Blueprint for Disaster: The Unraveling of Chicago Public Housing* (Chicago: University of Chicago Press, 2009); Arena, *Driven from New Orleans*; Vale, *Purging the Poorest*.

19. Michael Dougan and Don Fogleson, "Mayor Fires S.F. Housing Chief, Commissioners," *San Francisco Examiner* (March 3, 1996).

20. Leslie Goldberg, "Project's Tenants Put on Notice," *San Francisco Examiner* (March 4, 1996); Clarence Johnson, "A Pledge to Rid Projects of Crime: HUD Chief Also Says Jobs Won't Trigger Rent Increase," *San Francisco Chronicle* (March 16, 1996). Rachel Gordon, "Retired HUD Exec May Get SF Housing Post," *San Francisco Examiner* (August 8, 1996).

21. Gregory Lewis, "Acting Director Restores Faith in Public Housing," *San Francisco Examiner* (February 18, 1997). On the number of directors, see SFHA, *Minutes*, and Gregory Lewis, "Housing Control Returns to City," *San Francisco Examiner* (September 5, 1997).

22. SFHA, *Minutes* (November 9, 2000).

23. SFHA, *Minutes* (June 24, 1999).

24. In terms of SFHA employees, performance evaluations made it easier for management to fire them or contract out their jobs. SFHA, *Minutes* (March 10, 1994).

25. Quotes in SFHA, *Minutes* (May 26, 1994). SFHA, *Minutes* (April 14, 1994). See Catherine Bowman, "S.F. Housing Agency Workers Face Drug Tests," *San Francisco Chronicle* (March 6, 1996).

26. Catherine Bowman, "Housing Agency Laying off Staff: S.F. Organization Plans to Contract Out More Work," *San Francisco Chronicle* (June 4, 1996); Catherine Bowman, "Tight S.F. Housing Authority Budget Would Cut 138 Jobs," *San Francisco Chronicle* (June 25, 1996).

27. Al Gore promoted "reinventing government," though the phrase had roots in New Right writings. See Gore's "The Best Kept Secrets in Government: A Report to President Bill Clinton" (September 1996)." For reinventing government, see James A. Smith, *The Idea Brokers: Think Tanks and the Rise of the New Policy Elite* (New York: Free Press, 1991); David Osborne and Ted Gaebler, *Reinventing Government: How the Entrepreneurial Spirit Is Transforming the Public Sector* (New York: Addison-Wesley, 1992). For criticisms of reinventing government, see Peri E. Arnold, "Reforms Changing Role," *Public Administration Review* 55 (September/October 1995): 407–17; Ronald C. Moe, "The Reinventing Government Exercise: Misinterpreting the Problem, Misjudging the Consequences," *Public Administration Review* 54, 2 (1994): 111–22; and Ronald C. Moe and Robert S. Gilmour, "Rediscovering Principles of Public Administration: The Neglected Foundation of Public Law," *Public Administration Review* 55, 2 (1995): 135–46; Daphne T. Greenwood, "The Decision to Contract Out: Understanding the Full Economic and Social Impacts," (Colorado Springs: Colorado Center for Policy Studies, March 2014).

28. See SFHA *Minutes*. For Floresca working with the trade unions, see SFHA, *Minutes* (March 10, August 11, and October 13, 1994). For the kinds of jobs, see SFHA, *Minutes* (May 12, 1994). HUD even began giving small business loans to tenants through the Comprehensive Grant Program. See SFHA, *Minutes* (May 12, 1994). Margaret Weir, "Wages and Jobs: What Is the Public Role?" in Weir, *The Social Divide*; James P. Ziliak, ed., *Welfare Reform and Its Long-Term Consequences for America's Poor* (New York: Cambridge University Press, 2009). For the classic study of why social programs expand and contract in relation to labor needs and protest, see Frances Fox Piven and Richard Cloward, *Regulating the Poor: The Functions of Public Welfare* (New York: Vintage Books, 1993).

29. SFHA, *Minutes* (July 8, 1999); SFHA, "Resident Employment Plan: A Path to a Brighter Future," in SFHA, *Minutes* (June 22, 2000); Civil Grand Jury, City and County of San Francisco, "San Francisco Jails: An Investigative Visit" (June 26, 2006).

30. See SFHA, *Minutes* (March 1993 through the end of 1994). For discussion of ceiling rents to encourage wage work, and quote, see SFHA, *Minutes* (April 28, 1994). Weir, "Wages and Jobs"; Jane L. Collins and Victoria Mayer, *Both Hands Tied: Welfare Reform and the Race to the Bottom in the Low-Wage Labor Market* (Chicago: University of Chicago Press, 2010); LaDonna Pavetti, "Work Requirements Don't Cut Poverty, Evidence Shows," Center on Budget and Policy Priorities (updated June 7, 2016).

31. In general, TANF recipients have not fared well as affordable childcare, safe homes, and quality jobs remained elusive. Bianca Frogner, Robert Moffitt, and David Ribar, "How Families Are Doing Nine Years After Welfare Reform," in Ziliak, *Welfare Reform and Its Long-Term Consequences for America's Poor*, 140–72.

32. Catherine Bowman, "Critics Lambaste New Rules for Low-Income Housing: Higher Deposits, Tenants Must Pay for Damage," *San Francisco Chronicle* (January 22, 1996).

33. SFHA, *Minutes* (October 23, 1997); Ilene Lelchuk, "They Don't Call the Project Outta Control Anymore: Success of Renewal Using HOPE VI Is Evident All Around," *San Francisco Chronicle* (March 28, 2005).

34. Emelyn Cruz, "Federal Policy Allows Public Housing Tenants to Be Kicked out for Crimes Others Commit," *San Francisco Examiner* (August 23, 1998). Wendy J. Kaplan and David Rossman, "Called 'Out' at Home: The One Strike Eviction Policy and Juvenile Court," *Duke Forum for Law & Social Change* 3 (2011): 109–38.

35. Quote in Goldberg, "Project's Tenants Put on Notice"; Johnson, "A Pledge to Rid Projects of Crime."

36. SFHA, *Minutes* (August 10, 1995; and October 23, 1997).

37. SFHA, *Minutes* (August 10 and September 28, 1995). Rising SFHA evictions in SFHA, *Minutes* (September 7, 1995). Tenants challenged such evictions, but a legal case involving public housing tenants at the Oakland Housing Authority ruled the no-tolerance policy legal. See discussion of *Rucker v. HUD* in Eric Brazil, "HUD Drug Eviction Policy Upheld," *San Francisco Examiner* (February 15, 2000), and SFHA, *Minutes* (March 28, 2002).

38. For the prison industrial complex, see Christian Perenti, *Lockdown America: Police and Prisons in the Age of Crisis* (New York: Verso, 2009); Michelle Alexander, *The New Jim Crow: Mass Incarceration in the Age of Colorblindness* (New York: New Press, 2012).

39. SFHA, *Minutes* (June 23, 1994).

40. The report found problems with due process, exaggerated arrest records, effectiveness, and assessment. HUD Inspector General Report, "Actions Needed to Strengthen Management and Oversight of Operation Safe Home" (June 29, 2001), GAO-01–794.

41. SFHA, *Minutes* (March 9, 1995).

42. On oversight, see SFHA, *Minutes* (February 23, 1995). Jordan quote in SFHA, *Minutes* (April 13, 1995). Floresca quote in SFHA, *Minutes* (December 8, 1994). On Jordan's neoliberal ideas, see his letter to SFHA Commissioner Barbara Meskunas (April 12, 1995), in SFHA, *Minutes* (April 13, 1995); SFHA, *Minutes* (June 7 and 9, 1994); also see his public letter to SFHA tenants in Robert De Monte letter to Frank Jordan (December 19, 1991), Folder "1992 Corres," Box 1, Program Subject Files, R. J. De Monte, Regional Administrator, 1988–1992, NARA/SB, RG 207.

43. Quoted in Evans, "Privatization of Public Housing," 25–30. Also see Arena, *Driven from New Orleans,* for ways nonprofits expanded as a result of HUD's neoliberal policies.

44. Nancy Raquel Mirabal, "Geographies of Displacement: Latinas/os, Oral History, and the Politics of Gentrification in San Francisco's Mission District," *The Public Historian* 31, 2 (May 2009): 7–31; Karl Beitel, *Local Protests, Global Movements: Capital, Community, and State in San Francisco* (Philadelphia: Temple University Press, 2013). Although property taxes rose, the developers of live/work lofts skirted their tax obligation to the tune of millions of dollars. In 1999, the city of San Francisco was losing $5.5 million in school fees and $2.6 million in planning fees and developer subsidies because of the way the 1989 loft ordinance was written. See Tyche Hendricks, "Critics Say Developers Short-Change City by Millions on Schools, Affordable Housing," *San Francisco Examiner* (August 4, 1999).

45. Both quotes in David Talbot, "How Much Tech Can One City Take?" *San Francisco Magazine* (October 2, 2012).

46. Brian R. Mulry, "Potrero Hill Activists Continue to Fight the Powers That Be," and Alyssa Heartwell, "Making Ends Meet in San Francisco," both in *The Potrero View* (April 2007). Michael Webster explores these changes. See his "An Examination of Gentrification and Urban Change in San Francisco's Dogpatch," MA thesis (San Francisco State University, May 2011). For demographic data, see San Francisco Planning Department, "Profiles of Community Planning Areas" (San Francisco, 2002), chapter 6.

47. Evelyn Nieves, "In Old Mission District, Changing Grit to Gold," *New York Times* (January 21, 1999). The city's Latina/o population dropped from 109,504 to 98,891 from 2000 to 2005. Quote and data in Mirabal, "Geographies of Displacement," 14–15. Also see Rebecca Solnit and Susan Schwartzenberg, *Hollow City: The Siege of San Francisco and the Crisis of American Urbanism* (New York: Verso, 2001); Brian J. Godfrey, "Barrio Under Siege: Latino Sense of Place in San Francisco" in Daniel Arreola, *Hispanic Spaces, Latino Places: Community and Cultural Diversity in Contemporary America* (Austin: University of Texas Press, 2004); Christine Joy Ferrer, Krissy Keefer, and Stella Adelman, "The Beat of 24th and Mission," *Race, Poverty & the Environment* 20, 1 (2015): 106–113.

48. Quote and data in Mirabal, "Geographies of Displacement," 14–15.49. Jaxon Van Derbeken, "Battle over Gentrification Gets Ugly in S.F.'s Mission: Anarchist Arrested, Charged with Making Threats," *San Francisco Chronicle* (June 7, 1999), and Don Knapp, "San Francisco's Home $weet Home Dilemma," *CNN.com* (June 9, 1999). For Keating and the Yuppie Eradication Project, see "Space 1999: San Francisco's Mission Yuppie Eradication Project" (December 14, 2007). For the YEP poster, see http://www.infoshop.org/myep/cw_posters8.html. For other responses to Mission district gentrification, see Solnit and Schwartzenberg, *Hollow City*; and Godfrey, "Barrio Under Siege."

50. See www.galeriadelaraza.org and Solnit and Schwartzenberg, *Hollow City*.

51. Tom Wetzel, "San Francisco's Space Wars," *http://www.foundsf.org/index.php?title =San_Francisco%27s_Space_Wars_2001*; Beitel, *Local Protests, Global Movements*; Godfrey quote in "Barrio Under Siege," on 102.

52. Quote in Evelyn Nieves, "Blacks Hit by Housing Costs Leave San Francisco Behind," *New York Times* (August 1–2, 2001).

53. Venise Wagner, "Desperately Seeking Shelter That's Section 8 Compatible: Housing Subsidy Program Can't Keep Up with S.F.'s Soaring Rents," *San Francisco Examiner* (May 27, 1999); Stu Woo, "Some Left Out as Divisadero Corridor Shines," *Wall Street Journal* (January 12, 2012). See *Street Sheet* (especially May 1996).

54. *Street Sheet* (May 1996).

55. Erin McCormick, "Bayview Revitalization Comes with a Huge Price to Black Residents," *San Francisco Chronicle* (January 14, 2008); Nieves, "Blacks Hit by Housing Costs Leave San Francisco Behind"; Thomas Fuller, "The Loneliness of Being Black in San Francisco," *New York Times* (July 20, 2016).

56. "Report of the San Francisco Mayor's Task Force on African-American Out-Migration" (San Francisco, 2009). Also see Rachel Brahinsky, "Race and the Making of Southeast San Francisco: Towards a Theory of Race-Class," *Antipode* 46, 5 (2014): 1258–76.

57. Solnit and Schwartzenberg, *Hollow City*; Beitel, *Local Protests, Global Movements*. Quote in history of EDC at www.evictiondefense.org.

58. See history of SFCLT at www.sflct.org; for an example of SFCLT housing in Chinatown, see Cory Paul, "Chinatown Land Trust Helps Low-Income Housing," *San Francisco Chronicle* (June 30, 2009).

59. Jaron Browne, "Emails Show Regulators Conspiring with Lennar to Cover up Shipyard Development Danger," *San Francisco BayView* (March 23, 2011), and John Wildermuth, "Lennar Gives Bayview–Hunters Point $7.3 Million," *San Francisco Chronicle* (May 4, 2012).

60. Mirabal, "Geographies of Displacement"; documentary "See How They Run" (2003). Quote in Solnit and Schwartzenberg, *Hollow City*, 129. Also see Carl T. Hall, "SF Unions Going All Out for Brown: Mayor Sewed Up Support Early—Even Before Ammiano Entered Race," *San Francisco Chronicle* (December 7, 1999); Edward Epstein and John Wildermuth, "Brown in a Landslide: S.F. Rejects Ammiano, Hands Mayor Second Term," *San Francisco Chronicle* (December 15, 1999); Wetzel, "San Francisco's Space Wars"; Rick DelVecchio and John Wildermuth, "Homeowners Scared into Voting for Brown: Ammiano Seen as the Greater of Two Evils," *San Francisco Chronicle* (December 16, 1999).

61. Mirabal, "Geographies of Displacement"; Solnit and Schwartzenberg, *Hollow City*; Chester Hartman, *City for Sale: The Transformation of San Francisco* (Berkeley: University of California, 2002), 306–08. Proposition K would have made it easier to expand commercial and office space with no requirements for building more housing; Proposition L imposed building fees earmarked for housing, childcare, and public transit.

62. SFHA, *Minutes* (August 22 and September 12, 2002; April 11 and July 25, 2002; August 12, 2004). Woodruff and Brown quotes in SFHA, *Minutes* (May 25, 2006).

63. SFHA, *Minutes* (October 25, 2001).

64. Ibid.

65. The SFHA leased the land to TODCO and generated income from the project and the commercial spaces. Eugene Coleman advocated for the rights of the poor in the city, especially those in the South of Market. For the history of TOOR, see todco.org; Hartman, *City for Sale*, chapter 10; *TODCO Newsletter* (Fall 2002); "TODCO Opens New Affordable Senior Housing Center," *FogCity Journal* (January 13, 2006), http://www.fogcityjournal.com/news_in_brief/eugene_coleman_060113.shtml

66. Ilene Lelchuk, "Back Home in North Beach: Residents of Project Glad to Return After Renovation," *San Francisco Chronicle* (October 2, 2004), and SFHA, *Minutes* (April 27 and May 9, 2000).

67. James Sterngold, "Urban Housing Success Story Faces Budget Ax," *San Francisco Chronicle* (February 23, 2006). Also see the Atlanta Housing Authority, "HOPE: Atlanta Housing Authority 15 Year Progress Report, 1995–2010" (2011); Alex F. Schwartz, *Housing Policy in the United States* (New York: Routledge, 2014).

68. See MHDC and John Stewart Company websites: https://missionhousing.org and https://jsco.net. SFHA Commissioner Brown raised questions about how the John Stewart Company would benefit tenants and the SFHA, but the MHDC was actually charged with selecting the management company. For media praise of the project and new management and for the quote, see Heather Knight, "San Francisco: Infamous Projects Are Rebuilt and Reborn," *SFGate* (November 20, 2006).

69. Amy Lynne Howard, *More Than Shelter: Activism and Community in San Francisco Public Housing* (Minneapolis: University of Minnesota Press, 2014), chapter 2. Howard writes that tenant return rates were 52 percent at Valencia, 37 percent at Hayes Valley, 56 percent at Bernal Dwellings, and 41 percent at Plaza East. See Howard, *More Than Shelter*, fn 166 for chapter 2. For the loss of tenant community and activism, see chapter 2 in Howard, *More Than Shelter* and SFHA, *Minutes* (September 25, 2008; October 13, 2011; and June 14, 2012).

70. HUD, "HOPE VI Program Authority and Funding History" (updated March 2007). https://www.hud.gov/sites/documents/DOC_9838.PDF

71. SFHA, *Minutes* (May 25, 2006).

72. Heather Knight, "3 S.F. Public Housing Areas Getting Rebuilt," *SFGate* (March, 12, 2008). Also see hope-sf.org for the justification and plans.

73. Robert Selna, "Lennar Corp. Dominates Redevelopment in S.F./Hunters Point Deal Gives Firm City Hall Clout," *SFGate* (April 10, 2007). Also see Cecilia M. Vega, "Newsom Says He'll Ask Voters to Shell Out to Fix Public Housing: Federal Funding Cuts Mean Tighter Budget for S.F.'s Program," *San Francisco Chronicle* (September 23, 2006), and J. K. Dineen, "Hope SF to Start Work on 6,000 Units of Housing," *San Francisco Business Times* (updated November 22, 2009).

74. Jackson quote in Sarah Phelan, "Unanswered Questions," *The Guardian* (April 3, 2007); Nashelly Chavez, "Community Remembers Tenacious, Caring Spirit of Bayview Activist," *San Francisco Examiner* (January 26, 2016). Walker quote in Paul Hogarth, "City Sells Hunters Point to Lennar as Activists Revive Referendum," BeyondChron (April 17, 2007).

75. Heather Knight, "Agnos Expected to Get Housing Task," *SFGate* (March 21, 2007). SFHA, *Minutes* (October 13, 2005; January 12 and February 23, 2006).

76. Income data from the San Francisco Mayor's Office of Housing and Community Development: sfmohcd.org/2006-income-limits-housing-programs.

77. Santina, "Gentrification Rears Its Racist Head."

CONCLUSION

1. 2017 "Homeless Census" data in 2017 *San Francisco Homeless Count and Survey* (San Jose: Applied Survey Research, 2017); Matthew Desmond, *Evicted: Poverty and Profit in the American City* (New York: Broadway Books, 2016); Joseph Chamie, "As Cities Grow Worldwide, So Do the Numbers of Homeless," *YaleGlobal Online* (July 13, 2017). https://yaleglobal.yale.edu/content/cities-grow-worldwide-so-do-numbers-homeless

2. Mildred Van Reed to President Lyndon B. Johnson (December 22 and December 1965), Folder "310 Public Relations Assist. Req., 6 Jan 66," Box 9 1966, Subject Correspondence, 1966–1978, RG 207, NARA/CP.

ART CREDITS

× Figure I.1. San Francisco Housing Authority, Eighth Annual Report (no date).

× Figure 1.1. San Francisco History Center, San Francisco Public Library.

× Figure 1.2. Rebecca Solnit and Susan Schwartzenberg, *Hollow City: The Siege of San Francisco and the Crisis of American Urbanism* (New York: Verso, 2001). Map credited to Bart Wright. Used with permission.

× Figure 1.3. San Francisco History Center, San Francisco Public Library.

× Figure 1.4. San Francisco History Center, San Francisco Public Library.

× Figure 1.5. San Francisco History Center, San Francisco Public Library.

× Figure 1.6. San Francisco History Center, San Francisco Public Library.

× Figure 2.1. William and Catherine Bauer Wurster Papers, Environmental Design Archives, University of California, Berkeley.

× Figure 2.2. San Francisco History Center, San Francisco Public Library.

× Figure 2.3. San Francisco History Center, San Francisco Public Library.

× Figure 2.4. *Pencil Points.*

× Figure 2.5. San Francisco History Center, San Francisco Public Library.

× Figure 2.6. San Francisco History Center, San Francisco Public Library.

× Figure 2.7. San Francisco History Center, San Francisco Public Library.

× Figure 2.8. San Francisco History Center, San Francisco Public Library.

× Figure 3.1. San Francisco History Center, San Francisco Public Library.

× Figure 3.2. San Francisco History Center, San Francisco Public Library.

× Figure 3.3. San Francisco History Center, San Francisco Public Library.

× Figure 3.4. San Francisco History Center, San Francisco Public Library.

× Figure 3.5. San Francisco Housing Authority, *Eighth Annual Report* (no date).

× Figure 3.6. San Francisco History Center, San Francisco Public Library.

× Figure 4.1. San Francisco History Center, San Francisco Public Library.

× Figure 4.2. San Francisco History Center, San Francisco Public Library.

× Figure 5.1. San Francisco History Center, San Francisco Public Library.

× Figure 5.2. The San Francisco News-Call Bulletin newspaper photograph archive [graphic], BANC PIC 1959.010—NEG, Part 3, Box 274, 04-00-65.10:3. © The Regents of the University of California, The Bancroft Library, University of California, Berkeley.

INDEX